THE
LIES OF
GEORGE
W. BUSH

ALSO BY DAVID CORN

Blond Ghost: Ted Shackley and the CIA's Crusades

Deep Background

THE LIES OF GEORGE W. BUSH

MASTERING THE POLITICS OF DECEPTION

DAVID CORN

CROWN PUBLISHERS

Portions of this book appeared previously in different form in *The Nation*, TomPaine.com, and Alternet.org.

Published by Crown Publishers, New York, New York.
Member of the Crown Publishing Group, a division of Random House, Inc.
www.crownpublishing.com

CROWN is a trademark and the Crown colophon is a registered trademark of Random House, Inc.

Printed in the United States of America

DESIGN BY ELINA D. NUDELMAN

Library of Congress Cataloging-in-Publication Data is available upon request.

ISBN 1-4000-5066-9

10 9 8 7 6 5 4 3 2 1

First Edition

FOR WELMOED

Contents

When regard for the truth has broken down or even slightly weakened, all things will remain doubtful.

—St. Augustine

THE
LIES OF
GEORGE
W. BUSH

Introduction: A False Restoration

"Some people think it's inappropriate to draw a moral line. Not me. For our children to have the lives we want for them, they must learn to say yes to responsibility . . . yes to honesty."

—George W. Bush, June 12, 1999

George W. Bush is a liar. He has lied large and small. He has lied directly and by omission. He has misstated facts, knowingly or not. He has misled. He has broken promises, been unfaithful to political vows. Through his campaign for the presidency and his first years in the White House, he has mugged the truth—not merely in honest error, but deliberately, consistently, and repeatedly to advance his career and his agenda. Lying greased his path toward the White House; it has been one of the essential tools of his presidency. To call the 43rd president of the United States a prevaricator is not an exercise of opinion, not an inflammatory talk-radio device. This insult is supported by an all too extensive record of self-serving falsifications. So constant is his fibbing that a history of his lies offers a close approximation of the history of his presidential tenure.

While politicians are often derided as liars, this charge should be particularly stinging for Bush. During the campaign of 2000, he pitched himself as a candidate who could "restore" honor and integrity to an Oval Office stained by the misdeeds and falsehoods of his predecessor. To brand Bush a liar is to negate what he and his supporters claimed as his most basic and most important qualification for the job; it is a challenge, in a sense, to his legitimacy. But it is a challenge fully supported by his words and actions, as well as those of the aides and officials who speak and act for him. The list of falsehoods is long. And only one man bears responsibility for that—the fellow who campaigned in an airplane christened *Responsibility One*.

Does the truth matter to Bush? No more than winning office, gaining a political advantage, or prevailing in a policy dispute. He has lied not only to cover up inconvenient matters or facts, or out of defensiveness when caught in a contradiction or an uncomfortable spot. He has engaged in strategic lying—that is, prevaricating about the fundamental elements of his presidency, including his basic goals and his own convictions. He has used lies to render himself and his ideas more enticing to voters and the public. And that raises the question: has lying been critical to his success? Were Bush and his proposals—unadorned by fiction—not sufficiently appealing?

A liar in the White House is not a remarkable development. Most presidents lie, many brazenly and with impunity. Only a few have had to pay a political cost for their dissimulations. In 1840, William Henry Harrison, the Whig candidate for president, told potential voters he had been born in a log cabin. Not true at all. He was a scion of an aristocratic family, and he had grown up in a red-brick mansion on the James River in Virginia. But he won the contest. Twenty years later, Abraham Lincoln—his supporters hailed him as "Honest Abe"—was running for president, and advocates presented Lincoln to voters as a country lawyer. No—he had been reared in rural Illinois, but by the time he was a presidential wannabe, he had become one of the nation's leading attorneys, representing railroads and other corporations.

In more recent decades, presidents have lied to get their way or hide embarrassing truths. In a pre–Pearl Harbor fireside chat in 1941, Franklin Delano Roosevelt, looking to persuade Americans that the nation should side with Britain in its war against Nazi Germany, reported that a German submarine had launched an unprovoked attack on the USS *Greer*. Left unsaid was the fact that the *Greer* had been cooperating with a British naval effort to find the sub and destroy it. On August 9, 1945, three days after the United States struck Hiroshima with an atomic bomb, Harry Truman, in a radio speech, said, "The world will note that the first atomic bomb was dropped on Hiroshima, a military base. That was because we wished in this first attack to avoid, in so far as possible, the killing of civilians." Yet Hiroshima was a *city*, not a military base. Its population at that time included about 350,000 civilians. In May 1960, when the Soviet Union announced it had shot down an American U-2 spyplane flying over its territory, Dwight Eisenhower had his aides say that this aircraft had been only a weather plane that had wandered 1,500 miles off course. But after Moscow produced wreckage of the plane and the pilot of the aircraft, the Eisenhower administration publicly conceded it had been conducting U-2 overflights. At the time, many Americans were genuinely shocked that a White House had lied. Later, Eisenhower explained why he had subordinates spin for him during the U-2 episode: "When a president has lost his credibility, he has lost his greatest strength."

John Kennedy, while campaigning in 1960, declared that the United States was on the wrong side of a dangerous missile gap with the Soviet Union. But there was no missile gap in the Soviet's favor, and Kennedy had received classified briefings reporting that. In August 1964, Lyndon Johnson told congressional leaders that two American destroyers were attacked without provocation by the North Vietnamese in international waters in the Gulf of Tonkin. He asked Congress to immediately pass legislation approving a retaliatory attack, and Congress obliged. Years later, the public learned Johnson had misled Congress.

Richard Nixon lied about Vietnam (as a candidate he claimed he had a secret plan "to end the war, and win the peace," but he did not; as the president, he denied he was covertly bombing Cambodia, when he was). He lied about Watergate, too, declaring famously, "I am not a crook." Turned out he was, and, because he was caught lying, he became the first president to resign.

When the Iran-Contra scandal began to unfold in the fall of 1986, Ronald Reagan said that his administration "did not—repeat, did not—trade weapons or anything else for hostages" with Iran and that "there is no [U.S.] government connection" with the efforts to supply weapons to the Contra rebels fighting the Sandinista government in Nicaragua. He was wrong on both counts. Reagan, a champion falsifier who routinely got facts wrong about his own life and important policy matters (most air pollution is caused by trees and plants; submarine-launched nuclear missiles once fired can be recalled), later offered a new and highly original explanation for his Iran-Contra misstatements: "A few months ago I told the American people I did not trade arms for hostages. My heart and my best intentions still tell me that's true, but the facts and the evidence tell me it is not." That is, he lied because he was out of touch with reality.

Reagan's vice president—a fellow named George Herbert Walker Bush—also lied about Iran-Contra. When the Iran-Contra affair was first exposed, Bush denied he had been "in the loop." Yet government documents subsequently released disclosed that Bush had attended many high-level administration meetings on the Iran initiative. And in his private diary—which he managed to withhold from Iran-Contra investigators until December 1992, a month after he lost his reelection bid—Bush had written, "I'm one of the few people that know fully the details" of the Iran affair. More famously, during his acceptance speech at the 1988 GOP convention, Bush issued a solemn vow: "Read my lips: no new taxes." Two years later, in an attempt to address the budget deficit, he signed legislation raising taxes.

Bill Clinton tried unsuccessfully to escape scandal by lying. "I did not have sexual relations with that woman" has become one of the most well-known presidential falsehoods. The tortuously crafted remarks about his affair with intern Monica Lewinsky that he uttered while giving a deposition in a sexual harassment suit became the basis—or excuse—for a Republican impeachment crusade against him. Clinton survived, but his Monica lies tainted his presidency, divided the nation, and handed Bush and the Republicans ammunition to use in the 2000 presidential campaign. He earned less scorn and less trouble for the lies he told about other, more weighty matters. He promised an initiative on race relations and never produced one. On the campaign trail in 1992, he had pitched a "putting people first" agenda that emphasized federal public investments, but in office he embraced deficit reduction as his first priority. In 1998, Clinton visited Rwanda, the site four years earlier of a horrific genocide, and disingenuously remarked, "All over the world there were people like me sitting in offices who did not fully appreciate the depth and speed with which you were being engulfed by this unimaginable terror." The White House had been in-the-know about the massacre while it was occurring. But lying about genocide was apparently not as outrageous as lying about sex.

This very selective history demonstrates there are many varieties of presidential lies. Some concern grand policy matters, some concern secret government activity, some concern personal peccadilloes. Several presidents have misled the public about their health or their status as devoted family men. But what can be considered a lie? Sissela Bok, the author of *Lying: Moral Choice in Public and Private Life*, defines it simply as "an intentionally deceptive message in the form of a *statement.*" Intentionally? That may get Reagan off the hook—or any other president who truly believes his own spin. But because presidential lies matter more than most—they can lead to war, decide elections, break or make vital policy decisions—I would propose a slightly different standard for White House occupants. If a president issues a statement, he or she has an obligation to ensure the remark is truthful. The same applies to a presidential candidate who, after all, is seeking an office that comes with the ultimate power. It is not enough for a president or White House contender to *believe* what he is saying is true; he should *know* it to be true—within reasonable standards. And for the sake of judging presidents and presidential candidates, the statements of their aides and spokespeople should be measured using the same guidelines, for presidents often send out underlings to speak—or lie—for them.

Commanders-in-chief and presidential candidates do commit mistakes and misspeak. Given the amount of information they are expected to possess, this is only natural. Not every error or verbal miscue is a lie. But a president has a duty to acknowledge and correct any significant misstatement he or she utters—especially if that slip somehow worked to his advantage. An untruth that might have been spoken accidentally becomes a lie if a president and his aides permit it to stand.

In addition to serving as the leader of the nation and the head of the government, the president is an information source. He shares with the public the material gathered by the vast federal government, and often it is information about the most important matters confronting the nation. The public ought to expect a White House to pledge allegiance to accuracy. Citizens in a democracy not only have a right to truth in government, they have a need for it. Without good information, how can they make good decisions?

Yet lies seem essential in politics and government. In a cynical mood, George Orwell once wrote, "Politics itself is a mass of lies, evasions, folly, hatred and schizophrenia." That was unavoidable, he noted, because "political speech" is "largely the defense of the indefensible." Nixon at one point told his friend Leonard Garment, "You're never going to make it in politics, Len. You just don't know how to lie." Did he mean that politics is a down-and-dirty business? Or perhaps he believed that the voting public will not embrace a candidate who doesn't pander to popular biases and sentiments. Maybe Nixon thought that a leader in a complex and sometimes dangerous world did not always have the luxury of telling the truth. Long before Nixon contemplated the role of truth in politics, Plato referred to "noble lies"—falsehoods told by those in power that supposedly were for the public's own good.

In *The Prince*, Niccolò Machiavelli noted that honesty in leadership is not always desirable. "How praiseworthy it is that a prince keeps his word and governs by candor instead of craft, everyone knows," he wrote in the early 16th century. "Yet the experience of our own time shows that those princes who had little regard for their word and had the craftiness to turn men's minds have accomplished great things and, in the end, have overcome those who governed their actions by their pledges." Taking a dark view of human interactions, Machiavelli believed that a leader would always find an audience for his lies: "Men are so simple and so much inclined to obey immediate needs that a deceiver will never lack victims for his deceptions." And history's most famous political consultant observed that many "princes who broke faith" gained the advantage. But, he advised, "one must know how to mask this nature skillfully and be a great dissembler."

Which brings us to the current president of the United States. All presidents ought to be truth-tested. But George W. Bush has invited more than routine scrutiny. As a candidate, he maintained he was pursuing the presidency to return integrity to 1600 Pennsylvania Avenue. (A good son, Bush obviously believed integrity had been present prior to the arrival of the Clintons, despite irrefutable proof to the contrary.) Bush was leading a restorative cause (and also calling for massive tax cuts, the partial privatization of Social Security, and what he called education reform). He and his campaign strove to depict Vice President Al Gore, the Democratic nominee, as a say-anything serial fibber, the product of the weasel-words culture of Washington. A candidate who rises to power by denouncing lies warrants more attention when he engages in dishonest behavior.

And these days there is more reason than ever for a president to be beyond reproach. In perilous times, the nation needs a strong and credible leader. The president must be able to strike alliances overseas and inspire at home, in order to implement policies that protect the nation and enhance security in the United States and elsewhere. But if the president is a demonstrable fabricator, portions of the American public and some foreign leaders will be hesitant to rally around him.

Following the horrific attacks of September 11, 2001, Bush and his executive branch assumed greater powers. Congress authorized him to wage whatever war he deemed necessary against whatever forces he held responsible for the suicide-homicide attacks. A year later, Congress handed Bush the authority to launch a war against Iraq whenever he determined that military action was imperative. And he did so. Bush also reserved for himself and the federal government the right to conduct secret military tribunals, to detain non-citizen suspects or material witnesses indefinitely (while withholding information from the public about these detentions), and to monitor conversations between people held in federal prisons and their attorneys.

Because of September 11, Bush became the most powerful president in decades. As he moved to expand the war on terrorism to include military action against Iraq, his aides and outside-the-government champions occasionally suggested that Bush's decisions were informed by intelligence that could not be shared with the public. In essence, the argument was, trust us. In fact, in the middle of the public debate before the war against Iraq, late one night on a Washington street corner, Richard Perle, a hawkish adviser to the Pentagon, made the case for war to me with two words: "Trust me." Democracies are not supposed to operate that way, I replied. But Perle's we-know-best attitude was somewhat representative of the administration he was serving. Bush and his crew have embraced paternalistic secrecy as a virtue. Vice President Dick Cheney adamantly refused to tell the public (that is, the people he works for) what corporate lobbyists he met with while he was crafting the administration's energy plan. Attorney General John Ashcroft urged federal agencies to be as tight-fisted as possible when replying to Freedom of Information Act requests. The Justice Department drew up drafts of harsh anti-terrorism legislation—which challenged civil liberties—without consulting Congress. Bush and his aides have repeatedly noted that much of their war on terrorism must be conducted in the shadows, away from the prying eyes of the public and even from most members of Congress.

If Bush is going to lead the most secretive and opaque administration in years, he must demonstrate his trustworthiness at every turn, especially when he is guiding the country during a war. Lies and secrecy are a troubling mix. When Bush asserts the nation must resort to violence, the public ought to have full confidence in him. Yet as he tried to rally support for war against Saddam Hussein, he repeatedly misrepresented intelligence information. Such distortions—as well as Bush's distortions related to non-war matters—undermine (or should undermine) his credibility as he attempts to convince the public his decisions on war and peace merit support. Lying in office not only poses a potential political risk for Bush, a president who lies is a risk to the nation. He might steer the country into a war under false pretenses. Or, if he comes to be regarded as untruthful by a significant portion of the public, he might fail to rouse the country for military action that is indeed warranted. A liar in the White House is a national security threat.

Is George W. Bush more of a liar, less of a liar, than his predecessors? A better one, a worse one? Are his Cabinet members and aides more or less honest than those of previous chief executives? It may well be that Bush has pushed the envelope further than recent presidents. But if his consistent reliance upon deceptive arguments to support the major initiatives of his presidency is not unprecedented, it is still distinctive. Comparisons to previous administrations, though, are unimportant. Bush is the president the nation has now—at a point when honesty in government is needed as much, if not more, than ever. And he was the leader who—after winning office in a bizarre climax, having polled 500,000 fewer votes than his opponent—promised to bring the nation together, to work with political foes, to change the nasty tone of Washington. Such noble goals cannot be achieved by a president who soils the Oval Office with lies.

Bush, certainly, does not always lie. On the campaign trail, he stated he would stick with his tax proposal—which did not poll well—no matter what public opinion surveys said. He kept his word. He promised to confront Saddam Hussein. That happened. He said he would drill for oil in the Alaskan wilderness, seek a partial privatization of Social Security, and appoint conservative judges. Once in office, he moved in each of these directions. But this book is not a study of those instances when Bush spoke or acted honestly. A president wins no points for behaving properly. Integrity ought to be considered the default position. Lies deserve the attention and exposure.

There is the risk a volume of this sort can be seen as a one-note endeavor. Bush lied here, Bush lied there, Bush lied once again, and so on. But lies, in part, made this president, and lies frequently have been the support beams of his administration. An examination of Bush's lies turns out to be one way of charting and scrutinizing much of the Bush presidency. (And this book does not document every single lie.)

"Facts are stupid things," President Reagan once malapropped. He meant to say "stubborn." Indeed they are. It is beyond argument that Bush has lied more than once. This book will show he has trampled the truth often—without (as of yet) paying an obvious price. His lies did not turn off the 48 percent of the voting public that chose him or the significant majority of Americans who approved of his performance in office following the 9/11 attacks and the wars in Afghanistan and Iraq. But regardless of what he accomplishes during his tenure in the White House—be it four years or eight—a fair-minded reading of the record cannot escape the conclusion that Bush has failed to achieve what he claimed as one of his prime objectives. He has not been a president of integrity. The Bush White House has been no beacon of honesty. This president has treated the truth in the manner his predecessor treated an intern.

1. A Dishonest Candidate

"I have been very candid about my past."

"It's time to restore honor and dignity to the White House." So declared George W. Bush during the 2000 presidential campaign. In one of his first ads, an earnest-sounding Bush told television viewers in Iowa he would "return honor and integrity" to the Oval Office. His promise to escort these values *back* to 1600 Pennsylvania Avenue—after you-know-who had done you-know-what in the Oval Office and then *lied* about it—was often the emotional crescendo of Bush's stump speech. With solemnity, Bush told the crowds that, should he be fortunate enough to win the election, on the day of his inauguration he would not only lift his hand and swear to uphold the Constitution, he would swear to uphold the "honor and the integrity" of the presidency. His supporters ate this up and cheered wildly.

Bush's professed commitment to honesty was a constant chorus during the campaign. It was also a false claim. As he barnstormed across the country, Bush left a wide wake of distortions and deceits.

He was no pioneer in this regard. To campaign is to abuse the truth. Candidates exaggerate their assets, discount their liabilities, hype their accomplishments, downplay their failures. They hail their proposals and dismiss the doubts, often fiddling with the facts to do so. A certain amount of shiftiness is understandable, perhaps even acceptable. But in seeking the presidency of the United States, George W. Bush did more than fudge and finagle. He lied about the basics—about his past, about his record as governor of Texas, about the programs he was promising, about his opponents, about the man he was, and about the president he would be. Not occasionally, but consistently. Which meant he lied about a central element of his candidacy: that he was a forthright fellow who would indeed bring integrity to the Oval Office. His honest-man routine was a campaign-concocted illusion.

The many lies he told not only served his immediate interests (getting elected), they established the foundation for the deceptions that would come when he reached the White House. The origins of much of Bush's presidential dissembling can be found in the 2000 campaign. In that endeavor, Bush and his handlers fine-tuned a political style that included the frequent deployment of misleading statements, half-true assertions, or flat-out lies. Perhaps most importantly, during the campaign, Bush and his colleagues could see that lying worked, that it was a valuable tool. It allowed them to present Bush, his past, and his initiatives in the most favorable, though not entirely truthful, terms—to deny reality when reality was inconvenient. It got them out of jams. It won them not scorn but votes. It made the arduous task of winning the presidency easier. And the campaign, as it turned out, would be merely a test run for the administration to follow.

"I don't get coached."

Bush began his campaign with a lie. On June 12, 1999, he flew into Cedar Rapids, Iowa, and before several hundred spectators corralled into a hangar, announced he would be a candidate for the Republican presidential nomination. For months prior to joining the 2000 parade, Bush had been promoting himself as a "uniter-not-a-divider." In the hangar, he also presented himself as a tried-and-true moral leader. "Some people think it is inappropriate to draw a moral line," he said. "Not me. For our children to have the lives we want for them. They must learn to say yes to responsibility, yes to family, yes to honesty." The Texas governor, who had been reelected to his second term the previous November, maintained: "I've learned you cannot lead by dividing people. This country is hungry for a new style of campaign. Positive. Hopeful. Inclusive." He vowed, "We will prove that someone who is conservative and compassionate can win without sacrificing principle. We will show that politics, after a time of tarnished ideals, can be higher and better. We will give our country a fresh start after a season of cynicism."

Bush told his supporters and the assembled reporters, "I've learned to lead." As proof of that, he asserted, "I don't run polls to tell me what to think." *Take that, Bill Clinton.* No polls, no negative politics, no self-serving calculations, no ideological or partisan harshness, no more cynical spin, no more falsehoods. But it was all feigned.

Bush's announcement speech was evidence he would be mounting a truth-defying campaign. Before he delivered this kickoff speech, his campaign had held focus groups in South Carolina, Michigan, and California. At these sessions, according to Roger Simon, the chief political correspondent of *U.S. News & World Report,* the Bush operatives played footage of Bush and asked the people present to turn a knob one way if they liked what they were seeing and hearing and another way if they did not. All this led to a computer-generated graph line superimposed over the film, so Bush and his crew could determine which lines, words, and methods of delivery scored well and which ones stank. Political pros call this people-metering. Using this information, Bush's chief speechwriter, Michael Gerson, produced 16 draft versions of what would become Bush's standard campaign stump speech, according to the *New York Times.* True, Bush did not pledge *not* to use this particular device. But he certainly was eager to create the impression he was an I-am-what-I-am politician who would deliver, if nothing else, authenticity. In a later interview, he asserted, "I campaign the way I campaign. And I don't get coached." But do uncoached candidates use people-meters? And this was no anomaly. Toward the end of the campaign, *Time* would report that Bush was routinely using focus groups to test key phrases he used on the stump: "personal accounts," "school choice," "education recession."

Pretending to be a straight-shooter who eschewed the cynical mechanics of modern-day politics was but a small contradiction of the image Bush offered his followers in that Iowa hangar. Over the next 18 months, he would engage in business as usual—nasty ads, pandering, expedience-driven position-shifting, cover-ups, and assorted spinning. He would not deliver a "fresh start." Rather, he would embrace—though not in public—most of what he decried about politics. All this would be done to mount a false advertising campaign about a product he knew well: George W. Bush.

"I've got a record not of rhetoric, but a record of results."

As soon as Bush crashed the race—which already had a crowded field—he was the lead cowboy. He had the name, the money, the endorsements, the organization. And he had a clever slogan: he was the "compassionate conservative." The most dangerous threat Bush faced was himself—that is, his reputation as a less-than-serious, smirkful, syntax-challenged fellow who would rarely be mistaken for an intellectual heavyweight. And in the opening months of his campaign, he had a knack for providing the skeptics evidence. He called the Greeks "Grecians." He could not identify the leaders of Pakistan, India, and Chechnya. Asked which rendition of the Ten Commandments he preferred—Protestant, Catholic, or Jewish—he replied, "the standard one," suggesting he had no clue each religion recognizes different versions.

With his not-yet-presidential manner and his miscues on global matters, Bush faced the charge (from Democrats and some Republicans) that he did not possess sufficient candlepower for the job. But for the doubters, he had a stock response, which he would repeat throughout the campaign: look at my record. Bush was arguing that his stint as governor of the nation's second-largest state—with an economy larger than that of all but ten nations in the world—trumped his lack of foreign policy experience, his odd speech patterns, and his missing gravitas. His accomplishments in Texas were his credentials and showed he was both a fiscal conservative and a "compassionate" conservative. As he said at a Republican debate in Iowa, "I've got a record not of rhetoric, but a record of results. In my state, I led our state to the two biggest tax cuts in the state's history. Our test scores for our students are up." He also claimed Texas air had gotten cleaner on his watch, that he had passed a patients' bill of rights, that he had expanded a children's health insurance program. This was quite an impressive rundown—but it was counterfeit.

Being a champion of tax cuts—past and future—was one of Bush's key selling points. At one debate he called himself "a tax-cutting person." He bragged about those "two largest tax cuts" he achieved in Texas, and he boasted in a campaign ad, "we still have no personal income tax." Lowering taxes was Exhibit Number 1 in his claim he had been a successful governor.

But this declaration was part Texas tall-tale, and part muddy water. He had not had to do anything to keep Texas from adopting a personal income tax. An amendment to the state constitution—proposed and approved by a Democrat-controlled legislature before Bush took office—prohibited the imposition of an income tax without a voter referendum. Bush was assuming credit for a policy established before he had arrived in Austin.

As for those two big tax cuts, the true results were not much to boast about. Taxes were lowered for some, but much of the enacted tax cuts ended up being largely offset by other tax hikes made necessary by the cuts Bush was hailing. As he campaigned, Bush glossed over the real story of the Texas tax cuts and even mischaracterized the changes he had actually sought.

In 1997, Bush had proposed a major tax overhaul that would lower school property taxes but that would also *raise* the sales tax and impose a new business activity tax. The plan was a direct violation of a promise he had made in 1994, when he first ran for governor. That year, he pledged never to endorse raising the sales tax or creating a business tax. With his 1997 proposal, Bush did both. When grilled about this broken promise during the 2000 campaign on ABC News' *This Week*, Bush did not say, as might have been appropriate, that circumstances had changed between 1994 and 1997 and that he had been forced to reevaluate his position. Instead, he responded in an all-too-revealing fashion. He devalued his promise by remarking, "There are pledges all the time." Did that mean Bush believed it was okay to make pledges to get elected and not stand by them?

On the 2000 campaign trail, Bush was deceptive about the nature of his 1997 tax plan. He neglected to mention his attempt to boost the sales tax and to implement a new business tax. Nor did he note his package had not been accepted. He had been unable to persuade the legislature to greenlight his entire set of tax cuts and tax hikes. Instead, the lawmakers passed a $1 billion reduction in school property taxes. And these tax cuts turned out to be a sham. After they kicked in, school districts across the state raised local tax rates to compensate for the loss of revenue. A 1999 *Dallas Morning News* analysis of the state's 1,036 school districts found that "many [taxpayers] are still paying as much as they did in 1997, or more." Republican Lieutenant Governor Rick Perry told the newspaper, "The tax cut didn't stand the test of time as well as many of us would have liked for it to." He called the cuts "rather illusory." In 2003 a report released by the House Research Organization of the Republican-controlled Texas House of Representatives noted, "In 1997, then Gov. George W. Bush sought to revamp state taxes. . . . That effort was unsuccessful, and many of the concerns cited at that time remain unresolved."

The story was also more complicated with the 1999 tax cuts Bush also touted during his presidential bid. That year Bush sought $2 billion in property tax cuts. The legislature adopted a $1.3 billion reduction. But it was not relief for everyone. Much of the reduction was targeted to districts burdened by fast growth or construction-related debt. State Representative Paul Sadler, the Democratic chairman of the Texas House education committee, told the *Austin American-Statesman,* "If your district doesn't fall into one of these categories, you're not going to get as much benefit." According to the Texas Education Agency, property taxes dropped in only 36.5 percent of the districts; they stayed flat or went up in 63.5 percent. "As Bush sells the country on his tax-cutting prowess," Dave McNeely of the *American-Statesman* observed in 1999, "school districts back in Texas are raising local taxes anyway."

Sure, Bush had tried to slash *some* taxes (while trying to raise others), but the outcome had been unimpressive. And he was the guy claiming to be presidential material not on the basis of effort made but on results achieved. His efforts had not panned out. Perhaps more importantly than that, Bush's accounting of these episodes—taking credit for tax cuts that benefited a few and that created burdens for others—demonstrated he was not to be trusted when it came to talking about the all-important topic of taxes.

On the stump, Bush claimed that his stint in Texas proved he was also a guy who knew how to downsize Big Government. A Bush ad said he had "reduced the growth of state government to the lowest in 40 years." But according to the *Dallas Morning News,* Associated Press, and the *Washington Post,* during Bush's time in office, the state budget jumped from about $73 billion to $98.1 billion—a 34 percent leap that was hardly modest, and larger than the federal government's 21 percent growth rate.

■ ■ ■

As Bush misrepresented recent history to bolster his standing as a fiscal conservative, he did the same to demonstrate he was a "compassionate conservative" who had accomplished much in health-care. The Bush campaign's website portrayed him as having "led the nation in adopting a strong Patients' Bill of Rights." That was not the case. In 1995, Bush vetoed a patient protection act, which if passed would have made his state a leader in HMO reform. Two years later, Bush seriously considered vetoing a similar measure that included a provision allowing patients to sue HMOs for malpractice. Only after it became clear the Texas legislature would override his veto did Bush permit the bill to become law, and he did so without placing his signature on it. He had not led, he had not even signed the measure. He had been pushed. In fact, during the debate on the bill, according to *Salon*, State Senator David Sibley, a Republican and an oral surgeon sponsoring the legislation, had griped about the "governor's office," saying, "I can't make 'em happy no matter what I do unless I completely gut the bill."

To prove Bush cared about kids and their health needs, his presidential campaign maintained he had "signed legislation to create the Children's Health Insurance Program." And in an interview with CNN, Bush said, "We're spreading CHIPs, the CHIPs program out all across the state of Texas. We just passed the legislation necessary to do so." We? During Bush's tenure as governor, Texas had the highest number of uninsured children per capita in the nation, according to the *Houston Chronicle*. When the Texas legislature considered providing medical coverage to many of these kids in 1999, the Democrat-controlled House wanted the program to be available to children in families earning up to 200 percent of the poverty level (about $33,000 for a family of four). But Bush fought to limit eligibility to children from homes with incomes below $25,000. His lower cap would have prevented about 220,000 of the 500,000 uninsured children who were potentially eligible from qualifying for CHIP coverage. (At that time, Bush's number-one legislative priority was emergency legislation to provide a $45 million tax break to the oil-and-gas industry.) Eventually, the Democrats beat Bush on this front, and the 200 percent cutoff prevailed.

After the CHIP fight was settled, Texas state Representative Glen Maxey, a Democrat, claimed Bush told him, "Congratulations on children's health. You crammed it down our throats." And an account in *Time* made the point that Bush had dragged his heels in introducing CHIP to Texas and this delay had made possible the not-so-effective 1997 tax cuts: "Bush took his time to start up CHIP. . . . When CHIP finally did start . . . a total of five years had passed since the legislature first attempted to cover many of the same youngsters. The delay freed Texas from having to spend billions of dollars in matching state grants, leaving enough money for Bush to pass $1 billion in tax relief in the 1997 legislative session."

During the presidential campaign, Scott McClellan, a Bush spokesman, offered imaginative spin about the CHIP episode. Bush's push for a less extensive program, he said, had been "just a starting point." Did McClellan mean to suggest that Bush—who would adopt as a campaign slogan the cry "Leave no child behind"—had played politics with the health of 200,000 or so children? What if the legislature had accepted his "starting point"? Would Bush have said to those kids left out, sorry, it was merely a negotiating ploy?

Not only was Bush disingenuous about his health-care record, he wouldn't even admit the truth about how dire the situation was in Texas. When CBS News anchor Dan Rather asked Bush about Texas' low national ranking in medical insurance coverage for children (50th) and women (49th), Bush replied, "I think you can find all kinds of statistics to make all kinds of cases. I rest most of my case on that fact that people in Texas like the job I have done. . . . I don't know the statistics . . . but I do know there's a lot of women who are covered." It was a telling response. When confronted with the record—with facts— Bush chose not to address the actual (and embarrassing) statistics. Instead, he did a two-step, suggesting the numbers were wrong, while acknowledging unapologetically that he didn't know the details.

In embellishing his record in Texas, Bush falsely asserted the environment in the Lone Star State had improved on his watch, and that he was responsible for that. Weeks before entering the 2000 race, Bush remarked, "You've got to ask the question, is the air cleaner since I became governor? And the answer is yes." But a *Washington Post*

review of this claim concluded, "There is statistical evidence that the air in Texas cities is as foul—and perhaps more so—than when Bush took power in 1995. The frequency of smog alerts in Houston, Dallas, and Austin has risen steeply in the Bush years." Bush could point to a few categories of pollutants in which emissions had dropped, but there was no overall decline. The Texas Natural Resource Conservation Commission (which was headed by three industry-friendly officials Bush had appointed) maintained that industrial emissions were down 11 percent from 1994 to 1997, but Environmental Protection Agency figures indicated a 10 percent increase. Whichever of these statistics were correct, Texas still ranked first among all states in the number of days with health-threatening ozone levels, first in airborne carcinogens, and first in toxic air releases.

Of all his supposed achievements in Texas, Bush most enthusiastically talked up his education policy. "I've reformed education" in Texas, he proclaimed. Education was a subject with which Bush seemed thoroughly familiar, one of the few areas in which he was a details man. But he was once again dishonestly taking credit for actions for which he had not been responsible. As the *Fort Worth Star-Telegram* noted, "A review of the record indicates that the state's most important school reforms—including standardized tests and other accountability measures—took root long before Bush moved into the Governor's Mansion. Education experts, and even Bush aides, say that his predecessors are more responsible for improvements in Texas education." A *Los Angeles Times* investigation of the so-called "Texas miracle" reached the same conclusion. Yet Bush was not pursuing the White House as the official who *continued and didn't end* previously established measures. He was campaigning as *the* miracle-man.

When Steve Forbes, the millionaire publisher/candidate, threw stones at Bush's education record during a Republican debate, Bush told yet another fib. Forbes accused Bush of dumbing down standards "to the point where in Texas your SAT ranking has gone from 40th in the nation to 46th in the nation." Bush chuckled, "So many half stories, so little time." He then replied, "Test scores in my state, on the NAEP [National Assessment of Educational Progress] test, which compares state to state, showed dramatic improvement. And that's—

objective analysis after objective analysis has ranked Texas as one of the best education states in the country. ... One reason—our SAT scores have improved since I've been the governor. You need to get your research to do a better job."

But it was Bush's research that required fact-checking. Texas' NAEP scores, according to the National Center for Education Statistics, had risen significantly in only one category: mathematics. Not so on reading and science. On Forbes' point about the SATs, Bush had flipped the facts. According to the College Entrance Examination Board, the average verbal/math combined SAT score in Texas had *dipped* 3 points during Bush's administration; over the same period, the national average had improved 9 points.

It was true that in the years leading to the 2000 campaign Bush's state had drawn much positive notice in the education-policy community. But that was not because of its SAT scores. As a *Des Moines Register* truth-testing review of a Bush campaign ad maintained, "Student performance, as measured by the Texas Assessment of Academic Skills, has improved during his term. But Texas still lags behind many other states on various education indicators." Later in the campaign, a RAND Corporation study suggested that intensive drilling for the state's standardized tests—tests that Bush championed—might have artificially boosted the encouraging scores cited by fans of the state's testing-based education initiatives.

If Bush had wanted to boast accurately about his years as Texas' chief executive, he could have celebrated how he instituted a state food-aid program for elderly and disabled immigrants after Congress cut them off federal food stamps. Or how he pushed for a measure to speed up adoptions. Or how he signed legislation to raise the salaries for teachers and okayed a bill that forced medical insurers to treat mental illness more like physical health problems. He could have cited increased funding for child care used by mothers on welfare. But with his big-ticket claims to success—taxes, children's health, education, patients' protections, air quality—Bush was sharing one yarn after another. The intent was to sell himself as presidential material by establishing that he had already tackled the major policy dilemmas of

modern America. But to compose a compelling picture, he had to color outside the lines. Far outside the lines.

"He was always opposed to abortion."

Bush was an artful truth-dodger not only on the matter of his short record in government. He also shaved—or denied—the truth when it came to significant pieces of his past: his arrest record, his military service, and an apparent flip-flop on a critical social issue. In each instance, actions he had taken years previously held the potential, if fully exposed, to derail his presidential bid. In each case, Bush ducked trouble by dissembling.

During the 2000 campaign, I came across a 1978 interview with Bush in the *Lubbock Avalanche-Journal* newspaper. At that time, he was running for Congress in West Texas, and he had explained his political views to reporter Sylvia Teague. According to the newspaper, "Bush said he opposes the pro-life amendment favored by [his opponent] and favors leaving up to a woman and her doctor the abortion question."

This indicated Bush had once been on the side of abortion-rights advocates. But sometime after the 1978 campaign (in which he won the Republican primary but lost the general election), he reversed his position. During his successful 1994 campaign for governor, Bush said, "I will do everything in my power to restrict abortions." And as a presidential candidate, he was calling himself "pro-life" and supporting a constitutional amendment outlawing abortion. Yet his switch from "pro-choice" to "pro-life" had escaped public notice.

During the fight for the Democratic presidential nomination, Vice President Al Gore, who was campaigning as a champion of choice, took a big hit when news accounts revealed he had cast anti-abortion votes and expressed anti-abortion sentiments in the 1970s and 1980s. Bush's campaign had derided Gore for pulling a 180. "I think people want to see consistency with their leaders," said Mindy Tucker, a Bush spokesperson. Had Bush, too, shifted his abortion position in a direction more in line with his party's faithful?

When I asked the Bush campaign about the 1978 article, spokesman Dan Bartlett said, "We consider this a misinterpretation. He is pro-life. He was always opposed to abortion." You're saying, I remarked, that the reporter got it wrong? "We're saying this is a misinterpretation," he repeated.

The campaign had resorted to common subterfuge: claim the candidate was misquoted. There was no foundation for its assertion that Sylvia Teague had incorrectly recounted her interview with Bush. And Teague had gone on to become an award-winning investigative journalist at KCBS-TV in Los Angeles. She told me she was confident her story had been accurate. She did not recall Bush or his congressional campaign complaining she had misstated his position. Most campaigns would scream if a newspaper so thoroughly mangled the views of a candidate on such a sensitive issue.

The Bush campaign's "misinterpretation" explanation did not withstand close examination. In the context of the article, the disputed sentence made perfect sense. Bush had been contrasting himself to his Republican primary opponent, a Reagan-like conservative. First Bush noted his own conservative views, then he pointed out that he differed with his foe on abortion. But here was the killer: after saying, in Teague's account, that abortion should be a matter between a woman and her doctor, Bush added, "That does not mean I'm for abortion." Why would Bush have had to say those words if he had told Teague he was *opposed* to abortion rights?

Which scenario was more likely? A reporter with a good reputation reported the exact opposite of what a candidate said to her about abortion? Or a politician blurted out what he really thought, later reversed his position on a contentious issue to be more in tune with the activists of his party, and then lied about the switch? Yet by denying any abortion about-face had transpired, Bush evaded a confrontation with what would have been a highly uncomfortable truth.*

---

*During the campaign, Bush adopted an abortion position containing a glaring contradiction. He steadfastly declared his opposition to abortion when asked about the topic (which he rarely broached on his own accord). But he said he favored permitting abortion in cases involving rape, incest, and the life of the mother. At the same time, he professed support for the Republican Party's 1996 platform on abortion, which called for outlawing all abortions without exceptions. On ABC News' *This Week*, Sam Donaldson read the GOP platform to Bush: "The unborn child has a fundamental individual right to life which cannot be infringed. We support a human life amendment to the Constitution and we endorse legislation to make clear that the 14th Amendment's protections apply to unborn children." He then noted, "It does not say, 'with three exceptions.'" Bush replied, "Well, it doesn't say, 'without three exceptions,' either." Donaldson asked if Bush would recommend the three exceptions be added to the platform. "I am going to lead," Bush said, "and I'm going to recommend the platform stay the same."

"I did the duty necessary. . . . Any allegations other than that are simply not true."

In one of the more important ruses of his campaign, Bush misrepresented his military service and then offered dubious explanations in response to questions about it. His goal was to create the perception he had served honorably and legitimately in the National Guard during the Vietnam War, when the record suggested otherwise.

Soon after he entered the presidential race, the Associated Press discovered that Bush had not been honest about his military past when he had campaigned unsuccessfully for Congress in 1978. Back then, in an ad in the *Lubbock Avalanche-Journal*, he boasted he had served "in the U.S. Air Force and the Texas Air National Guard where he piloted the F-102 aircraft." But Bush had done time only in the Guard, not the Air Force. When AP asked Bush's presidential campaign about this, the Bush crew could have taken the opportunity to set the record straight. Instead, Bush spokeswoman Karen Hughes told AP that the advertisement had been "accurate," considering the time Bush had spent on alert and in training. "As an officer," she maintained, "he was serving on active duty in the Air Force." Bush himself remarked, "I was in the Air Force for over 600 days." Not so, according to a definitive source— the Air Force. The AP reported that "the Air Force says that Air National Guard members are considered 'guardsmen on active duty' while receiving pilot training. They are not, however, counted as members of the overall active-duty Air Force. . . . Anyone in the Air National Guard is always considered a guardsman and not a member of the active-duty Air Force." The 1978 ad had been a distortion, and Bush and Hughes refused to concede that.

Bush's two-decades-old exaggeration of his Vietnam-era service— which received scant media notice—was not his sole problem on this front. Prior to becoming an official 2000 contender, he had been dogged by questions concerning his reason for joining the Guard and his good fortune in snagging a spot, which protected him from being drafted for Vietnam. And his answers—before and during the 2000 campaign—often had a less-than-truthful, tinny sound.

Bush had long denied that anyone rigged the system for him when he joined the Air National Guard in 1968. At that time, he was finishing his final semester at Yale (and losing his student deferment) and the

Vietnam War was escalating. The National Guard was widely viewed as a way to escape being drafted. Naturally, Guard slots were prized by young men answering the call of self-preservation. Past Texas Guard officials have said that at that time there were long waiting lists. And connections helped. In Houston, so many sons of prominent families were joining the 147th Fighter Group of the Texas Air National Guard that the group would later be dubbed the Champagne Unit, according to Bill Minutaglio's biography of Bush, *First Son*. That was the fighter wing Bush entered. And he said he did so without the help of his father, then a congressman, or any other person of clout. In March 1999, *The Boston Globe* quoted him: "Did I receive preferential treatment? There were some pilot slots available, and I was chosen. I sought and was chosen."

Yet on September 26, 1999, Ben Barnes, a former Speaker of the Texas House of Representatives, revealed to the *New York Times* that during the Vietnam War he often received requests to help men find a way into the National Guard. One such entreaty, he said, had come in for Bush. A Houston oilman named Sidney Adger, a friend of Bush's father, had asked Barnes to pull strings for George W. According to Barnes, he then contacted the brigadier general in charge of the state's Air National Guard. What happened after that? Barnes wouldn't say. And the general and Adger were dead.

Perhaps Bush hadn't known about any behind-the-scenes favoritism. He now told reporters that if someone had exerted influence on his behalf, they had not informed him (and he added that his father-the-congressman had done nothing). It might have been that the Air National Guard itself had decided, without prompting, that it wouldn't hurt to do a favor for the son of a congressman. No preferential treatment, as Bush repeatedly said? Maybe it was in the eye of the beholder, and this beholder hadn't seen it. But other Bush statements about this chapter in his life were much more subject to dispute.

Why had he sought a Guard slot? Had it been to elude the draft? "At the time I wanted to fight . . . and I was willing to train for whatever experience came my way," he said in March 1999. But in 1998 he had explained his rationale differently, telling *USA Today*, "I wanted to be a pilot. I heard there were pilot slots open in units in Houston. I joined." In 1994, according to *The Texas Monthly*, when asked if he had turned toward the Guard to avoid Vietnam, Bush responded, "Hell no. Do you think I'm going to admit that?" But in 1990, according to a *Houston Chronicle* story published in 1994, Bush said, "I was not prepared to shoot my eardrum out with a shotgun in order to get a deferment. Nor was I willing to go to Canada. So I chose to better myself by learning how to fly airplanes." This explanation sure sounded like the words of someone who had been primarily concerned with evading the draft, not a person who had "wanted to fight." Moreover, when Bush entered the Guard, he had to say on his application papers whether he was willing to volunteer for overseas duty. He checked the box that read "do not volunteer." In a 1999 interview with the *Washington Post*, Bush claimed he did not recall doing so. Two weeks later, his campaign released a statement from a former Air National Guard officer who said Bush "probably" had been advised by Guard officers not to volunteer for an overseas assignment.

The stories that came out in mid-1999 about Bush's Guard service—which focused on how he had managed to enlist—were speedbumps, not potholes, for his campaign. But a page-one report published by the *Boston Globe* in May 2000 added a new and more disturbing layer of mystery to Bush's military history, and it offered more evidence that Bush had been knowingly dishonest about his time as a guardsman.

In Bush's campaign autobiography, *A Charge to Keep*, he wrote that he had completed his pilot training in 1970 and "continued flying with my unit for the next several years." But according to copies of his military records obtained by the *Globe,* Bush stopped flying during his final 18 months of service in 1972 and 1973. More curious, the records indicated Bush had not reported for his Guard duty during a long stretch of that time. That raised a question that could cause Bush much trouble: Had a man who now wanted to be commander-in-chief gone AWOL when he served in the Guard?

In May of 1972—with two years to go on his six-year commitment to the Guard—Bush moved to Alabama to work on the Senate campaign of a family friend. He asked the Guard for permission to do "equivalent training" at a unit there, and he won approval to join temporarily a unit at Maxwell Air Force Base. But that unit had no airplanes, no pilots. It could not provide the training that Bush, who had done well as a fighter jet pilot in Houston, needed. Albert Lloyd Jr., the Texas Air Guard's personnel director at the time, told the *Globe* that he was mystified by the 1972 decision to allow Bush to pull duty in such a unit. (No preferential treatment?) But the Air Reserve Personnel Center in Denver, according to an investigation published by TomPaine.com, ultimately disallowed this transfer. And for months, Bush put in no Guard time. In the meantime, he lost his flight status for failing to submit to an annual physical examination. (Bush campaign aides, trying to explain this point, said Bush did not take a physical because he was in Alabama and his personal doctor was in Houston. But, as the *Globe* noted, "Flight physicals can be administered only by certified Air Force flight surgeons, and some were assigned at the time to Maxwell Air Force Base in Montgomery, where Bush was living.") For failing to take a physical, Bush was grounded. In September 1972, he asked to do duty at a unit in Montgomery; permission was granted.

The tale at this point becomes odder. The commander of the Montgomery unit and his administrative officer, in interviews with the *Globe*, said they had no recollection of Bush ever reporting. Lloyd noted that if Bush had performed duty in Alabama, "his drill attendance should have been certified and sent to Ellington [Air Force Base in Houston], and there would have been a record. We cannot find the records to show he fulfilled the requirements in Alabama." Odder still, when Bush went back to Texas after the November election, he apparently did not return to his unit at Ellington. His annual performance report, dated May 2, 1973, noted, "Lt. Bush has not been observed at this unit" for the past year. The unit's administrative officer at the time later said he believed Bush had been in Alabama for the entire year—which had not been the case. In May, June, and July 1973, Bush pulled 36 days of duty at Ellington—a large amount of time in a short period—before receiving permission to end his service early. He was off to Massachusetts to attend Harvard Business School.

So where was W? Did he skip out on the Guard in Alabama? Did he abandon his Houston unit in late 1972 and the first four months of 1973? Bush wouldn't talk to the *Globe*. But campaign spokesman Dan Bartlett said Bush recalled doing duty in Alabama and "coming back to Houston and doing duty, though he does not recall if it was on a consistent basis." Once the story broke, Bush said, "I did the duty necessary. . . . Any allegations other than that are simply not true." At a June 23, 2000, press conference in Alabama, a reporter asked if Bush recalled what work he had done in the Alabama Guard. "No, I really don't," he replied. "But I was there." Two days later, Bush's campaign acknowledged that it had failed to find any documents proving he fulfilled his duty in Alabama. (The campaign later located one undated document without Bush's name that it maintained showed Bush had put in one day's duty with the Montgomery unit. But that record was not conclusive, and, if accurate, could also mean that Bush had gone weeks without reporting.)

Bartlett told reporters that campaign inquiries would turn up former Guard members who could corroborate Bush's presence in Alabama. Yet the campaign produced no such witnesses. (The Montgomery unit had contained 600 to 700 people.) And Bush provided not one name of a former comrade in Alabama. He did point to an ex-girlfriend as a witness. But *The New Republic* reported that she said she remembered Bush telling her he was obliged to perform duty in Alabama, not that she knew for sure he had.

Bush's military service was not as he had portrayed it in his autobiography. And it was further evidence he did not honor his vows. When he enlisted with the Texas Air Guard, he signed a pledge: "I, George Walker Bush, upon successful completion of pilot training plan to return to my unit and fulfill my obligation to the utmost of my ability. I have applied for pilot training with the goal of making flying a lifetime pursuit and I believe I can best accomplish this to my own satisfaction by service as a member of the Air National Guard as long as possible." Bush did not serve "as long as possible." He received pilot training—at the expense of the U.S. government—and then cut out on his unit, heading to Alabama where, at the least, he did not put his training to any use. He failed to arrange for a flight physical (so as to be fully ready to serve), and, once back in Texas, he flew no more for the Guard. He then ended his service prematurely. Bush had not been faithful to the Guard, and on the campaign trail, he refused to be honest about that.

■ ■ ■

"Trust me. If there was a time bomb sitting out there, it would have been discovered by the Clintons in 1992."

Along with his iffy military record, there was another embarrassing episode in Bush's past—this one involving unlawful behavior—that he had managed to keep secret prior to the campaign. But when it was exposed, he would again employ guile in a blatant (and somewhat ridiculous) attempt to escape what appeared to be a lie previously told.

For years, Bush had acknowledged his tendency to drink too much before he cast off the booze when he turned 40, which was about the time he became a born-again Christian. But he adamantly refused to explain the particulars. Had his drinking been a serious problem? He wouldn't answer that. Unlike other politicians of his generation, he declined to say whether he had used marijuana. As he put it when campaigning for governor in 1994, according to the *Texarkana Gazette*, "What I did as a kid? I don't think it's relevant. . . . Did I behave irresponsibly as a kid at times? Sure did. You bet." His definition of *kid* seemed a bit liberal.

Concerning his more wild days, Bush adopted a best-defense-is-a-good-offense stance. He branded any questioning of his personal past illegitimate rumor-mongering. He equated being asked about the booze-and-drugs issue with being targeted by unfair innuendo. "I'm not ready for rumors and gossip," Bush told *USA Today*. "I'm ready for the truth. Surely people will learn the truth." What insincerity. He was claiming he wanted people to know the truth about him, but he would not answer a whole set of questions about his past.

One concealed truth Bush had not been "ready for" exploded on November 2, 2000, five days before Election Day. A Maine television channel reported that in 1976, Bush, then 30 years old, was arrested in Kennebunkport, Maine, for drunken driving. He had admitted to the arresting officer he had been drinking. He paid a $150 fine and had his driving privileges revoked in Maine. After the story broke, at a campaign press conference (his first in a month), candidate Bush acknowledged the report was accurate, and he said that he had never publicly revealed the DWI conviction out of concern he would set a bad example for his twin girls. In the same press conference, Bush maintained,

"I have been very candid about my past." This was obviously not a factual statement, since Bush had neglected to disclose this arrest while supposedly being "very candid about his past."

As the story developed, the issue became not his post-youth crime, but one question: Had Bush lied to keep his arrest record a secret? Wayne Slater, a reporter for the *Dallas Morning News* and a longtime Bush watcher, recalled he had asked Bush in a 1998 interview whether Bush had ever been arrested after 1968. Slater told his media colleagues on the Bush campaign plane that Bush had said no. Slater also remembered that later in that 1998 interview Bush indicated he was about to return to this subject. But as Bush began to say something, Karen Hughes cut in, and Bush said nothing else on the topic.

While Slater was sharing this account, Hughes, several rows away, was presenting her own version to reporters "nervously," according to *New York Times* correspondent Frank Bruni. This was her line: not only had the governor not said anything false to Slater, he had somehow conveyed an accurate impression that an episode like the 1976 bust had occurred. Hughes, according to UPI, maintained that Bush in the 1998 interview with Slater "was hinting that something had happened. That's why I stopped the conversation." *Washington Post* reporter Dana Milbank subsequently wrote that Hughes told the journalists, "I think the implication Wayne was left with was that in fact the governor was acknowledging that he had in fact been arrested." Notice the two "in facts" in one sentence. As Bruni quipped, "An accurate impression of an unacknowledged event? It was an awfully weird concept."

This was spin at its most frantic. But that was the Bush camp's story. During a press conference, Hughes said Slater "was clearly left with the impression that the governor—an accurate impression that the governor had been involved in some incident involving alcohol." And she noted that on another occasion, in 1996, Bush "was asked directly had he ever been arrested for drinking, and the governor replied, quote, 'I do not have a perfect record as a youth.'" That vague response supposedly was evidence Bush had not outright lied about this arrest. But his 1996 answer had not been responsive. And had he been a "youth" at the age of 30?

However he had ducked Slater's question, he had indirectly lied about the DWI incident to another Texas newspaper. In November 1998, Bush told the *Fort Worth Star-Telegram* there was nothing of note to uncover in his past: "Trust me. If there was a time bomb sitting out there, it would have been discovered by the Clintons in 1992. And if they couldn't have found it, it darn sure would have been discovered in 1994, or discovered in '95, '96, '97, or now."

Had Bush forgotten about his arrest? There was even reason to suspect he had taken deliberate steps in the recent past to keep this time bomb buried. In 1996, Governor Bush was called for jury duty in Travis County, and he publicly expressed his eagerness to be a good citizen and serve. But then he ran into a problem: the jury questionnaire asked if he had "ever been accused, or a complainant . . . in a criminal case." According to a report by *Newsweek*'s Michael Isikoff, Bush left the answer blank. And as a potential juror he faced a serious hazard. During jury selection, he likely would be asked whether he had ever been arrested for drunk driving. (Travis County handled a large number of DWI cases.) Having been informed that Bush would have to answer questions about his past, Alberto Gonzales, Bush's chief counsel, orchestrated a legal maneuver that resulted in Bush being excused from duty.

The case at hand involved a topless dancer on trial for drunken driving, and Bush showed up at the courthouse, claiming he was raring to go. "While Bush chatted with reporters," *Newsweek* noted, "Gonzales consulted with the judge in chambers. Gonzales raised an unusual argument: as governor, Bush had a potential conflict because he one day might be asked to pardon the defendant." The county prosecutor let Bush off the hook, and the defense attorney agreed to be the one to ask for Bush's dismissal. So in public it appeared as if the defense had requested Bush be bounced. He left the courthouse saying he was "glad to do my duty."

On the long and trying campaign trail, Bush misrepresented his tenure as governor and notable episodes in his past to concoct a certain image (or escape a certain image) and to establish an appeal to voters. All this belied his strategically important claim to be the candidate of honesty. So, too, did his manner of campaigning. He was not, as he and his campaign maintained, a candidate who shunned partisan finger-pointing, blame-gaming, and mudslinging. He freely adopted negative campaigning. And he wasn't lying just about himself and his campaign style. He was lying about what might happen should he become president. While asking voters to trust him, Bush dissembled about crucial policy proposals that could have—and would have—tremendous consequences for the entire nation and the world beyond.

2. A Dishonest Campaign

"I'm a uniter, not a divider."

From the start of the campaign, Bush said he would remake American politics. He was the candidate who denounced down-and-dirty attack ads, the plain-talking Texan who bemoaned partisan assaults and name-calling, the presidential contender who yearned to change the harsh tone of the national discourse. During a GOP presidential debate, Bush proclaimed, "One thing that makes the American people cynical is negative advertisement on TV. That's one thing that causes people to turn away from politics." Moments later, he added, "I'll run positive ads. And I'm darn sure not going to do to a candidate what this man [Steve Forbes] did to Bob Dole in 1996." That is, viciously attack a fellow Republican. Bush and Senator John McCain, another presidential aspirant, then shook hands and vowed not to hurl ads against each other. But Bush would toss all the lofty sentiments—and his handshake with McCain—onto the scrap heap when McCain, the maverick, reform-minded war hero from Arizona, threatened to snatch the Republican nomination out of Bush's hands. To win, Bush would manhandle the truth.

The primary season began well for Bush, the front-runner. He predictably placed first in the Iowa caucuses on January 24, 2000. But in the influential New Hampshire primary, on February 1, McCain upset the leader, 49 to 31 percent, and Bush—supposedly the candidate of inevitability—was suddenly in trouble. He had to win the next major contest, which was coming in South Carolina in two-and-a-half weeks. No negative campaigning? Forget about it.

Bush hit the Palmetto State with an anti-McCain bang. On February 3, he appeared at a campaign rally with J. Thomas Burch Jr., the chairman of a marginal outfit called the National Vietnam and Gulf War Veterans Coalition. Burch lambasted McCain for "always" opposing veterans legislation, including measures concerning Agent Orange, health care, and the Gulf War. "He was the leading opponent in the Senate," Burch groused. "He had the power to help these veterans. He came home, he forgot us. We need leadership in Washington, and we need yours, Governor Bush."

Cozying up to Burch was a clever move for Bush. South Carolina was home to a large population of retired military people, and the McCain camp was hoping they would fall in behind the former POW. Bush, who had escaped Vietnam by doing time (kind of) in the Air National Guard, needed to prevent that; he had to make the vets of South Carolina think twice about McCain. How better to do that than with a veterans advocate assailing McCain for being AWOL on veterans issues? There was one problem: Burch was lying. McCain had actually co-sponsored the Agent Orange Act that became law. He also had testified in favor of legislation to provide compensation to Gulf War vets struck by unexplained illnesses. But how did Bush respond to Burch's malicious and deceitful attack? When Burch finished, Bush shook his hand and said, "Thank you, buddy."

Perhaps Bush was not up to speed on McCain's record on veterans affairs. But after press accounts noted Burch had lied about McCain *and* after five senators who had fought in Vietnam (including two Republicans) called Burch's allegations "absolutely false," Bush still refused to repudiate Burch or to apologize. He stuck to this stance, even following Burch's admission that he could not back up his charges about McCain. Instead, Bush campaign spokesman Tucker Eskew cynically brayed, "The McCain campaign is squawking because we hit them where they hurt. McCain and the media created a myth of the [pro-McCain] military monolith [in South Carolina], and we exploded that. We challenged him on his greatest point of pride, and they stomped their feet, pointed fingers, and whined." So much for the honor, decency, and integrity Bush had promised.

The Burch blast was merely an opening shot. In South Carolina,

McCain became the target of a trash-talking effort unprecedented in recent years. The mud was being thrown with hurricane force. Leaflets, e-mails, faxes, phone calls—all conveying the nastiest, unsubstantiated rumors about the man. That McCain had been brainwashed by the Chinese and turned into a real-life Manchurian candidate when he was a POW in Vietnam. That his adopted daughter from Bangladesh was actually a love child he had sired with a black prostitute. That he had infected his wife with venereal disease and driven her to become a drug addict. That his wife was mobbed up. That there had been an abortion in the McCain family.

The Bush campaign claimed it had nothing to do with the sleazy anti-McCain efforts. But the McCain camp (and many other political observers) suspected Bush's people were behind some, if not much, of this foul barrage. In *Bush's Brain*, a biography of chief Bush strategist Karl Rove, journalists James Moore and Wayne Slater note, "Although Rove denied responsibility, there clearly resonated in the dirty tactics a pattern familiar in Rove's history." Most telling was that Bush—who had trumpeted his disgust for below-the-belt politics—did not speak out against this covert smear crusade. "Whenever Bush was questioned about these hardball tactics," *New York Times* correspondent Frank Bruni recalled, "he did not respond with a full-throttle exhortation that they cease and desist. He instead offered a woe-is-me testimonial that he too was being attacked, by groups like the Sierra Club and the National Abortion and Reproductive Rights Action League." But these outfits were not asserting Bush and his family were psychotic, morally debased, and wracked by sex scandals.

Whether the Bush campaign was in league with the anti-McCain death squads in South Carolina, the Bush organization, in its public actions, was going mean. After countenancing an untrue attack on McCain's record on veterans issues, the Bush machine zeroed in on McCain's standing as a reformer who assailed the influence of big-money and lobbyists in politics and government. One of its many attack ads claimed McCain "solicits money from lobbyists with interests before his committee and pressures agencies on behalf of contributors." But, as NBC News reported at the time, Bush had raised five times as much in contributions from lobbyists as McCain. The Bush campaign, according to Moore and Slater, made "push-poll" calls that asked harsh questions about McCain. (Bush aides maintained they were only making phone calls that chastised McCain for his own "negative campaign tactics." In one advertisement, McCain had compared Bush's trustworthiness to that of Clinton's—a low blow in a GOP primary.) In an effort to rile up South Carolina's social conservatives, an important voting bloc, the Bushies, Moore and Slater report, sent direct-mail pieces to potential Republican voters saying that McCain wanted to erase the anti-abortion plank from the GOP platform—which was not true.

What of the handshake and the no-negative-ads pledge Bush had previously accepted? He claimed McCain had broken the promise first by airing ads in New Hampshire asserting Bush's tax plan would eat up the federal budget surplus. Bush argued that McCain's commercials were "not the truth" and that he had been forced to "vigorously . . . defend my record." Bush, though, was attacking a foe, not defending himself. Besides, he had not vowed to abstain from negative ads *only* if McCain did as well. As the comfortable front-runner, he had assailed negative campaigning since entering the race. When he needed to resort to such ugly tactics . . . now, that was different. "My ads aren't negative," Bush maintained. "My spots are to make sure that I clarify exactly who I am and what I believe." Yet Bush was referring to a string of spots that included one that described McCain's campaign as "crawling with lobbyists." Conservative leader William Bennett, who was neutral in the Republican presidential contest, observed that the Bush campaign was being "disingenuous" and "inaccurate" in South Carolina.

Bush was quick to make excuses for his not-so-positive/whatever-it-takes campaign, even if that entailed clumsy efforts to fiddle with the truth. During the battle of South Carolina, this self-styled uniter-not-a-divider—who was desperately seeking the support of religious-right voters—spoke at Bob Jones University, an evangelical Christian school that banned interracial dating and was a hotbed of anti-Catholicism. Bush subsequently came under attack for having appeared before these bigoted social conservatives, and he responded by misrepresenting his visit there. His speech at the school, Bush said, "gave me a chance to speak out on interracial dating, for starters. You wouldn't have known my views on interracial dating, would you, had I not gone." And Bush told CNN, "I denounced the policy at Bob Jones." Both statements implied that Bush had criticized his hosts at Bob Jones for their wrongheaded views on interracial hand-holding. Yet during his speech at the school, Bush had said not a word about the dating ban and the school's ugly and divisive prejudices. He had only repudiated the bigotry at a later news conference in response to a challenge from a reporter. He had not done so on his own volition or while among the social conservatives.

In South Carolina, Bush walloped McCain 53 to 42 percent. Mean-spirited campaigning, brutal ads, dishonest statements, divisive tactics—all those things that Bush said he stood against—had served him well. But the race was not over. And Bush kept up the negative and misleading attacks in order to finish off McCain. In Michigan, he deployed an especially inventive tactic. He complained that McCain had unfairly branded him as anti-Catholic. But that was not true. The McCain campaign had only put out a phone message whacking Bush for having visited Bob Jones University. It pointedly informed listeners that the school was led by a man who had called "the pope the anti-Christ, the Catholic Church a satanic cult." An outraged Bush griped that McCain was "paying for calls that call me an anti-Catholic bigot." (At first, the McCain campaign did not acknowledge it was behind these calls, but then confessed.) But the McCain telephone message had not slammed Bush for being "an anti-Catholic bigot." It had noted—accurately—that Bush had courted votes at a school run by bigots. Bush was misrepresenting the script to come across as a victim, to win sympathy. This was a clever and sophisticated form of negative campaigning: accuse your opponent of going negative by falsely claiming he is lying about you.

After McCain won the Michigan primary 50 to 43 percent, the Bush campaign again battered the truth as it attempted to vanquish McCain. In New York, Bush aired a radio ad in which a breast cancer survivor condemned McCain for having opposed funding for two breast cancer programs in the state. The spot was as unscrupulous and misleading as political ads get. McCain had not fought against breast cancer research, as the ad suggested, and his campaign cited numerous times he had voted for cancer research. Long a critic of congressional pork, McCain had opposed an appropriations bill that in a behind-closed-doors process had been stuffed with money for hundreds of programs. He had voted not against a cancer research measure but against a sloppy, lazy, and non-transparent form of legislating that was often abused by influential members of Congress. And what made the ad even more disgraceful was that McCain's sister was a breast cancer survivor then in remission.

When Bush was told about McCain's sister, he callously replied, "All the more reason to remind him what he said about the research that goes on here." Even CNN commentator Robert Novak—no McCain fan—said of this particular assault, "That really is going too far." A "cheap shot," observed the *Philadelphia Inquirer*.

The nasty tactics and the hypocrisy never caught up to Bush. On March 7, he crushed McCain in most of the Super Tuesday states, including New York, clinching the nomination. That night, Bush vowed to "reform Washington and renew the spirit of the country." In his first weeks as the presumptive nominee, he reiterated his pledge to change the tone of politics in America. And he insisted that during the primary battle, "I didn't take the negative tone." But at the same time, Bush was redeploying his negative campaign skills against his next opponent, Al Gore. In February, according to Moore and Slater, Bush's pollster Fred Steeper had conducted a poll that showed voters could be persuaded that Gore had "questionable integrity." During a March 12 press conference, Bush—the candidate who declared he did not make decisions based on polls—premiered a new campaign line. "The vice president," Bush charged, "is someone who will say anything to get elected." To make sure this would be the message of the day, he repeated this phrase four times. Bush was moving quickly to define the remaining campaign as a contest in which *the other guy* was the liar.

"I believe everybody ought to get a tax cut."

With the Republican contest over, Bush wasn't done lying. For months he had been fibbing about his policy proposals—about their real costs, about whom they would benefit, about their consequences. Now that he was the all-but-coronated Republican nominee, he was expected to further detail and promote the ideas he wanted to carry into the White

House. This meant it was time to continue and intensify the false marketing of his policy initiatives.

His brashest policy was a package of supersized tax cuts, which included a reduction in income tax rates across the board, abolition of the estate tax, and doubling the child credit. The Bush campaign maintained these tax cuts would pose no problem for the nation's budget because a large surplus would more than cover them. But his numbers did not add up—that is, despite his claim to the contrary, they added up to more than the surplus.

Bush's aides described his tax cuts as a $1.6 trillion, ten-year plan (after it was revised in May 2000).The projected ten-year U.S. budget surplus at the time was $4.6 trillion, with about half of it coming from Social Security and Medicare. But Bush had pledged not to touch the $2.4 trillion Social Security trust fund. That left him $2.2 trillion to play with. In his economic plan, according to information on his campaign website, Bush proposed to devote $900 billion of that non–Social Security surplus to new federal programs in education, health care, and other areas and to debt reduction.* That meant there was $1.3 trillion available for his tax cuts—assuming this surplus would indeed materialize. The math was simple: Bush's $1.6 trillion tax cuts would place the U.S. budget $300 billion in the red. But Bush employed a fudge factor to hide this hole. He claimed he would achieve $200 billion in savings due to unspecified "government reforms." That would still cause a ten-year budget gap of $100 billion, rather than $300 billion—a huge amount of money, but for Bush, close enough for government work.

The true fiscal effect of his tax cuts, though, could well be more severe. The $1.6 trillion price tag excluded a hidden cost of over $300 billion in additional interest payments on the national debt that would have to be made over ten years. Tax cuts lead to either budget deficits or smaller surpluses; in either case, there is less money available for paying down the national debt. Consequently, more interest has to be paid on the national debt. In real terms, then, Bush's tax cuts would

---

*Bush's budget plan disingenuously did not include the unspecified costs of big-ticket proposals he was championing during the campaign, such as partial privatization of Social Security, an accelerated missile defense program, and a Medicare prescription drug benefit. Together, these three initiatives could cost close to $2 trillion. If enacted, they would certainly leave much less surplus—perhaps none—to use for tax cuts.

soak up about $1.9 trillion of the estimated surplus. If Bush had accurately labeled his tax proposal a $1.9 trillion plan, he would have ended up with a $600 billion deficit—not a result befitting a candidate who championed fiscal responsibility.

Bush was misleading on more than the financial impact of his bold tax cuts. His characterization of who would gain from them was even more underhanded. In pitching his proposal, he often declared, "I believe everybody ought to get a tax cut." But his plan did not provide relief to "everybody." Millions of low-income families—in which the earners paid payroll taxes but not income taxes—would receive nothing from Bush's tax cuts. As CNN's Brooks Jackson reported, "While Bush promises relief for the working poor, the fact is, his income tax cut would give no relief at all—zero—for millions of working families who earn too little to pay income taxes, but who do pay payroll taxes for Social Security and Medicare. That's no help for roughly 20 million working families, the bottom 22 percent." In justifying his tax proposal, Bush also liked to say, "I believe, as a matter of principle, that no one in America should pay more than one-third of his or her income to the federal government." But he was making something out of nothing. The highest income tax rate was indeed 39.6 percent, but that applied to income after deductions. As the *Washington Post* noted, "Virtually no one pays that much [one-third] including many people making more than $1 million."

Bush's biggest whopper on taxes came when he stated, "The vast majority of my tax cuts go to the bottom end of the spectrum." That estimate was wildly at odds with several analyses of where the money would really go. One report done by Citizens for Tax Justice (CTJ), a liberal outfit that specialized in distribution analysis, figured that 42.6 percent of Bush's $1.6 billion tax package would end up in the pockets of the top 1 percent (people with annual incomes above $319,000). Half the rewards would go to the top 5 percent ($130,000 and above). As for Bush's "bottom end," the lowest 60 percent would net 12.6 percent. The average middle-income taxpayer would receive $453; the average top 1 percenter, $46,072. CTJ would have to have been off by 1,700 to 6,000 percent (depending on how one defined "bottom end") for Bush's "vast majority" remark to come close to being true. The *New York Times*, the *Los Angeles Times*, ABC News, and NBC News each reported that Bush's tax-cuts package produced the results CTJ calculated.

Bush's assertion that the bulk of his tax cuts flowed toward the bottom was one of the most important and insidious lies of his campaign. Gore accused Bush of an unfair and unwise bias in favor of the wealthy; McCain had similarly complained. How did Bush counter such serious charges? He did not offer an analysis showing the CTJ numbers were wrong. That was because he couldn't. The CTJ estimate had to be mostly on the money. Key and costly provisions in Bush's tax plan—ending the estate tax and dropping the higher income tax rates—could only benefit wealthier Americans. So to deal with the criticism that his plan was a boon for millionaires, Bush took another course: he devised an imaginary friend—a mythical single mom–waitress, who was supporting two children on an income of $22,000, and whom he talked about often.

How unfair it was, he exclaimed, that this woman faced a higher marginal tax rate than a lawyer pulling in $220,000 a year. Bush did have a point—at least, a theoretical one. The lawyer was already in the top bracket; each extra dollar she made was taxed at the same rate. But if the waitress moved up the income ladder, she could see her new dollars taxed at a higher rate, as her Earned Income Tax Credit decreased and as she headed toward a higher bracket. Bush said he wanted to remove the tax-code barriers that kept this waitress from reaching the middle class. And he insisted that if his tax cuts were passed, "she will pay no income taxes at all." His argument sounded good, as if it was truly motivated by compassion. But it was fraudulent.

When *Time* magazine asked the accounting firm of Deloitte & Touche to analyze precisely how Bush's waitress-mom would be affected by his tax package, the firm reported that she would not see any benefit because she already had no income tax liability. Bush's plan, by their numbers, did zilch for her. (The same study reported that Bush's favorite woman would gain $878 from Gore's tax proposals, which included expanding the Earned Income Tax Credit and making the child-care tax credit refundable.) And only about 3.5 percent of Bush's tax cut, according to CTJ, was even aimed at individuals in single-waitress-land—those making between $13,600 and $24,400 a year. The average person in that income range would have an extra $187 a year due to Bush's plan—spending money, but not enough for him or her to achieve the "social mobility" Bush was promising.

Bush's professed concern for this waitress and the marginal rates faced by the working poor was a cynical scheme—a way for him to say *something* to defend himself against the charge that his tax cuts were a handout for the rich. Had he truly cared about low-income workers, he could have structured a tax package that would help them with, say, payroll taxes. Instead, he was attempting to hide tax cuts for the wealthy behind the apron of his make-believe waitress. Not only was she fictitious, so were his claims about his tax package.

Another glaring policy distortion Bush hawked was his Social Security plan. Well, it wasn't really a plan. It was a collection of four "principles." The first three were conventional promises for an American politician: no change in benefits for people currently retired or nearing retirement; no dipping into the Social Security trust fund; no increase in the payroll tax. But his last "principle" was new-world territory: personal retirement accounts for young people. Other conservatives had long advocated such a device, which would allow a worker to take a portion of his or her payroll tax and place it in a fund that invests in stocks and bonds and that meets what Bush called "basic standards of safety and soundness." Bush declared this could "save" an imperiled Social Security program. He also claimed Gore, by bitterly attacking this proposal, was "spreading fear and panic."

But it was Bush who was spreading panic. Visiting one senior center, he told his audience that "if we do nothing to reform the system, the year 2037 will be the moment of financial collapse." That was hyperbole. The year 2037, according to official forecasts, would not bring the crash of Social Security. That was the year when the Social Security trust fund would run out of money and the system would only be able to cover about 70 percent of its obligations. This would mark a serious crunch time for Social Security, but not its imminent destruction. The same forecasts noted that Social Security could continue to pay out that amount of benefits for 40 or so years. Yet Bush made it seem as if the system would be a complete bust for older Americans. On PBS, he told Jim Lehrer, "It's more likely" that younger workers would "go to Mars than to receive a check from the Social Security system." That was undeniably untrue.

But Bush was hyping a Social Security crisis for a reason: to sell his privatization plan as crucial to the program's future. And a critical falsehood in his Social Security rap was what he left unsaid. Bush never explained how partial privatization would affect what remained of the Social Security program.

He had avoided issuing a detailed plan, but most proposals for private retirement accounts called for shifting 2 points of a worker's 12.4 percent payroll taxes to such accounts. Consequently, Social Security would lose about 16 percent of its revenues. What would that mean for beneficiaries? Despite the widespread view that Social Security is a pension plan, it is a pay-as-you-go system in which current taxes cover the benefits distributed to current recipients. How could Bush yank money out of a system heading for trouble in 2037 and render it more financially stable? If he used the Social Security surplus to fund these new retirement accounts, he would shorten the time before the "moment of financial collapse." Diverting Social Security funds into personal retirement accounts, according to the Center on Budget and Policy Priorities, would cause the so-called trust fund to run dry in 2023, not 2037.

Bush suggested Social Security would be on a sounder footing with partial privatization because the personal retirement accounts would have a higher rate of return. "Right now," he said, "the real return people get from what they put into Social Security is a dismal 2 percent a year. Over the long term, sound investments yield about a 6 percent return. Investing that 4 percent difference, over a lifetime, can show dramatic results. A worker who invests even a limited portion of his or her paycheck could, over a career, end up with hundreds of thousands of dollars for retirement."

It was not that simple. Bush was assuming a constant 6 percent average for all investors over all periods of time. He did not acknowledge that life for a given individual may not average out so neatly. And Social Security's rate of return included disability and survivor's benefits—which accounted for a third of the program's payments. Comparing Social Security (and its paltry-but-guaranteed 2 percent return) to a stock fund (with its not-for-certain 6 percent return) was misleading, for the latter does not have to provide these other benefits. The many Social Security recipients who received non-retirement benefits earned a tremendous rate of return, several times higher than the 2 percent average Bush derided. And those "hundreds of thousands" of retirement dollars Bush dangled were not adjusted for inflation.

Investors who managed to do well with retirement accounts *might* pocket enough to cover or exceed a decrease in Social Security benefits. But, certainly, Bush could not guarantee all Social Security recipients would be so fortunate.

Bush skipped past the possible downsides of partial privatization, especially the prospect of reductions in benefits. Was this lying by omitting the inevitable? If funds were pulled from Social Security, the guaranteed benefits for some recipients would have to be cut back. But Bush avoided this dicey question. At one point, his chief economic adviser, Larry Lindsey, did tell *Newsweek*, "Reductions in the guaranteed amounts of benefits that will go to [retirement] plan participants are absolutely obvious. So I will say it." Then, in a letter to the magazine, Lindsey tried to unsay it, claiming he was quoted in a "misleading way." In subsequent interviews, Lindsey refused to answer questions about decreases in benefits.

"Social security is . . . a test of presidential candidates—a measure of seriousness and resolve," Bush said. At least he didn't say a test of candor. If he truly considered it a measure of seriousness and resolve, how could Bush merely propose "principles," rather than present a plan with specifics? How could he sidestep the costs and difficulties associated with this approach? Where would the money come from for the transition costs, estimated to be $1 trillion? Bush had a team of economic advisers—Lindsey included—who could have done all the calculations for him. But he stayed away from actual numbers. Though one of his speeches on Social Security had been entitled "A Defining Promise," Bush purposefully declined to define fully his proposal. He was dishonestly ignoring the challenges posed by his own principles.

Bush's questionable policy claims also extended to the plan he offered to help Americans without health insurance. "Every low-income, working family in America must have access to basic health insurance—for themselves and for their children," he stated. "I believe we can help these Americans. We can start by making a basic health plan more affordable." His solution was a tax credit for families making less than $30,000 that would pay for 90 percent of the cost of an insurance policy, up to $2,000 a year. "This Family Health Credit," he said, "will help to buy a basic policy . . . enough to ensure against sudden poverty. And a lot more peace of mind." And his website noted, "If a family earning $30,000 purchases a health insurance plan costing $2,222, the government will contribute $2,000 [90 percent] and the family will pay just $18.50 per month [$222 annually, or 10 percent]."

Health care for less than twenty bucks a month? That seemed a swell deal. And Bush spoke as if his plan would work for the tens of millions of Americans who could not afford coverage. But the proposal was based on a fantasy: a $2,222 health plan. Adequate health coverage was more likely to run in the $5,000 to $6,000 range, according to Families USA, a health-care advocacy group. Presumably, Bush's policy experts knew that. They just ignored this inconvenient wrinkle. Under the Bush plan, a $30,000-a-year family would still have to be able to part with up to $4,000 to buy adequate insurance. (It would also have to shell out additional funds to cover deductibles and co-payments.) The *Washington Post* editorialized, "The subsidy he proposes is too low to reduce significantly the number of people in the country without health insurance. The plan in that sense is a shell." And *USA Today* argued, "The Bush tax credits would expand coverage to 3 million or 4 million uninsured Americans [out of 40-plus million] at most." Bush may have, as he said, believed "we can help" the millions of uninsured. But contrary to the impression he tried to create, he offered a plan that left most of them at risk.

"America better beware of a candidate who is willing to stretch reality in order to win points."

Presidential contests often develop simplistic narratives. In 2000, a dominant plotline pitted Gore the too-smart, lying chameleon versus Bush the not-so-bright down-home charmer. While Bush contended with media questions about his intelligence, Gore had to deal with press reports labeling him a truth-stretcher. Gore had taken several unfair hits. For instance, remarks that he made in December 1999 at a New Hampshire high school were misquoted by the *Washington Post* and the *New York Times* in such a fashion to make it seem he wrongfully had asserted he was the fellow who uncovered the infamous Love Canal toxic waste scandal. And given the flood of lies and distortions from Bush, the press's obsession with Gore's fabrications was out of balance. But the vice president had brought much of this on himself. Caught red-handed in earlier fund-raising scandals, he had offered slippery answers. He also had flung false accusations at his primary opponent, former senator Bill Bradley.

The Bush campaign—headed by the candidate who pledged to change the tone of American politics—tried mightily to encourage the depiction of Gore as a clumsy, self-promoting fibber. After media reports challenged Gore's claim that his mother-in-law's arthritis medicine cost three times what he paid to obtain the same medication for his aging dog, Bush remarked, "The country needs an honest dialogue without exaggerations. I have always been concerned about Vice President Gore's willingness to exaggerate in order to become elected. . . . This is not what a leader does. A leader doesn't try to exaggerate in order to win." Bush laid it on thick: "America better beware of a candidate who is willing to stretch reality in order to win points." And when the Republican Party put out an ad slapping Gore for "reinventing himself," Bush defended the spot, maintaining (once again) Gore "is a fellow that will say anything" and "exaggerate in order to win." Asked whether this ad squared with his promise to "change the tone," Bush replied, "I read where someone said this is going to cost me the election, this ad. Let's let the public judge." It appeared that Bush would stand by results, not principles. "This is politics," he said.

During the most dramatic high-profile moments of the campaign— the Republican convention and the three presidential debates— Bush would exaggerate and fabricate. In his acceptance speech in Philadelphia, Bush pushed his Social Security privatization plan, without mentioning the $1 trillion or so in transition costs. A lie of omission. He said his tax cuts were based on the principle that "those with the greatest need should receive the greatest help." A lie of false impression. The candidate who visited Bob Jones University and whose campaign employed in-the-gutter ads called for more "civility and respect" in politics—and then derided Gore for practicing "the politics of the roadblock," "reinventing himself," "running in borrowed clothes," and being a fearmonger. A lie of hypocrisy. He also dishonestly blamed Clinton and Gore for weakening the military: "If called on by the commander-in-chief today, two entire divisions of the Army would have to report, 'Not ready for duty, sir.' " An out-and-out lie.

Bush was mischaracterizing outdated information; the problem, if there had been one, had been resolved the previous year. (Weeks after the convention, Richard Armitage, a key Bush national security adviser, acknowledged on CNN these divisions were "ready for duty.")

At the first Bush-Gore mano-a-mano—held October 3 at the University of Massachusetts in Boston—Gore once again got nailed for making inaccurate statements. He mentioned that he had "accompanied" James Lee Witt, the head of the Federal Emergency Management Agency, to Texas when major fires broke out there. Wrong. He had been with Witt on many other trips, but not that particular jaunt, during which he had traveled with a Witt deputy. "He made up the story," Karen Hughes exclaimed after the debate, according to *U.S. News & World Report*'s Roger Simon. "The president of the United States cannot do that . . . the president cannot go to a meeting with a foreign leader and simply make things up that aren't true." But Bush had lied about far more important matters during that same debate.

In his opening statement, Bush laid out his grand economic plan: "I want to take one half of the surplus and dedicate it to Social Security, one quarter of the surplus for important projects. And I want to send one quarter of the surplus back to the people who pay the bills" in tax cuts. His math, again, was way off. The projected ten-year surplus was still $4.6 trillion. A quarter of that would be $1.15 trillion. Yet Bush was proposing a tax-cuts package that he now claimed cost $1.3 trillion—but that was over *nine* years, not the customary ten years used for budget projections. Were he to count the extra interest payments the tax cuts would cause *and* include its full ten-year cost, the total draw against the surplus would be $1.9 trillion—much more than a quarter of the surplus. He had shaved $750 billion off the cost of his tax cuts so they would appear reasonable and affordable.

At another point in the debate, Bush promoted partial privatization of Social Security by noting it offered younger workers "a better rate of return so that they'll have a retirement plan in the future." But a few days later, *Wall Street Journal* reporter Jacob Schlesinger wrote, "Here is what the Texas governor and his campaign don't say: Social Security's number-crunchers actually found that none of [the Bush-type retirement plans] can save the program only by tapping into higher stock-market returns." The sort of system Bush was endorsing,

Schlesinger added, would have to "supplement market accounts with deep cuts in promised benefits, a multitrillion-dollar infusion of new revenue, or some combination of these. Spinach, anyone."*

In this first debate, Bush lied to pump up his ideas, and he lied to tear down his opponent. He ridiculed Gore's proposed budget plan for creating "20,000 new bureaucrats." This was a disingenuous remark based on phony calculations. Bush said he got the stat from the Senate Budget Committee. He did not mention that this estimate had been produced by *Republican* staff members of the committee, who had employed a loaded methodology. These GOPers had calculated the current ratio of employees to expenditures within the federal government and then applied that ratio to *their* own cost estimates of Gore's new spending proposals. But, as the *Washington Post* reported, the number of federal workers had decreased by 15 percent in the previous decade, even though federal spending had risen 40 percent. It was unquestionably misleading to peg the number of federal employees to the size of the budget.

Bush not only fudged numbers, he tried to pass off outright fiction as fact. Refusing to accept Gore's invitation to endorse a campaign finance reform bill, Bush exclaimed, "This man has outspent me." Not even close. Bush had spent more than $121 million on his campaign—more than double the $60 million Gore doled out. (And in the July-to-October period, the Republican Party had banked $100 million to the Democrats' $55 million.) Was Bush misinformed about his own campaign spending figures? Or had he intentionally dissembled?

In back-and-forth concerning each candidate's proposals for Medicare, Bush made another false statement, declaring that "all seniors are covered under prescription drugs in my plan." Yet according to Bush's own campaign website, only seniors with incomes below $11,300 would receive full coverage. Seniors with incomes beneath $14,600 would have partial coverage. Other seniors could receive about 25 percent of the premium costs for a drug plan—but that would not help individuals who could not afford the remaining 75 percent of the drug plan's cost. And a Bush initiative that would give states $48 billion over four years for medications for seniors would help seniors with incomes

---

*One Bush ad proclaimed, "President Bush will keep the promise of Social Security. No changes. No reductions. No way." But there was no way that could be done.

above $14,600 only after their drug bill topped $6,000 a year. Bush's plan offered coverage mainly to the poorest seniors, not "all seniors."

As politicians like to do in debates, Gore referred to a 70-year-old man named George McKinney, who was in the audience and who could not afford the medications he needed. McKinney's income was $25,000, and he regularly trekked to Canada to buy lower-priced prescription drugs. Gore noted that under his own plan, half of McKinney's prescription drug costs would be paid "right away" and that McKinney "would not get one penny" from the Bush program. Bush was outraged. "Under my plan," he replied, "this man gets immediate help with prescription drugs." Bush was wrong. According to the criteria detailed on his campaign website, McKinney would only receive assistance once he had already spent $6,000—almost one-quarter of his income—on medications.

Gore zeroed in on this: "They get $25,000 a year income. That makes them ineligible." How did Bush get out of this fix? With sarcasm. "Look," he said, "[Gore] is a man who's got great numbers. He talks about numbers. I'm beginning to think not only did he invent the Internet but he invented the calculator." The audience laughed, and Bush continued: "It's fuzzy math. It's a scaring—trying to scare people in the voting booth."

Bush, though, was trying to fool people, misleading seniors about an issue of critical importance to them. Did he not understand his own proposal? Or was he purposefully deceiving seniors? In either event, he escaped Gore's trap with a quip. And he escaped punishment for a deception-ridden debate performance. The reviews of the face-off—written within the media-created framework that Gore was a liar and Bush was a dunderhead—generally held that Bush had done fine by managing not to drool, while Gore had sighed excessively and had, once more, been caught not telling the truth.

In the next two debates, Bush uttered other self-serving embellishments. (And, yes, Gore offered his own.) When Gore claimed Bush did not support a strong national patients' bill of rights, Bush declared, "It's not true. . . . I brought Republicans and Democrats together to do just that in the state of Texas." But that was a dusty exaggeration from the campaign trail, for Bush had not even bothered to sign the legislation for which he was now assuming credit. And in the final debate, Bush proclaimed, "When you total up all the federal spending [Gore] wants to do, it's the largest increase in federal spending in years, and there's just not going to be enough money." As the *Boston Globe* noted the next day, "While Bush is correct that Gore's spending proposals exceed his, the combination of Bush's spending plans and tax cuts would eat up more of the surplus than Gore would with his more modest tax cut and his larger spending plans." Bush, with his immense tax cuts, was actually the surplus-buster, yet in a black-is-white fashion he was accusing Gore of recklessly spending all the surplus.

Bush had spoken wildly untruthfully about his campaign spending, his prescription drug plan, his proposed tax cuts, his record in Texas, and Gore's economic plan. Yet he was comfortably jetting around the nation in a plane his campaign had dubbed *Responsibility One* after the first debate (in a dig at Gore), while Gore had to contend with charges he was an opportunistic, self-aggrandizing fibber. Truth is, there were two liars in the race, but only one had to defend himself continuously on the integrity front.

In the homestretch of the campaign, Bush and his aides fired off a host of falsehoods. A Bush ad claimed, "Al Gore's prescription drug plan forces seniors into a government-run HMO." The *Washington Post* concluded, not true: "Bush misrepresents the Vice President's drug plan. . . . In fact, many analysts say Bush's plan, while providing choices, would encourage more seniors to join cost-conscious HMOs." At an office-equipment factory in Wisconsin, Bush denounced Gore for wanting "to grow the size of the federal government." But Bush's own spending proposals—$500 billion or so to Gore's $818 billion— would also "grow the size" of the government. Campaigning in Macomb County, Michigan, Bush claimed that if $1 trillion of the Social Security surplus were placed into personal accounts for younger workers, it would turn into $3 trillion by 2016. But that would only be true if the rate of return were nearly 8 percent or more—which was hardly guaranteed—and this number did not take into account infla- tion. (Months earlier, Bush had assumed a 6 percent rate of return when praising personal retirement accounts.) During a campaign rally in Missouri, Bush decried the critics of his Social Security plan and let slip one of those revealing gaffes for which he had become famous: "This frightens some in Washington because they want the federal government controlling the Social Security like it's some federal program."

Bush also held fast to his tax and budget proposals and kept insisting that "most of the tax reductions go to the people at the bottom end of the economic ladder." Eight Nobel laureates and 300 other economists signed a letter arguing, "The costs of the tax cuts, combined with Bush's proposed spending increases, would more than exhaust the projected surplus outside of Social Security and Medicare." They also claimed Bush's tax proposal "would shift after-tax income to high-income persons who have already gained the most from the current economic boon."

At a speech in Pittsburgh, 12 days before Election Day, Bush declared, "Good leaders create a climate of honesty and integrity." Yet he had not done so as a candidate. His campaign did have its truthful moments. He accurately noted—more than once—that Clinton and Gore had failed to deliver on their 1992 promise of a middle-class tax cut. (Once in office and confronted with worse-than-expected budget numbers, Clinton traded in the tax cut for a deficit-reduction plan. Bush was correct in pointing out that the number of uninsured Americans had increased during the Clinton-Gore years. (He might not have been the most appropriate person to raise this concern, but that was another issue.) He, no doubt, was sincere in pledging to direct more money to the military and to bring Texas-style education to the entire nation. He did appear committed to the foreign policy stands adviser Condoleezza Rice and others drafted for him. He was, as he claimed, a fan of permitting religious groups to become more involved in the delivery of government-funded social services.

In a limited fashion, Bush was the "different kind of Republican" he proclaimed to be. He truly appeared to enjoy visiting inner-city schools and having his photo taken with children of color even as these events were clearly orchestrated for political advantage. As Frank Bruni put it, "A reporter covering Bush could bet his 401(k) on certain truths: if Bush attended a Republican fund-raiser in a hotel ballroom packed with rich, fleshy white men, his advertising team and their cameras were nowhere to be found. If he took a walk through a Hispanic neighborhood in Santa Ana, California, there would be a film crew populous and frenetic enough to tackle a David Lean epic." It was not unreasonable of Bush to question Gore's veracity. And maybe Jesus Christ was, as Bush said in one GOP debate, his favorite philosopher.

But so much of Bush's campaign was dishonest—including his promise to be honest. He was a big-government candidate, too—just not as big as Gore. He didn't level with the public about his Social Security plan or his tax cuts proposal. His fundamental numbers did not track. He exaggerated past accomplishments as much as, if not more than, Gore. Though he proudly vowed he would not engage in divisive campaigning, he readily turned to the sort of brutal politics he condemned. When the crunch hit, he forged political alliances with liars and bigots. He claimed his proposals were more compassionate—that is, more helpful to less fortunate Americans—than they were. He fudged details about his National Guard service and survived a last-minute round of questions concerning his truthfulness during the DWI episode. Without lies, what chance would he have had?

His self-professed honesty was a false positive. But it sure worked. His promise to restore honor and integrity to the White House helped net him 50,456,002 votes. (An Election Day exit poll found that 25 percent of voters considered "honesty" the "most important thing to consider" when voting, and 80 percent of them voted for Bush.) This was not enough for him to place first—Gore was the choice of 50,999,897 voters—but it was enough to win 246 electoral votes outright in a race where 271 meant victory. And the initial count in the swing state (oh so literally) of Florida (25 electoral votes) placed Bush ahead by 1,784 votes, or .03 percent. Bush had lied his way into a bizarre runoff—in which his lies would once again be crucial to the outcome.

3. Sudden-Death Lies

"[The votes] have not only been counted, they've been counted twice."

J ames Baker landed in Florida with a lie. Two days after Election Night ended unresolved, with Bush barely ahead of Gore in Florida, this wily and formidable power-lawyer/politico/diplomat became the CEO of Bush's sudden-death effort. As soon as he hit the Sunshine State, Baker was declaring, "We've had a vote. We've had a count. We've now had a recount with respect to which there are no charges of irregularity, and yet the other side is now saying, 'We want yet another recount.' Third count of the same ballots." During his first press conference in Florida, Baker proclaimed that the votes "have not only been counted, they've been counted twice. . . . Nobody's going to dispute that."

Baker was establishing the cardinal tactics of his mission: lie, distort, and, above all, stick to the story. And he had already crafted what would be the never-changing essence of the Bush argument during the 36-day-long post-election drama: the votes were counted *and* recounted, Bush was ahead at the end of each tally, and Gore couldn't accept this and was trying, illegitimately, to stretch out the process and forestall the inevitable.

But what Baker claimed as indisputable—two complete and full tallies of the vote affirming Bush the winner—was indeed open to dispute. It was not what had actually happened. The Florida vote had not been subjected to a complete recount. In the weeks ahead, whenever

Bush partisans claimed a recount had confirmed Bush's victory, they would be speaking untruthfully.

Florida law required a "recount of the votes cast" if the margin was less than half of 1 percent. Bush's initial lead was .03 percent of the 5.9 million votes recorded. As the law mandated, on the morning of November 8, the state Division of Elections—overseen by Secretary of State Katherine Harris, co-chair of the Bush campaign in Florida—sent out a memo to the counties calling for a mandatory recount. But such a recount never occurred. Eighteen of the state's 67 counties did not reprocess the ballots; most of them merely rechecked the math from their Election Night tabulations. These 18 counties accounted for about one-quarter of the state's total vote.

What might have happened had all the 1.5 million ballots in these 18 counties been run through the counting machines a second time is anyone's guess. Still, this supposedly statewide (but actually partial) recount caused Bush's lead to drop sharply to 327.

Baker's assertion that every ballot had been counted by a machine at least twice—which the Bushies recited ad nauseam—was false. It may be that Bush, Baker and company did not realize they were spreading misinformation. This discrepancy was not widely noted at the time, and the Gore campaign apparently never double-checked the automatic recount. But given the close ties between the Bush campaign and Florida's Division of Elections and Department of State, it is not unreasonable to wonder whether Baker or other members of Bush's vast legal team had an inkling that Bush had lucked out during the automatic recount. In any event, Bush and Baker had an obligation to ascertain that the statements they were making during the critical post-election period were accurate. Yet the core of their argument was an utter myth.*

---

*Considering the bitter partisan divide caused by the Florida fray, it is worth noting that this view of the automatic recount—detailed in Jeffrey Toobin's *Too Close to Call*—is not the exclusive property of the left or Bush antagonists. In his book *At Any Cost,* Bill Sammon, the conservative White House correspondent for the conservative *Washington Times,* writes: "The enduring myth of Florida's first recount is that all sixty-seven counties tallied their ballots by machine, employing a uniform, statewide standard. In reality, some ballots were counted by machine, while others were tallied by hand. Some counties didn't bother counting the ballots in any fashion. Instead, election officials simply ran tests on the computer software that had been used to tabulate the votes on Election Night. Or they examined tally sheets to double-check that all the precincts had added up properly."

■ ■ ■

If elections are too often win-at-all-costs battles full of truth-mangling, the Florida conflict was nuclear warfare. Bush and Baker may have been unaware their primary line of attack was based on a falsehood, but Baker and other Bush-backers were willing to say whatever they could—true or not—to thwart any reevaluation of the original results.

Case in point: Palm Beach, where the use of an unusual "butterfly" ballot led to thousands of Gore supporters either mistakenly voting for Reform Party candidate Patrick Buchanan or disqualifying their ballots by errantly punching holes for both Gore and Buchanan. To prevent the Palm Beach screwup from threatening Bush's win, Baker and the Bush campaign disseminated false information. Baker maintained this kind of ballot had been used before in Florida "elections" and that this time "there were not complaints until after the election." One of his colleagues later noted, "It is not fair to wait until the votes have been counted and then, if you don't like the outcome, to say . . . there was something wrong with the form of the ballot." Yet such a ballot had not been used before in a contested race. Fourteen years earlier, a butterfly ballot had been handed out for yes-no constitutional amendment questions. And complaints about the ballot had begun pouring in early on the morning of Election Day 2000—before results were known—and they continued throughout the day, as befuddled voters exited their voting stations and poll workers and Democratic officials became increasingly concerned.

Campaign spokesperson Ari Fleischer, trying to pooh-pooh the problem in Palm Beach, issued a statement that claimed, "Palm Beach County is a Pat Buchanan stronghold, and that's why Pat Buchanan received 3,407 votes there." Fleischer assailed Democrats for "politicizing and distorting these routine and predictable events." He added, "It's important that no party to this election act in a precipitous manner or distort an existing voting pattern in an effort to misinform the public." But this was exactly what Fleischer and the Bush campaign were doing. To truth-test Fleischer's statement, *Salon*'s Jake Tapper read it to Buchanan's Florida coordinator, Jim McConnell. "That's nonsense," McConnell replied. He placed the number of Buchanan activists in the county at 300 to 500 and denied Palm Beach was

Buchanan country, as did Buchanan himself. "I do believe a number of those votes cast for me were clearly intended for Al Gore," Buchanan said.*

The ballots-have-been-counted-and-recounted line Baker ceaselessly pitched was but one-half of a dishonest two-part argument. The other portion involved dismissing the legitimacy and accuracy of the manual recounts Gore had requested. Days into the Florida fracas, Baker blasted Gore for "attempting to unduly prolong the country's national presidential election through endless challenges to the results." He asserted that the Gore campaign's request for "recount after recount after recount" will "destroy . . . the traditional process for selecting our presidents." But at that point Gore was behind by 327 votes statewide and had asked for hand counts in four counties. Did that amount to "endless challenges"? Gore, of course, had a team of his own aiming to do whatever it could to prevail. The Democrats would also mislead and fudge when necessary. But the election was not officially over. Absentee ballots were still coming in—and would be counted—until midnight on November 17, and Gore's manual recount requests were in accordance with state law. Baker was attempting to use extreme, untruthful rhetoric to establish a context in which Gore would be seen as a sore loser desperately trying to subvert the system and tear the country apart in order to achieve an undeserved victory.

The Bush crew was ferocious in its attempt to undermine the manual recounts, and Baker and his colleagues would not let facts interfere. Appearing on *Meet the Press* on November 12, Baker scoffed at these recounts: "Now the other side wants to proceed with a manual recount in a few selected counties that are predominantly Democratic under a procedure that has no standards, no uniform rules. . . . The country is

---

*Separate reviews conducted in 2001 by the *Palm Beach Post* and a consortium of media outfits (including the *Wall Street Journal,* the *New York Times,* CNN, Associated Press, and others) found that the butterfly ballot had cost Gore a net loss of over 6,000 to 9,000 votes—far more than the amount of votes quibbled over during the recount phase. The evidence was strong—undeniable—that had it not been for the butterfly ballot, Gore would have taken the state. Yet this ballot had created a problem that could not be remedied by any sort of recount.

moving toward automated voting machines because that's the best way to get the most accurate result."

It was true that the Gore campaign—with its battle cry of "count every vote"—had only pursued manual reviews in four counties that leaned Democratic. This move smacked of opportunism and cherry-picking. But that was how Florida state law worked. A candidate got to request hand counts where he or she wanted. Bush could have demanded manual reviews in his favorite counties. But since he was ahead, even if barely, his campaign had decided it was in his interest to block any and all manual recounts. To do that, they disingenuously assailed the notion that a manual review could yield accurate results.

With manual recounts, Baker exclaimed, "The electoral officials look at the ballots and simply divine the intent of the voter. . . . That's extraordinarily inaccurate." And he repeatedly remarked, "Machines are neither Republicans nor Democrats, and therefore can be neither consciously nor unconsciously biased." He complained that there were "simply no standards to guide" the manual inspection of ballots—even as election officials in several counties were attempting (albeit with difficulties) to establish standards. Referring to a recount that had started in Palm Beach County, Fleischer remarked, "What's happening in Palm Beach is exactly why our nation switched from hand counting ballots to the more precise, less subjective counts done by precision machines."

The recount-bashers were swimming against the truth. On November 17, the *New York Times* published a front-page story featuring interviews with officials in companies that manufactured counting machines for punchcard ballots.* These experts estimated the error rate for these devices at between .1 percent and 1 percent or more (which may have been optimistic, on their part). Given that these sort of machines tallied 3.45 million votes in Florida, this suggested that, theoretically, between 3,450 and 34,500 votes could have been misread—which was many more votes than the actual margin between Bush and Gore. The newspaper noted, "Ultimately, industry officials

---

*Punchcards require voters to push a stylus through a perforated hole to knock out a chad. The ballots are then fed through a machine that records the numbers of holes created. With optical-scan ballots, voters use a pen to mark their preference. The punchcard system—which is less accurate than the optical-scan system—was used in about 60 percent of the state. The four recount counties had used punchcard systems.

said, the most precise way to count ballots is by hand." Robert Swartz, president of Cardamation, which had been producing punchcard readers for 25 years, said, "The important thing here is that there may be no way to get a 100 percent accurate count by a machine. It is totally reasonable that the most accurate way to do it is a carefully run recount." Todd Urosevich, a vice president of Election Systems and Software, Inc., remarked, "A manual recount can be extremely accurate." The *Times* added, "Election officials in several states said a manual recount was a simple and reliable way to correct mistakes in the computerized counts." Kimball Brace, president of Election Data Services, told the *Washington Post* that with punchcards, "the only way to positively know how many votes were cast for each candidate is to do a manual recount."

Scientific experts outside of the vote-counting industry seconded this view. Two officials of the Association for Computing Machinery—Lauren Weinstein and Peter Neumann—issued a statement on hand counts. (Neumann was one of the top computer scientists in the country.) "As is well known to election officials and voting system vendors, but historically not advertised to the public at large," they said, "all voting systems are subject to some degree of error—electronic and mechanical systems alike. Punchcard-based systems are no exception. . . . In general, so long as the interested parties both have observers participating in manual recounts to assure a consensus on the interpretation and tabulation of the cards, manual recounts provide the MOST reliable mechanism for counting these cards accurately, particularly due to the common hanging chad problem. . . . Indeed, manual counting is still prevalent today in England and Germany." Weinstein and Neumann recommended that all votes in Florida be counted manually, a position the Gore gang would adopt late in the game. "If the will of voters is not to be subjugated to technical flaws over which they have no control," the two maintained, "this would be the only fair course."

The Bush team's moral outrage over hand counts was not in sync with a provision in a Texas law—signed by Bush in 1997—that called for manual reviews in close elections. "A manual recount," the law read, "shall be conducted in preference to an electronic recount." When asked about this embarrassing and inconvenient Texas law, Bush surrogates lied. Baker said, "Under the Texas statute, there is provision for a manual recount, but it is subject to uniform rules and objective standards." Bush lawyer Ted Olson, according to Jake Tapper's book on the recount, *Down and Dirty,* told a federal court, while trying to stop the hand counts, that the "Texas provision, which has been mentioned for obvious reasons, has a list of very specific standards."

The Texas law—Section 127.130 of the Election Code—did state that a vote counted if "at least two corners of the chad are detached" and "light is visible through the hole." But it also granted vote counters a fair amount of discretion, noting that a vote must also be tallied if "an indentation on the chad from the stylus or other object is present and indicates a clearly ascertainable intent of the voter to vote; or the chad reflects by other means a clearly ascertainable intent of the voter to vote." These parts of the Texas law were similar to the Florida law that allowed local officials to establish standards to judge intent. Baker had misled the public, and Olson had misled a federal judge.

"We have a responsibility to conduct ourselves with dignity and honor . . . to respect the law."

All this slipperiness with the truth was fully embraced by the governor. On November 15, Bush went on television to counter an earlier Gore appearance and dissembled himself. "My campaign," he said, "supported the automatic recount of all the votes in Florida." This was misleading in the sense that Bush had no choice regarding that recount. It was as if he were saying he supported stopping at red lights. "Additional manual counts of votes that have been counted and recounted," he maintained, "will make the process less accurate, not more so." He also declared, "Everyone in Florida has had his or her vote counted once." That was not so. As manual reviews would show, some of the punchcard ballots that had not registered a presidential vote when passed through the counting machines on Election Night—so-called undervotes—did contain a hole clearly indicating a vote had been missed. Much debate had occurred—and was still occurring—over what could be discerned as a vote during a manual recount. A hanging chad? A punctured chad? A dimpled chad? A pregnant chad? But there was no denying that some undervote ballots (and there were

10,500 of them in Miami-Dade County alone) had not been read properly. Maybe only a few. But this was a contest in which a few could change the balance.

Bush also pushed another phony argument developed by the Republicans: "Each time these voting cards are handled the potential for errors multiplies." His loyalists had been characterizing ballots as fragile pieces of paper. When ballots were reviewed, Bush advocates suggested, chads might fall out. That was incorrect. After the Florida mess was over, I examined ballots used in Miami and found they were rather sturdy items. Routine handling in no way could cause an unpunched chad to escape a card. As David Leahy, the Miami-Dade County elections supervisor—who had been no friend to Democrats—told me, "You can run a ballot through a reader 100 times and you'll never get any chads inadvertently punched out. The ballot won't disintegrate on the basis of normal handling."

Bush finished up his remarks with a call to decency: "We have a responsibility to conduct ourselves with dignity and honor. We have a responsibility to make sure that those who speak for us do not poison our politics. And we have a responsibility to respect the law, and not seek to undermine it when we do not like its outcome." But he and his partisans would violate these very standards.

When the Florida Supreme Court, nearly a week later, ruled unanimously that hand counts had to be included in the state totals, overturning a previous Katherine Harris order, it was bad news for the Bush camp, and Bush reacted by blasting the judges. "We believe," he said, "the justices have used the bench to change Florida's election laws and usurp the authority of Florida's election officials." Bush's harsh critique was out of step with his admonition of the previous week "to respect the law, and not seek to undermine it when we do not like its outcome." During a brief Q & A with the press, Bush added, "The legislature's job is to write law. It's the executive branch job to interpret law." No, interpreting law is what courts do. The state court had been handed the job of sorting out conflicting state statutes: one providing for manual recounts (which can take time to complete); one calling for a relatively quick certification of the vote. Bush might have argued the court had interpreted wrongly and should have put time concerns ahead of counting concerns. Instead, he showed he did not take his own noble words seriously and attacked the judges, complaining "the court cloaked its ruling in legalistic language." What other kind of language would judges use?

Bush called for honorable conduct during the fractious post-election playoff, and he acknowledged his own obligation to ensure his advocates "do not poison our politics." So how did he respond when his loyalists acted in an unseemly—if not violent—fashion? With silence. On November 22, as election officials in Miami-Dade County were preparing to kick off a manual recount, a Republican crowd gathered at the Stephen P. Clark Government Center to protest the review. What happened precisely and how it affected the county's recount would become matters of contentious debate. The *New York Times* reported the demonstration "turned violent on Wednesday after the canvassers had decided to close the recount to the public. Joe Geller, chairman of the Miami-Dade Democratic Party, was escorted to safety by the police after a crowd chased him down and accused him of stealing a ballot." (Geller had only been holding a sample ballot.) "Upstairs," the newspaper continued, "in the Clark Center, several people were trampled, punched or kicked when protesters tried to rush the doors outside the office of the Miami-Dade supervisor of elections."

Following the disturbance, the elections board canceled the hand-counting. David Leahy, the elections supervisor, said the protest was one factor in this decision. (He later maintained he had been misquoted in this regard.) Republicans, as the *Times* put it, "scoffed at the accusation that they had been engaged in a scheme of intimidation, saying the protest had been nothing more than a spontaneous manifestation of people's anger." Responding to the charge the event had been engineered, Representative Clay Shaw, a Fort Lauderdale Republican, told the *St. Petersburg Times*, "That's nonsense. The thing was spontaneous. To think that this was orchestrated high up in the Republican Party is nuts." Paul Crespo, a Bush campaign official, said the event was made up of "irate citizens" and had been "impromptu and spontaneous."

But the ruckus was not the spontaneous action of local citizens, and the intent of the protesters went beyond declaring disgust. The mob, made up of scores of people, included at least a dozen Republican operatives who had been flown to Florida as part of an organized campaign to supply foot-soldiers for the Bush recount endeavor. Many of these ringers were congressional aides recruited by Representative Tom DeLay, then the House majority whip. While this group of politicos-posing-as-protesters were in the Clark Center—*Wall Street Journal* columnist Paul Gigot reported—two GOP observers there called Congressman John Sweeney, a New York Republican who had headed south to be a warrior for Bush. They told him the canvassing board was moving the recount behind closed doors. (The board would still allow representatives from each party to witness the proceedings.) "Shut it down," Sweeney ordered. The congressman later told Associated Press, "What I essentially told my people is, 'You've got to stop them.'"

Protesting the decision to shield a recount from a prying (even if unruly) public was justified. But the event grew ugly, and Bush never publicly said anything, nor publicly chastised his supporters for engaging in distinctly uncivil behavior organized to interfere with the process and poison the atmosphere. Days afterward at a Bush campaign press conference, Fred Bartlit, a Bush attorney, maintained the event had been "noisy and peaceful . . . There were babies in the crowd. There were little kids there. There was, in some ways, a holiday atmosphere." Maybe Fright Night. At a Thanksgiving Day party for the Republican ringers—where Wayne Newton sang "Danke Schoen"—Bush and Cheney spoke by speakerphone to their troops and, according to the *Wall Street Journal*, made "joking references" to the Miami incident.

Throughout all the craziness of the post-election squabble, Bush and his associates held tight to their falsehoods. When Harris on November 26 certified election results that had Bush winning by 537 votes, Bush declared, "The election was close, but tonight, after a count, a recount, and yet another manual recount, Secretary Cheney and I are honored and humbled to have won the state of Florida." There had been no full recount, nor, as he suggested, a true manual recount, either statewide or in the four counties where Gore had requested hand counts. Only two of those counties—Volusia and Broward—had their new tallies included in the results. And when the state Supreme Court subsequently ordered an immediate statewide manual recount and cut Bush's lead to 154 votes, an upset Baker once more disingenuously claimed that Bush had already "won this election . . . over a count, a recount, a manual recount, and perhaps another recount."

Then the U.S. Supreme Court weighed in. On December 9, as Florida was beginning the court-ordered review of 43,000 under-votes, five of the nine justices granted Bush a stay. The recount was suspended. Three days later, the same five justices, who were each Republican appointees, settled the election, ruling the Florida Supreme Court had erred in ordering manual recounts across the state. Gore conceded the next day.

It will never be known definitively which candidate would have tri-umphed had Florida's voting system been able to handle such a tight election or had the U.S. Supreme Court not intervened.* But it is clear that Bush and his team succeeded in one of the oddest and tightest presidential races with a strategy that manipulated and mauled the truth. And in victory, Bush further demonstrated he had no qualms about the gap between his rhetoric and his actions.

An hour after Gore told the public, "It's time for me to go," Bush appeared at the podium in the chamber of the Texas House of Representatives. Now that the bare-knuckled street-fighting was done, he portrayed himself as a uniter. "The spirit of cooperation . . . is needed in Washington," he said, noting, "I am optimistic we can change the tone in Washington, D.C. . . . Our nation must rise about a house divided. Americans share hopes and goals and values far more important than any political disagreements." But in the same speech, he reiterated his devotion to policy proposals that divided the nation, that split Democrats and Republicans in Congress, and that he had presented dishonestly: privatization of Social Security and large tax cuts that would richly reward the wealthy. In his first moments as

---

*The ballot review conducted in 2001 by the major media consortium produced differing results, depending on the counting standards used. In one scenario, Bush won by 400, not 537 votes. Others had Gore triumphing by 42 to 427 votes. (None of these took into account the 6,000 or more votes Gore lost due to the butterfly ballots.) My own three-day review of Miami undervote ballots found that creating standards for manual recounts was possible. I happened to favor a tight standard, such as counting only dislodged chads, or slapping a ballot on a light table and seeing if a beam passes through whatever mark might be on the chad. Using a strict standard, I concluded that Gore would have picked up only a few extra votes from a manual review of the Miami undervotes, not enough (in this county) to overturn the statewide results.

president-to-be, Bush extended to the public and his political foes nothing concrete to launch the bipartisanship he claimed to hold dear. Instead, he offered duplicitous platitudes. But he was remaining true to lies that had smoothed his path to power and that would again be unleashed once he was in the Oval Office.

4. Lying in Office

"This is my solemn pledge: I will work to build a single nation of justice and opportunity."

On a cold, wet and muddy day, George W. Bush appeared on the steps of the U.S. Capitol and recited the presidential oath of office. His inaugural address offered no surprises. He referenced his basic campaign pledges: to cut taxes, to "reform" Social Security, to "reclaim America's schools," to boost the military budget. He said that he would adopt a foreign policy that shows "purpose without arrogance." He noted that God was the "author" of "our nation's grand story of courage and its simple dream of dignity." And in the aftermath of his irregular victory, he renewed his vow to be a uniter-not-a-divider. "Sometimes our differences run so deep," he remarked, "it seems we share a continent, but not a country. We do not accept this, and we will not allow it. Our unity, our union, is the serious work of leaders and citizens in every generation. And this is my solemn pledge: I will work to build a single nation of justice and opportunity." He would do so, he asserted, by promoting civility. "America, at its best, matches a commitment to principle with a concern for civility," he observed. "A civil society demands from each of us goodwill and respect, fair dealing and forgiveness."

Yet in the first acts of his presidency, Bush again revealed that his professed fealty to unity and civility was a lie, that his devotion to politics and to policies that served the constituencies and special interests that had embraced his presidential bid trumped any desire to overcome national "differences." It was his right to be as political as he wanted to be, to cater to his own backers. But he was trying to have it both ways, waving a flag of unity, while taking divisive actions to advance the agendas of his supporters.

This was evident when Bush, before he assumed office, announced he would nominate John Ashcroft, the former Republican senator from Missouri and an ardent social conservative, to be attorney general. While discussing this Cabinet pick during a pre-inauguration television interview with Barbara Walters, Bush demonstrated, unintentionally, that unity and civility mattered much less to him than political calculations.

Ashcroft—who lost his seat the previous November after being outpolled by a governor who had died in a plane crash—had been one of the most forceful ideologues in the Senate. He had even flirted in 1999 with the notion of running for president as *the* candidate of the religious right. His record of die-hard positions extended beyond opposing abortion rights, several common forms of contraception, gun control, and gay rights. He had praised a "neo-confederate" magazine (*Southern Partisan*) that had published an apologia for slavery, celebrated the assassination of Abraham Lincoln, and hailed Ku Klux Klan leaders. In a 1998 interview with that magazine, he had called on "traditionalists" to defend Jefferson Davis, Robert E. Lee, and Stonewall Jackson, the leaders of the pro-slavery South. He had met with a leader of the Council of Conservative Citizens (a group that considered African-Americans intellectually inferior to whites and opposed interracial marriage) to discuss the plight of a member imprisoned for conspiring to kill an FBI agent. He had blasted Missouri Supreme Court Judge Ronnie White, a prominent African-American jurist, as "pro-criminal" in a successful attempt to derail his nomination to the federal bench. He had congratulated a professional football star for having publicly remarked that America had turned away from God by permitting homosexuality to "run rampant." Appearing at Bob Jones University in 1999, Ashcroft proclaimed that America "is unique among the nations" and "the place where mankind has had the greatest of all opportunities to approach the potential that God has placed within us" because "we have no king but Jesus." (Such a comment implied that Americans who do not worship Jesus do not share in the responsibility for whatever it is that makes the United States special.)

At the Republican convention in 1992, he denounced Democrats for having written God out of their platform and for attempting to turn the "traditional family . . . into any two people at the same address."

Ashcroft was entitled to his views, but these were unquestionably the actions and words of a polarizing figure. Don't like how a judge, who often supported the death penalty, ruled in several other capital crime cases? Rather than explain your opposition, just label him "pro-criminal." Have a disagreement with the Democrats? Call them godless. Naturally, Democrats, civil-rights organizations, African-American groups, gay-rights advocates, and others screeched in protest after Bush tapped Ashcroft. Bush was within his rights to select a brash fundamentalist for one of the most influential and powerful posts in his Cabinet. But he had promised over and over to bring the country together. How could he believe he was doing that while appointing Ashcroft the nation's top lawman? Did Bush not realize that nominating Ashcroft would provoke a bitter fight?

That was precisely what Barbara Walters wanted to know, when she asked him, "Did you really expect [Ashcroft] to be as much of a lightning rod?"

"Yes," Bush replied.

Walters had him in a trap. "You really did?" she countered. "And you did it anyway, even though you talk about wanting to unite?"

She was right. Would-be uniters and proponents of civil debate do not try to shove lightning rods up the backsides of their opponents. A snared Bush retorted, "It doesn't mean that we can't unite the nation once we put somebody in place who can do the job." Bush seemed to be saying, *I'm a uniter who knowingly creates rifts, and then, once I have my way, I go back to proclaiming myself a uniter.* Choosing Ashcroft while avowing political healing signaled Bush was not telling the truth when he claimed a serious commitment to achieving unity and changing the tone in Washington.

In the opening weeks of his administration, Bush did initiate several publicized overtures to Democrats. He invited some to the White House, often recruiting them to work with him on his education bill and his proposal to allow faith-based groups to receive federal funding. And he appointed Democrat Norman Mineta, a Clinton administration commerce secretary, to one of the less prominent Cabinet slots (transportation secretary). But this was mostly tactical bipartisanship—

useful and convenient for Bush. When the issue was whether he would honor his eloquent rhetoric (by not appointing a divisive attorney general) or promote his own political interests (by throwing social conservatives a meaty bone), he went with what was best for number-one.

No one had forced Bush to say he would work to bridge the nation's differences. He had assumed that task on his own. But when pressed, Bush acknowledged making a critical decision that he realized would create rancor. He broke his inauguration day promise before declaring it.

"It is my conviction that taxpayer funds should not be used to pay for abortions."

Lies adorned several early Bush initiatives, especially the most controversial ones. In the opening weeks of his presidency, Bush dishonestly explained an anti-abortion decision, falsely characterized criticism of his first major policy proposal, and tried to mislead the public about an attempt to roll back new environmental protection.

On his first workday, Bush signed a directive reviving a controversial 1984 Ronald Reagan order known as the Mexico City Policy, which had been rescinded by Clinton. This policy prohibited U.S. government family-planning funds from going to overseas groups that provide abortion services, lobby for abortion rights, or counsel pregnant women that abortion is an option. In a two-paragraph announcement, Bush noted, "It is my conviction that taxpayer funds should not be used to pay for abortions or advocate or actively promote abortion, either here or abroad."

But the funds in question—$425 million in foreign aid—did not underwrite abortion-related activity. This money could only be used by these groups for their family-planning activities that did not involve abortion or abortion-rights advocacy. A 1973 law rendered it illegal for any organization to use U.S. government funds to pay for abortions overseas. Yet the Bush White House sold the reinstatement of the policy as a direct step in defunding abortions overseas. At a White House press briefing, Bush press secretary Ari Fleischer defended the directive by saying that Bush "did not support use of taxpayer dollars to fund abortion abroad." He made that point at least three times during this session.

One reporter tried to force Fleischer to address this distinction: "Is the president aware that under the 1973 law, the use of American money for abortions abroad is banned? This money isn't used for abortions." Fleischer replied: "I would urge you to wait until you read the executive order, and then you'll be able to see this for yourself." With that answer, Fleischer ignored the essential issue. (The executive order would not be issued until March 28, and in no way explained why the Bush White House had promoted the policy's revival with misinformation.)

Fleischer also said Bush "thinks that this will help make abortion more rare." That seemed, at best, wishful thinking. Though Bush promised the money would be sent to other family-planning groups, his action was expected to result in the defunding of existing family-planning programs, which could lead to a rise in unwanted pregnancies and a subsequent increase in abortions. Maurice Middleberg, director of health and population programs for CARE, told the *Washington Post* at the time, "This has to have only bad consequences for the health of the women and children that we serve, and for the abortion rate." (CARE did not engage in abortion promotion but still opposed the Mexico City Policy.)

The truth was that the Mexico City Policy was not about reducing abortions. It was about punishing international family-planning organizations—some of which also provided gynecological services and engaged in AIDS prevention in poverty-wracked nations—for promoting or discussing abortion, even though they relied on non-federal funds for that work. A cynic would have been justified to note that Bush's directive was issued the same day that scores of thousands of anti-abortion activists had come to Washington for their annual protest against *Roe v. Wade*.

Had Bush wished to be forthright, he could have said, "It is my conviction that any group that actively supports abortion rights should be penalized and denied taxpayer assistance for its other endeavors." Or he could have argued that if you sent money to an organization's family-planning program, the group would be able to divert other funding to its abortion-related activities. But if Bush had depended on that reasoning, he would have undermined a basic premise of his own faith-based initiative, which sought to funnel federal funds to religious organizations offering social services in the United States. In response to critics who had questioned this proposal for violating the separation of church and state, Bush had maintained that the government could indeed hand money to a religious outfit to underwrite the group's social services without abetting its religious functions. (Money for soup kitchens, but not for proselytizing between courses.)

But a week after Bush reimposed the Mexico City Policy, a journalist asked Fleischer if "there is not a double standard at work here." Under the Mexico City policy, a taxpayer opposed to abortion would not have to see his or her taxes subsidize even the non-abortion family-planning activities of organizations that support abortion rights. Yet Bush's faith-based initiative would require a taxpayer to finance the social-services activity of a religious group that might also try to convert people to a religion this taxpayer considered wrongheaded or offensive. Fleischer responded by misconstruing the question: "I think you misstated the [faith-based initiative] program. There won't be any focus on conversion. That's not what the programs do." But no double standard? No, Fleischer said.*

"Critics of testing contend it distracts from learning. . . . If you test a child on basic math and reading skills and you're 'teaching to the test,' you're teaching math and reading."

Three days into his presidency, Bush released his blueprint for education reform. A cornerstone of the plan was more testing for students. In order to ensure "accountability and high standards," Bush called for annual reading and math "assessments" (read: tests) for every child in grades 3 to 8. Using these tests as the key measurements, states and

---

*In early 2003, the Bush administration revised the Mexico City Policy and announced that money from Bush's global AIDS initiative would be available to international organizations that did promote or perform abortions, as long as their anti-AIDS programs were separate from their abortion-related activities. AIDS activists praised the move. But it did raise an obvious question: Why give money to groups involved with abortion for their AIDS work, but not for their non-abortion family planning and gynecological services?

districts would monitor schools. Schools that did not make "adequate yearly progress for one academic year" would be identified as needing improvement. A school that did not meet "adequate yearly progress after two years" would be designated a "failing school," and it would have to implement "corrective action" and offer a choice of another public school to its students. If a school screwed up for three years, low-income students could use federal funds to transfer to a better public school or a private school. A voucher system of sorts would kick in.

Judging schools on strict standards sounded reasonable. "Without yearly testing, we don't know who is falling behind and who needs help," Bush said. Yet some education specialists had challenged the efficacy of so-called "high stakes" testing. Bush and his education secretary, Roderick Paige, responded to testing naysayers by mischaracterizing their arguments and belittling their points. Testifying before Congress, Paige declared, "Those who say that testing is the problem, rather than lack of learning, are really suggesting that we lower our expectations because some kids can't learn." In his first address to Congress, Bush said, "Critics of testing contend it distracts from learning. They talk about 'teaching to the test.' But let's put that logic to the test. If you test a child on basic math and reading skills and you're 'teaching to the test,' you're teaching math and reading, and that's the whole idea."

Appearing at an education roundtable at Sullivant Elementary School in Columbus, Ohio, on February 20, Bush derided the testing critics, claiming that some opposed testing because they believe "there's no role for government" and that others maintained testing was "racist." He added, "We need to be results-oriented people. All we're asking is, Is it working? What are the results." The next day, at an elementary school in Knoxville, Tennessee, he declared, "We must measure because we want to know. We want to know when there is success."

Bush was grossly misrepresenting the case against testing. As *New York Times* columnist Richard Rothstein noted, academic studies of annual school testing had indicated that such testing was sometimes a poor and unreliable means of evaluating schools. (The studies had been conducted by Thomas Kane, an economist at the conservative Hoover Institution, and Douglas Staiger, a Dartmouth College economics professor.) "Under President Bush's proposal," Rothstein wrote, "commonplace measurement error could cause states to identify as 'failing' some schools that don't deserve the label." These studies noted that tiny sampling errors could skew scores and keep them from representing a school's true performance. One year's fourth grade at any given school, for example, could greatly differ in ability from the next year's fourth grade. Random events—bad weather, say—could affect test results. A school's average could change from Monday to Tuesday. Taking a test on a particular day would only provide an inexact snapshot, not an accurate picture of the quality of education being provided at that school. These cautionary studies raised the prospect that the Bush initiative could end up being counterproductive, by punishing good schools (with bad scores) and rewarding bad schools (with good scores).

Bush and Paige wanted no part of this debate and forged ahead. A year later, after tough negotiations with Congress, Bush signed the No Child Left Behind Act, an education bill somewhat different than he had proposed but one that retained the key testing provisions. Low-income students in failing schools would be eligible to receive taxpayer-financed tutoring or transportation to other schools. And schools deemed failing would have to take remedial steps, eventually replacing their principals and teachers.

A year after the legislation's passage, education officials across the nation faced a crisis, thanks to the testing and rating provisions of Bush's education plan. Thousands of schools, perhaps a majority of the nation's schools, were registering as failing. Here's how the *Washington Post* explained the complicated—but not unforeseen—situation: "The problem . . . is that the law also requires school systems to raise the achievement levels of students in each of five racial and ethnic subgroups, as well as among low-income students, those with limited English skills and disabled students every year. Any deviation from steady improvement in any of the subgroups for two consecutive years results in a school being called low-performing [that is, failing]. Accountability experts say that requirement, coupled with the year-to-year deviations that typically occur in standardized test results, means that schools would often be deemed low-performing for what amounts to statistical —rather than educational —reasons." And the *New York Times* reported, "The formula used to identify underperforming schools is so unwieldy that President Bush described a Michigan elementary school he visited last year as 'excelling' just three months before it was declared below standard." Testing skeptics—whom Bush and Paige had mocked—had, it turned out, been right to worry. Bush had oversold yearly testing as a problem-free solution to education ills and had painted an incomplete and false picture of the criticisms leveled against testing-centric reform so that this critique could be ignored rather than addressed. Subsequently, a mess ensued.*

"We pulled back [the arsenic standard] so that we can make a decision based upon sound science."

Soon after he had settled into the White House, Bush demonstrated that on environmental matters he was fully in tune with the corporate interests that had underwritten much of his presidential campaign and that he was willing to mislead the public to defend himself on this front. In March 2001, Christine Todd Whitman, head of the Environmental Protection Agency, announced the EPA was withdrawing a new standard for arsenic in drinking water developed during the Clinton years and issued two days after Bush assumed office. The decision to trash this standard produced howls of protests, a flood of editorial cartoons, and jokes on late-night talk shows. It was Bush's first major PR nightmare—and the first lie for which his administration took a hit.

From its initial minutes in power, the Bush team had attacked recent

---

*In June 2003, the Houston school system—hailed as the leader of the so-called Texas miracle in education and a model for Bush's No Child Left Behind Act—was embarrassed by the revelation that it had been rigging statistics to show schools were performing better than they were. A state audit of 16 middle and high schools found that thousands of dropouts had been wiped off the books, and it recommended lowering the ranking of 14 of these schools from the best to the worst. The audit also said that Houston's entire school system should be labeled "unacceptable." The New York Times reported, "Some here are questioning whether the [education] miracle may have been smoke and mirrors. . . . And they are suggesting that perhaps Houston is a model of how the focus on school accountability can sometimes go wrong, driving administrators to alter data or push students likely to mar a school's profile—through poor attendance or low test scores—out the back door." Paige, who was in charge of the Houston school system from 1994 through 2000—before becoming Bush's education secretary—refused to comment on the dropout undercounting.

environmental protections. On inauguration day, Andrew Card, Bush's chief of staff (and a former lobbyist for the automobile industry), issued a memo to all federal agencies ordering a 60-day freeze on the rush of new rules that had been finalized by the Clinton administration at the end of its term. This suspension covered several environmental standards, such as a regulation to minimize raw sewage discharges. The new administration also delayed implementing a standard protecting wetlands, weakened a rule instituting energy efficiency standards for air conditioners, and suspended new regulations on mining pollution. And Bush dumped a campaign promise to seek reductions in carbon dioxide emissions, the primary cause of human-induced global warming.

But it was the arsenic-in-water decision that came to symbolize the new president's relationship with the environment. And his administration's explanation for it could not survive scrutiny.

"I want to be sure," Whitman said when stopping the arsenic standard, "that the conclusions about arsenic in the rule are supported by the best available science. When the federal government imposes costs on communities—especially small communities—we should be sure the facts support imposing the federal standard." She was accusing the EPA of having crafted a standard that was not based on the "best available science." That was a harsh charge.

The new standard had lowered the permissible amount from 50 parts per billion (ppb) to 10 ppb. Whitman conceded that most scientists agreed the 50 ppb standard was not safe, but she asserted there was no consensus on a safe level. "The scientific indicators," she maintained, "are unclear as to whether the standard needs to go as low as 10 ppb." The agency, she said, would study the issue further. Days later Bush implied that the new standard had been irresponsibly rushed through, when he said, "At the very last minute my predecessor made a decision, and we pulled back his decision so that we can make a decision based upon sound science and what's realistic."*

---

*That same day, while addressing a dinner of radio and television correspondents, attended by several thousand, Bush joked, "I appreciate the members of the press. I think you serve a very useful purpose, especially tonight. As you know, we're studying safe levels for arsenic in drinking water. To base our decision on sound science, the scientists told us we needed to test the water glasses of about 3,000 people. . . . Thank you for participating."

But the new arsenic standard was no rush job unattached to reasonable scientific findings. The EPA had worked for a decade on establishing the 10 ppb standard. Congress had directed the EPA to establish a new standard, and it had authorized $2.5 million a year for studies from 1997 through 2000. A 1999 study by the National Academy of Sciences had concluded that the 50 ppb standard "could easily" result in a 1-in-100 cancer risk and had recommended that acceptable levels be lowered "as promptly as possible." Policymakers within the EPA had thought that a 3 parts per billion standard would have been justified by the science, yet they took cost considerations into account and went for the less stringent 10 ppb level.

Chuck Fox, a former EPA assistant administrator for water, pointedly noted that the Bush administration was being disingenuous when it claimed it was seeking a standard supported by a scientific consensus. What could be more sensible than a consensus-based rule? But as Fox explained, "There rarely is consensus on such numbers. The 10 parts per billion standard for arsenic, however, is widely supported by drinking water utilities, state scientists, public health officials and environmentalists, though not by the mining industry, some Western states and some scientists. Regulators always strive for consensus, as I did. But it is simply not possible to achieve absolute consensus in this case, so we opted for the scientifically sound standard that would protect public health." The new EPA standard was identical to one adopted earlier by the World Health Organization and the European Union.

But Whitman asserted that a one-size-fits-all 10 ppb standard might impose hardships on states—such as New Mexico and others in the Southwest—where there were higher natural levels of arsenic. (The EPA estimated the cost of compliance at $200 million a year.) That might have been cause for granting water systems in these states exemptions and more time to come into compliance with the new standard. Instead, Bush and Whitman were sticking with a one-size-fits-all cancellation.

When the media jumped on this issue, Whitman tried to take the arrows for Bush. A month after the arsenic decision was announced, she appeared on *Meet the Press* and claimed she had blocked the standard without any input from the White House. "I never talked to the White House about this one," she said. "I never read or talked to any of the industry groups. This was purely my decision. In fact, when we told the White House we were going with it, they pushed back. They said, 'Are you sure this is what you want to do? Is it the right thing?'"

Yet Whitman's I-did-it-my-way line would be contradicted by other accounts. A subsequent investigation conducted by the Senate Committee on Governmental Affairs (when it was in the hands of Democrats) unearthed a March 14 e-mail from the EPA's drinking water protection division noting, "EPA is discussing with White House staff the recommendation for a proposed withdrawal of the arsenic standard." Another e-mail the committee reviewed—this one from the acting deputy assistant administrator for science to the agency's arsenic team—noted it "was made very clear that" delaying the arsenic rule "was not a science but a policy decision."

The decision appeared to have been a political calculation as well, worked out by the White House—in contravention of a Bush pledge. As a candidate, Bush had said he would not decide key policy matters on the basis of politics. During a campaign speech in Kalamazoo, Michigan, he declared, "A responsible leader is someone who makes decisions based upon principle . . . principles that will not change, no matter what happens in the course of someone's political career." But one former White House insider maintained politics dictated the arsenic decision. In his book *The Right Man*, David Frum, who had been a Bush economic speechwriter, reported that Karl Rove, Bush's chief political adviser, had "pressed for reversal" of the arsenic standard. "Bush," Frum explained, "had come within a few hundred votes of carrying New Mexico in 2000, and the right decision on arsenic might carry the state in 2004. [White House communications director Karen] Hughes resisted. Arsenic was scary, arsenic in water even scarier, and the wrath of the environmentalists scariest of all. Hughes proved to be right. The attempt to shift five electoral votes Bushward handed the national Democrats their most devastating anti-Bush message of 2001."

Several months after the EPA suspended the standard, the National Academy of Sciences produced a new study concluding the 10 parts per billion standard was scientifically justified but possibly not tight enough. The administration could no longer harbor hope for a looser standard, one more friendly to the mining industry and New Mexico utilities. And Bush and his advisers had by then realized they had stepped into a big cowpie. In an August interview with ABC News,

Bush said of the arsenic standard suspension, "I think we could have handled the environmental issue a little better."

Six weeks after the NAS study was leaked to the press, the EPA announced Whitman's final decision on an acceptable level of arsenic in drinking water. After all that review, the administration had found that—what do you know?—10 parts per billion was exactly the right level for a workable rule. Not 5, not 15, but the original 10, even though the most recent NAS report—the latest in "best available science"—had suggested that the 10 ppb level might not adequately safeguard water drinkers. "We are reassured," Whitman said, "by all of the data that . . . a standard of 10 ppb protects public health based on the best available science and ensures that the cost of the standard is achievable."

The arsenic episode not only exposed the Bush administration's bias against scientifically based environmental regulations but made clear the White House was ready to dissemble in order to cover for policy (and political) decisions that were tough to support in public.* But no issue caused Bush to churn out fabrications and distortions more so than his proposal for massive tax cuts. The battle over his tax plan was the most significant event of his first months in office. And in crusading for these cuts, Bush would deploy some of his most outrageous and consequential lies. Quite literally, they would be the costliest lies of his presidency.

---

*Another regulatory matter that occurred at the same time indicated the same. In March 2001, Bush signed into law a measure passed by the Republican-controlled Congress that repealed workplace ergonomics standards that had been ten years in the making. These standards had been targeted by an extensive lobbying campaign mounted by business and industry groups. Explaining his decision, Bush said, "I was pleased to sign a bill that got rid of needless regulations." Opponents of the standards had argued they were too costly for businesses. But "needless"? Was that the truth? Not according to the best available science. In January, the National Academy of Sciences had released a report estimating that one million people a year took time off work to treat or recover from "work-related musculoskeletal pain or impairment of function" and that these injuries cost the economy between $45 billion and $54 billion a year. When Bush killed these health and safety rules, he promised to "pursue a comprehensive approach to ergonomics." A year later, his administration unveiled a so-called "comprehensive approach" that merely relied on voluntary "guidelines" for a number of unspecified industries.

5. Tax Policy Cheat

"Tax relief for everybody . . . while still reducing our national debt and funding important priorities."

When it came to the central policy proposal of his campaign, Bush stayed true to his word. As a candidate, he had said his priority would be tax cuts. But because his much-criticized plan had never registered substantial support in public opinion polls and because he had won office under questionable circumstances, many political observers wondered if Bush, a president without an obvious mandate (for tax cuts or anything else), would stick with his controversial and divisive plan.

He did. His third week in office, Bush unveiled what he called a "tax relief" package. (According to former Bush speechwriter David Frum, Karen Hughes always insisted that Bush's proposal be billed as "tax relief," rather than "tax cuts.") The ten-year plan was close to what Bush had hawked on the campaign trail: across-the-board reductions in income tax rates, canceling the estate tax, doubling the child tax credit (and extending it from families earning $110,000 a year to families making $200,000), and ending the so-called marriage penalty.

The package was big, and Bush tossed out plenty of arguments for it. The tax cuts, as he portrayed them, would assist middle-income Americans, net the average family $1,600, help millions of low-wage earners reach the middle class, save family farms and family-owned businesses, and rev up the recently gone-sluggish economy. And there was no reason to fret about the cost of his plan; there was, he said, more than enough surplus to cover the tab—and still provide money for other needs. Bush called his plan "tax relief for everybody, in every bracket . . . while still reducing our national debt and funding important priorities." But most of this was false. Bush was replaying the distortions and misrepresentations he had developed during the campaign.

"The bottom end of the economic ladder receives the biggest percentage cuts."

During a radio address on February 3, 2001, Bush claimed his plan "reduces taxes for everyone who pays taxes." Then, at a White House event on February 5 featuring families from different tax brackets, Bush asserted that "the bottom end of the economic ladder receives the biggest percentage cuts" from his tax package.* "My plan," he proclaimed, "addresses the struggles of American families." On another occasion, Bush maintained, "We must give low-income families fairer treatment," and he said that "six million families, one out of every five families with children, will no longer pay federal income taxes at all under our plan."

His rhetoric made it seem he had designed his tax cuts foremost to aid the beleaguered working poor. But the numbers told a different story. Shortly after Bush sent his tax plan to Congress, Citizens for Tax Justice released an analysis of its benefits. During the campaign, CTJ had calculated that Bush's tax proposal awarded 43 percent of its tax give-backs to the top 1 percent. Now CTJ's analysis showed that the Bush proposal was even more skewed toward the upper class.

The top 1 percent (those with annual incomes over $373,000) would pocket 45 percent, once the tax cuts were fully in place. The top 5 percent (over $147,000) would receive nearly 53 percent. The top 20 percent ($72,000 and above) would bag almost 72 percent. On the other end, the bottom fifth ($15,000 and below) would see 0.8 percent of the "relief." The lower 40 percent ($27,000 and less) could expect to share 4.3 percent. The middle fifth ($27,000 to $44,000) would be handed 8.4 percent. By the way, CTJ estimated that Bush and his wife, Laura,

---

*When a reporter asked why Bush had no family present representing the top bracket, Bush replied, "Well, I beg your pardon. I'm representing—I got a little pay raise coming to Washington from Austin; I'll be in the top bracket."

would personally save about $100,000 a year on their taxes—almost double the average gain for a taxpayer in the top 1 percent.

Using a different model, the Center on Budget and Policy Priorities derived similar numbers. This outfit also calculated that over 12 million low- and moderate-income families—almost a third of all families— would not gain any tax relief from the Bush plan. This was because these families had no income tax liability, though they still paid other federal taxes. An example: a two-parent family of four pulling in $25,000 a year would normally pay $3,825 in payroll taxes (including the employer's share) and additional excise taxes. This family would qualify for an earned income tax credit of $1,500, leaving it with a federal tax bill of at least $2,325—none of which would be relieved by the plan Bush touted as reducing "taxes for everyone who pays taxes." Bush should have said his tax cuts would help "everyone who pays *income* taxes." And sometimes he did specify that. But often he promised his package would help *all* taxpayers, an inaccurate description that rendered his proposal more far-reaching and generous than it was.

After Bush was bashed during the campaign as a reverse Robin Hood, his team was sensitive to the rich-guys-make-out critique of the Bush tax plan. And they crafted two counterattacks. One was the claim, as Bush put it, that "the greatest percentage of tax relief goes to the people at the bottom end of the ladder." The other was an analysis showing that the top 1 percent would not receive *such* a large chunk of the tax cuts. Both of these defenses were tricks predicated on unsubtle distortions.

The first trick relied upon Bush's use of the word "percentage." It was true that if a lower-income taxpayer were to receive an income tax decrease under the Bush plan, he or she probably would see a greater percentage of their income tax liability disappear than would a millionaire. But that had nothing to do with Bush's concern for the working poor. It was because low-income earners pay so little income tax to begin with. As the Center on Budget and Policy Priorities put it, "A two-parent family of four with income of $26,000 would indeed have its income taxes eliminated under the Bush plan, which is being portrayed as a 100 percent reduction in taxes." A 100 percent reduction did seem momentous. But here was the punchline: the family owed only $20 in income taxes under the existing law. Its net tax bill, though, was over $2,500. So that twenty bucks represented less than 1 percent of all its taxes. Big deal. Bush's "greatest percentage" line was meaningless in the real world, where people paid their bills with money, not percentages.

Talking about percentage reductions was a dishonest attempt to divert attention from the distribution analyses that made the tax plan look like Christmas for the well-to-do. Similarly, the Bush White House's claim that six million low-income families would have their federal income tax bills wiped out meant less than it appeared. If many of these families owed small amounts of income tax, it would be no great accomplishment to remove them from the income tax rolls.

Trick number two involved a chart released by the White House showing that the top 1 percent would pocket a mere 22.3 percent of the tax cuts. ("Richest 1% Will Get 22% of Cut, Bush Says," read a *Washington Post* headline.) That meant Bush's tax cuts were half as loaded for the rich as Citizens for Tax Justice and others purported. But one had to read the fine print, starting with the chart's title: "Income Tax Burden by Income for Calendar Year 2005." The White House was performing two cons at once. It excluded the impact of the proposed estate tax repeal, which was about one-fifth of Bush's tax plan and which only "relieved" the wealthy, and it was not taking into account the top-bracket income tax rate cuts scheduled for 2006, which also obviously favored the well heeled. The chart was a transparent effort to engage in the most creative of accounting by ignoring the big-ticket items of consequence to the rich.

This White House chart was about as phony and as blatant as spin gets in Washington. Except perhaps for when the Republican Party and industry groups arranged a demonstration in support of the Bush tax cuts. The National Association of Manufacturers sent out a memo to business outfits that urged lobbyists to show up at the Capitol Hill rally wearing hard hats and non-business attire: "WE DO NEED BODIES—they must be DRESSED DOWN, appear to be REAL WORKER types, etc."

"My plan unlocks the door to the middle class for millions of hardworking Americans."

In selling his tax cuts, Bush observed that "the country has prospered mightily over the past 20 years. But a lot of people feel as though they have been looking through the window at somebody else's party. It is time to fling those doors and windows open and invite everybody in. . . . Above all, my plan unlocks the door to the middle class for millions of hardworking Americans." Bush kept referring to that single-mom waitress—remember her from the campaign?—pulling in $22,000 or so a year, who pays a higher marginal tax rate than someone making $200,000 a year. His package, he asserted, would address this "unfairness." And he argued that "it's as if our nation had erected a toll booth right in the middle of the road to the middle class, making it hard for people to access the middle class." His tax plan would topple that tollbooth and usher this waitress and millions of others into the middle class. In one presidential address, Bush asked his audience to imagine this Everywoman in a diner carrying coffee and toast to a female attorney earning $250,000 a year: "Both of these women . . . deserve a tax cut. Under my plan, both of these women . . . will get one. For the waitress, our plan will wipe out her income tax bill entirely."

But just as Deloitte & Touche had concluded during the campaign, the Center on Budget and Policy Priorities calculated that this waitress, at $22,000 a year, would receive no reduction in her taxes under Bush's proposed legislation. If she managed to earn $25,000, she *might* pick up a few hundred dollars, depending on her child-care costs. But an extra $200 would hardly place this woman on the highway to middle-class ease. In the meantime, the lawyer in the diner would pocket between $3,100 and $8,400 a year from Bush's plan.

"We will return $1,600 to the typical American family with two children."

The check was in the mail. That was how Bush made it seem when he vowed, "We will return $1,600 to the typical American family with two children." But the $1,600 figure was based on two proposed changes not scheduled to be fully in place until 2006: doubling the child tax credit from $500 to $1,000 (a savings of $1,000 for a couple with two kids) and dropping the 15 percent tax rate to 10 percent for the first $12,000 in income (a $600 savings). Yet according to Citizens for Tax Justice—yes, here it was again—85 percent of families would receive either no tax cut or one less than $1,600. As the Center on Budget and Policy Priorities explained, "To qualify for this full $1,600 tax cut, a married couple with two children would need income of about $39,200 in that year." Bush more or less confirmed this when he said, "Working families earning between $35,000 and $75,000 will keep anywhere from $600 to $3,000 more each year." Families in that income range would be in the top half of all earners. Most of the bottom 60 percent, though, would not receive a $1,600 check. By Bush's standards, then, a majority of American families were not "typical." And taking inflation into account, that $1,600 would be worth less than $1,600 when it finally showed up.

Bush's emphasis on the $1,600 check was deceptive in another way. The two provisions he used to reach his $1,600 figure comprised only one-third of his total plan. Put another way, his $1,600 claim justified less than one-third of his overall proposal. If his aim were to assist these "typical" families, he could have done so with a much smaller tax-cuts package. And much of the projected cost of these two measures covered benefits slated to go to high-income families. The CBPP estimated that 3 percent of the benefits from the child tax credit expansion would accrue to the bottom 40 percent, but nearly half would go to families in the top fifth, which were, by definition, untypical.

"To keep family farms in the family, we're going to get rid of the death tax."

In his February 3 radio address, Bush boasted that his tax package would "eliminate the death tax"—the Republican term for the estate tax—"saving family farms and family-owned businesses." Weeks later, while swearing in his secretary of agriculture, Ann Veneman, Bush pledged to be a "friend to the American farmer." And he would show his friendship in his tax plan: "To keep family farms in the family, we're going to get rid of the death tax." His argument was that because family farms and other family businesses sometimes had to be liquidated to pay the estate tax, the estate tax was driving family farmers off their spreads. If that were so, Bush's proposed repeal of this tax might have been justified. But it wasn't so.

Using statistics from the congressional Joint Committee on Taxation, the Center on Budget and Policy Priorities noted that the estate tax covered a mere 1.9 percent of estates. That was because the tax only applied to estates valued above $675,000 (and that cutoff amount was already scheduled to rise to $1 million by 2006). Estates of any size could be bequeathed to a spouse free of taxes. And a couple could pass on an estate worth $1.35 million to an heir without cutting in Uncle Sam. The estate tax only concerned a small number of wealthy Americans, of whom only a few had to worry about family-owned businesses. The CBPP noted that "farms and family-owned business assets account for *less than four percent* of all assets in taxable estates valued at less than $5 million." And family-owned businesses and farms were already eligible for special treatment, including doubling the exemption level.

Had Bush been truly concerned about family farms, he could have raised the exemption further or called for new rules to cover the small percentage of estates that involved a family-owned business. Dumping the entire tax—which accounted for almost 20 percent of his total tax package—was not necessary to address the purported problem. It was as if Bush wanted to raze an apartment building because something was off-kilter in one unit.

But was there even a small problem in that unit? Did the estate tax force anyone to sell the farm? In early April, the *New York Times* published a front-page story that concluded it had not. Referring to an Internal Revenue Service analysis of 1999 returns, the paper noted that "almost no working farmers" owed any estate taxes. According to the newspaper, "Neil Harl, an Iowa State University economist whose tax advice has made him a household name among Midwest farmers, said he had searched far and wide but never found a farm lost because of estate taxes. 'It's a myth,' he said." Even one of the leading advocates for repealing estate taxes, the American Farm Bureau, said it could not cite a single example of a farm lost because of estate taxes. Lloyd Brown, president of Hertz Farm Management in Nevada, Iowa, which operated more than 400 farms in ten states, told the *Times* that none of his clients or anyone he knew had encountered problems due to the estate tax. As the paper pointed out, under the current tax laws, a farm couple could pass a farm worth $4.1 million to their heirs untaxed, as long as the beneficiaries continued farming for ten years. In Iowa, the average farm was then worth $1.2 million. The only real impact of the estate tax that any of the farm experts could identify was that it forced some farmers to hire lawyers and purchase life insurance policies used to offset possible estate taxes.

Bush, then, was calling for a tax cut of nearly $300 billion to solve a problem that did not exist. Not that some taxpayers wouldn't gain greatly from the repeal. "The overwhelming majority of beneficiaries [of abolishing the estate tax] are the heirs of people who made their fortunes through their businesses and investments in securities and real estate," the *Times* explained. Bush could have pressed for ending the estate tax by claiming (rightly or wrongly) it unfairly burdened rich Americans or that it amounted to double taxation (even though many of the estates in question included capital gains that had escaped taxation). But Bush found it more useful to claim he was helping the beloved family farmer—which he wasn't.

The day after the *Times* disassembled Bush's rationale for ending the estate tax, Ari Fleischer was conducting his daily press briefing, and Russell Mokhiber, the editor of *Corporate Crime Reporter,* tossed him a straightforward but challenging question. Noting that the newspaper had found no instances when a family farm had been lost because of estate taxes, Mokhiber asked, "So what did the president mean when he said, We are going to get rid of the death tax to keep farms in the family?"

This is how Fleischer replied: "Well, one of the reasons for that is that farmers have to go through a tortuous process just to keep the farm in the family hands. And there is no reason that farmers, or anybody else, should have to go through these tax avoidance schemes, should have to get financial planners. You shouldn't have to get an estate planner just because you work the land. . . . If you abolish the death tax, people won't have to hire all those planners to help them keep the land that's rightfully theirs."

This was a textbook example of Washington double-talk. Fleischer's boss had falsely asserted it was necessary to kill off estate taxes to preserve family farms. Caught in a $300 billion lie, the White House was now saying the reason to abolish the tax—a move that *also* would be a blessing to the richest 2 percent of Americans—was to spare farmers the pain-in-the-ass of estate planning. How considerate.

"There is enough money."

To prove his tax cuts were responsible, Bush had to demonstrate that the projected ten-year budget surplus was large enough to cover them. "There is enough money," he said to White House reporters in late January. And in an address to a joint session of Congress, he maintained his budget, even with his tax cuts and his promise not to touch the Social Security surplus, would still leave "almost a trillion dollars . . . for additional needs." During a radio address, he asserted, "My plan reduces the national debt . . . so fast, in fact, that economists worry that we are going to run out of debt to retire." But to get the numbers to line up right, the White House engaged in two shifty actions at once: it lowballed the fiscal impact of the tax cuts, and it hyped inflated projections of the budget surplus.

The Bush administration said the cost of the tax cuts would be $1.6 trillion over ten years—which would leave much of the surplus untouched and available for other purposes. But the White House's cost estimate ignored two key elements. It did not include the presumed cost of fixing a design flaw in the Alternative Minimum Tax, which was created to make sure corporations could not use loopholes to escape all their tax liability. This glitch was about to cause the AMT to be applied to middle-class taxpayers, and it would bring in $200 billion in revenues. The Bush administration was counting this money as offsetting the cost of its tax-cuts package, which it actually predicted to be $1.8 trillion. But with most tax experts assuming the out-of-control AMT would be reined in, Bush's number-crunchers could not honestly count on that $200 billion in revenue to lower the price tag of his tax cuts. The Bush estimate also did not include the higher federal interest costs that would result from the tax legislation. Put this all together, according to the Center on Budget and Policy Priorities, and Bush's proposed tax cuts could be expected to draw $2.1 trillion over ten years from the projected surplus.

But how large was that surplus going to be? In its dying days, the Clinton administration on January 16 issued an estimate of $2.4 trillion for the non–Social Security surplus over the coming ten years. But then on January 31, the Congressional Budget Office released a forecast projecting a $3.1 trillion surplus. The Bush crowd declared this indicated his tax plan was affordable and would cause no deficits. Using the CBO figure for the surplus and its own too-modest estimate of the tax plan's costs, the White House could claim that Bush's package would consume only slightly more than half the available surplus. That hardly seemed reckless.

But the Brookings Institution, the Concord Coalition, and the Center on Budget and Policy Priorities—policy groups of different political stripes—each pointed out that the CBO included in its calculations various tax increases and program cuts that were highly unlikely to occur. It also counted in its estimate the $400 billion Medicare surplus, which Congress had designated off-limits for financing tax cuts or other programs. When the Center on Budget and Policy Priorities used real-world assumptions, the available surplus became $2.0 trillion—less than the estimated full cost of Bush's tax cut. The analysts of the Concord Coalition and the Brookings Institution believed this surplus estimate was *overstated*, perhaps by several hundred billions of dollars.

All surplus estimates are best-guess projections, a fuzzy number by definition (as subsequent events would tragically confirm). Slower economic growth or higher growth in health-care costs could cause the surplus figure to shrivel—just as an unpredicted boom could create a fatter surplus. As the CBO noted, "The longer term outlook is . . . unusually hard to discern at the present." And Alan Greenspan, the Federal Reserve chairman, observed that recent changes in the economy rendered budget projections "subject to a relatively wide range of error." Yet estimates are what the policymakers and politicians have to work with. And according to the realistic numbers, Bush's tax plan, contrary to what he was saying, would gobble up the entire surplus.

What about funds for his promised military buildup? Or for the expanded (but yet unproven) ballistic missile defense system he advocated? That could consume a hundred billion dollars. What about the $1 trillion in transition costs for the Social Security privatization plan Bush wanted? What about money for the prescription drug benefit for the elderly he claimed to favor? What about unforeseen needs? Bush could have argued he wanted to devote *all* the available surplus to his tax cut. But that would have seemed rash. Rather, he fudged. The White House underestimated the tax cuts by about half a trillion dollars; it overestimated the surplus by about $1 trillion. Thus, everything fit. But only if one didn't look too closely. In truth, he was close to busting the bank.

"Immediate tax relief will provide an important boost at an important time for our economy."

Bush pitched his tax cuts as an effective pick-me-up for a stalled economy. He maintained it would "help jump-start the American economy." In a speech to Congress, Bush declared "tax relief is urgent" and necessary to address the "faltering" economy. But much of the Bush tax-cuts package was, as the tax-writing committees in Washington say, back-loaded. The biggest cuts would not kick in for several years—when the projected surpluses (and, Bush, too) might not be there and when the economy might be performing fine or not. Only about $20 billion of Bush's tax cuts were to go into action in the first year. That would barely provide any nudge to a $10 trillion economy. Peddling this tax plan as a direct and immediate remedy for current economic ailments was outright deceptive.

After months of political tussling, congressional Democrats—who mostly opposed Bush's tax-cuts bonanza—forced Bush to add an immediate tax rebate to the whole shebang: a $300 check for single taxpayers, $600 for couples. (It was not truly a rebate against taxes already paid, but an advance refund against 2001 taxes. But both congressional Democrats and the White House repeatedly referred to the checks as rebates.) The purpose of the so-called rebate was to provide about $60 billion in instant stimulus to the economy. Bush, embracing the argument of the Democrats, declared this "immediate tax relief will provide an important boost at an important time for our economy." That was a highly debatable proposition (whether made by a Republican or a Democrat). A study by the Economic Policy Institute, a liberal-leaning outfit, had concluded that $90 billion in such "rebate" checks would boost consumer spending by 1.3 percent. The checks lauded by Bush and the Democrats would probably increase consumption by less than 1 percent—which would likely do little to juice up the economy. After all, could a 0.6 percent tail wag a $10 trillion dog of an economy?

In the end, none of Bush's misrepresentations, deceptions, phony stats, and disingenuous make-believe hindered his unrelenting drive for "tax relief." In fact, they smoothed the course for him. Could he have won passage of the plan had he sold his package as mainly targeted to the wealthy? Could he have rallied support by decrying the estate tax as an accounting inconvenience for a small minority of family farmers? Could he have succeeded had he not camouflaged this massive tax reduction for the rich with his insistence he was providing "relief" to all, including his cherished single-mom waitress?

But Bush triumphed. In May, the Republican-controlled Congress passed his plan, with 12 Democratic senators crossing party lines to vote for his lies. (Two Republican senators—John McCain and Lincoln Chafee—voted nay.) During the legislative shuffle, Bush had been forced to agree to a trimming that dropped the total sticker price (as calculated by the White House) from $1.6 trillion to $1.35 trillion, though the cost including extra interest payments would be about $1.65 trillion.

The final cost would likely be even higher. As the congressional debate was finishing, the crafty Republicans in control of the House and the Senate added a sunset provision to the bill, under which the tax cuts in the package would expire at the end of 2010. This was not done to allow future legislators the opportunity to reconsider the controversial tax cuts. The point was to juggle the numbers to squeeze the tax cuts into the $1.35 trillion slot available under existing budget law. In pulling this stunt, the Republicans, with no protest from Bush, sliced away from the package's cost the revenue that would be lost in the last year of the decade-long period used for measuring tax legislation.

But this expiration date was a sham. No political observer believed it would survive. Would a future Congress—or a future president—permit these tax cuts to end and claim responsibility for a large tax boost? No way. An outraged Paul Krugman, columnist for the *New York Times*, wrote of this ploy: "They simply waved their hands" and made hundreds of billions of dollars "disappear from the accounting. . . . This is white-collar crime, pure and simple."

With the budget hawks of the Concord Coalition at this point estimating that the ten-year, non–Social Security surplus to be $2.2 trillion, even Bush's downsized tax package would likely end up consuming most, if not all, of the projected surplus. What had happened to Bush's assurance that he would preserve a trillion-dollar cushion? Forget about it. And any shock to the system—or new spending initiative—could lead to a return of federal budget deficits.

Bush had denied there was any reason for such prudent worrying. In

March, he had declared, "we can proceed with tax relief without fear of budget deficits, even if the economy softens." In April his White House predicted a $125 billion surplus for the year (excluding Social Security). But three months after his tax cuts were enacted, Bush was proven 100 percent wrong. At the end of August, the Congressional Budget Office released the bad news. The year's surplus had disappeared. The CBO predicted the federal government would run a deficit in 2001 of $9 billion and have to tap into the Social Security surplus to cover the shortfall.

Who or what was to blame for this dramatic reversal of fortune, this sudden loss of the surplus? The CBO estimated that two-thirds of the lost surplus was the result of the final tax cuts package. The other third was attributable to the weak economy. What about the trillion-dollar contingency fund Bush had guaranteed? Poof—its 2001 portion had vanished. What about Bush's vow not to tap the Social Security surplus? That, too, was defunct. And Bush's claim that he would be reducing the national debt so fast that economists would be concerned? No reason to worry now. Instead, Bush would be steering the federal budget in the opposite direction. He had broken his major budget-related promises—to cause no deficits, to enact affordable tax cuts, to preserve a rainy-day fund, to bring down the national debt, to honor the Social Security lockbox.

Weeks before the CBO announced the return of deficits—but when it was clear such a reckoning was coming—Bush had started to back-pedal. "Well," he remarked, "I've said that the only reason we should use Social Security [surplus] funds is in case of an economic recession or war." But that was not what his campaign platform had stated. It was not what he had told the public while fighting for his tax cuts. He had clearly pledged that his tax cuts would not contribute to deficits, that they would not necessitate a raid on the Social Security trust fund.

Could these broken promises have been worth the plan's supposed benefit to the economy? The direct relationship between taxes and an economy's performance is a topic of contentious debate. Perhaps the tax cuts would, as Bush claimed, improve the long-term prospects of the economy. But that was more a matter of faith than reason. In the case of the "rebate" checks—which Bush and Democrats had hailed as potent stimulus for an ailing economy—subsequent research indicated they did little to boost demand for goods and services. According

to surveys conducted by Matthew Shapiro and Joel Slemrod, economists at the University of Michigan, only about 25 percent of the 92
million taxpayers who received a check spent it. The rest saved the
money or used it to pay off debt. By Shapiro and Slemrod's numbers,
this supposed stimulus measure had pumped less than $10 billion
into the economy; by macro-economic standards, that was virtually
nothing.

The passage of his tax plan was a tremendous victory for Bush. A
man who had barely made it to the White House (and who still
inspired questions and jokes about his competence and intelligence)
had in four months rolled the Democratic opposition and achieved his
number-one objective. He had—using deceit as ammunition—pulled
off a political blitzkrieg. And the consequences were damn real: the
wealthy would retain hundreds of billions of dollars, the federal government would have fewer resources, and the surplus—which could
have been used for a prescription drug benefit or some other purpose—would be eviscerated.

Bush's victory, though, was marred (in political terms) by the news
that Senator Jim Jeffords, a moderate Republican from Vermont,
would leave the GOP and ally himself with the Senate Democrats.
This dramatic defection would transfer control of the Senate to the
Democrats and place Bush's other major initiatives at risk. With the
Senate in Democratic hands, Bush could expect to have a tough time
gaining congressional support for partially privatizing Social Security,
for oil drilling in Alaska, or for building a missile defense system. But
he would not give up these desires. The fights would continue—and so
would the lying.

6. **High-Octane Lies**

"The American people need to have an
honest assessment of [energy] issues."

On May 17, 2001, Bush flew on *Air Force One* to St. Paul, Minnesota,
where he toured an innovative power plant, one using both conventional and renewable energy sources to generate low-cost electricity.
Later that day, he traveled to Iowa and visited a research center
exploring new and more efficient ways to produce energy. At each stop
he praised the merits of conservation. Had the former oilman gone
green (or gone Gore)? No, this was more a trip of calculation than of
transformation. Bush had hit the road to rally the public behind his
new "comprehensive energy plan," and in doing so he was purposefully conveying a false impression.

In his first week in office, Bush had asked Dick Cheney to lead a
task force to draft an energy agenda. Now the plan was done, and
Bush was conducting these photo ops to unveil the 163-page document. "Today," Bush proclaimed, "I outlined over 100 solutions or
proposals as a solution to the problems we face." And he characterized
his plan as one based primarily on conservation: "I've laid out an initiative that said first and foremost we better be conservationists in the
country." He noted his plan would "require manufacturers to build
more energy-efficient appliances."

But there was much more to the plan than conservation. "We also
need," Bush said, "to come up with additional supplies." Pointing to
the rolling blackouts then under way in California, he maintained that
the nation was facing a severe energy shortage and had to build more

power plants and explore reviving nuclear energy. He called for drilling in Alaska's Arctic National Wildlife Refuge. Decrying the impact of high energy prices on "the average family budget," he claimed his administration had "developed a sound national plan to help meet our energy needs this year and every year." And Bush urged all partisans to come together: "Just as we need a new tone in Washington, we also need a new tone in discussing energy and the environment, one that is less suspicious, less punitive, less rancorous. We've yelled at—we've yelled at each other enough; now it's time to listen to each other, and to act."

To listen to Bush, one would have thought that his energy plan was written to confront a looming crisis and that it laid out a blueprint for a ready-to-roll Apollo-like project for conservation, contained scores of new and innovative ideas to beef up energy supplies, and was the product of bull sessions attended by environmentalists, industry representatives, and policy experts. But none of that was true.

"America in the year 2001 faces the most serious energy shortage since the oil embargoes of the 1970s."

Was there any crisis in the first place? The opening page of the Cheney document referred to "our nation's energy crisis," asserting that "America in the year 2001 faces the most serious energy shortage since the oil embargoes of the 1970s." It warned of "a fundamental imbalance between supply and demand." The first page also featured a graph that supposedly illustrated the nightmare to come. Charting projected energy consumption over the next 20 years, the graph showed demand heading from 100 quadrillion British thermal units (BTUs) to nearly 130 quadrillion BTUs, while in the same period domestic energy production stayed flat at about 74 quadrillion BTUs. It sure did look as if the country was about to be smacked by a big energy gap, requiring a tremendous boost in energy imports.

But with this chart, the White House was being unjustifiably melodramatic—if not deceptive—for this illustration made the gap appear larger than it might well end up being. The estimates for the increasing energy consumption were from the U.S. Energy Information Administration. But the energy production data was courtesy of the Sandia National Laboratories, a quasi-governmental entity engaged in energy technology research. Why use these two sources this way? Was it because if the chart had relied on EIA figures for consumption *and* production, the difference between the two would have been substantially less?

Sandia's energy production projection was based on the dubious assumption that production would grow in the coming 20 years at the same rate as it had in the 1990s—meaning production would hardly expand at all. The 1990s had been a time of low energy prices, which had led to less investment in energy, lower rates of development, and no overall increase in production. With energy prices now higher, production would presumably expand. In fact, the EIA was predicting 18 percent growth in production between 1999 and 2020. Had the graph consistently used EIA data, the gap between consumption and production would have been less severe, rising in 20 years from 27 quadrillion to 40 quadrillion BTUs, but not to the 50 quadrillion BTUs the graph showed. The need for imported energy supplies would still grow, but at a slower pace than the Cheney report contended.

W ere Bush and Cheney hyping a crisis to pave the way for their favorite energy policies? There was no question the United States could have used a comprehensive energy strategy to confront present and future problems involving energy prices, supplies, and pollution. Gas prices were relatively high, and the power shortages in California that led to blackouts were worrisome. But, as was later confirmed by a Federal Energy Regulatory Commission investigation, the problems in California were partly the result of underhanded manipulations engineered by price-gouging electricity companies, including the soon-to-be-infamous Enron.

In reality, the energy picture was not as grim as Bush and Cheney maintained. *Forbes* magazine wrote that "there is no energy crisis and there is little reason to expect there will be." The magazine took issue with Cheney, noting he had recently claimed, "As a country, we have demanded more and more energy. But we have not brought online the supplies needed to meet that demand." Yet *Forbes* politely reported, "The facts are something different. Between 1980 and 2000, despite a 90 percent increase in real gross domestic product (GDP), energy consumption increased by just 25.6 percent. . . . The energy price increase was tiny compared to non-energy prices, which rose by 119 percent." Writing for Knight Ridder newspapers, reporter Ken Moritsugu observed, "To call the current situation a crisis is an exaggeration." Citing industry figures, he noted that power companies had built or expanded 123 power plants in the 14 months prior to Bush's energy push and that 197 new plants were under construction. "That pace of construction," he wrote, "is enough to meet the upper end of the Bush administration's estimate that the country will need 1,300 to 1,900 new power plants over the next 20 years."*

The Bush-Cheney paper seemed to be purposefully overstating the case. It even referred to a supposedly urgent problem that didn't exist. The report said that New Hampshire might well experience electricity blackouts within months. Yet officials there, the *Boston Globe* noted, reported that New Hampshire had an energy surplus and was exporting 13 percent of its power to other states. When asked to justify the report's claim, Andrew Lundquist, the executive director of the Cheney task force, acknowledged the report was wrong on New Hampshire and told the *Globe* that the task force's intention had been to point out that "the electricity situation in New England is tight." But, the newspaper reported, Lundquist "could not specify which states are expected to have a problem." And Richard Kennelly, energy project director for the Conservation Law Foundation in Boston, maintained that the energy situation in New England "is just fine and getting better." He noted that 9 power plants had opened in the region in the previous year and 13 more were under construction.

So maybe there wasn't a full-fledged national crisis. But what about

---

*The Bush-Cheney estimate for new power plants overlooked other possibilities. A Department of Energy study in 2000—"Scenarios for a Clean Energy Future"—found that an aggressive policy promoting energy efficiency and renewable power sources could cut the projected increase in energy consumption per capita by almost 20 percent in the coming two decades. That would keep the nation's energy consumption at about the 2000 level and greatly reduce the need for new plants.

the middle-class families Bush and Cheney claimed to be fretting about? Did the United States have to drill more, burn more coal, and fire up more nuclear power plants to lift the oppressive financial burden on these people? Not according to the Cheney report. A chart on the first page of chapter two actually refuted the notion there was a serious crunch. It showed that the current percentage of household income spent on energy was lower than at any time between 1970 and 1995, and far less than the 8.0 percent high that had occurred in the early 1980s. The chart did indicate that since 1998, household income used to pay energy bills had increased from 3.8 percent to 4.8 percent. But this tick-up was attributed to both higher oil prices *and* record cold temperatures in 2000.

Had energy prices risen? Yes, but Bush was overstating the problem. The bottom line was that there was no pressing energy crisis. Yet Bush and his crew were trying to scare the country into believing an energy emergency was at hand.*

"We need to conserve."

Despite efforts by White House PR specialists to play up the conservation piece of Bush's energy message, reducing consumption was hardly the central feature of the plan. "We need to conserve," he said when he unveiled his energy plan. But a couple of weeks earlier, Cheney had callously dismissed conservation as a serious policy option. In a speech, he had said, "To speak exclusively of conservation is to duck the tough issues. Conservation may be a sign of personal virtue, but it is not a sufficient basis for a sound, comprehensive energy policy." But conservation advocates did not contend that conservation alone would adequately address the country's energy needs. And Cheney's disparaging remarks drew much flak; the White House felt the sting. So it was no surprise that two-and-a-half weeks later, Bush was trying to come

---

*Time proved Bush and Cheney had indeed been fearmongers. No immediate energy crisis ensued in the months or years after the Cheney report was produced. Writing in March 2003, *New York Times* columnist Paul Krugman observed, "Within months after the Cheney report's release, stock analysts were downgrading energy companies because of a looming long-term capacity glut. In short, Mr. Cheney and his tough-minded realists were blowing smoke: their report described a fantasy world that bore no relation to reality."

across like the conservationist-in-chief, depicting his energy plan as a roadmap for conservation. But this was all spin—manufactured for political purposes and not close to an accurate reflection of Bush and Cheney's true policy.

As the *New York Times* noted, "While in his public comments [Bush] always started with talk of conservation, the report itself was much more specific when it came to tapping new supplies." The numbers proved that Bush was not serious about conservation and alternative energy. Under his plan, funding for renewable energy could potentially double over ten years. "But," as the *Times* reported, "the estimated $10 billion commitment over that period is below what the Clinton administration had projected spending for roughly the same period, and well below what energy experts say would be required to make some cutting-edge energy technologies commonplace."

The Bush-Cheney energy plan did include more chapters and recommendations on conservation and renewable energy than on expanding conventional energy production. But the parts of the plan devoted to conservation and environment-friendly energy contained fewer commitments to specific and extensive actions than those sections that cried out for expanding traditional energy supplies. The report, for example, urged increasing the energy efficiency of homes and offices—in order to reduce the demand for new power plants—but it proposed no hard-and-fast goals. (Months earlier, the Bush administration had relaxed energy-efficiency standards for new air conditioners—a move that the Natural Resources Defense Council, an environmental group, estimated would force the construction of more than 40 power plants by 2020.) In a similar bob-and-weave, Cheney's document noted that raising the fuel efficiency standards for automobiles in the 1980s had been a positive step, but then avoided a decision on whether to increase the current standards, which were at a 20-year low.*

Moreover, the Bush-Cheney report's purported devotion to conservation and renewable energy was at odds with Bush's own federal budget. The budget he had submitted a few weeks earlier slashed funding for energy efficiency and renewable energy and cut spending on

---

*A month after the report came out, Cheney, while visiting a GM research facility in Michigan, said that the administration had no plans to implement higher fuel efficiency standards: "I'm one of those who believes very deeply in the market, and I think we have to be very careful not to pass artificial, unfair standards that sound nice."

research and development for solar, wind, and hydroelectric power by about 50 percent. How sincere, then, was the White House's newfound concern for conservation?

The true spirit of this energy plan—concocted by an administration led by two former oil industry executives—was found not in its nods toward conservation and renewable energy but in its calls for more coal mining, additional oil drilling, and a revived nuclear industry. (Cheney's paper did not offer any new ideas on what to do about the lethal radioactive waste produced by nuclear power plants.) The document also urged easing pollution regulations for power plants, refineries, and pipelines in order to enhance production. And even Bush's EPA, after reviewing a late draft of the document, had challenged this part of the Cheney blueprint, accusing it of presenting misleading information that happened to benefit the oil industry. In a memo to Cheney's task force, EPA Associate Administrator Tom Gibson complained that within the plan,

> costs of compliance with environmental requirements are over-stated, several inaccurate statements and opinions are presented as factual, and no citations are provided for many of these statements. We are very concerned that this language is inaccurate and inappropriately implicates environmental programs as a major cause of supply constraints in the United States' [oil] refining capacity. Such a conclusion, in our opinion, is overly simplistic and not supported by the facts.

When the final plan was released, it still contained much of the material the EPA considered misleading. Bush's talk of conservation was but green camouflage for a plan that embraced the biases and needs of traditional energy producers.

"The notion that somehow developing the resources in ANWR requires a vast despoiling of the environment is provably false."

The most controversial plank in the Bush-Cheney energy plan was its recommendation for drilling in Alaska's environmentally sensitive Arctic National Wildlife Refuge. This proposal also inspired some of the administration's most imaginative lies. The White House knew it would face a fight on this subject. Environmentalists and Democrats had long opposed developing this coastal plain—a wildlife area, a calving home for some 129,000 caribou, and an important habitat for many species of birds. To counter the opposition, the Bush crowd developed an impressive-sounding but misleading factoid. In advance of the energy plan rollout, Cheney deployed it during an April 30 speech. "ANWR," he said, "covers 19 million acres, roughly the size of South Carolina. The amount of land affected by oil production would be 2,000 acres, less than one-fifth the size of Dulles Airport. The notion that somehow developing the resources in ANWR requires a vast despoiling of the environment is provably false."

To the contrary, Cheney's statement was provably false. The oil that might be found beneath ANWR would not be gathered in one contained 2,000-acre area. According to a 1998 report of the U.S. Geological Survey, the main collections of oil in this area lay in more than 30 deposits spread across the refuge's northern coast, a 1.5-million-acre strip of territory. And the 2,000-acre figure did not reflect the large infrastructure—including roads and pipelines—that would have to stretch across ANWR to capture whatever oil lay under the tundra. As *Time* magazine noted, "[O]nly the space of the equipment touching the ground is counted [in the 2,000-acre estimate]. Each drilling platform can take up as little as 10 acres. The pipelines are above ground. For space purposes, [the 2,000-acre calculation] . . . counts only the ground touched by the stanchions holding up the pipe. Road widths are also conveniently left out of the space limit." By Cheney's method of measurement, a car would take up only several square inches of space—the area where the rubber hit the road.

Then there was the *big* lie—that drilling in ANWR would make a crucial difference in the energy security of the nation. Earlier in the year, Fleischer said Bush believed it was necessary to open ANWR to drilling "so that we can secure America's energy needs." He also noted that extracting the oil in ANWR was one step to take to make sure "we're not dependent on foreign sources." And Fleischer said, "The supplies that come out of there are so massive, they will last for an extended, long period of time." Bush, too, characterized his proposal to drill in Alaska as a way to counter over-reliance on foreign sources "to diversify supply, not only for national security reasons, but for international reasons, as well."

But the available numbers did not confirm such grand assertions. In 2000, the United States consumed 19.7 million barrels of oil per day, of which 10.4 million were imported, according to the Energy Information Administration. The best estimates of ANWR's output, according to the EIA, was that the amount of extracted oil *could* reach between 250 and 800 million barrels a year—seven to twelve years after development begins. The total amount of "technically recoverable" oil that could be obtained was estimated by the U.S. Geological Survey as between 5 and 16 billion barrels. On the low end, that would be the equivalent of nine months' of national oil consumption, and on the high end, slightly more than two years' worth. And those time spans would be less, if as Bush and Cheney maintained in their own report, U.S. energy consumption did increase by the time ANWR began producing oil.*

The ANWR oil would not be an insignificant amount, but it would have only a small and temporary impact on the nation's need for foreign oil. The EIA predicted that if ANWR yielded the mean amount—the middle of the estimated range—drilling there would lower the amount of oil the country would have to import by only 2 percent, from 62 percent to 60 percent of the nation's oil needs in 2020. This 2 percent drop, while perhaps important, did not jibe with the Bush administration's statements about enhancing energy security. The Bush-Cheney energy plan noted—without recommending it—that "an increase in the average fuel economy of the on-road vehicle fleet by three miles per gallon would save one million barrels of oil a day." This would be more than some ANWR estimates. As *Forbes* put it in May 2001, "Whatever the merits of this plan environmentally, the case remains that just slight increases in automobile fuel efficiency would conserve far more oil than the U.S. could ever hope to extract from the Alaskan preserve."

---

*The 5 billion to 16 billion estimate did not take into account the costs of extraction. The USGS also calculated what it called "economically recoverable oil" (oil that could be obtained by economically feasible means). And it found that if one assumed the price of a barrel of oil would run between $15 and $25 in 1996 dollars (the range of prices over the previous 15 years), the mean level of probable ANWR oil production would be between zero and 5.6 billion barrels. Under the most optimistic scenario, the production of "economically recoverable oil" might peak at about 10 billion barrels.

"My plan helps people in the short term and long term by recognizing the problem and by expediting energy development."

Bush extolled his energy plan as quick relief for the nation's energy woes. He claimed it would address "energy needs this year." This year? But most of the plan's proposals, if implemented, would not affect energy markets for years. As for Bush's claim that his energy plan contained over 100 solutions, many of these were actions already in progress. Some were requests to federal agencies to further study problems. And others were short on specifics. One of these "solutions" called for Bush to direct his science advisers "to review and make recommendations on using the nation's energy resources more efficiently." Another was a recommendation that Bush "direct the Secretary of Energy" to develop fusion energy. How exactly should the secretary do this? The report didn't say. A third "solution" was the suggestion that Bush "make energy security a priority of our trade and foreign policy." In other words, the plan's "solutions" section was padded.

"It's time to listen to each other."

When Bush launched his energy plan, he nobly talked up the importance of all participants in the energy debate paying heed to one another. Yet he and Cheney had not been keen on listening to environmentalists when the plan was being drafted. In February 2001, the Green Group—a collection of the leading environmental outfits in Washington—requested separate meetings with Cheney and Energy Secretary Spencer Abraham to discuss the energy proposals under construction. Both men slammed the door on the greens. Abraham's office claimed his schedule was too "busy." But over a year later, Energy Department documents—released in response to a suit filed by a consortium of public interest groups—showed that Abraham had possessed enough time to meet with 109 executives, trade association leaders, and lobbyists from the energy industry while the plan was being drafted. He had huddled with execs from the American Coal

Company, ExxonMobil, BP/Amoco, Shell, ChevronTexaco, and half a dozen nuclear power companies.*

As for Cheney, he passed off the Green Group to Andrew Lundquist, his energy task force staff director, and Lundquist waited nearly two months before seeing the enviros. The session, according to the Natural Resources Defense Council (one of 14 groups represented at the meeting), lasted less than an hour and was mostly consumed by introductions, not policy specifics. Not until June 5, six weeks after the plan had been issued, did Cheney meet with a delegation of environmentalists.†

Bush's call for a wide-open and respectful debate with plenty of listening was hokum. His White House wouldn't even say to whom it had listened. Cheney refused to release the names of the industry reps who had been allowed to meet with him and his task force to plead their case. Asked by House Democrats to find out who had conferred with Cheney and the task force, the General Accounting Office—the investigative arm of Congress—requested that the Cheney task force produce records identifying the people who had met with it and notes from these meetings. Cheney and the White House said no. At one White House press briefing, a reporter asked press secretary Ari Fleischer, "You know what the perception is, don't you, that only Big Oil has contributed [ideas for the energy plan] and wouldn't you want to wipe that out" by saying who had met with Cheney's task force? Fleischer replied, "I don't think that's the perception." The reporter shot back, "Yes, it is." And Fleischer countered, "Among some people."

The GAO, in an unprecedented move, sued the White House, and Cheney and the GAO slugged it out for nearly a year. During that time, the White House repeatedly claimed it was standing on principal and protecting the president's ability to receive confidential and unfettered advice. "In order for people to give me sound advice," Bush said during the GAO-Cheney standoff, "that information ought not to be

---

*When the Center for Responsive Politics investigated the list of people Abraham had chatted with, it found that 18 of the individuals and groups had contributed a total of $16.6 million to the Republican Party over the previous two years.

†In January 2002, Cheney appeared on *Fox News Sunday* and said of his energy task force work, "I talked to energy companies, I talked to labor members, talked to environmentalists." He was trying to make it appear he had solicited advice from environmentalists while drafting the report and neglected to mention he had spoken to the enviros only *after* his energy plan was out the door.

public. Somebody is not going to walk into the Oval Office thinking that the conversation is going to be public and give me good, sound advice." But the GAO was not being that intrusive. Its lawsuit merely demanded a list of the several hundred people who had huddled with Cheney's energy posse. For the legal battle, the GAO had scaled back its initial request and was no longer seeking minutes or transcripts of the task force's meetings.

And why did Bush assume that people would feel uneasy providing him "sound advice" on policy if they knew the public were to be told they had met with the president? Might it have been that White House officials preferred to keep their sessions with industry executives and lobbyists private—particularly after drafting a plan that catered to many of these interests? Bush's argument was more appropriate for a mob boss than for a leader who had called for a "less suspicious" debate. One could even contend that Bush generally ought to have been wary of receiving advice from anyone not willing to be seen entering the White House through the front door. At one point, while explaining why the Bush White House was entitled to hold closed-door meetings with industry representatives, Fleischer remarked, "The Constitution was, of course, drafted in total secrecy."

This GAO–White House dispute went on until a federal court in December 2002 ruled that the GAO lacked sufficient grounds to compel Cheney to turn over task force records. Shortly after that, GAO Comptroller General David Walker decided not to appeal and dropped the suit, citing as one factor Republican threats to cut his funding if he pursued the case. (A similar lawsuit filed by the Sierra Club and Judicial Watch, a conservative government-watchdog group, continued in the federal courts.)

"Eleven of those twelve [Sierra Club] proposals are, in fact, almost identical to provisions in the Bush plan."

The Bush-Cheney energy plan, not surprisingly, generated a storm of complaints. Environmentalists howled. Democrats whacked it. House Democratic leader Richard Gephardt snorted, "It looks like the ExxonMobil annual report and maybe that's really what it is." Jerry

Taylor, director of natural resource studies at the libertarian Cato Institute, urged conservatives to "just say 'no' to the energy plan," blasting it as "corporate welfare." Writing in *The National Review,* he maintained the nation was "currently in the midst of a power-plant construction boom," one that "will probably produce an electricity glut in the near future." The *New York Times* editorialized, "President Bush's long-awaited energy plan is as flawed and one-sided as its advance notices suggested it would be. Its 105 separate provisions include several potentially useful proposals aimed at improving energy efficiency and modernizing the country's power grid and pipelines. . . . But on the whole it is an alarmingly unbalanced piece of work whose main objective seems to be to satisfy the ambitions of the oil, gas, and coal industries, either by easing environmental rules or by opening public lands for aggressive exploration." A CNN/*Time* poll, conducted days after the plan became public, found that only 38 percent of people thought Bush was doing a "good job" on energy policy; 49 percent rated his performance "bad." And *Time* provided evidence for those who believed that politics, more than honest policy needs, had fueled the Bush energy plan. The magazine reported that a Republican pollster had used polls and focus groups to test certain words, phrases, and ideas for Bush's energy plan. (Remember Bush's claim that he didn't need polls or focus groups to help him make decisions? He apparently only used them to find the right words and concepts.)

How did the man in charge of the plan respond to the criticism? Disingenuously. Cheney felt the need for political cover and attempted to wrap himself and his plan in the flag of the Sierra Club. Appearing on *Meet the Press* three days after the plan's release, he was asked about a television commercial put out by environmental groups that blasted the Bush-Cheney energy proposals. "It's fascinating," Cheney replied. "I went back and I did a little analysis this week. The Sierra Club recently put out a set of energy proposals for how to deal with the energy problem in this country, twelve proposals; eleven of those twelve proposals are, in fact, almost identical to provisions in the Bush plan." Cheney really liked this argument. He said the same thing that day on *Face the Nation,* and repeated the assertion in speeches before corporate audiences.

Was it a lie? Or a desperate lie? Several months later, when NBC

News asked Cheney if the administration's "friends at the energy companies had unfairly influenced his energy plan," he once again shot off the Sierra Club line. This time, the Sierra Club responded with a side-by-side comparison showing that Bush and Cheney had not adopted its 12-point agenda. The group had urged raising the fuel economy standard for cars from 27.5 to 40 miles per gallon by 2012; the task force had called only for studying the issue. The Sierra Club had advocated doubling federal spending on energy efficiency and creating a tax credit to promote energy-efficient buildings; Bush and Cheney merely recommended "appropriate" funding for efficiency research and no tax credit for buildings. The Sierra Club proposed generating 20 percent of electricity with renewable sources by 2020; Bush and Cheney's plan aimed at 2.8 percent. And so on. "If the Bush administration really thinks their energy plan includes eleven of twelve Sierra Club solutions," quipped Sierra Club executive director Carl Pope, "then Arthur Andersen"—the accountants for Enron—"must be checking their math."

There was something in particular about drilling for oil in ANWR that drove Bush officials to trim facts and exaggerate. In an August 2001 interview, Fox News host Tony Snow asked Interior Secretary Gale Norton if it was true that ANWR was a birthing ground for caribou and a sanctuary for birds and waterfowl. "The area," Norton replied, "is sometimes calving grounds for the caribou, but this year, for example, they didn't use the area at all. They calved in Canada. And that has happened last year, several times in the past." That answer—which said nothing about the birds—suggested that when it came to birthing, the caribou could take or leave ANWR. But the U.S. Fish and Wildlife Service—a component of Norton's Interior Department—had found that there had been caribou "calving concentrations" within ANWR "for 27 of 30 years," according to a May 15, 2001, letter the FWS sent to a U.S. senator. There was no doubt that ANWR was an important area for caribou.

In that same interview, Norton, repeating one of the major fibs told by drilling advocates, claimed that opening up that stretch of wilderness to oil extraction would produce 700,000 new jobs—and that these jobs would be spread across the United States. (That was a lot of employment for just 2,000 acres!) What Norton did not say was that this job estimate came from an 11-year-old study commissioned by the American Petroleum Institute—not an unbiased source. And according to *Time,* economists had complained that this report "wildly inflates the employment potential." Eban Goodstein, an economist at Lewis and Clark College, told the magazine, "It's just absurd" and predicted real job growth would be less than one-tenth of that estimate.

On August 2, 2001, Republicans in the House, with the help of several dozen Democrats, passed a gigantic energy bill that in several respects mirrored the Bush-Cheney plan. It okayed drilling in ANWR and offered $33.5 billion in various tax credits and breaks—about 80 percent of which would benefit oil, gas, coal, and nuclear energy firms. The bill included a slight increase in vehicle fuel efficiency, rather than a proposal for a sharper boost that the GOP leaders had beat back.

Democrats slammed the bill as a fiscally reckless payoff to energy companies that had contributed to Bush and the Republicans in the previous election. The tax breaks were about three times the amount Bush had requested, and they included provisions—such as tax incentives for oil and gas production—that Bush and Cheney had not proposed. Still, Bush supported the bill. But the legislation went nowhere in the Democrat-controlled Senate. When Congress adjourned following the 2002 elections, the energy bill was dead, with the White House and its allies on Capitol Hill vowing to revive it in the coming year. And a year and a half later the lies of ANWR were called upon again as part of a GOP effort to pass just that portion of the energy plan— but to no avail. In March 2003, the Senate voted 52 to 48 against opening the Alaskan refuge to drilling.

Two weeks before Bush issued his doomed energy plan, he was speaking with reporters in the White House about the upcoming release. "We will be honest with the American people," he said, "and the American people need to have an honest assessment of the issues." That honesty was never delivered. Nor would it be on another energy-and-the-environment issue that concerned the possible fate of the world: global warming.

7. **Hot Air**

"We must address the issue of global
climate change."

O n June 11, 2001, Bush stood on a stage set up in the Rose Garden
and declared, "My administration is committed to a leadership role on
the issue of climate change." But in his first months in office, he had
not been leading on the issue of global warming. He had been proposing policy retreats, not policy advances. And U.S. allies around the
world were harshly criticizing him for his do-nothing approach to a
worldwide threat that could cause massive flooding, the extinction of
species, the spread of disease, famine, and other severe consequences.
So the White House had decided to position Bush as a president dedicated to confronting the frightening prospect of climate change. But
positioning is not the same as policy-making. Once more, Bush was
relying on photo-op rhetoric. His goal was not to create effective policy;
it was to avoid taking a hit for a stance that defied science but that allied
Bush with big business and anti-regulation ideologues.

The Bush White House's record on climate change began with a
broken promise. During the 2000 campaign, Bush called for reducing
the United States' emissions of carbon dioxide, a leading global warming gas. This statement had seemed unusual for Bush, given his image
as the candidate of Corporate America, much of which opposed
mandatory reductions of greenhouse gases. Sure enough, as soon as
Bush had settled into the White House, he tossed aside this campaign
pledge. Bush also declared in March 2001 that he was opposed to the
Kyoto Protocol, the 1997 global warming accord. This treaty—signed

by President Clinton but never submitted to the Senate for ratification—called for industrialized nations to cut their emissions of greenhouse gases to below 1990 levels by 2008 to 2012. Bush claimed it would be too costly for the United States—which was producing about 25 percent of the planet's human-source greenhouse gases—to abide by the treaty. He also criticized the agreement for demanding that industrialized nations lessen emissions before developing countries, such as India and China.

To defend his retreat from the treaty, Bush cited "the incomplete state of scientific knowledge of the causes of, and solutions to, global climate change." He was claiming the science was too iffy to warrant a strict regime of emissions reductions. But at the time, the scientific consensus—reflected in various reports of the Intergovernmental Panel on Climate Change (IPCC), an international body of thousands of scientists assembled by the U.N. and the World Meteorological Organization—was rather firm. That large consortium of scientists held that global temperatures were indeed on the rise and might climb 10 degrees Fahrenheit this century and that this increase was, to an unspecified degree, a result of human-induced emissions. A small number of contrarian scientists argued otherwise or questioned the computer models used to produce these findings, but it was undeniable that most experts believed human-caused global warming was occurring. They also generally agreed that the consequences of a 10-degrees increase would be terrible—rising sea levels, the dislocation of coastal populations, the spread of tropical diseases, the eradication of species, severe weather, drought, the disruption of ocean currents—and that countering human-caused global warming would require extensive emissions cuts soon.

Bush's abandonment of Kyoto had provoked an international outcry. Perhaps seeking cover, he called for more studies, including a report from the National Academy of Sciences. But when that additional information came in and further weakened Bush's position, his administration responded by lying.

In early June 2001, the NAS released the report Bush had requested, and the opening lines read:

Greenhouse gases are accumulating in Earth's atmosphere as a result of human activities, causing surface air temperatures and subsurface ocean temperatures to rise. Temperatures are, in fact, rising. The changes observed over the last several decades are likely mostly due to human activities, but we cannot rule out that some significant part of these changes are also a reflection of natural variability. Human-induced warming and associated sea level rises are expected to continue through the 21st century.

If Bush reached the last paragraph of the first page, he would have read, "The committee generally agrees with the assessment of human-caused climate change presented in the IPCC . . . report."

Case closed. Global warming caused by emissions was real. But rather than accepting the analysis it had commissioned, the Bush White House tried to mislead the press and the public about the NAS study. Fleischer maintained that the report "concludes that the Earth is warming. But it is inconclusive on why—whether it's man-made causes or whether it's natural causes." That was not spinning. That was prevaricating. The study blamed "human activities" while noting "natural variability" might be a contributing factor as well.

A day later, Fleischer fine-tuned his message. He said that Bush welcomed the report and agreed that temperatures were on the rise. But then Fleischer fixated on the fact that "uncertainties remain" as to how much global warming could be directly attributed to human activity. This was more sophisticated spin. Focus on the question marks, not the exclamation points. Concede human-caused warming was occurring, but dwell on the finding that scientists could not precisely measure how much warming was the result of cars, power plants, and the like. It looked as if even this report was not going to compel Bush to engage in any action.

But the White House then adopted a slightly different—but disingenuous—course. On June 11, as Bush was leaving town to meet with European allies seething over his rejection of the Kyoto accord, he delivered his Rose Garden remarks on global warming. He acknowledged the existence and dangers of climate change, but, like Fleischer, he emphasized the unknowns: "We do not know how much our climate could, or will, change in the future. We do not know how fast change will occur, or even how some of our actions could impact it." True enough. Yet he appeared to be saying that near-perfect knowledge was required before extensive remedies could be implemented:

"The policy challenge is to act in a serious and sensible way, given the limits of our knowledge." Mandatory reductions remained out of the question. He blasted the "unrealistic" Kyoto pact for being "not based upon science"—which was more of a mantra than an argument. (Actually, several prominent climate scientists believed the Kyoto treaty did not go far enough.) But Bush conceded, "We recognize the responsibility to reduce our emissions." He pledged his administration would craft an alternative to the Kyoto accord. This "science-based" alternative, he asserted, would use high-tech and market-based approaches "to reduce" greenhouse gas emissions. He promised to be a leader. "This is an administration," he said, "that will make commitments we can keep, and keep the commitments that we make."*

Was Bush really committed to "a leadership role"? Was he serious about reducing emissions? Or was this a feint to counter the torrent of criticism he had drawn? A month later, when diplomats from more than 180 countries gathered in Bonn for talks on global warming, the U.S. team, led by EPA administrator Christine Todd Whitman, arrived with no proposed alternative to the Kyoto accord. No leadership yet. When over 160 nations met five months later in Morocco, in November 2001, to hash out details of the global warming treaty, the United States was a no-show. And still, there was no Bush substitute for the Kyoto agreement.

Finally, on February 14, 2002, Bush was ready to be a leader—or pretend to be. That day, at the headquarters of the National Oceanic and Atmospheric Administration, Bush stood at a podium in front of a blue backdrop on which the phrases "Cleaner Air" and "Brighter Future" had been emblazoned over and over, top to bottom, side to side. No news photographer could snap a shot of him without those optimistic and happy words appearing in the frame. By now, this PR tactic was old hat for the White House's image experts. They had long

---

*According to Bush speechwriter David Frum, before Bush delivered this speech, two White House aides—John Bridgeland and Gary Edson—spent two months crafting a far-reaching alternative to Kyoto. The pair, Frum wrote, "cobbled together an ambitious program of controls and trading permits intended to lower American carbon dioxide emissions by almost as much as Kyoto demanded, without international supervision or pay-offs to foreign entities. They pushed their program all the way onto the president's desk before anyone else got much of a look at it. . . . Their policy was tossed aside, the speech they wanted the president to deliver was ripped to shreds, and a new one was hastily cobbled together that promised to take the issue seriously—and study it some more."

made sure that the *message du jour* would be spelled out—literally—in photos of Bush.

As he unveiled his long-awaited global warming plan, Bush remarked, "We must address the issue of global climate change." But instead of a plan to reduce emissions he offered an illusion. His program would actually allow for an increase in the production of global warming gases. If this artifice stood, the future would be warmer, but not necessarily brighter.

Describing his plan, Bush made certain to note that "scientific uncertainties" remained. But he said, "We can begin now to address the human factors that contribute to climate change." ("Now"? Why not a year ago? The science had not changed dramatically.) He maintained that America was committed to stabilizing greenhouse gases at a level that would not be harmful to the atmosphere. "Our immediate goal," Bush said, "is to reduce America's greenhouse gas emissions relative to the size of our economy."

This was sleight of hand. *Relative to the size of our economy?* Since the U.S. economy was generally growing, even if it had been sluggish of late, this meant emissions could continue to rise, as long as the rate of increase was below the rate of economic growth. The other industrialized nations, with the Kyoto accord, were calling for real reductions (below 1990 levels). Bush was pushing for slower increases (above 2000 levels). This was not a meaningful alternative to the Kyoto Agreement. It was more of an accounting ruse.

Bush's proposed emissions slowdown was not even mandatory. He said he intended to achieve his "goal" through voluntary action—mainly, tax credits to encourage companies and individuals to decrease emissions. His plan would even grant businesses that produce greenhouse gases tax credits for merely monitoring and reporting their emissions, not necessarily for reducing their output. These firms could then sell their pollution credits to other companies, which could use the credits to increase their emissions. Overall, Bush's plan would not force a single greenhouse gas polluter to do a thing. The net result: no guaranteed reduction of emissions.

"This will set America on a path to slow the growth of our greenhouse gas emissions," Bush said, "and, as science justifies, to stop and then reverse the growth of emissions." He still was refusing to acknowledge that the current science—according to most experts—

already justified reducing emissions. In his June 11, 2001, remarks, Bush had promised to develop an alternative to Kyoto that would lower emissions. This plan was no such thing.

"Addressing global climate change will require a sustained effort over many generations," Bush said at NOAA. That, too, was somewhat misleading, suggesting there was plenty of time. The IPCC scientists maintained that dramatic effort had to begin with the current generation and that if strong actions were not adopted soon, the opportunity to redress global warming might be lost. Bush could have said, There is no way I'll support reductions because I believe the cost to the economy will be too great. Instead, he developed a position and language that made it look as if he favored reducing greenhouse gases when he was actually endorsing further emissions.

The issue would not fade, and Bush would continue to dissemble. In June 2002, Bush's EPA quietly sent to the United Nations a climate report. (This study was required under an early climate-change treaty signed by Bush's father.) The paper noted the United States in the decades ahead would experience dramatic environmental changes due to global warming: heat waves and other extreme weather, loss of wetlands and coastland, pest outbreaks, increased air pollution, water shortages. Bush dismissed the 268-page study, contemptuously remarking, "I read the report put out by the bureaucracy." And he reiterated his opposition to the Kyoto process. Days later, Fleischer admitted Bush had not read the report.

So Bush had told a little lie about reading the report. More significantly, Fleischer insisted there remained "considerable uncertainty" on the causes of global warming. Nevertheless, he said Bush's climate change proposal "can reduce the problem of greenhouse gases and global warming." He did not explain how increasing emissions (albeit at a slower pace) would ameliorate damage to the atmosphere.

The following February, several industries responded to Bush's voluntary program by announcing commitments to limit the growth of their emissions. Secretary of Energy Spencer Abraham crowed that the administration was on its way to meeting Bush's goal of an 18 percent decrease in the growth rate of greenhouse gas emissions. Was this proof that Bush's leadership had paid off (on his very limited terms)? Not entirely. The electric utilities industry—responsible for 40 percent of the nation's emissions of global warming gases—was vowing it would reduce its emissions growth rate by only 3 to 5 percent over a decade. Yet the Energy Information Administration had previously predicted that the industry on its own—without Bush's program—would lower its emissions growth rate by 7 percent in that time. Bush's plan had made little difference.

Days after that less-than-impressive announcement, the National Academies' National Research Council issued a report that assailed the Bush administration on global warming research. The government's research plan, the study noted, lacked "a guiding vision, executable goals, clear timetables and criteria for measuring progress, an assessment of whether existing programs are capable of meeting these goals, explicit prioritization and a management plan." The expert panel—convened at the administration's request—reported that Bush's 2004 budget proposal "appears to leave funding relatively unchanged" for global warming initiatives, despite promises to increase it.

The panel also complained the Bush administration was focused on scientific questions that were already resolved. "In some areas, it's as if these people were not cognizant of the existing science," panel member William Schlesinger, dean of the environment and earth sciences school at Duke University, said. "Stuff that would have been cutting-edge in 1980 is listed as a priority for the future." And the report found that the administration was continuing to trump up uncertainty about the impact of human activity on global warming. In courteous terms, the panel was saying to Bush, Knock it off, already.

Shortly after the report came out, British Prime Minister Tony Blair rebuked Bush for not doing enough to forestall global warming. "There will be no genuine security," Blair observed, "if the planet is ravaged." He pledged to cut England's total emissions by 60 percent by mid-century, going further than the Kyoto accord timetable. In the spring of 2003, the White House edited an EPA report on the state of the environment to eliminate and dilute key sections on global warming. In one instance, according to the *New York Times*, the White House struck a reference to a 1999 study confirming an increase in global temperatures and replaced it with a reference to a study underwritten by the American Petroleum Institute that questioned this conclusion. EPA officials decided to drop the entire global warming section, rather than accept the White House's changes.

Bush had assured the public that he would "address" global warming, that his administration would assemble a plan to "reduce" emissions, and that he would assume "a leadership role." He did none of that. He did not address; he exacerbated. He did not reduce; he approved increases. He did not lead. Instead, he emitted misleading hot air.

8. **Stem Cells and Star Wars**

"This allows us to explore the promise and potential of stem cell research."

Come Bush's first summer in the White House, his presidency had lost steam. It wasn't that Bush's lies had slowed him down. But his agenda had thinned out since his tax cuts success. His faith-based initiative was stalled. Social Security privatization had been kicked over to a commission. Instead of promoting major policy proposals, the White House was planning a fall program—dubbed "Communities of Character"—that would include such touchy-feely measures as encouraging email between grandparents and their grandchildren and urging newspapers to publish more positive stories.* But two serious—perhaps life-and-death—research matters were sitting on Bush's desk. Each required a decision, and each would cause Bush to mislead the public. This administration, it seemed, never tired of putting politics ahead of facts and science.

---

*On July 9, 2001, the Bush White House held a senior staff retreat. In a letter later published in *Esquire,* John Dilulio, who headed the White House Office of Faith-Based and Community Initiatives in 2001, noted, "An explicit discussion ensued concerning how to emulate more strongly the Clinton White House's press, communications, and rapid-response media relations—how better to wage, if you will, the permanent campaign that so defines the modern presidency regardless of who or which party occupies the Oval Office. I listened and was amazed. It wasn't more press, communications, media, legislative strategizing, and such that they needed. . . . No, what they needed, I thought then and still do now, was more policy-relevant information, discussion, and deliberation." And Bush had promised that his White House would not be one of spin and politics.

■ ■ ■

For months, Bush had been approaching a moment of reckoning when he would have to resolve a knotty moral, scientific, and political dilemma: What to do about human stem cell research?

Human stem cells are cells in an early stage of development with the potential to grow into any one of the more than 200 different types of human cells. If stem cells are extracted from a blastocyst—the small cluster of cells that forms in the days after an egg is fertilized—they can be cultured into self-replicating lines of cells. This is a rather difficult process, but, when successful, it can produce stem-cell lines of value to medical research. The scientific community's consensus is that research employing stem cells may assist those seeking cures and treatments for a host of awful diseases, such as Parkinson's, Alzheimer's, diabetes, and cancer.

Human stem cell research has been controversial for some because researchers harvest the cells from week-old human embryos in a manner that destroys the embryos. The main sources for these embryos are fertility clinics that use in vitro fertilization to help couples conceive. Usually the fertilization procedure creates more embryos than are placed within the potential mother, and often there are leftovers that remain frozen in labs and are eventually discarded. Catholic church leaders, fundamentalist Christians, anti-abortion activists, and others who believe life begins at conception oppose stem cell research because it is predicated on the destruction of embryos. And that, to them, is the taking of human life.

Congress had banned federal funding of embryo experimentation in 1995. But by 1999, Clinton had been edging toward permitting federal funding of stem cell research, providing the government didn't underwrite the actual extraction of stem cells from embryos. But nothing had been decided by the time Bush entered the White House. He inherited the issue. It was now his call.

A problem for Bush was that in courting Catholic and anti-abortion voters during the 2000 election he had thrown in with the anti–stem cell crowd. "I oppose federal funding for stem cell research that involves destroying living human embryos," he had declared. But the politics of the stem cell debate were not as either/or as that of the conflict over abortion. Prominent conservatives who opposed abortion, including several Republican senators, were beseeching Bush to approve federal funding of stem cell research. Cheney and White House Chief of Staff Andrew Card favored stem cell research, as did many of the Republicans' biggest donors. Secretary of Health and Human Services Tommy Thompson was another cheerleader for stem cell research. Nancy Reagan, whose husband was suffering from Alzheimer's, was a high-profile fan of this research, and numerous patient advocacy groups were urging Bush to allow federally funded scientists to engage in stem cell research.

The White House let it be known that Bush was studying the issue, consulting with scientists and ethicists, and wrestling with the moral complexities of the topic. As Frum put it, "He did something I had never seen him do: He brooded."

On August 9, 2001, in what was his first nationally televised prime-time speech as president, Bush, looking less than comfortable, revealed his decision on stem cells. He acknowledged the research potential and the crucial role federal funding could play in developing such research. He also noted, "Embryonic stem cell research is at the leading edge of a series of moral hazards." He laid out "two fundamental questions: First, are these frozen embryos human life, and therefore, something precious to be protected? And second, if they're going to be destroyed anyway, shouldn't they be used for a greater good?"

Stand on a moral and theological principle? Or give a boost to potentially lifesaving research? Bush cut the difference—and he justified the verdict with false information.

"As a result of private research," he said in his speech, "more than 60 genetically diverse stem cell lines already exist. They were created from embryos that have already been destroyed, and they have the ability to regenerate themselves indefinitely, creating ongoing opportunities for research. I have concluded that we should allow federal funds to be used for research on these existing stem cell lines, where the life and death decision has already been made."

Some commentators hailed this compromise—funds for research using old lines, not for research using new—as Solomonic. Others called it a copout. After all, Bush did not explain why fertility clinics should be allowed to toss unused days-old blastocysts (or embryos) into the garbage, while researchers could not obtain consent and make use of them. But Bush's argument rested on his assertion that there were already 60 available lines for which the key moral question (destroy a potential life or not) had become moot. He noted that these lines were sufficient to achieve progress, suggesting it was not necessary to create new lines. "This allows us to explore the promise and potential of stem cell research," he said, "without crossing a fundamental moral line."

The 60 lines were crucial to Bush's dilemma-straddling position. Had there not been enough pre-existing lines, there would have had been no escape route for Bush. He would have had to decide between encouraging the creation of additional lines (which would offend important political constituencies) and imposing a virtual ban on this research (which would cause him to be accused of thwarting potential cures and treatments for millions of Americans). As he pondered before the speech, he had asked the National Institutes of Health how many lines were available for researchers. In late July, according to *Newsweek,* the NIH told Bush there were 30. That estimate was consistent with the figure used in a report on stem cells issued earlier that month by the NIH. But this total may have been an inflated—or wildly optimistic— amount. In a June letter to Tommy Thompson, a lawyer for several scientists working in the field had pointed out that only about six stem cell lines had been described in the scientific literature.

By the estimate of many scientists, the 30 lines the NIH claimed existed were not enough to support effective research. As the Associated Press had noted, researchers required a large number to ensure that the "basic biological discoveries are universal and not characteristics that are unique to the limited number of cell lines." One prominent expert had informed Bush that at least 100 lines were needed. And John Gearhart, a developmental biologist at the Johns Hopkins School of Medicine, told the *Washington Post* weeks prior to the speech, "You may have to establish hundreds of lines to get the few you'd want to have."

Look again, Bush ordered the NIH. And the agency searched further. On August 2, according to Stephan Hall, a science journalist who later wrote about this in the *New York Times,* the NIH reported to the White House that approximately 60 lines existed *or* were in development. But Bush ignored the crucial distinction between established lines and lines under development and focused on the total number. With 60 lines, Bush had his out.

He also had a completely false argument, for the 60 lines did not really exist.

Bush's count was immediately questioned. Douglas Melton, chairman of cellular and molecular biology at Harvard University, told the *Los Angeles Times*, "I do not know of 60 existing cell lines. I haven't counted them up, but I believe that there's closer to 10. And some of those 10 cell lines don't grow well at all and are largely useless." John Hopkins' John Gearhart said to the *Baltimore Sun*, "I am absolutely puzzled by this report of 60 cell lines." And Evan Snyder, a neurologist and stem cell researcher at Harvard Medical School, was quoted in the *Chicago Tribune* comparing Bush's decision to "Congress telling Bush they'll fund his defense budget but only if he uses World War II armaments. Those existing cell lines were generated with old technology. What if next week we find a new gene or growth factor that creates stem cells that are safer and more effective? The president has banned them."

In an interview with Bush, ABC News' Claire Shipman noted, "There's been some criticism today that when you said there are 60 existing stem cell lines, that those stem cell lines are worldwide and that there only may be a dozen available in the United States, and some people are saying, 'He wasn't completely forthcoming about that.'" Bush replied, "I'm telling you what the people at the NIH told me, and I suggest the skeptics talk to the people who are on the front line at research. The NIH thought there was ample amount of stem cell lines to work with." In a subsequent radio address, Bush maintained these 60 lines could do the trick: "They have the ability to regenerate themselves indefinitely."

The Sunday after Bush's speech, Thompson hit *Meet the Press* to hail and defend Bush's decision. And he addressed the doubts about those 60 lines: "There's a lot of questions about, you know, the viability of these cell lines. And let me just explain that a little bit. . . . There are 60 that we know of, real, viable, robust embryonic stem cell lines across the country, around the world. . . . We have checked and we have double-checked after the president made his statement."

Double-checking was not what it used to be. A *Washington Post* review backed up the initial criticism and found that "at least one-third of the 64 embryonic stem cell colonies approved for funding under a new Bush administration policy are so young and fragile it remains unclear whether they will ever prove useful to scientists." The NIH had identified Göteborg University in Sweden as the home of the world's largest collection of embryonic stem cell lines, reporting it had developed about 19 lines. But neurobiologist Peter Eriksson, a member of the stem cell team there, told the *Post* that at most only three of the 19 batches could be considered true stem cell lines. "I was a little surprised to see the NIH calling them 19 lines," he commented. "Maybe they misinterpreted a little bit." And the university's three actual lines had been alive for only half a year and had not yet demonstrated the ability to turn into all the major human cell types. That was an indication they might not even be full-fledged stem cells. "It's a little bit exaggerated," Eriksson remarked, "to say we have 19 lines. I think [the NIH] probably kept a relatively low bar."

Other labs named by the NIH as keepers of stem cells reported that their holdings were not yet ready for use in research. "At Reliance Life Sciences in India," the *Post* noted, "four of the seven cell lines included in the NIH tally have barely cleared the first hurdles in the long process of proving their identity and usefulness as stem cells. The three remaining lines are even younger and could easily 'peter out,'" said Firuza Parikh, founder and director of the Bombay-based research firm." In addition, CyThera Inc., a small biotech firm in San Diego, which supposedly owned the largest collection of stem cell lines in the United States (nine), noted that it was at least several months away from being able to provide a single colony to researchers. (The company later told *Newsweek* that it was not ready to analyze its stem cell lines to determine if they could be of value to researchers.)

The scientific reality was much different than what Bush and Thompson had claimed. Bush had said 60 stem cell lines existed that could be regenerated "indefinitely." Thompson had noted they were "robust" and "viable for research." Yet many of them were barely alive and not even actual stem cells. And there was another issue: it was unclear how many of these lines would be made available to researchers by the companies and institutions that held them. Bush and Thompson had given the impression that researchers would have 60 lines to choose from. But that depended on their owners.

When Bush had referred to the 60 lines in his speech, he probably believed the estimate was accurate. After all, what did he really know about the science of stem cells? That was the count the NIH had relayed. (Perhaps the NIH had felt pressure to craft as liberal an estimate as possible.) But what did the Bush administration do once that number was shown to be greatly inflated? It clung to its original, misleading claim. Take the disappearing stem cells of Göteborg University. Thompson declared, "There are 19 lines. They're in different areas of production and replication." Did Thompson know more about their status than the researcher in charge of these lines? And at one press briefing, a reporter asked Fleischer, "There's a question of there not being enough stem cell lines that are viable. What if there aren't enough viable stem cell lines? Will the White House consider changing its position?" Bush's press secretary ignored the latest information and maintained that "according to the National Institutes of Health, there are some 60 to 64 lines."

One day later, Thompson, in testimony before Congress, conceded that only about two dozen lines were ready for research, but insisted that most of the other lines would mature into usable colonies by the time federal funds became available nine months down the road. And when asked by Katie Couric of the *Today* show whether these in-development lines of unconfirmed stem cells could be termed "robust and viable for research," Thompson replied, "That is the case." The Bush administration was holding firm to the 60-line myth. Otherwise, Bush would have to revisit the issue and be forced to make a painful choice.

In subsequent months, the other lines did not materialize *and* the number of available lines decreased. A year after Bush's speech, *USA Today* reported, "Of the original 64 stem cell lines counted by officials at the National Institutes of Health last August, only five are now fully available to researchers, according to institutions that own rights to the self-replicating colonies of cells. Twelve others are available with some limitations, according to the NIH. More than a dozen of the stem cell lines remain largely untested; many of the others may never be available because of reasons ranging from legal disputes over ownership to medical problems with the colonies." The newspaper also reported that "the few lines of stem cells available to researchers lack sufficient genetic diversity to provide researchers with a full understanding of how they work." At a Senate hearing in September 2002, scientists—including Robert Pedersen of Cambridge University—complained that while the NIH had by then listed 78 available stem cell lines, only 17 or less were usable. Toward the end of 2002—long after stem cell research had faded as a hot-button issue—the NIH quietly cut its stem cell list to nine lines. At that time, Peter Berg, a Nobel laureate at Stanford, accused the Bush administration of deliberating impeding stem cell research. "I think it is scandalous," he told the *Milwaukee Journal Sentinel,* "how little has actually been promoted by the NIH. It's very hard to escape the conclusion that this has been put on a very slow track to please the White House."

By April 2003, researchers had developed a new technique for growing human stem cells. The older lines—the ones available for research under Bush's guidelines—had been bred using mouse cells. But these mouse cells could transfer mouse viruses and microbes to the human cells, and that limited the possible use of the human stem cells cultivated in this manner. The new process did not mix mouse cells with human cells. Yet the new-and-improved lines created by this method were off-limits to most stem cell researchers, since a majority of these scientists relied upon federal grants. Bush's rule permitted such researchers to work only with the lines developed before his speech. "This is the conundrum we're caught up in as federally funded researchers under the Bush policy," George Daley, a Harvard University stem cell biologist, told the *Washington Post.* "We want to do the basic research that works towards cures, but we cannot use the newly derived, latest, and best cell lines, which puts us at a disadvantage." And that month the *New York Times* reported that only 11 stem cell lines were then currently available for federally funded researchers. "Scientists foresee the need to create other lines," the paper noted. And one leading stem cell expert, who declined to speak for attribution, told the paper that researchers might eventually need between 100 and 1,000 lines to achieve effective results.

From 64 lines to 11. What a difference. Yet Bush never admitted he had gotten it wrong. More importantly, he refused to confront the implications of his erroneous estimate. Instead, he said nothing as his aides kept disseminating disinformation about the number of stem cell lines. Bush was willing to let them engage in deception, as he placed important medical research at risk—all to avoid political risk.

"Of course, we're not going to deploy a system that doesn't work."

While wrestling with the complexities of the brave new world of biotech, Bush was facing another controversial issue of science-and-politics: Star Wars, the sequel. In the summer of 2001, his administration was considering moving quickly toward deployment of a limited, test-model missile defense system. It supposedly would be able to shoot down a small number of nuclear missiles launched at the United States. But in seeking to create a favorable context for this momentous decision, Bush and his aides again stretched the truth: they overstated the threat and oversold the remedy.

During the campaign, Bush had promised he would revive the national missile defense program that President Ronald Reagan had embraced and beefed up in 1983. Yet after almost two decades of research—costing $84.5 billion (in 2001 dollars), according to the Center for Strategic and Budgetary Assessments—no proven model existed. Still, candidate Bush vowed to "build and deploy missile defense to protect America's homeland and our allies." Such a statement implied an effective system could indeed be built—which was not yet true. Bush did not say he would *try* to develop a system that could blast incoming nuclear missiles and, if successful, that he would then field it. He said he would install one. Was that campaign poetic license? Perhaps. But he was generating unrealistic expectations and exploiting false hopes.

Once in the White House, Bush remained devoted to his pie-in-the-sky campaign pledge. A week after the inauguration, newly sworn in Defense Secretary Donald Rumsfeld said of Bush, "He intends to deploy." And the Bush administration signaled it wanted to rip up the 1972 Antiballistic Missile Treaty in order to be able to pursue a missile defense without any restraint. That accord limited the United States and the Soviet Union (now Russia) to two missile defense sites and permitted much but not all testing of missile defense systems. This talk of a unilateral retreat from a fundamental arms control treaty rattled Moscow, Beijing, and European allies.*

On May 1, 2001, Bush officially launched his missile defense crusade with a speech in which he argued a limited missile defense system was needed because "today's most urgent threat stems not from thousands of ballistic missiles in Soviet hands, but from a small number of missiles in the hands of . . . states for whom terror and blackmail are a way of life." He reported that Rumsfeld "has identified near-term options that could allow us to deploy an initial capability against limited threats. In some cases, we can draw on already established technologies." He peddled missile defense as a weapon that "can strengthen deterrence by reducing the incentive for proliferation." And he tried to counter the criticism he was proceeding in a reckless and unilateral fashion. "These will be real consultations," he pledged. "We are not presenting our friends and allies with unilateral decisions already made." All of these were untrue statements.

The *most urgent threat*? That was an unambiguous declaration. Was a nuclear missile being lobbed at the United States by some rogue leader the most pressing danger the nation faced? Certainly, it was a worry, but the number-one threat? In February 2000, Robert Walpole, the national intelligence officer for strategic and nuclear programs, had testified to Congress that the intelligence community believed the missile threat was growing but was not the paramount challenge for the United States. "In fact," he said, "we project that in the coming years, U.S. territory is probably more likely to be attacked with weapons of mass destruction from non-missile delivery means (most likely from non-state entities) than by missiles, primarily because non-missile delivery means are less costly and more reliable and accurate. They can also be used without attribution."

In other words, terrorists wielding nuclear, chemical, and/or biological weapons in storage containers, trucks, airplanes, or freight packages warranted more concern than a dictator with a missile. A 1999 report by the National Intelligence Council noted that "non-missile delivery options . . . probably would be more reliable than ICBMs . . .

---

*Arms control experts and missile defense critics maintained that the ABM Treaty did not truly constrain the administration's missile defense efforts at this point, and they accused the White House of exaggerating the accord's impact in order to justify its decision to withdraw from the treaty.

probably would be more accurate than emerging ICBMs over the next 15 years," and "would avoid missile defenses."

Did Bush know something about the missile threat from rogue states that the intelligence community did not? If so, he did not indicate that in his speech or in subsequent remarks. And as missile defense skeptics often argued, if a rogue leader were eager to do the United States harm, would he choose to do so with a ballistic missile? Such weapons are expensive and hard to develop and maintain. Also, the origins of any missile attack would be easy to determine. Which means the regime that launched an attack would be toast. Taking issue with Bush, former senator Sam Nunn, a hawkish Democrat, remarked, "The most serious threats right now are not a missile from a third world country that has a return address. If we end up spending a huge amount of money on defending limited attack from three or four countries in the world—three, four, five missiles—and we don't have money left over to try and get the [nuclear] weapons and materials and know-how [that exist in the former Soviet Union and elsewhere] under control, we could end up with a more dangerous situation in ten years than we have now."*

During his speech, Bush noted that Rumsfeld was putting together a good-to-go system, and, in doing so, he spoke as if ballistic missile defense was essentially a tried-and-tested proposition. He neglected to mention that significant components had not been developed and that those that had were not ready for prime time. Two of the three tests of the main missile defense component—an interceptor missile that destroys an incoming missile by crashing into it—had failed in the past year. The one success that had occurred, according to *Defense Week,* came in a test in which the target missile had been specially equipped with a beacon that made it easier for the interceptor to locate it during

---

*Nunn was indirectly referring to a Bush campaign lie. While running for president, Bush had praised the Nunn-Lugar program, which Nunn had co-created with Republican Senator Richard Lugar. This program funded measures that increased security for nuclear weapons in Russia, that assisted the destruction of Russian fissile material, and that sought to provide legitimate employment for former Soviet weapons scientists who otherwise might be tempted to sell their services to a would-be proliferator. Bush had vowed to "ask the Congress to increase substantially our assistance to dismantle as many of Russia's weapons as possible as quickly as possible." But the Bush White House, in its proposed budget for fiscal year 2002, cut funding for Nunn-Lugar by 15 or so percent, about $117 million. This slash came after a bipartisan task force had called for a fourfold funding increase for these efforts.

the middle portion of its flight. And a July 2001 test—initially proclaimed a success by the Pentagon—was also carried out in this manner. The use of this beacon, *Defense Week* noted, "raises new questions about the realism of the exercises." Though ballistic missile defense was not yet being tested under real-world conditions, Bush was pitching the program as vital and viable protection for the nation, rather than *possible* protection.

Bush's claim that missile defense could curtail proliferation was another questionable assertion, if not an actual falsehood. What he meant was that if the United States deployed a limited system that could shoot down a small number of incoming ballistic missiles, there would be less reason for a foe of America to develop and build such weapons. But the intelligence experts had concluded the opposite. The 1999 National Intelligence Council report noted, "We assess that countries developing missile also will respond to U.S. theater and national missile defenses by deploying larger forces, penetration aids, and countermeasures." And a classified National Intelligence Estimate warned in August 2000 that deployment of a U.S. missile defense system could provoke China to expand its nuclear arms from about 20 long-range missiles to up to 200 in order to ensure the relevance of its nuclear arsenal. (A Chinese nuclear buildup, the intelligence analysts noted, could prompt India and Pakistan to accelerate their nuclear efforts.) The intelligence community also reported that countries developing ballistic missiles would be able to develop the technical means to evade missile defenses.

And Bush's promise to hang up his cowboy hat and consult with allies was belied by the facts. A month before his speech, Bush had declared, "I've assured our allies that we will consult with them, but we're moving forward to develop systems." As one European diplomat commented after the speech, "If Bush has already decided to go ahead with breaking the ABM Treaty and building his project, then how are we supposed to believe that these consultations have any meaning?"

Bush was gung-ho about missile defense, but naturally he did not want to appear to be racing off half-cocked. In mid-June, at a press conference in Brussels, he remarked, "And to those who suggest my administration will deploy a system that doesn't work are dead wrong. Of course we're not going to deploy a system that doesn't work. What good will that do? We'll only deploy a system that does work, in order to keep the peace."

That sounded sensible, but it wasn't official policy. A week earlier, Rumsfeld had said, "We will likely deploy test assets to provide rudimentary defenses to deal with emerging threats. We will likely continue to improve the effectiveness of any deployed capabilities over time." That is, the administration was planning to field missile defense components before they could be assumed to be in working order. They would be deployed for testing *and* operational purposes.

In July 2001, Deputy Defense Secretary Paul Wolfowitz, demonstrating that the administration was serious about rushing ahead, noted that the Pentagon wanted to turn a "testbed" at Fort Greely, Alaska, into a "very rudimentary" national missile defense system, as early as 2004. "Very rudimentary" was a clever phrase—code for "not yet working." And "very rudimentary" might have even been an optimistic description. Testifying before the Senate that month, Philip Coyle, the Pentagon's director of operational testing and evaluation from 1994 to 2001, observed, "Development of an effective NMD [national missile defense] network, even one with only a limited capability to intercept and destroy long-range missiles, will take a decade or more. This is for simple technical and budgetary reasons." (Some scientists opposed to missile defense maintained that an effective system could never be developed and deployed, due to technical hurdles that could not be overcome.) It did appear as if Bush—contradicting himself—was going to deploy a system that was not operational in any meaningful sense of the term.

Whatever the merits of missile defense or lack thereof, Bush was not being honest with the public. His policy was a gamble: let's spend tens of billions of dollars and start to deploy a system that may ultimately not do what I claim it will do. Perhaps the threat (distant or not) justified such an early deployment of a maybe-it-will-work system. Perhaps the naysayers were wrong, and over time the technological obstacles would be surmounted and the kinks worked out. But there was no guarantee this strategic holy grail could be obtained. Bush and Rumsfeld did not give the American public the benefit of a realistic assessment. They did not own up to the fundamental uncertainties.

In December 2001, Bush yanked the United States out of the ABM

Treaty as he had threatened. A year later he made his missile defense plans official: he announced his administration would indeed field a limited missile defense system at bases in Alaska and California by October 1, 2004. "While modest," Bush remarked, "these capabilities will add to America's security." Modest, for sure. The system still had not been demonstrated to work, its testing had yet to occur under real-world conditions, and necessary components (including the required computer networks) remained to be developed. None of that prevented Bush from proclaiming the Pentagon would "deploy missile defenses capable of protecting not only the United States and our deployed forces but also our friends and allies." Is it a lie to say you will definitely deliver what might never exist?

Two months after that announcement, the Pentagon's office of operational testing and evaluation released a report noting that the core element of Bush's missile defense system "has yet to demonstrate significant operational capability." In the report, Thomas Christie, the head of the office, observed, "I recognize and agree, in principle, with the desire to field new capabilities as soon as possible, but that desire should be tempered with the responsibility to ensure that the weapons will not put Americans at risk." Forget phony protection, he was suggesting the dash to deploy a non-working system could damage U.S. national security. At this time, the administration—for obvious reasons—was considering exempting its missile defense program from a law that requires the Pentagon to certify a system has undergone the appropriate operational tests before it goes into production.

In May 2003, with construction under way on a system in Alaska and California that would include ten anti-missile interceptors, the administration released a policy fact sheet noting, "The United States will not have a final, fixed missile defense architecture. Rather, we will deploy an initial set of capabilities that will evolve to meet the changing threat and to take advantage of technological developments." That was bureaucratese for saying, We're going to slap something together. As Fred Kaplan, a longtime defense writer, observed in *Slate*, "For the administration to start deploying a missile defense system before devising an architecture is no different from a construction firm starting to hammer nails, put up joists, and lay out a roof before knowing the style or size of a house." At about the same time, the Pentagon canceled nine of twenty missile defense tests it had scheduled over the coming five years. One of the canceled trials was scheduled to occur months before the initial deployment in October 2004, and it was supposed to test a crucial element of the system. In response to the cancellations, Senator Carl Levin, a longtime critic of ballistic missile defense, remarked, "The decision to field an as-yet-unproven system has been accompanied by a decision to eliminate or delay the very testing that must be conducted to show whether the system is effective."

In June 2003, a General Accounting Office report warned that because the missile defense program was being rushed, the Pentagon was "in danger of getting offtrack early and introducing more risk into the missile defense effort over the long term." This was more evidence that Bush's overeagerness was bad for U.S. security. The report noted that the system now scheduled for early deployment included components "that have not been demonstrated as mature or ready." The GAO added, "Testing to date has provided only limited data for determining whether the system will work as intended in 2004."

Despite Bush's assurance he would *only* deploy a system that works, he kept moving unflinchingly toward fielding an unproven and unreliable missile defense. And the 2004 price tag for his missile defense program was $9 billion.

With stem cells and missile defense, Bush and his aides misrepresented the state of the science. In the case of stem cells, that allowed him to duck a dicey and politically perilous decision. In the case of missile defense, he provided himself cover for plowing ahead without appearing rash. In each instance, the gambit worked. By speaking untruthfully, Bush had been able to restrict a promising field of scientific inquiry that key Bush constituencies considered an abomination and to revive a costly and uncertain weapons program craved by his military advisers and his conservative base. With missile defense, Bush was obsessing over a threat that the intelligence experts considered secondary. Their threat assessment—not heeded by Bush—would prove all too accurate on September 11.

9. **September 11**

"We must uncover every detail and learn every lesson of September the 11th."

O̤n the morning of September 11, 2001, when the second airliner crashed into the World Trade Center, it was shockingly and painfully evident the United States was under attack. Immediately—and for the first time in 60 years—the citizens of an assaulted America looked to their president to lead and protect them from presumably a foreign threat that had managed to reach the territory of the United States. As the buildings collapsed, as the Pentagon burned, as the death toll was estimated, as a wounded nation contended with trauma and grief, Americans also looked to Bush for answers. Who did this? Why did they want to murder American civilians? How could they have eluded aviation security and U.S. intelligence, hijacking four airplanes at once, and crashing three of them into these targets? What did all this mean? If ever there were a time when the nation—and the world—needed an American president who was credible and trustworthy, this was the moment.

The horrific 9/11 attacks would change the country and George W. Bush. His smirk would disappear. He would speak and act with seriousness and determination. He would rally the country, impress many Americans as a bold, purposeful and confident wartime leader, and establish a new bond with much of the public. But after September 11, he would not change his less-than-faithful relationship with the truth. He would grow in many ways, but he would not become a more honest leader.

The assault upon the United States presented the country with multiple challenges. How to respond. How to move forward as a society. How to understand the event. And understanding was crucial to the other challenges. In order to reach sound decisions on how to react, on how to strike back effectively, on how to protect America from future attacks, the public needed solid information on the murderous perpetrators, their intentions, the systems failures that had allowed them to succeed, and past, present, and future vulnerabilities. Much sophisticated knowledge did exist, inside and outside the government, about the attackers, the reasons for the assault, and the security weaknesses the plotters managed to exploit. But as many Americans and others yearned to make sense of this evil and transforming event, Bush elected to share with the public a misleadingly simplistic explanation of this catastrophe. And throughout the post-9/11 era, he would continue to misrepresent what was perhaps the most consequential tragedy to befall America.

It began on the night after the attacks. That evening, Bush addressed the nation for about four minutes from the Oval Office, the first time he had ever done so. He had already been briefed that Osama bin Laden, the leader of an Islamic fundamentalist terror network, was probably responsible for this heinous deed. But U.S. intelligence had not yet assembled proof. So even though news accounts were reporting that bin Laden was indeed the prime suspect, Bush, in his televised remarks, would not name names. But he did attempt to explain the event. "America was targeted for attack," he said, "because we're the brightest beacon for freedom and opportunity in the world." The next day at the Pentagon, Bush remarked that the United States was hit "because we embrace freedom." On September 13, he said of the yet-unidentified enemy, "These people can't stand freedom. They hate our values. They hate what America stands for." At a moving commemorative service at the National Cathedral on September 14, Bush noted, "They have attacked America because we are freedom's home and defender."

And on it went. Bush kept maintaining the United States had been attacked because of its love of freedom—even before he felt comfortable naming the culprits. After the Bush administration acknowledged on September 14 that bin Laden was the prime suspect, Bush two days later explained to the public that al Qaeda was "a large, broad organization, based upon one thing: terrorizing. They can't stand freedom. They hate what America stands for."

Was the motivation behind bin Laden's murderous jihad against the United States merely, as Bush suggested, that bin Laden despised the United States for embodying freedom? Nothing else? Perhaps Bush had initially resorted to simplistic rhetoric as a quick way of grappling with an unprecedented calamity. But in subsequent days, as Bush had additional time to ponder the catastrophe, he continued to depict the attacks in these superficial terms.

In a September 20 speech, Bush rhetorically asked, "Why do they hate us?" It was an important question. Not because the answer might excuse the mass murder of 9/11. It was important because Americans needed to comprehend the hatred that produced these terrorists—and, more significantly, that caused many Arabs and Muslims to hail the plotters—so that they would be able to evaluate policy options for dealing with a long-term threat to the United States. But Bush's own answer to his question was woefully narrow: "They hate our freedoms." And he said of al Qaeda, "Its goal is remaking the world and imposing its radical beliefs on people everywhere." Bin Laden's followers, he told the public, yearned "to kill all Americans."

This was all shallow analysis. Bush was offering the public no more than a comic-book interpretation of the event. It covered up complexities and denied Americans information crucial for developing a full understanding of the attacks. His account was oblivious to history and facts. In the view Bush furnished, bin Laden was a would-be conqueror of the world, a man motivated solely by irrational evil, who killed for the purpose of destroying freedom.

The record—and the experts—told quite a different story than the one Bush was supplying to the American public. According to terrorism experts and the State Department, bin Laden's goals were not global domination, slaughter for slaughter's sake, or the repression of freedom in the West. He was working to achieve specific geopolitical objectives, as he pursued a theological Yankees-go-home crusade.

Bin Laden's aim was to chase the United States out of the Middle East. He considered the presence of U.S. troops in the land of Islam (such as U.S. forces in Saudi Arabia) an abomination. He wanted to force Washington to end its support of autocratic Arab regimes in order to ease the way for a fundamentalist takeover of the region. Issuing a 1998 fatwa that urged the murder of American civilians and military personnel, bin Laden said this must be done "in order to liberate the al-Aqsa

Mosque [in Jerusalem] and the holy mosque [Mecca in Saudi Arabia] from their grip, and in order for their armies to move out of all the lands of Islam, defeated and unable to threaten any Muslim." A 1998 State Department fact sheet, put out by the department's counterterrorism coordinator, noted that "bin Laden and his network seek to provoke a war between Islam and the West and the overthrow of existing Muslim governments, such as Egypt and Saudi Arabia. . . . Bin Laden's goal in his own words is to 'unite Muslims and establish a government which follows the rule of the Caliphs,' which he believes he can accomplish only by overthrowing nearly all Muslim governments, driving Western influence from these countries and eventually abolishing state boundaries."

Outside-government experts also have depicted bin Laden as being motivated by policy designs (perverse as they were) related to Middle East politics. "His message is simple," Bruce Hoffman, director of the RAND Washington office, testified before Congress in 2002. "According to bin Laden's propaganda, the U.S. is a hegemonic, status quo power; opposing change and propping up corrupt and reprobate regimes [in the Middle East] that would not exist but for American backing." In his book *Holy War, Inc.*, Peter Bergen, a former CNN producer and the first journalist to arrange a television interview with bin Laden, writes,

> Why is bin Laden doing what he is doing?. . . . Bin Laden is not some 'AY-rab' who woke up one morning in a bad mood, his turban all in a twist, only to decide America was the enemy. . . . In all the tens of thousands of words that bin Laden has uttered on the public record there are some significant omissions: he does not rail against the pernicious effects of Hollywood movies, or against Madonna's midriff, or against the pornography protected by the U.S. Constitution. Nor does he inveigh against the drug and alcohol culture of the West, or its tolerance for homosexuals. . . . Judging by his silence, bin Laden cares little about such cultural issues. What he condemns the United States for is simple: its policies in the Middle East. Those are, to recap briefly: the continued American military presence in Arabia, U.S. support for Israel, its continued campaign against Iraq, and its support for regimes such as Egypt and Saudi Arabia that bin Laden regards as apostates from Islam.

With the September 11 attacks, Bergen notes, "bin Laden hoped to ignite anti-American sentiment in Muslim countries that would cause the downfall of governments and replace them with Taliban-style theocracies."

In their book, *The Age of Sacred Terror*, Daniel Benjamin and Steven Simon, who were counterterrorism officials at the National Security Council in the late 1990s, observe that "al Qaeda hijacked four airplanes and used them to inflict harm on the country that it perceived as the greatest enemy of Islam, with the aim of forcing that country to change its policies." And after the September 11 massacres, bin Laden purportedly gave an interview to a Pakistani journalist and said, "I ask the American people to force their government to give up anti-Muslim policies." In a December 27, 2001, videotape, bin Laden explained why he had targeted Americans: "If their economy is destroyed, they will be busy with their own affairs rather than enslaving the weak peoples."

Bin Laden was maniacal and murderous, an "evildoer," as Bush accurately tagged him. But he had specific reasons for his foul actions. His principle goal was to transform the Islamic world, not to annihilate the United States and slay its people. His key objection was to United States' policy, not its political, social, and cultural values. Bin Laden did not seem to care what Americans did at home. He wanted to push them out of Arabia so he could create a regional, fundamentalist theocracy—hardly a laudable end, but one much different than crushing freedom in the West.*

Rather than acknowledge the realities of bin Laden's war on America, Bush attempted to create and perpetuate the war-on-freedom myth. Why? Was this how he saw the situation? Was he unaware of the past and the details? A cynic might wonder if he took this course to prevent reconsideration of the United States' position in the Middle East. After all, if U.S. support for hard-liners in Israel and autocrats in

---

*In April 2003, Deputy Defense Secretary Paul Wolfowitz essentially acknowledged that 9/11 was not about U.S. freedom. The *Los Angeles Times* reported, "The effort to contain Hussein after the [1991] Gulf War left thousands of U.S. troops in Saudi Arabia. Their presence, Wolfowitz said, is 'one of Osama bin Laden's principal recruiting devices.' Bin Laden's 1998 fatwa, or religious decree, calling for the killing of Americans, Wolfowitz notes, cites the presence of 'crusader forces'—U.S. troops—in the Muslim holy land of Saudi Arabia, and U.S. bombing runs on Iraq, as reasons for jihad—or holy war—against the United States."

Saudi Arabia stirred vile terrorists to strike America, might the American public question the policies that prompted such reactions? And though the attacks were mounted by only a handful of people, a large number of Arabs and Muslims voiced support for bin Laden after the attacks. Did they hate us, too, because of the freedoms Americans enjoyed? Or were there other matters that had created such ill will against the United States? The limited explanation Bush made available for public consumption—that this was a battle between freedom and evil—did not cover the widespread anti-American sentiment that was exposed and fueled by bin Laden's strike against America. It kept deeper and hard-to-address problems out of the picture.

Maybe Bush needed—or thought the public needed—a self-affirming, easy explanation that offered what Bergen calls "psychological satisfaction." Or maybe a general disdain for nuance led Bush to see and cast the conflict in grandiose and theatrical terms. But it certainly was in Bush's interest for Americans to believe that "they" hate America because America loves freedom, not that "they" hate America because of its government's policies.

In the wake of the savage attacks of 9/11, Bush did not need to justify using force against the mass-murdering bin Laden and his allies. A strong and clear response was warranted. But by developing a mythic, simple, black-and-white, and reality-challenged narrative—the freedom-versus-evil plotline—Bush established a false context for his new war on terrorism and the actions that might come after the initial assault upon bin Laden and al Qaeda.*

---

*Calling his response a "war on terrorism" that would "eradicate the evil of terrorism" was also conceptually disingenuous for Bush. This, no doubt, sounded noble and reassuring to many Americans. But terrorism is a methodology—used for centuries by various forces. After he left the White House, Bush speechwriter David Frum bemoaned this device: "All this talk of fighting 'terrorism' made as much sense as a war against 'sneak-attackism' would have made after Pearl Harbor. Terror was a tactic, not an enemy." Yet Bush told Congress, "Our war on terrorism begins with al Qaeda, but it does not end there. It will not end until every terrorist group of global reach has been found, stopped and defeated. . . . And we will pursue nations that provide aid or safe haven to terrorism. Every nation in every region now has a decision to make: either you are with us or you are with the terrorists." Was Bush actually committing the United States to military action against terrorist outfits around the world unconnected to 9/11 or al Qaeda *and* the nations from which they operated? Only he could say if this was the truth.

"No one could have conceivably imagined suicide bombers burrowing into our society."

Bush also failed to level with the American public on another central element of the 9/11 disaster: what had happened—or not happened—on the U.S. side that allowed bin Laden to succeed so thoroughly and monstrously. The question rang out on September 11: why hadn't the U.S. government, with its assorted intelligence agencies, seen this coming? Had the country's gargantuan national security apparatus not picked up a whiff of this scheme? Had the best minds of the intelligence community been unaware such an assault was possible? After the attack, the Bush administration's position was, we had no clue; this was so far out of the box, it was unforeseeable. The Sunday after 9/11, Bush remarked, "No one could have conceivably imagined suicide bombers burrowing into our society and then emerging all in the same day to fly their aircraft—fly U.S. aircraft into buildings full of innocent people, and show no remorse."

He was wrong. Such a scenario had been imagined and feared by terrorism experts in and out of the U.S. government. Plots of this sort had previously been uncovered and thwarted by security services in other nations—in operations known to U.S. officials. Moreover, the Bush White House had received a warning in July 2001 that bin Laden was about to mount a major attack. Yet after 9/11, Bush and his aides did not share this important back-story with the public; they even attempted to cover up what Bush himself had been told about a possible al Qaeda attack. The White House also at first discouraged the congressional intelligence committees from conducting a what-went-wrong investigation, arguing that the government was too busy fighting the new war and should not be bothered with pesky inquiries from Congress. And Bush initially opposed legislation to establish an independent commission that would examine, among other topics, the pre-9/11 performance of U.S. intelligence agencies and his own administration. He showed little interest in accountability.

For eight months after the calamity, Bush managed to avoid public scrutiny over whether his administration and the Clinton administration had ignored hints or leads that possibly could have prepared the U.S. government for such a nightmare. His no-one-could-have-imagined-this line stood. Then in early May 2002, Associated Press reported that an FBI agent in Phoenix in July 2001 had written a classified memo suggesting that a group of Middle Eastern aviation students might be linked to terrorists. The AP revealed that no action had been taken in response to the memo. Next came the revelation that an FBI counterterrorism agent, trying to figure out the intentions of Zacarias Moussaoui, a suspicious aviation student arrested in August 2001, had speculated Moussaoui might have been planning to fly an airliner into the World Trade Center. The bureau, though, had not vigorously pursued the Moussaoui case.

The FBI's lackadaisical response to these pre-9/11 leads sparked a firestorm of criticism. But Bush was not directly drawn into the controversy until May 16, 2002. That day the White House confirmed a CBS News report revealing that on August 6, 2001, Bush (while vacationing at his Texas ranch) had received an intelligence briefing noting that Osama bin Laden was interested in hijacking airliners and looking to strike the United States directly. A political dust-up ensued, with Bush critics suggesting Bush had inadequately responded to that information and maybe missed a chance to prevent the 9/11 attacks. "There were two separate FBI reports plus a CIA warning, none of which were coordinated," Senator John McCain noted. "The question is, if all three had been connected, would that have led to more vigorous activity?" *Newsweek* observed, "The fact that the nation's popular war president might have been warned a little over a month before September 11—and that the supposedly straight-talking Bushies hadn't told anyone about it—opened up a serious credibility gap for the first time in the war on terror."

At this point, the White House, overreacting to what was a media overreaction, went into full spin-and-attack mode. Cheney denounced Democratic criticism of the administration's handling of the August 6 briefing as "thoroughly irresponsible . . . in a time of war." During a hastily called press conference with combative White House reporters, National Security Adviser Condoleezza Rice played down the importance of the August 6 briefing. She claimed it had not been a "warning," but a short and vague "analytic report" that merely mentioned hijacking "in the traditional sense" as one tactic that interested bin Laden. She asserted that the briefing—which the White House refused to make public—had contained no specific information upon which

Bush could have ordered action. That may well have been true. But Rice then reiterated a falsehood Bush had stated months earlier: "I don't think anyone could have predicted that these people would take an airplane and slam it into the World Trade Center." That day, Fleischer said the same: "Never did we imagine what would take place on September 11th, where people used those airplanes as missiles and as weapons."

The truth was that a 9/11-like attack had been predicted—more than once. The Clinton and the Bush II national security teams had not paid full attention to hints going back to 1995. That year, a Pakistani terrorist linked to bin Laden was arrested in the Philippines, and he said that he planned to use training he obtained at flight schools in the United States to fly a plane into CIA headquarters or another federal building. Information about his scheme was shared with the United States. And before his arrest, Algerian terrorists connected to al Qaeda hijacked a plane, hoping to crash it into the Eiffel Tower. (French commandos killed the hijackers at a refueling stop.) Those two episodes should have served as a warning to U.S. intelligence that bin Laden or others were considering a 9/11 type of operation. The CIA and the FBI (and other intelligence outfits) ought to have been chasing after intelligence related to plots of this sort. But nothing like that happened.

There was more: in 1998 terrorism analysts briefed Federal Aviation Administration officials on scenarios in which terrorists would fly planes into U.S. nuclear plants or commandeer cargo planes and crash them into the World Trade Center, the Pentagon, the White House, the Capitol, and other targets. In 1999 a public report prepared for the National Intelligence Council, an affiliate of the CIA, by the research division of the Library of Congress noted, "Suicide bomber(s) belonging to al-Qaida's Martyrdom Battalion could crash-land an aircraft packed with high explosives (C-4 and semtex) into the Pentagon, the headquarters of the Central Intelligence Agency (CIA), or the White House. Ramzi Yousef [the mastermind of the 1993 World Trade Center bombing] had planned to do this against the CIA headquarters." Two years later, in July 2001, Italian authorities warned the United States that bin Laden agents might try to use an airliner to attack Bush and other Western leaders at the Genoa summit.

The Bush administration's who-could-have-known cover story—thin already—became weaker when the congressional intelligence committees released a preliminary report from their 9/11 joint inquiry in September 2002. It revealed that the national security establishment had plenty of warnings—more so than publicly known—that al Qaeda had considered using airplanes as weapons. "While this method of attack had clearly been discussed in terrorist circles," the intelligence committees stated, "there was apparently little, if any, effort by Intelligence Community analysts to produce any strategic assessment of terrorists using aircraft as weapons." It was not, as Bush and Rice had suggested, that the intelligence community had failed to imagine the horrors of 9/11; it had failed to act upon clues in its possession.*

More damning for Bush was a paragraph that appeared in the committees' preliminary report on page 23. It reads,

> A briefing prepared for senior government officials at the beginning of July 2001 contained the following language: "Based on a review of all-source reporting over the last five months, we believe that UBL [Usama bin Laden] will launch a significant terrorist attack against U.S. and/or Israeli interests in the coming weeks. The attack will be spectacular and designed to inflict mass casualties against U.S. facilities or interests. Attack preparations have been made. Attack will occur with little or no warning."

This was a much more to-the-point briefing than the August 6 one that had caused all the fuss months earlier. But who were the "senior government officials" who had received this warning? And what had they done in response? The report did not say.

That was because the Bush administration wanted to block the public from finding out. Prior to the report's release, CIA Director George

---

*In August 2002, *Time* reported that the Bush administration had paid little attention to an extensive plan to "roll back" al Qaeda, one developed by Richard Clarke, chair of the interagency Counter-Terrorism Security Group, toward the end of the Clinton administration. The Clarke proposals, the newsmagazine noted, "became a victim of the transition process, turf wars and time spent on the pet policies of new top officials. The Bush Administration chose to institute its own 'policy review process' on the terrorist threat." That review process was coming to a close in early September 2001. At that point, *Newsweek* and other media accounts noted, Rumsfeld and Ashcroft were far more engaged with their own policy priorities (national missile defense for Rumsfeld; traditional crimebusting for Ashcroft) than counterterrorism.

Tenet instructed the congressional intelligence committees not to reveal whether this warning had been presented to Bush. As the committees' report explained, "According to the [director of central intelligence], the President's knowledge of intelligence information relevant to this Inquiry remains classified even when the substance of that intelligence information has been declassified." That is, the administration was willing to declassify intelligence reports for the committees, but it insisted on keeping classified whether this material had (or had not) been shared with Bush or anyone else at the White House.

This was an absurd stance. The administration was saying that it was okay to tell the public about top-secret information gathered before September 11. But it was arguing that national security would be endangered if the world were told those reports had been brought to the attention of Bush or his aides. If there had been a secrecy-meter for the secrecy-loving Bush White House, this move would have pegged the needle in the red zone. After all, if the information that was shared with Bush was made public—in this case, the dramatic July 2001 warning—how could Bush's awareness (or unawareness) of that information be considered a vital secret?

The reason for this maneuver appeared obvious: to avoid further debate on what Bush did or did not know prior to 9/11—and how he reacted to what he was told. What headlines might have ensued had a congressional report revealed that Bush was told two months before 9/11 that a "spectacular" attack was weeks away?

Speaking to reporters—including me—after a joint hearing of the intelligence committees, Senator Bob Graham, a Florida Democrat who chaired the Senate panel, said that classifying this type of information "is new to me. . . . I do not understand how, as a blanket reason, that serves national security interests." Was the White House trying to cover up an embarrassment? a reporter inquired. With a smile, Graham replied, "I'm not in the psychotherapy business." Asked if a reader could assume that prior to being censored the report originally read "the president and White House officials" in the many spots where it now referenced "senior government officials," Graham nodded his head without saying anything. He added, "If the underlying information has been declassified, I see no reason that who received it should be classified. How else do you hold people accountable?"

Precisely. The intelligence committees' job was to examine and judge how the government performed prior to 9/11—and to tell the public what happened. A key part of that mission was determining what information reached the White House and how Bush and his aides reacted. But a president who liked to champion responsibility was abusing—or stretching—the classification system to prevent a public evaluation of how he and White House officials had handled their own responsibilities. (By the way, when Rice spoke to reporters in May 2002 about the August 6, 2001, intelligence report Bush received, she did not disclose the July warning or say anything about having received intelligence indicating a "spectacular" bin Laden attack involving "mass casualties" was nearing.) The administration had mounted a cover-up just as the 2002 congressional elections were approaching. And Bush and his national security team received little, if any, flak regarding the July 2001 warning.

The intelligence committees' final 9/11 report, released in July 2003, noted that the White House still claimed the public could not be told about warnings that might have reached Bush. It also hinted (strongly) that the August 6, 2001, briefing that Rice had dismissed as an "analytic report" (one which the White House would not release) had said that bin Laden supporters were planning attacks in the United States. The committees concluded that 9/11 might have been prevented had the CIA and FBI better handled information in their possession.*

Regarding 9/11, Bush never embraced the notion of full disclosure. After months of opposing a bill to establish an independent 9/11 commission, he finally relented, but only once he had won the right to

---

*Tenet encountered no trouble for misleading the public about 9/11. In February 2002, while testifying in Congress, he declared that September 11 "was not the result of the failure of attention and discipline and focus" on the part of the CIA. But the intelligence committees noted the CIA had mishandled crucial information regarding two suspected terrorists who ended up on Flight 77, the airliner that was flown into the Pentagon. On different occasions in 2000 and 2001, the CIA learned these men were either heading toward the United States or already in the country, but it did not alert the FBI, which had an informant in San Diego in close contact with the two. This allowed the pair to go about their business and prepare for the attacks beyond the notice of the FBI. "There were numerous opportunities," the committees said, "during the tracking of these two suspected terrorists when the CIA could have alerted the FBI and other U.S. law enforcement authorities to the probability that these individuals either were or would soon be in the United States. That was not done." No one can ever know what would have happened had the agency red-flagged two of the nineteen 9/11 hijackers 18 months before the attacks. But this was a monumental failure of attention and focus.

choose its chairman. The day before Thanksgiving 2002, Bush announced he had selected for the job former Secretary of State Henry Kissinger, a symbol to many of excessive secret government, and Bush declared, "We must uncover every detail and learn every lesson of September the 11th." How phony. (Kissinger lasted two weeks in the job and resigned after being assailed for refusing to release the names of the clients of his international consulting business. Bush replaced him with former New Jersey Governor Thomas Kean, a moderate Republican with no extensive national security experience.)

Bush and his aides had misled the public about the aims of the 9/11 mass murderers and about the information possessed by the national security community before the attacks. And his administration had stopped the public from discovering what Bush and his advisers were told prior to the strikes. This was not the behavior of a person who favored uncovering "every detail" and learning "every lesson." It was conduct of a man who did not want the full truth known.

"[We are] taking every possible step to protect our country from danger."

Bush's war on terrorism was not all lies. His administration accurately pegged bin Laden and al Qaeda as the responsible criminals. It correctly noted the operational and intimate ties between bin Laden and the Taliban rulers of Afghanistan. Bush's case for war in Afghanistan was based on facts and well-founded inference. But the Bush administration would dissemble about other 9/11 matters, some sweeping, some small —to reassure, to cover mistakes, and to win policy disputes.

The day after the attacks, the White House hurriedly put out false information to protect the president. The issue was his whereabouts on September 11. Bush had been in Florida that morning, and instead of hurrying back to the helm, Bush had hopscotched around the country on *Air Force One* before returning to Washington in the evening. This dallying had prompted criticism. In response, the White House maintained Bush had been unable to come back to Washington immediately because the White House had received a "real and credible" threat about *Air Force One*. A threatening phone call seemed a reasonable explanation for the delay. But two weeks later, Associated Press reported, "Administration officials said they now doubt whether there was actually a call made threatening the president's plane." CBS Evening News reported that the call "simply never happened."

This was not an episode of great importance, but the post-9/11 period was a time when the country deserved full honesty from the Bush administration, particularly concerning the government's efforts to protect the country. Understandably, Bush and other officials did not want to draw attention to some of the nation's weaknesses. But in key instances they offered false assurances and were not straight with the public about vulnerabilities that existed and needed to be confronted.

In fact, false reassurance was something of an administration theme in the post-9/11 days. Transportation Secretary Norman Mineta, for one, professed that aviation "safety is always of paramount importance." Always? The U.S. government had long taken a less vigilant view toward safety than its European counterparts. In many European nations, airline and airport safety was the duty of the government. In the United States, it was often relegated to private contractors that paid their employees low wages and that employed screeners who received minimal training. Efforts to raise these wages and to submit screeners to FBI background checks had been successfully opposed by these companies. After September 11, Congress considered aviation security legislation that would make 28,000 airport screeners federal employees. Bush lobbied passionately against this measure. But once Congress approved the bill, Bush signed it and declared the law an "important step."

Trying to comfort the public, Health and Human Services Secretary Tommy Thompson told *60 Minutes* on September 30, "We're prepared to take care of any contingency, any consequence that develops for any kind of bioterrorism attack." But following his appearance on the show, ABC News reported that senior administration officials were privately saying that "Thompson dramatically overestimated the U.S. readiness to deal with such an attack." An unidentified CIA official told the network, "If they were being completely honest with the American public about the dangers posed by biological weapons, it would cause panic."

The nation was not close to being prepared. Two days before Thompson maintained on CBS that all was well, the General Accounting Office had released a study on bioterrorism preparedness.

It reported finding "deficiencies in capacity, communication, and coordination elements essential to preparedness and response, such as workforce shortages, inadequacies in disease surveillance and laboratory systems, a lack of regional coordination and compatible communications systems." State and local officials, the GAO said, "reported a lack of adequate guidance from the federal government on what it means to be prepared for bioterrorism."

Thompson could not avoid reality for long. Three days after the *60 Minutes* broadcast, he appeared before a Senate committee and essentially acknowledged that the government would not be able to handle a biological attack. A "regional or national response to a health emergency involving bioterrorism," he conceded, "will also require that additional capacities be in place . . . before the disaster strikes."

But on October 4, when the first news about anthrax hit, Thompson again misrepresented a matter of bioterrorism. After Robert Stevens, a photo editor at a supermarket tabloid published in Florida, contracted inhalation anthrax, Thompson suggested at a White House briefing that there was no evidence of terrorism, that this was an "isolated" case, and that Stevens may have been infected when he drank water out of a stream. But according to a report of the Century Foundation Homeland Security Project, "Experts said such a means of transmission had never been documented." And by the time Thompson made these remarks, Dr. Larry Bush, who had diagnosed Stevens, had concluded his patient had been exposed to anthrax via the postal system. When he heard Thompson claim the infection might have happened naturally, he was surprised. He later told the *New York Times:* "I thought: 'Wow. His first statement is wrong. Why did he say that? It was a major disservice. He should have said: 'We have a case of anthrax. It is very concerning. I don't have the details, but we will investigate it as bioterrorism.' "

On October 11, Bush told the public that the government was "taking every possible step to protect our country from danger." That clearly was rhetorical excess—understandable excess during a trying period, but still misleading. Wasn't it important for the public to know—and debate—what actions were not being adopted? Public health experts, for instance, warned that a weak public health infrastructure—which might be called upon to react to a bioterrorism attack—needed a massive upgrade. Dr. Mohammed Akhter, the executive director of the American Public Health Association, testified in Congress that "state and local health departments are not fully prepared to deal with an attack" of bioterrorism. Of 3,000 local health departments, 10 percent did not have email capability. Most departments were funded only to be open nine-to-five on weekdays. "If a bioterrorist attack occurred on a Friday afternoon," Akhter noted, "there would be no report of it until Monday morning under the current staffing profiles of most health departments." Yet there was no talk from the Bush administration of a full-scale effort to fortify the public health system. Nor did the administration, after 9/11, embrace the proposals of a Department of Energy task force that earlier in the year had called for spending $30 billion on programs "to secure and/or neutralize in the next eight to ten years all nuclear weapons-usable material located in Russia and to prevent the outflow from Russia of scientific expertise that could be used for nuclear or other weapons of mass destruction."

Plenty of steps went not taken. A report written by security and government experts at the Brookings Institution noted that much went undone in the year after 9/11. The unfulfilled tasks "range," the study said, "from creation of a new networked intelligence capability that tries to anticipate and prevent future terrorist actions, to greater protections for private infrastructure like chemical plants and skyscrapers, to a much stronger Coast Guard and Customs Service.... They also include obvious steps that should have been taken soon after the 9/11 tragedy but were not—such as making sure first responders can communicate over commonly accessible radio networks during emergencies, hastening development of port security plans, and improving security transportation networks aside from airports." This group reported (a year after the attacks) that Customs "still only inspects less than 5 percent of all cargo entering the country, even if it has become savvier about which small percentage to examine." These experts complained that the "federal budget has not been updated to reflect the emergence of homeland security as a priority for policymakers," and that Bush's homeland security budget for fiscal year 2003—about $38 billion—was about $7 billion short of what was necessary.

The Brookings study—as did a General Accounting Office report—identified security at chemical plants as a priority concern being unaddressed. The United States contains 12,000 chemical facilities. About 123, according to the EPA, handle toxic chemicals that, if released, could potentially threaten one million people. The Brookings study maintained, "These chemical facilities are not adequately protected against terrorist attack." And the GAO warned in March 2003, "No one has comprehensively assessed the security of chemical facilities." The EPA had tried to establish regulations to bolster security at these sites, but administration lawyers thwarted the effort by arguing the EPA did not have the authority to do so.

In an October 2002 article, EPA chief Christine Todd Whitman and homeland security czar Thomas Ridge wrote that mandatory government regulations were needed for security at these facilities. "Voluntary efforts alone are not sufficient to provide the level of assurance Americans deserve," they observed. Yet several months later—as the chemical industry lobbied against mandatory regulations—the Bush administration was preparing legislation that emphasized voluntary compliance with standards. And those standards were to be drafted by a chemical industry trade group, not the government. Not only was the Bush White House moving slowly in response to this top-of-the-list vulnerability, at this point it was ignoring the advice of Ridge and Whitman and heeding the pleadings of industry.

Every possible step? Not really. The Brookings report indirectly took issue with Bush's claim that his administration was doing all that was doable. "The federal government," it concluded, "after a respectable start in 2001, did not on the whole distinguish itself in its homeland security efforts in 2002. . . . [F]or every important step that has been taken, an equally important one has been neglected."

And the situation did not improve subsequently. In July 2003, an independent task force sponsored by the Council on Foreign Relations (CFR) and chaired by former senator Warren Rudman, a Republican, issued a frightening report declaring, "The United States remains dangerously ill-prepared to handle a catastrophic attack on American soil." It noted that fire departments across the country were short on radios and breathing apparatuses, police departments did not have the protective gear that would be needed to safely secure a site following an attack with weapons of mass destruction, public health labs lacked basic equipment and expertise to adequately deal with a chemical and biological strike, and most cities could not identify hazardous materials used in a terrorist attack. The task force calculated that America would "fall approximately $98.4 billion short of meeting critical emergency responder needs over the next five years if current funding levels are maintained." (Another report issued about this time by the Partnership for Public Service found that the government was nowhere near ready to handle a bioterrorism attack, due to a woeful lack of medical and scientific expertise within the federal agencies responsible for biodefense.) The report of the CFR task force ominously concluded, "If the nation does not take immediate steps to better identify and address the urgent needs of emergency responders, the next terrorist incident could have an even more devastating impact than the September 11 attacks." Not too indirectly, this study undermined Bush's assertion that everything possible was being done to protect America.

"It's not time to worry about partisan politics here in America."

In the shock-filled days following 9/11, Washington reverberated with earnest-sounding calls from both parties for bipartisan cooperation. Though Bush had repeatedly proven as a candidate and as a president that his claim to be a uniter-not-a-divider was worthless, September 11 provided him another chance and a unique opportunity to make good on his previous promises. This was a moment when the nation could reasonably expect political leaders to rise above politics-as-usual. And Bush acknowledged that. "It's not time to worry about partisan politics here in America," he declared. "It is time for our government to continue to work together." But as the capital resumed its business—now dominated by responses to the attacks—policy disputes arose. And the post-9/11 Bush handled them as did the pre-9/11 Bush. He lied, blamed, and attacked. Not even a national tragedy caused him to change his habits. Especially when tax cuts were at stake.

In early October, Bush proposed what he called an economic stimulus plan between $60 and $75 billion. (Congress had already passed a $45 billion package of disaster spending.) A rough outline of his plan included $15 billion in assistance for the unemployed. The rest would be tax cuts—including accelerating reductions in income tax rates scheduled for 2004 and 2006—and tax breaks for businesses. This proposal was yet another tax plan that could only be supported with fibs. As *The Economist* reported, "The Bush White House is once again playing games with numbers. The $75 billion pricetag for the stimulus refers only to fiscal 2002. Since several of its provisions are permanent, the overall fiscal cost will be higher. . . . Given the scarcity of details, it is hard to quantify the cost of the whole tax package precisely, but it could be up to $300 billion over ten years—a tad more than Mr. Bush's $75 billion figure."

The supposed point of this plan was to rejuvenate the post-9/11 economy. But the Center on Budget and Policy Priorities maintained the provision accelerating income tax reductions made "little sense as a stimulus measure." Dropping the 28 percent rate to 25 percent ahead of schedule, it explained, "would benefit only the top quarter of households and be of greatest benefit to the top five percent. These households tend to save rather than spend much of the new income they receive, so this change is unlikely to have a substantial stimulative impact. This proposal seems designed to lock in tax rate reductions so policymakers will not have the option of deferring or canceling them when the recession ends, the need to meet budget targets returns, and policymakers confront serious medium- and long-term budget problems."

Bush, as could be expected, claimed he was helping the middle class. "The income tax rate reduction," he asserted, "affects those making $27,000 to $65,000 a year—hardworking Americans who could use help." Technically, that was true. It did *affect* them—but not by much. A Citizens for Tax Justice analysis found that taxpayers in the $28,000-to-$46,000 range (the middle 20 percent) would on average in 2002 receive $11, and account for 0.8 percent of this particular tax cut. Those in the $46,000-to-$75,000 category (the second highest quintile) would pocket on average $98 and claim 6.6 percent of the tax cut. The top 1 percent ($384,000 and above) would receive $16,275 on average and account for 55.3 percent of the tax cut. These were not tax cuts targeted to the middle class.

Bush's 9/11 stimulus plan bogged down in Congress. Republicans in the House wanted to go further with business tax breaks.* The Democrats controlling the Senate were opposed to the tax cuts favoring the well-to-do. And Bush's so-called stimulus plan died in early February 2002. Bush, who had called for an end to partisan bickering after 9/11, immediately sought to blame the Democrats for being more mindful of politics than the national interest. "It seems like to me," he said, "that we ought to focus on what's best for the country, work together. . . . We can't let politics dominate Washington, D.C." But Bush had been playing politics just as much as the Democrats. He could have yielded by dumping the non-stimulative tax cut provisions Democrats opposed and preserving the rest of the package, but he fought as hard for his tax ideas (and his constituencies) as did the Democrats for theirs.

Bush's Republican Party went further than pointing fingers. It aired ads blasting five Senate Democrats who were in reelection battles. The spots lambasted them for being "partisan Democrats [who] put their interests ahead of national interests" by opposing Bush's post-9/11 tax cuts. Bush appeared in each ad, asserting, "There's something more important than politics and that's to do our job." With the country still recovering from 9/11, Bush, who had decried negative ads and the Washington blame-game, was participating in partisan hit ads. When Ari Fleischer was asked, "Why is the president appearing in a very sharply partisan political ad," he replied, "I have a hard time classifying it as sharply partisan."

This was hardly the first time a Bush administration official had, in the post 9/11 period, acted in a partisan or harsh manner. When civil libertarians—Democrats and Republicans—criticized Bush administration moves (such as a plan to try, and possibly execute, foreign terrorists in secret military tribunals), Attorney General John Ashcroft declared that critics who "scare peace-loving people with phantoms

---

*When the House Republicans crafted their own version of a stimulus bill, they included a corporate tax rebate going back to 1986, the year this tax was established. Under their plan, profitable companies would receive big refunds. IBM, for instance, would recoup $1.4 billion; Ford, $1.0 billion; General Motors, $833 million; General Electric, $671 million.

of lost liberty . . . only aid terrorists, for they erode our national unity and diminish our resolve." He was practically calling the critics traitors.*

Bush also interjected politics and falsehoods into what became his most prominent domestic response to the 9/11 attacks: the creation of the Department of Homeland Security. In October 2001, Bush appointed Pennsylvania Governor Tom Ridge to head up a new White House office on homeland security. But some congressional Democrats advocated going much further by creating a new federal department on homeland security that would combine various, existing agencies. Bush said no. At an October 24 press conference, Fleischer dismissed the idea, explaining there "does not need to be a Cabinet-level Office of Homeland Security." For months, Bush opposed a new Cabinet department. During a March 19, 2002, briefing, Fleischer maintained, "Creating a Cabinet office doesn't solve the problem." At a May 17 news conference, he again declined to endorse congressional proposals for a new department.

Then on June 6, 2002, in a surprise move, Bush proposed creating the Department of Homeland Security. Why the turnaround? By this point, Ridge and his new operation were being increasingly criticized, and the administration was under attack for having failed to pick up on possible 9/11 clues. "By reversing course, indeed by calling for a department larger than any of his critics had been seeking," the Brookings Institution report noted, "the President regained the initiative." Of course, Bush would not concede political motivations. In

---

*In the weeks after 9/11, Ashcroft fibbed and overstated his case while pushing the so-called USA Patriot Act, which included provisions granting new surveillance, search and wiretap powers to federal law enforcement officials. He suggested the legislation was needed to allow the feds to catch up to modern technology, noting, "Law enforcement tools created decades ago were crafted for rotary telephones, not email, the Internet, mobile communications and voice mail." But the wiretap laws were updated in 1986, 1999, and 2000, and they applied to e-mails, the Internet, and mobile telephones. The situation was not as dire as he had portrayed it. Ashcroft further argued that the Patriot Act would merely extend the same roving wiretap authority used in criminal cases to foreign intelligence cases (such as those involving suspected terrorists). But the authority requested by the act differed from the pre-existing authority; it dropped the requirement that the FBI had to ascertain that the target of a wiretap was actually using a particular phone or computer before tapping it (which protected innocent people from being wiretapped).

announcing his plan for the most massive reorganization of the federal government in 50 years, Bush mentioned neither his previous opposition nor the pending Democratic-backed legislation to set up such an entity. He even made it seem this was his idea. He urged Americans to pressure Congress "to support my plan."

The House and the Senate quickly went to work on the legislation. But Senate Democrats and the White House clashed over Bush's attempts to deep-six workplace protections for the new department's employees. To score points in this quarrel, Bush exaggerated. Arguing that he needed flexibility to deal with absurd workplace rules, he claimed that port inspectors, backed by their union, had refused to carry radiation detectors and that Customs employees had resisted providing their personal telephone numbers for use in emergency situations.

But his anecdotes were not right. The National Treasury Employees Union, which covers the Customs inspectors, had at first argued the previous January that the radiation devices should remain voluntary until Customs employees were properly trained how to use them. Then, on April 8, 2002, the union sent a letter to the Customs commissioner that read, "This is to confirm that NTEU does not object to the agency's proposal." The dispute had been resolved amicably. (The *Washington Post* noted that in griping about the radiation detectors, Bush had "taken some liberties.") And the phone-number fight had involved a Customs plan to create a centralized database of every Customs employee's home address and phone number. The NTEU had raised privacy objections to the database before September 11. But after the attacks, the union had dropped its opposition. And the union explained in its defense that it had only objected, pre-9/11, to establishing a central database; Customs employees already were providing emergency contact information to their managers. In other words, Bush had misrepresented the union's now-discarded position to obtain an advantage in a political brawl.

While engaged in the debate over the homeland security department, Bush was also relying on whoppers to advance another 9/11 initiative: terrorism insurance. After the attack, he had pushed legislation that would provide the insurance industry up to $90 billion a year to cover costs it might incur due to a catastrophic terrorist attack. Such a law would lay the foundation for an enormous taxpayer bailout of the insurance industry should another 9/11 occur. (The September 11 attack generated an estimated $30 to $40 billion in claims.) To sell this bill, Bush claimed that following September 11, "many insurance companies stopped covering builders and real estate owners against the risk of terrorist attack. The lack of terrorism insurance has delayed or canceled more than $15 billion in real estate transactions. The $15 billion worth of delay has cost 300,000 jobs—jobs to carpenters and joiners, bricklayers, plumbers, and other hardworking Americans." Terrorism insurance, he exclaimed, had become "basically extinct."

Much of this was untrue, and the numbers Bush was hurling—which he used as if they were government estimates—were far from reliable. As the *Washington Post* reported, "The $15 billion figure comes from the Real Estate Roundtable, a trade group that is leading the fight for the legislation and whose members have much to gain. After pleas earlier this year from the White House for 'hard evidence' to make its case for terrorism insurance, the roundtable got the information from an unscientific survey of members, who were asked to provide figures with no documentation." The 300,000-jobs number was also shaky. The White House said it got the estimate from the carpenters' union. But a union official told the *Post* that it appeared the White House had "extrapolated" the number from a Transportation Department study that looked at highway construction, not real estate.

"Do we know of a single job being delayed because of [a lack of terrorism insurance]?" Michael Dugan, an AFL-CIO official, remarked to TomPaine.com. "No." And the Consumer Federation of America noted that while the future of the insurance industry and terrorism insurance had been unclear in the months after 9/11, a year later terrorism coverage was available in most cases. Prices were high, CFA reported, but rates were falling, with some insurers apparently still "price-gouging." But the insurance industry, post-9/11, was in strong financial shape. No crisis existed. Nevertheless, Congress approved the bill. When Bush signed it into law, he proclaimed it would "get our hard hats back to work." But there was no solid evidence many—if any—hard hats had been affected in the first place by a 9/11 insurance problem.

In the weeks before the 2002 elections, Bush—the self-proclaimed scourge of divisive politics—had no qualms about using the homeland security bill as political ammunition to divide and conquer. At campaign appearances, he repeatedly assailed Democrats for supporting workplace protections for the employees of the new department, and he did so in an acrimonious manner, claiming his foes were willing to sacrifice the safety of the citizenry. At a stop in New Jersey in late September, Bush accused the Senate Democrats of being "more interested in special interests in Washington and not interested in the security of the American people." Democrats complained about this ugly attack, but Bush would go on to repeat the line. A reporter sarcastically asked Fleischer whether Bush was "trying to bring Democrats and Republicans together essentially by saying if you don't agree with me then I'm going to tell America you don't want to protect America." Fleischer replied that Bush was engaging in a "legitimate policy debate," adding what Bush had said was "not out of any malicious feelings" about the Democrats.

In mid-October, Bush attended a fund-raiser for Representative Saxby Chambliss, a Georgia Republican trying to unseat Democratic Senator Max Cleland, and he blamed Democrats—and Cleland by association—for trying to "tie the hands of this president and future presidents to be able to carry out one of our most solemn duties, which is to protect the homeland." He was accusing Democrats of placing the country at risk. And Bush was in complete sync with his party's electoral strategy. At the time, Chambliss was airing a television ad that flashed photos of bin Laden and Saddam Hussein as it assailed Cleland for supposedly voting against "homeland security" and lacking the "courage to lead." The Republicans were smearing Cleland, a Vietnam vet who had lost three limbs in a grenade accident, as being weak on national security.

Branding Democrats foes of homeland security ended up being effective strategy for Bush and the Republicans. The GOP retained its narrow majority in the House and regained control of the Senate—in part due to Chambliss's nasty victory over Cleland. And once the political dirty work was done, Bush lied in denying that any untoward politics had occurred. He maintained that his party's candidates had fared well because of their clean campaigns. "Their accent was on the positive," he remarked. "If you want to succeed in American politics, change the tone." But that was bunk. Just ask Cleland. Bush had decidedly not changed the tone while stumping for GOPers who had hit low and hard. As the *Washington Post* noted, "some of [Bush's] handpicked candidates ran tough negative campaigns. . . . Bush occasionally joined in the attack." Here was more proof that Bush was incapable of telling the truth about his own style of politics.

Congress passed the Department of Homeland Security bill after the election, with the dispirited Senate Democrats losing out on the workplace protection provisions. Bush signed the measure on November 25, declaring, "We are taking historic action to defend the United States and protect our citizens." Was Bush right to imply that the creation of the department would lead to better protection of U.S. citizens? The Brookings Institution's security experts were doubters. "The department," they noted, "will not in and of itself make Americans safer. To the contrary, the complexity of merging so many disparate agencies threatens to distract from other, more urgent security efforts. Moreover, excessive focus on organizational matters during the past year was one reason Congress has so far failed to pass a federal budget for homeland security for 2003. Even assuming that budget is soon passed, valuable time will have been lost in buttressing our national defenses against terrorist attacks." This criticism— coupled with Bush's unexplained about-face on the issue—suggested that Bush's most significant domestic response to 9/11 had been designed largely as an act of political protection rather than one of honest policy.

September 11 had transformed the U.S. government, reshaped American politics, and altered the nation. It would lead to two wars, if not more. And while much about Bush had changed, much had stayed the same. He still defied facts and distorted the truth when it served his interest. He still claimed to be a positive-toned leader but without hesitation employed negative tactics. The immense challenges created by 9/11 had not prompted Bush to rethink his reliance upon divisive and deceptive politics. They had caused him to embrace it further.

10. **Afghanistan**

"[The] oppressed people of Afghanistan will know the generosity of America."

On October 7, 2001, Bush honored his promise to punish al Qaeda and its allies. That Sunday, U.S. and British forces struck targets within Afghanistan in an effort to wipe out the terrorists and the Taliban rulers of that nation who had refused to hand over bin Laden and his comrades. Bush had not had to present much of a case for war. His decision to attack was justified by the facts of September 11. But that did not mean the Afghanistan campaign would be free of the lies and misrepresentations that accompany most wars and many Bush endeavors. His administration would shave the truth to pump up results and downplay setbacks and fatal mistakes. But Bush's most troubling dissembling of this war would come when he repeatedly claimed he was dedicated to rebuilding and reviving Afghanistan. This promise was an integral part of Bush's Afghanistan campaign from the start. When he announced the U.S. bombing campaign there, he vowed that the "oppressed people of Afghanistan will know the generosity of America." Yet the actions of his administration would demonstrate that this grand commitment was no high priority.

Though the war was at first tough slogging, the Pentagon and the White House cast events in as favorable a light as possible. That was to be expected, and it entailed highly selective presentations. On the first day of the bombing campaign, General Richard Myers, chairman of the Joint Chiefs of Staff, told reporters that 15 bombers, 25 carrier fighter jets, and 50 cruise missiles had been used in the opening salvo. That was not a huge force, but one capable of hitting scores of sites. Myers, though, did not inform the reporters that the Pentagon had derived only 31 targets for its to-do list, according to Bob Woodward's insiders' account, *Bush at War*. Thirty-one targets, after all, would hardly have seemed an impressive amount. At that briefing, a reporter asked Rumsfeld, "Could you give us a sense of how many targets you've hit?" The defense secretary replied, "No. We have no way to discuss the outcome of this operation." He certainly could have discussed the number of targets struck. But, as Woodward notes, Rumsfeld did not wish to reveal to the public "the smallness of the operation."

It is often tough for a commander to be honest in public about war developments. And when Bush and Rumsfeld knew the war was not going well, they offered Americans upbeat appraisals. At an October 23 National Security Council meeting that Bush attended, the participants were told, according to Woodward, that the anti-Taliban Northern Alliance (the Bush administration's on-the-ground partner in the war) had gained little territory. Worse, the CIA was reporting that the number of Taliban soldiers at a crucial frontline had increased by thousands. That day, though, Bush publicly stated, "We're making great progress on the ground." Four days later, Bush and his war council held a teleconference dominated by more bad news. Tenet reported his operatives were making no headway in the south. Rumsfeld expressed deep disappointment with the Northern Alliance. And the Bush officials discussed a Defense Intelligence Agency memo that concluded neither Mazar-e-Sharif, a strategically important city, nor Kabul, the capital, could be taken by winter.

The next morning, October 28, Rumsfeld, appearing on ABC's *This Week*, was asked, "Is the war just not going as well as you had hoped it would at this point?" His answer: "No, quite the contrary. It's going very much the way we expected when we began. . . . The progress has been measurable. We feel that the air campaign has been effective." And at his daily briefing the next day, Rumsfeld maintained frustration had not yet set in. That evening, though, at a meeting of Bush's war council, according to Woodward, Condoleezza Rice said, "We can't afford to lose. The Taliban proved rougher than we thought."

Yet on November 9, the Northern Alliance took Mazar-e-Sharif. Four days later, it seized control of Kabul. The Taliban was on the run. The Bush war council was surprised by the sudden collapse of the Taliban. But on November 27, when it was clear the Taliban had been routed, Rumsfeld told reporters, "What was taking place in the earlier phases was exactly as planned."

A president at war has to cheerlead and command, as do members of his national security team. Perhaps overly or unduly positive pronouncements can be justified as a cost of war. Yet no one had forced Rumsfeld to hold daily press conferences and become a media star celebrated for his supposedly straight-to-the-point manner, even though he was frequently spinning. What was less forgivable and less obligatory was Rumsfeld's duplicity on an inescapable fact of warfare: civilian deaths.

"If we had hit a village causing widespread death that was unintended, we would have said so."

From the beginning of the war, Bush and his aides repeatedly said the Afghanistan operation was not targeted at the Afghan people but at the Taliban and al Qaeda. And they pledged to try to limit civilian casualties. Yet the Bush administration wounded its own credibility on this front by consistently failing to be honest about the civilian deaths and injuries that occurred due to the actions of the U.S. military.

Rumsfeld displayed the administration's disingenuousness when he delivered a short lecture on the subject at a December 4 briefing. "One of the unpleasant aspects of war," he remarked, "is the reality that innocent bystanders are sometimes caught in the crossfire, and we're often asked to answer Taliban accusations about civilian casualties. Indeed, one of today's headlines is, quote, 'Pentagon Avoids Subject of Civilian Deaths.' The short answer is that that's simply not so."

Though he sounded as if he was making a good case for his point, Rumsfeld then proceeded to prove the offending headline's accuracy. "With the disorder that reigns in Afghanistan," he said, "it is next to impossible to get factual information about civilian casualties. First, the Taliban have lied repeatedly. They intentionally mislead the press for their own purposes. Second, we generally do not have access to sites of alleged civilian casualties on the ground. Third, in cases where someone does have access to a site, it is often impossible to know how many people were killed, how they died, and by whose hand they did die."

Look at the World Trade Center, he continued. The number of dead there was still shifting: "If we cannot know for certain how many people were killed in Lower Manhattan, where we have full access to the site, thousands of reporters, investigators, rescue workers combing the wreckage, and no enemy propaganda to confuse the situation, one ought to be sensitive to how difficult it is to know with certainty, in real time, what may have happened in any given situation in Afghanistan. . . . What we at the Pentagon try to do is to tell the press what we do know that's accurate, and we try to say what we don't know. . . . We lost thousands of innocent civilians on September 11th, and we understand what it means to lose a father, a mother, a brother, a sister, a son or a daughter, and we mourn every civilian death."

Rumsfeld's remarks, seemingly heartfelt, were an exercise in profound cynicism. Discovering the truth about civilian casualties in Afghanistan was not the impossible task he had depicted. Nor were the only claims of civilian casualties coming from the Taliban, who obviously could not be believed. As Rumsfeld was asserting there was no way to assess civilian casualties, *Washington Post* reporter Susan Glasser was developing a story based on a visit to Jalalabad's Public Hospital No. 1. In the previous four days, the hospital had taken in 36 patients who said they were victims of the U.S. bombing strikes that had targeted villages southwest of Jalalabad. This was an area where Osama bin Laden and al Qaeda remnants were thought to be hiding in cave compounds. The hospital had also received 35 dead. One of the injured was Noor Mohammed, a boy who had lost both eyes and both arms. He said he had heard the sound of an airplane overhead, ran from his room, and did not know what happened next. Glasser found other wounded children from families who claimed they had been struck by bombs while in their mud houses.

Days earlier, the *New York Times* had run a dispatch from Tim Weiner, a Pulitzer Prize winner, reporting that U.S. bombers flying over this area of Tora Bora had struck three villages, killing dozens of civilians. Weiner quoted the local law-and-order minister and the region's defense minister, who each maintained these attacks had occurred. Survivors interviewed by Weiner spoke of horrible losses in these areas. "The village is no more," said a man named Khalil. "All my family, 12 people, were killed. I am the only one left in this family. I have lost my children, my wife. They are no more." Another survivor said she had lost 38 relatives; another estimated up to 200 were dead.

Mistakes, as Rumsfeld said, happen in war. But a government that maintains it is dedicated to avoiding such mistakes and to assisting the people who are harmed by these mistakes has a responsibility to be forthright about such errors. If the administration was sincerely concerned for Afghan civilians, wouldn't it at least acknowledge their suffering? Rather than admit the truth about civilian deaths, Rumsfeld's Pentagon denied everything. Rear Admiral Craig Quigley, chief spokesman for the U.S. Central Command, said that American bombers had hit their targets twenty miles away from these villages: "If we had hit a village causing widespread death that was unintended, we would have said so. We have been meticulous reporting whenever we have killed a single person."

The day after Weiner's account appeared, Rear Admiral John Stufflebeem was questioned at the daily Pentagon briefing about civilian deaths around Tora Bora. He replied, "I have seen the press reports about alleged civilian casualties, and I would just ask us all to remember that this was orchestrated by the Taliban, and therefore it's not clear to us in fact were there innocent civilians who in fact may have been injured." (Note the double "in fact.") The admiral added, "We know for a fact that these were legitimate military targets in that area that were struck. We know that there was terrific traditional, consistent planning to ensure that only these targets were struck. We know there were no off-target hits, so there were no collateral damage worries in this series of strikes. And therefore I can't comment on the civilian casualties because I don't know them to be true."

Yet Richard Lloyd Parry, a reporter for the London-based *Independent* visited the area and found homes replaced by craters, a cemetery containing 40 freshly dug graves (some, he was told, contained only body parts), and a fragment bearing the words "Surface Attack Guided Missile AGM 114." And this was not a unique episode. Weeks earlier, residents of the hamlet of Thoral told *Washington Post* reporter Molly Moore about a missile attack that had hit a trailer and a house, killing 21 members—mostly children—of two farming families. The Pentagon insisted its target had been a Taliban command center and that all its bombs had landed on that center.

Truth is often difficult to ascertain in war. But it was clear that Stufflebeem and Rumsfeld were not speaking truthfully. The reports of these casualties in the Tora Bora region were not, as Stufflebeem maintained, "orchestrated by the Taliban." The information was coming from officials of the government that had replaced the Taliban. And Rumsfeld was engaging in champion dissembling when he maintained that the Pentagon could not possibly determine whether civilian casualties had occurred in war-torn Afghanistan. The U.S. military may not have been able to discern civilian-death figures with the same precision it claimed for its bombing, but it could have done better than denying they had occurred. It could have done what Weiner and the other reporters did: ask people on the ground. Instead, the Pentagon insulted survivors and local (non-Taliban) Afghan officials by dismissing their reports as nothing but Taliban propaganda. It was not, as Rumsfeld asserted, "impossible to get factual information about civilian casualties." His military just did not bother.

In the following weeks and months, as the U.S. military continued to pursue al Qaeda and Taliban remnants in Afghanistan, the pattern would hold. U.S. forces would mistakenly kill civilians (or forces allied with the new, pro-U.S. government of Hamid Karzai), and the Bush administration would try to cover up or dodge responsibility. In December, a U.S. airstrike blew up a convoy of tribal elders on their way to Karzai's inauguration, killing 12 people. The Pentagon insisted the attack had been legitimate, but Karzai himself complained about the strike.

On January 23, U.S. Special Operations forces raided two small compounds in a town 100 miles north of Kandahar. Up to two dozen people were killed; 27 were captured. The Pentagon claimed its targets were Taliban soldiers, and Rumsfeld pointed to the raid as proof the United States was still on the trail of terrorists. Days later, however, media reports, based on interviews with local residents, tore apart the official account. The townspeople said that one of the compounds was being used as a weapons depot for a local disarmament drive, and that the Afghans killed and snatched by the Americans were not Taliban or al Qaeda but troops loyal to the interim government of Kabul. The Pentagon, in automatic-pilot fashion, defended the operation, contending nothing had gone wrong. "We take great care to ensure we are engaging confirmed Taliban or al Qaeda facilities," a spokesman told the *New York Times*. But after Afghan officials kept complaining that innocent troops had been killed and apprehended, the Pentagon gradually backtracked, and Rumsfeld on February 4 finally acknowledged that "friendly" Afghan forces *might* have been killed during the raid. Forty-eight hours later, the Americans released the 27 Afghans it had grabbed at the compounds, and the Pentagon announced that not one was a Taliban or al Qaeda fighter.

Yet Rumsfeld still refused to concede the mission had been a "mistake." He said it was the result of an "untidy" situation. How could killing up to two dozen innocent people not be a "mistake"? This was the sort of dishonesty that was so transparent it was hard to call it a lie. (In Afghanistan, the CIA did concede the error by doling out $1000 to each family of the Afghan soldiers killed in the raid. The relatives of civilians killed in other U.S. military screwups were not so fortunate.)

By April 2002, civilian casualties in Afghanistan had become a political issue in that country. Afghans who had been injured or had lost family members due to errant U.S. bombs protested in front of the U.S. embassy in Kabul, calling for official investigations and compensation. President Karzai said, "It would be good for the United States to help out the families." And in the United States, a small band of columnists, members of Congress, and public interest do-gooders were urging Bush to provide financial assistance to Afghan victims. At a press conference in Kabul, Zalmay Khalilzad, Bush's special envoy to Afghanistan, discussed the subject: "I can assure you that we try our darned best to avoid hitting innocent targets—that's not what we're about. But mistakes do happen. When charges are made, we investigate. And then we do the right thing to respond to the needs of those who have suffered." But that was precisely what had not been happening. There had been no investigations of civilian deaths. No money for the hundreds, if not thousands, of Afghan victims (with the exception of the botched raid on the two compounds). Bush's representative in Afghanistan had lied.

When a U.S. AC-130 gunship on July 1 attacked a compound in the village of Kakrak, killing 54 people, mostly women and children attending a wedding celebration, the Pentagon yet again denied any wrongdoing. Reporters once more collected credible eyewitness accounts of a massacre. Afghan government officials expressed outrage. Then the Pentagon slowly changed its story, conceding its warplane had fired on these civilians but maintaining that the assault had been in response to anti-aircraft fire. In a telephone conversation with Karzai, Bush, according to the White House, expressed his "sympathies" to the victims' families. But he did not apologize or offer compensation. "He certainly did express the tragedy of the situation," a White House spokesperson said.

This time, the administration did promise a comprehensive inquiry. The U.S. Central Command report released two months later stuck to the Pentagon's most recent explanation: the airstrike had been provoked by anti-aircraft fire. The report asserted that the "AC-130 aircraft, acting properly and in accordance with the rules, engaged the locations of those weapons. Great care was taken to strike only those sites that were actively firing that night." But the report acknowledged that when an investigative team visited the two sites where most of the women and children were gunned down, it did not find "the presence of any anti-aircraft weapons or even a significant presence of shell casings from any weapon." According to eyewitness accounts obtained by journalists, there had been no anti-aircraft fire from the compound and civilians had even been chased by the U.S. aircraft. Only those present in Kakrak that horrible night—on the ground and above—could know, with certainty, the truth. But the Pentagon's case was, to be generous, weak.

In 2002, Senator Patrick Leahy, a Vermont Democrat, managed to slip $1.25 million into the budget of the U.S. Agency for International Development to assist Afghan civilians who had lost relatives, limbs, homes, or businesses due to U.S. bombing. The goal was not to hand out compensation to specific people—which would create a precedent unacceptable to the Pentagon and the State Department—but to target relief to areas that were known to have suffered losses because of U.S. military action. Yet by the spring of 2003, none of these funds had been spent. For instance, the hamlet of Madoo had been bombed for several days in December 2001, as American forces attacked bin Laden's cave complex at Tora Bora. Much of the town was destroyed; an estimated 55 of its 300 residents were killed. Seventeen months later, 30-year-old Niaz Mohammad Khan, one of the survivors, told the *Washington Post*, "Our houses were destroyed. We want to rebuild, but we don't have the money. . . . We need water for our land. We need everything. People come and ask us questions, then go away. No one has helped."

"Our responsibilities to the people of Afghanistan have not ended."

Bush mostly let the Pentagon handle the progress reports on the war and the responses to civilian casualties. But on the subject of his administration's postwar commitment to Afghanistan and its people, Bush spoke often and eloquently. He repeatedly noted his dedication to the reconstruction of this poor and beleaguered nation. A month into the war, he promised, "America will join the world in helping the people of Afghanistan rebuild their country." After the Taliban had been chased out, he said, "Our responsibilities to the people of Afghanistan have not ended." Referring indirectly to his father's abandonment of Afghanistan following the Soviet withdrawal from that country in 1989, Bush declared, "America and our allies will do our part in the rebuilding of Afghanistan. We learned our lessons from the past. We will not leave until the mission is complete." When Karzai visited the White House in January 2002, Bush hailed "America's enduring commitment to Afghanistan's future."

Bush did take steps toward honoring his promise. Days after the war broke out, he asked schoolchildren to send one dollar each to the White House for a fund that would help Afghan children. And he promised $320 million in humanitarian aid (up from $170 million the United States had budgeted for Afghanistan assistance in 2001). But his commitment ended up being not so enduring.

The first signs came in December 2001, with administration officials noting the United States' postwar role in Afghanistan would be limited. "We don't want to get involved in intrusive nation-building,"

Richard Haass, the State Department's director of policy planning told the *San Francisco Chronicle*, "and we want other nations to provide the bulk of resources for rebuilding." Somehow Bush had neglected to mention his desire to be a *limited* minority partner in the reconstruction effort—estimated to cost $10 to $15 billion over ten years—whenever he had promised to stand by Afghanistan. Then, in March, Bush visited a Northern Virginia high school to celebrate a volunteer program sending material, sewing machines, and funds to Afghanistan for use in producing school uniforms. At the same time, however, administration officials were maneuvering to restrict peacekeeping operations in Afghanistan.

Sewing machines were, no doubt, useful, but peacekeepers were needed more. For months, Karzai had pleaded for expanding the international peacekeeping force in his country. These troops—about 4,500 soldiers from 17 nations but not the United States—were patrolling only Kabul and its environs. With lawlessness and violence mounting in other parts of the lightly governed country, Karzai and U.N. Secretary General Kofi Annan were appealing for a larger peacekeeping contingent that could cover areas beyond the capital. After considering backing a plan to double this force (even though the State Department had advocated beefing it up to 25,000 troops), the Bush administration said no.

On March 15, Rumsfeld, defending this decision, maintained "there is not a serious security problem" in Afghanistan. Yet four days later, Tenet and Vice Admiral Thomas Wilson, head of the Defense Intelligence Agency, told the Senate armed services committee that severe economic, social, and political problems plagued the country. Wilson noted there was "a very widespread probability of insurgency-type warfare" in Afghanistan's rural areas and cities. Al Qaeda and Taliban leftovers were strong, they said, and posed what Tenet called "a long-term issue." And a report by the International Crisis Group (ICG), a private research organization specializing in conflict resolution, concluded that a failure to expand the peacekeeping force would risk "seeing Afghanistan again slide toward factional fighting." The ICG recommended boosting the peacekeepers to 25,000 to 30,000 troops to cover the main cities of Afghanistan and vital transportation routes. An enhanced peacekeeping presence, said ICG president Gareth

Evans, was necessary to "allow the country's internal political process and security forces to develop."

But the Bush-Rumsfeld argument was, there was no need for this. That seemed a lie designed to cover up the White House's and Pentagon's unwillingness to participate or deal with an expanded peacekeeping force while U.S. forces still roamed through Afghanistan in search of Taliban and al Qaeda loyalists. But the lack of security and stability outside Kabul carried life-and-death implications for Afghans. On March 20, 2002, Bush had boasted, "We've prevented mass starvation because we've moved a lot of food into the region." Yet Kenneth Bacon, president of Refugees International and, formerly, Clinton's Pentagon spokesman, said security in parts of Afghanistan was so bad that aid workers could not safely operate and food was not reaching starving Afghans. In August 2002—shortly after an unsuccessful assassination attempt against Karzai—the Bush administration finally dropped its opposition to expanding the peacekeeping force, but it still refused to provide U.S. troops or additional U.S. funds for this operation. By then, though, other nations were no longer interested in increasing the size and range of the peacekeepers. "The absence of U.S. leadership has doomed any serious international peacekeeping role outside of Kabul," Larry Goodson, a professor of Middle East Studies at the U.S. Army War College, subsequently wrote in the *Journal of Democracy*.

The security situation in Afghanistan did not improve in the first half of 2003. As *New York Times* correspondent Carlotta Gall noted in April, "In a very real sense, the war here has not ended. . . . Nearly every day, there are killings, explosions, shootings and targeted attacks on foreign aid workers, Afghan officials, and American forces, as well as continued feuding between warlords in the regions. No clear picture exists of who will provide the security to stop the bloodshed."

Bush offered more double-talk than dedication when it came to rebuilding Afghanistan. During an April 2002 speech at the Virginia Military Institute, he proclaimed that by helping to rebuild Afghanistan, "we are working in the best of traditions of George Marshall." What an overstatement. His administration fell far short of

Marshall Plan standards. When the U.S. Agency for International Development, the government outfit in charge of helping Afghanistan, asked for $150 million more for assistance in Afghanistan, the bean-counters at the White House Office of Management and Budget approved only $40 million, signaling no massive relief-and-reconstruction plan would be forthcoming.

On October 11, 2002—the anniversary of his send-a-buck-to-Afghanistan program—Bush said, "We want to be a continuing part of the new era of hope in Afghanistan." The U.S. government, according to a White House fact sheet, had provided $588 million to "humanitarian assistance and reconstruction" during the previous year. But according to the White House figures, about half of that—and maybe much more—had gone to emergency relief, not reconstruction. With the rebuilding tab estimated to be $1 to $1.5 billion a year, the Bush administration was covering but a small slice of the reconstruction costs. "Rather than getting out there in a leadership role and saying, 'We need a Marshall Plan,' and fighting for it, they've taken a minimalist approach," remarked Joel Charny, a vice president of Refugees International. Peter Tomsen, a U.S. special envoy and ambassador to Afghanistan during the first Bush administration, complained that the administration's 2003 budget for U.S. Agency for International Development programs in Afghanistan was less than it had been in 2001. Writing in the *Washington Post*, Tomsen noted that Bush "does not even have a comprehensive Afghanistan budget request before Congress, and there is no high-level coordinator providing interagency coherence on Afghan policy. No major roadwork has yet started in Afghanistan." He continued, "The effusive praise of American aid programs in Afghanistan, by both White House and USAID representatives, clearly demonstrates their ignorance of the reality on the ground."*

In November 2002, Bush did sign the Afghanistan Freedom Support Act, which authorized spending $3.3 billion in economic, political, humanitarian, and security assistance for Afghanistan over four years. But he did so with little fanfare—understandably, for the legislation was actually a vote of no-confidence in Bush's handling of Afghani-

---

*During one congressional hearing, Andrew Natsios, the Bush-appointed head of USAID, was asked how much money USAID needed to do its job in Afghanistan and elsewhere. According to *Boston* magazine, Natsios replied, "I can't mention numbers, if I want to keep my job."

stan reconstruction. It had been authored by Senator Chuck Hagel, a Nebraska Republican, who had cordially but firmly decried the Bush administration's efforts in Afghanistan as disappointing. But just because the bill was signed, that did not mean a lot more assistance would start flowing to Afghanistan. In the world of government budgets, authorizing funding is not the same as supplying the money. For instance, the law said $500 million *could* be used to fund and possibly expand the peacekeeping force in 2003. But then there was no money for peacekeepers in Bush's 2003 budget.

"The President was willing to go along with authorizing funding for greater security," said Mike Jendrzejczyk of Human Rights Watch, "but not to follow up with providing actual money." In one version of its budget proposal for 2003, the Bush administration neglected to ask for any assistance funds specifically for Afghanistan. USAID had wanted about $200 million, according to a Senate aide who tracked this issue, but the White House Office of Management and Budget said no, explaining that there were still 2002 funds unspent. "The OMB decision," this aide said, "bore little relation to the needs and capabilities on the ground." Facing criticism, the administration finally requested about $100 million. But Congress, believing this was meager, tripled the amount. Hagel, who remained critical of the Bush administration for not doing enough for Afghanistan, noted, "It's not even close to being adequate."

The administration was proposing more money—$657 million—for 2004. And in a supplemental spending bill in spring 2003 it requested an additional $320 million to use that year—more than half of which, though, would go to training the barely functioning Afghan military. But time was quickly passing for Bush to make a difference in Afghanistan. That was the message of a lengthy article Larry Goodson of the U.S. Army and War College contributed to the January 2003 issue of the *Journal of Democracy* (published by the National Endowment for Democracy, a foundation created by Congress and funded by the U.S. government). In this polite but compelling indictment of Bush's postwar actions in Afghanistan, Goodson observed that the United States and the rest of the world appeared to be "losing interest" in aiding Afghanistan's transition. Goodson, who had been a consultant to the *Loya Jirga* that chose Karzai president, noted that the $1.8 billion pledged in early 2002 by the United States and the international community for rebuilding that year "was less per capita than was spent in Bosnia, East Timor, Kosovo, or Rwanda. Moreover, most nations were slow meeting their pledges, and about 75 percent of the $1.5 billion that was spent on aid to Afghanistan in 2002 went to pay for short-term humanitarian assistance," not reconstruction projects. Bush and the world community had been keeping their fingers in the dike, not developing a better Afghanistan.

Afghanistan was a mess, according to Goodson. There was a resurgence in warlordism. Karzai had little power outside Kabul. "Most Afghan leaders today," he wrote, "derive their authority from a combination of appeals to Islam, illicit economic activities (such as the opium trade), and gunmen." What had happened to Bush's "new era of hope"? It did not exist.* In May 2003, hundreds of Afghans protested in Kabul, chanting "Death to Bush" and "Long Live Islam." At the time, the government had not paid its workers for months, unemployment was rampant, major roads remained unusable, and violence still wracked the nation. "Of course, the people see that nothing has been done," Deputy Interior Minister Hilaluddin Hilal told *The Washington Post*. "This is a problem for the government of Afghanistan. If the U.S. would help rebuild Afghanistan, then the organizers [of the protest] wouldn't have so many people joining them."

In his article, Goodson concluded, "Many of the political challenges facing Afghanistan might be resolved through greater international— meaning U.S.-led—commitments to peacekeeping and nation-building. On both these vital issues, U.S. policy has been overly hesitant." He added, "If the events of the past year are any indication . . . Washington has been slow to take the right steps to lead."

---

*A Human Rights Watch report released in November 2002 found that "the human rights situation in most of the country remains grim.... This has happened not simply because of the inherent difficulties of rebuilding an impoverished, devastated country, but because of choices the United States and other international actors have made, and failed to make. In most parts of the country, security and local governance has been entrusted to regional military commanders—warlords—many of whom have human rights records rivaling the worst commanders under the Taliban.... American military forces have maintained relationships with local warlords that undercut efforts by U.S. diplomats and aid agencies to strengthen central authority and the rule of law." In particular, the report cited a warlord named Ismail Khan, whose regime crushed political dissent and whose security forces engaged in torture and beatings. The previous spring, Rumsfeld had visited with Khan and called him "an appealing person....He's thoughtful, measured and self-confident."

In late July 2003, Bush administration officials said that the White House intended to seek $1 billion in near-term aid for Afghanistan. If the money did appear, this would be a significant amount, though long overdue. The announcement was acknowledgment (implicit, of course) that Bush had not done enough to date for Afghanistan. But perhaps it marked a shift in the administration's attitude toward Afghanistan— from neglect to engagement. Previously, Bush had frequently declared his concern for Afghanistan's future and his devotion to its reconstruction. But for nearly two years, he had shortchanged it. His soaring rhetoric had been backed by insufficient funds. It remained to be seen if Bush—after having written Afghanistan a bad check—would finally (and belatedly) make good on his word.

11. White-Collar Lies

"I first got to know Ken [Lay in 1994]."

On January 10, 2002, as George W. Bush was about to hold an Oval Office meeting with members of his economic team, he told one of the largest whoppers of his presidency.

Before closing the doors and tending to business, Bush was speaking to White House reporters and pushing the message of the day: *Bush cares about the economy.* And this day, he especially cared about the bankruptcy of Enron, a Texas-based energy firm and the seventh-highest-valued company in the country. It had gone belly-up the previous month, causing thousands of Enron employees to lose their jobs and their retirement funds, as the firm's stock lost $26 billion in market value in just seven weeks (and nearly $80 billion over the course of a year). The once high-flying, much-acclaimed Enron had been run as a scam that relied upon accounting chicanery, secret partnerships, and complicated, convoluted and shady derivatives trading. In October, it had reported a third-quarter loss of $638 million. In November, it had admitted inflating its profits by $600 million over five years. And, before Enron's collapse, the prestigious accounting firm of Arthur Andersen had awarded its seal of approval to the company's sleight-of-hand finances (and then destroyed incriminating documents). On top of all that, Enron had paid no income taxes in four of the past five years, via the use of hundreds of overseas tax havens and other devices.

One of its more notorious misdeeds had been preventing workers from selling the Enron stock in their retirement portfolios as the firm was tanking. Company executives, though, had dumped over a billion dollars' worth of their own shares. Enron chief executive officer Ken Lay had even advised employees to buy more stock as the company was heading toward ruin, claiming the low price of the stock made it a great value. But he had pocketed an estimated $50 million in oh-so-prescient sell-offs in the months before Enron's crash. And Enron—though it was not yet proven at this point—had manipulated energy supplies in California and contributed to the electricity crisis that had cost the state's consumers billions of dollars. Enron was one of the most appalling corporate scandals in the country's history—and its demise preceded a long line of corporate smashups to hit the nation in 2002.

With the Enron debacle still in the headlines, it was quite natural for Bush to tell the White House reporters that this very day he was diligently responding by convening a working group that would analyze corporate disclosure rules and regulations. Referring to Enron's dramatic implosion, he remarked, "The administration is deeply concerned about its effects on the economy."

Bush also had reason to be deeply concerned about Enron's effect on George W. Bush. The president had for years been wired into Enron and Lay. Enron had pumped hundreds of thousands of dollars into Bush's campaign accounts, making the company the most generous patron of Bush's political career. In the aftermath of September 11 and the defeat of the Taliban, Bush's approval rating was soaring. But the Enron scandal loomed as a potential threat to Bush. It was a reminder of one pre-9/11 rap against him: he cared more about CEOs than working stiffs. Now, his number-one CEO pal had become a national symbol of corporate greed and boardroom bamboozlement. But rather than tell the truth about his dealings with Lay, Bush elected to lie.

When a reporter asked Bush whether this working group meeting was an attempt to "inoculate" himself from the Enron virus, Bush replied, "First of all, Ken Lay is a supporter, and I got to know Ken Lay when he was a head of the—what they call the Governor's Business Council in Texas. He was a supporter of [Governor] Ann Richards in my run [against her] in 1994, and she had named him head of the Governor's Business Council, and I decided to leave him in place, for the sake of continuity. And that's when I first got to know Ken and worked with Ken, and he supported my candidacy for—and—but this is what—

what anybody's going to find, if—is that this administration will fully investigate issues such as the Enron bankruptcy."

This statement was as dishonest as Enron's own disclosures—and just one of many assertions that Bush and his aides would make about Enron and Bush's own adventures in the private sector that could not survive a close audit.

Bush's relationship with Lay went back—maybe way back—before Bush became governor of Texas. It was utterly implausible that Bush *first got to know* Lay *after* the 1994 election as he had claimed. The public record indicated Bush and his family's interactions with Lay—whom Bush had called "Kenny Boy"—predated that campaign. In 1989, Lay spearheaded a drive to convince the first President Bush to locate his presidential library in Houston. "That's when I probably spent a little more quality time with George W.," Lay told the *Dallas Morning News* in the summer of 2001. In 1990, Lay co-chaired a host committee for a G-7 economic summit held by Bush the First. Lay was a sleepover guest at the first Bush White House. He also headed the local host committee for the 1992 Republican National Convention in Houston, where Bush the elder, the incumbent president, was renominated. According to the *Houston Chronicle*, "Lay worked closely with George W. Bush" at the convention.

In a March 2001 interview with PBS—before the Enron disaster started—Lay had claimed a longer and tighter connection with Bush than Bush acknowledged:

> I've been a strong financial and political supporter of, first, President Bush Sr. when he was running for president [unsuccessfully in 1980]. . . . And then certainly when he ran for president and was elected in 1988. [I'm] very close to the family, to Barbara Bush and the kids. When Governor Bush—now President Bush—decided to run for the governor's spot, [there was] a little difficult situation. I'd worked very closely with Ann Richards also, the four years she was governor. But I was very close to George W. and had a lot of respect for him, had watched him over the years, particularly with reference to dealing with his father when his father was in the White House and some of the things he did to work for his father, and so did support him.

And in a video of an October 2000 meeting of Enron employees, according to the *Houston Chronicle*, Lay noted, "I strongly supported [Bush] when he ran for governor of Texas both times." Lay's comments jibed with a letter Bush sent him in 1997, in which he referred to Lay as one of his "old friends."

Yes, during the Texas gubernatorial campaign of 1994, Lay had been a supporter of Richards, as Bush had maintained. But Lay had been *more* of a supporter of Bush. He and his wife donated $47,500 to Bush, while contributing $12,500 to Richards, according to Texans for Public Justice, a campaign finance reform outfit. And Enron's political action committee and executives—including Lay—gave a total of $146,500 to Bush that year (and $19,500 to Richards).

From 1994 on, Lay and his wife donated generously to various Bush causes. This included $122,500 for both of Bush's gubernatorial campaigns, $100,000 for his presidential inauguration, and $250,000 for the presidential library of Bush I. According to the Center for Responsive Politics, Enron and its executives handed Bush $736,680 for all his political campaigns, his election-recount fund, and his inaugural gala. In 1996, the Lays and George and Laura Bush chaired a fundraiser for a literacy charity sponsored by Barbara Bush. (In 1997, both Bush and his father were filmed for a going-away video for Enron's president, Rich Kinder. In the video, Father Bush tells Kinder, "You've been fantastic to the Bush family. I don't think anybody did more than you did to support George." George W. says, "Don't leave Texas. You're too good a man.") During the 2000 campaign, Bush campaign staff and Bush's parents flew on Enron corporate aircraft, and Lay was a Bush campaign "pioneer"—a fundraiser who collected at least $100,000 for Bush. In the 2000 election cycle, Lay donated over $275,000 to the Republican Party, and Enron kicked in over $1 million, including $250,000 for the GOP's national convention. The day after Bush's presidential inauguration, Lay attended a private lunch at the White House. A free lunch was the least Bush could do for him.

Bush even had a business connection with Enron—a connection he had once denied.

As it happened, in 1994, when Bush was first running for governor, I was introduced to a former public works minister of Argentina, Rodolfo Terragno. He claimed that when he headed the ministry in

1988, George W. Bush, whom Terragno did not know personally, called and pressured him to award a pipeline contract worth hundreds of millions of dollars to Enron. Terragno, who said he resisted this and subsequent importuning, could not provide proof the call had occurred. But he came across as a credible person, noting he would not forget a call from an American whose father was vice president and about to become president.

I contacted Bush's gubernatorial campaign and asked whether Bush had spoken to Terragno on Enron's behalf and whether Bush ever had *any* business relationship with Enron. Bush aide Karen Hughes faxed me a terse statement: "The answer to your questions are no and none. Your questions are apparently addressed to the wrong person." An Enron spokesperson said, "Enron has not had any business dealings with George W. Bush." (In 1992, Enron was able to obtain a significant stake in Argentina's pipeline system.)

But Bush had done business with the company. As the Enron scandal was raging in 2002, I received a tip from the son of a former Enron officer and discovered records showing that a firm headed by Bush had been a partner in an oil well with Enron in 1986. Back then, Bush was a not-too-successful oilman running Spectrum 7, a privately held oil venture facing financial trouble. He owned about 15 percent of the company. In October of that year, Enron Oil and Gas Company, a subsidiary of Enron Corporation, announced it had completed a well producing both oil and natural gas in Martin County, Texas. Ten percent belonged to Spectrum 7. To spell it out: George W. Bush and Enron Oil and Gas were in business together in 1986—when Ken Lay was head of Enron.

How did this deal come about? How long did it last? Was that the only project in which Bush and Enron were partners? I called the White House to ask, and received no response. An Enron spokeswoman said, "I can't tell you anything about" that well, explaining that Enron "sold all its domestic exploration and production assets about two years ago to EOG Resources" and probably did not retain records on that well. As for the possibility Spectrum 7 invested in other Enron ventures, she noted, "You're referencing something that happened in 1986. I can check, but we're pretty short-staffed now." (She never called back.) A spokeswoman for EOG Resources (formerly Enron Oil and Gas) said, "If we did have any records on that well, it would be nothing that we would share with the public." After I posted a story about the Enron-Bush partnership, White House communications director Dan Bartlett told *The New York Times* that Bush "has no recollection of this specific deal."

The existence of this 1986 Enron-Bush venture undermined the 1994 statements from Bush and Enron denying any business relationship between the scion and the company. Did any of this mean the relationship between Bush and Lay stretched back to the mid-1980s? The deal could have happened without contact between the two. But most company heads would be interested to know that the son of the sitting vice president (whose presidential campaign they had supported) had invested in one of their enterprises. Given Enron's penchant to amass political ties in order to win and protect business opportunities, it was hard not to wonder if this Bush-Enron partnership involved special arrangements. In any event, the Enron–Spectrum 7 deal—whether Bush remembered it or not—was another reason for him to be nervous about the ongoing Enron scandal.

The reasons for White House apprehension extended beyond Bush's coziness with Lay and Enron, for he was not the only official in his administration who had been intimate with Enron. Chief economic adviser Lawrence Lindsey and trade representative Robert Zoellick had served on an Enron advisory board as paid consultants. Attorney General John Ashcroft had received over $57,000 in political contributions from Enron and Lay (and, thus, had to recuse himself from the biggest white-collar case in recent history). Karl Rove, Bush's top adviser, had recommended political consultant and former Christian Coalition whiz kid Ralph Reed to Enron when the Bush presidential campaign had been courting Reed. Subsequently—perhaps consequently—Reed won a big-money contract at Enron.* The lobbying firm of Edward Gillespie, a top Bush campaign adviser, pocketed more than a half-million dollars working for Enron in 2001. Key consultants to then House majority whip Tom DeLay were hired for $750,000 to work on an Enron-backed electricity deregulation cam-

---

*In an October 23, 2000, memo to Enron, obtained later by the *Washington Post*, Reed pitched a PR project to the firm—for which he wanted to be paid $380,000—and offered this classic observation: "In public policy, it matters less who has the best arguments and more who gets heard—and by whom."

paign after DeLay suggested to Enron that they be retained. Thomas White, whom Bush appointed secretary of the army, had served as vice chairman of Enron Energy Services when alleged accounting irregularities occurred in that division. Marc Racicot, Bush's hand-picked chairman of the Republican Party, had been a lobbyist for Enron. James Baker had been a consultant to Enron. Bush's brother Neil (the sibling once cited by federal regulators for conflict-of-interest violations regarding a failed savings and loan) had attempted to do business with Enron in Kuwait.*

"If they came to this administration looking for help, they didn't find any."

Despite his long-time ties to the company, what first drew Bush into the Enron unpleasantness was the news, which broke in January 2002, that Lay in late October 2001 had called both Treasury Secretary Paul O'Neill and Commerce Secretary Don Evans to discuss his company's plight. The White House claimed the administration did nothing to help Bush's friend and underwriter. Perhaps the company's close rela-tionship with many in Bush's circle had prevented the Bushies from trying to rescue the company. How could anyone in the Bush adminis-tration claim it was assisting Enron for the right reasons as opposed to favoritism? Who would believe that?

But Bush indirectly helped Lay and Enron by not saying anything critical about the business once it had become clear the firm had been one massive con-job that had screwed over its workers. Only after hearings were under way in Congress and Republicans had started fretting the White House was vulnerable to charges it had been too comfy with Enron did Bush, on January 22, 2002, clear his throat and say he was "outraged" by the company's collapse. And he

---

*The Clinton administration also had been in the hayloft with Lay and Enron. The company gave the Democrats hundreds of thousands of dollars and won much-coveted seats on overseas trade missions headed by Ron Brown and Mickey Kantor, Clinton's secretaries of commerce. It obtained favorable decisions from the U.S. Overseas Private Investment Corporation and the Export-Import Bank. The Federal Energy Regulatory Commission issued orders that helped Enron compete in the electricity market. Enron lobbied for establishing an international trading system for greenhouse gas emissions, and the Clintonites subsequently supported this concept.

revealed that his mother-in-law had lost $8,000 by investing in the company.*

Bush advisers told the *New York Times* that Bush "did not act sooner to denounce Enron because he and his aides were inundated with questions about ties between the administration and Enron officials." That was a ridiculous explanation. Had Bush himself been busy researching all those press queries? And had he needed the help of his aides to say something tough about Enron? In this period Bush did have time to watch a football game (and faint after gagging on a pretzel) and to spend a whole day with Tom Brokaw for a NBC special, *Inside the Real West Wing*. He even discussed Enron with Brokaw. "My Justice Department is going to lead a full investigation," he promised. But he had no cross words for his old friends.

Bush's unconvincing condemnation of Enron did not stop the questions from coming. During a brief session with reporters in the Rose Garden on January 28, Bush was asked if his administration had afforded Enron special treatment, particularly regarding the energy plan Cheney had produced the previous year. "Enron had made contributions to a lot of people around Washington, D.C.," Bush answered. "And if they came to this administration looking for help, they didn't find any." That may have been the case during Enron's final days—when Lay was on the phone to members of Bush's cabinet—but that was not true during the preceding months when Enron was not yet radioactive.

Before Enron's crack-up, the Bush administration had been of tremendous assistance to the company on several fronts: appointments to the Federal Energy Regulatory Commission, the California energy crisis, a billion-dollar contract dispute Enron had in India, and, indeed, the energy plan. And there were several signs that much of this assistance had been neither accidental nor coincidental, but had occurred because of the association between Enron and the Bush gang.

When it came time to appoint commissioners to the Federal Energy

---

*One previous comment by O'Neill had made it seem that the administration's position on Enron was, no big deal. O'Neill remarked, "Companies come and go. Part of the genius of capitalism is people get to make good decisions or bad decisions, and they get to pay the consequences or enjoy the fruits of their decisions." The conniving and dishonest executives who had made the "bad" and probably illegal decisions pocketed millions; those out of the decision-loop—the workers—were forced to live with the "fruits" of these decisions: unemployment and downsized pensions. What genius.

Regulatory Commission—a body of much importance to Enron—Bush in March 2001 happened to select two people who had been pushed by Lay: Nora Mead Brownell and Pat Wood III. Each was a fan (as was Lay) of electricity deregulation.

Three months later, Curtis Hebert Jr., an FERC commissioner who had been appointed chairman by Bush in January 2001, told the *New York Times* that Lay had offered him a deal: agree with Enron's view on electricity deregulation and the firm would support him so he could keep his job at the commission. Lay recalled the conversation differently, claiming Hebert had requested Enron's support at the White House. But a senior FERC official informed the newspaper that he had witnessed the telephone conversation and had heard Hebert rebuff Lay's quid pro quo offer. Hebert, a free-market conservative who also supported states' rights concerning utilities issues, maintained he turned Lay down. "I was offended," he said, noting he realized that Lay could use his influence with the Bush administration to force Hebert out of the chairmanship. Three months later—in what could not have been called a surprise move—Bush replaced Hebert with Wood, a former oilman. In 1995, Bush had tapped Wood for a spot on the Texas Public Utility Commission—after he was recommended by none other than Lay.

Naming members to the regulatory body that oversees operations of your own company is a neat feat for a CEO. Had the campaign bucks doled out by Lay won him influence with the Bush White House? Lay told the *Times* his generosity with contributions "probably helps" him gain access to government officials, but he insisted he only supported candidates "I strongly believe in."*

I n early January 2002, the White House—which had refused for months to release any information about the deliberations of the Cheney energy task force—did disclose that Enron representatives had

---

*It made sense for Lay to believe in Bush. As Texas governor, according to the New York *Daily News*, Bush signed an energy deregulation bill that Enron had lobbied for and that "opened huge markets for Enron. Bush set up a panel that met in secret and granted exemptions to allow power plants to exceed legal pollution limits. Enron got plenty." And according to *Pipe Dreams*, Robert Bryce's book on the Enron fiasco, Governor Bush, at Lay's urging, called his friend Republican Governor Tom Ridge of Pennsylvania to put in a good word for Enron when it wanted to sell power in Ridge's state.

met six times with Cheney or his energy policy staff, before and after Cheney had drafted the administration's energy plan. One of these sessions was a tête-à-tête between Cheney and Lay.*

In these meetings, Enron had the opportunity to sell the White House on energy policies that would be good for Enron. Asked about the Enron-Cheney chats—were they a sign of favoritism?—Fleischer replied, "The president thinks that access should be across the board. And that's why the Sierra Club, for example, as you know, met repeatedly with the energy task force." What a lie. Sierra Club officials had met once with Cheney but only *after* the task force had crafted and released its energy plan. "Unlike Enron," Carl Pope, the executive director of the Sierra Club, noted, "the Sierra Club never met with the energy task force or made any recommendations to it."

Did the White House sessions pay off for Enron? The Cheney-Lay get-together, in retrospect, appeared especially useful to Enron. On April 17, 2001, the two huddled and, according to an Enron memo later publicized by the *San Francisco Chronicle,* Lay presented Cheney with a list of suggestions for the White House energy plan. He also expressed his company's view on how the administration should respond (actually, not respond) to the energy crisis then under way in California. That state had been hit by rolling blackouts and electric bills ten times the normal amounts (or more). The crisis was costing the state tens of billions of dollars, and some Californian officials were calling for caps on wholesale prices. In his meeting with Cheney, Lay, whose company sold power to California, argued against price caps; his memo claimed that even temporary price restrictions "will be detrimental to power markets and will discourage private investment."

The following day, Cheney, in a telephone interview with the *Los Angeles Times,* spoke out against caps, asserting (Lay-like) that they would discourage investment. He blamed price caps for California's fix: "Frankly, California is looked on by many folks as a classic example of the kinds of problems that arise when you do use price caps." But Cheney was confusing different types of price caps. The price caps he derided were limits imposed by the state on consumer rates; some

*In a May 3, 2002, letter to Senator Joseph Lieberman, Alberto Gonzales, the White House counsel, disclosed 18 additional contacts in 2001 between Enron and the White House concerning Enron.

analysts argued that these caps had left ill-prepared California utilities short of funds to buy power from energy producers. But the price cap then being sought by state officials was a limit on *wholesale* prices, which would be imposed on companies that produced electricity and sold it to California utilities. Many of these firms happened to be based in Texas and were supporters of Bush. And at the time they were enjoying profits rising by 400 to 600 percent. Did Cheney not understand the difference between the two kinds of caps? Cheney was even dead-set against a temporary wholesale price cap. "Six months? Six years?" he said in the interview. "Once politicians can no longer resist the temptation to go with price caps, they usually are unable to ever muster the courage to end them. . . . I don't see that as a possibility."

Perhaps this was no more than an instance of corporate-minded minds thinking alike, but Lay could have been forgiven had he concluded that his White House string-pulling had netted results.

Bush, too, would criticize price caps. And the electricity crisis would continue unabated for weeks, sucking billions of dollars out of California—until FERC finally approved limited wholesale price caps in June 2001. But, as would later be revealed, Enron and other energy companies had been manipulating the Golden State's energy market, exacerbating the crisis to drive prices—and their profits—up. Two years after the rolling blackouts, a FERC investigation concluded, "Enron and its affiliates intentionally engaged in a variety of market manipulation schemes that had profound adverse impacts on market outcomes." FERC's report noted that Enron and other profiteering energy traders "used a variety of techniques, including submitting false information, creating false transmission congestion, and importing and exporting power into and out of California." One Enron division, according to FERC, had generated more than $500 million in speculative profits for the firm by manipulating gas and electricity prices. Knowingly or not, Cheney and Bush had abetted this gigantic billion-dollar rip-off.

During the April 17 meeting with Cheney, Lay also had pitched ideas for the energy plan, handing Cheney a memo detailing what Enron wanted in Cheney's blueprint. When Lay's memo became news in January 2002, Mary Matalin, a Cheney aide, stated, "Well, it turns out that somehow a San Francisco paper got a copy of the memo of items that Enron wanted in the energy plan . . . and lo and behold, of the eleven items they wanted, nine did not end up in the plan." But the minority staff members of the House of Representatives committee on government reform reached a different conclusion.

Their study noted that the Lay memo identified policy recommendations in *eight* not eleven areas and the final energy plan "adopts all or significant portions of Enron's recommendations in seven of the eight areas." Sure, it was Democrats making the charge. But this report—which dealt with the highly technical energy matters of interest to Enron—was more detailed and, consequently, more persuasive than Matalin's assertion. And shortly after the energy plan came out in 2001—months before Enron became controversial—the *New York Times* had reported in a matter-of-fact way, "Mr. Cheney's report includes much of what Mr. Lay advocated during their meeting."

In another more elaborate report, the committee's minority staffers—who worked for Representative Henry Waxman, the ranking Democrat on the committee—maintained that "there are at least 17 policies in the White House energy plan that were advocated by Enron or that benefited Enron financially." Certainly, the committee staff noted, the plan's policies did not benefit Enron exclusively, and some provisions might have "independent merit." But these pursuers of the Bush-Enron connection concluded, "It is unlikely that any other corporation in America stood to gain as much from the White House energy plan as Enron."

The Bush administration undeniably provided direct assistance to Enron by attempting to help the company resolve a dispute in India concerning a megadeal that had gone sour. In 1992 Enron and India began working on what Enron claimed would be the largest liquefied natural-gas-fired power plant in the world. The $2.9 billion Dabhol project was situated in Maharashtra state and partly financed by the U.S. Export-Import Bank and the Overseas Private Investment Corporation. (In 1993, the World Bank had concluded the plan was "not economically viable" and deserved none of its financing.) For years, the plant generated controversy in India; locals complained about the terms of the deal, its environmental impact, human rights violations committed by security forces guarding the facility, and the cost of the power it would produce. In 1999, the plant, after much political tussling, was turned on, but the power it produced, according to *The Financial Times,* was more expensive than domestic producers. In early 2001, the Maharashtra state government stopped paying for the power and sought to cancel the purchase agreement. Enron soon began an arbitration process, shut down the plant, claimed the state owed it tens of millions of dollars, and hoped to sell its interest for $2.3 billion.

During its first year in the White House, Team Bush had been slugging away for Enron and its Dabhol endeavor. In April 2001, Secretary of State Powell discussed Enron's derailed deal with India's foreign minister. About this time, the *Washington Post* reported, the White House amended a draft proposal written by the State Department for the energy plan to include a provision encouraging oil and gas production in India that could end up helping Enron there. By June, the National Security Council was coordinating an interagency effort—at one point called the "Dabhol Working Group"—to push India to settle the conflict. On June 27, Cheney met with the leader of India's opposition party and brought up the Dabhol squabble. According to the *Washington Post,* which later obtained a collection of administration memos and emails related to the Dabhol plant, an NSC email the next day reported, "Good news is that the Veep mentioned ENRON in his meeting with Sonia Gandhi yesterday." Another email indicated the NSC was helping Lay win an invitation to dinner with Indian officials.

On July 24, Christina Rocca, the U.S. assistant secretary of state for South Asia, applied pressure when she addressed a meeting of Indian officials in New Delhi: "By any reasonable international standard, the level of foreign investment here remains much lower than it could or should be. . . . From an American perspective, as I'm sure you've all heard before, many of India's problems in this regard can be summed up in one five-letter word: Enron." In September, the administration tried to nudge the World Bank "to express concern" to the Indian government about Dabhol.

Even after 9/11, the White House maintained its intense interest in this matter. Cheney was again briefed on the Enron-Dabhol situation before meeting with India's foreign minister in early October. And Bush was supposed to broach the subject in early November during a conversation in Washington with India's prime minister. But the day before the meeting, Enron disclosed it had grossly overstated its profits by $600 million, and the Enron meltdown was in full swing. The Dabhol dispute was yanked from Bush's agenda for the meeting.

During the Clinton years, Enron, which had donated to Democrats as well, had received help for its difficult Dabhol project from senior-level officials. And after the Enron scandal broke, the White House pointed to the Clintonites' previous involvement as evidence that it was routine for government officials to assist U.S. firms overseas, especially when U.S. taxpayer-financed institutions have loans at stake. But the-Clintons-did-it-too argument did not provide Bush much wiggle room. He was the one who had declared that *if* Enron had approached his administration seeking help, *it didn't find any.*

But Enron had come. That was documented. And it had found help on crucial items. That, too, was a fact. Perhaps the Bush administration would have taken exactly the same actions on these issues had it not been dealing with a CEO and a firm that had showered Bush with money for years. But Bush chose not to make that case. Instead, he went with a dishonest, blanket denial.

By mid-March 2002, the Enron scandal no longer dominated the Sunday talk shows or overwhelmed White House briefings. There was news about the indictments of Enron's accountants and continuing coverage of which Enron exec knew what when. But the political dimension of the scandal had slipped from view. A big question was whether the Democrats who controlled the Senate would conduct a thorough and extensive inquiry with high-profile hearings. Without a push from the Senate Democrats, a congressional aide said at the time, "Enron fades here, unless there are new dramatic revelations regarding the [secret Enron] partnerships." On March 21, Senator Joseph Lieberman, chairman of the governmental affairs committee, announced he was issuing subpoenas seeking information about "Enron's communications with the White House or other federal agencies" since 1992. But in a statement, he noted, "We are trying . . . to understand what government agencies knew about Enron's practices and whether there was anything they could have or should have done to prevent the company's collapse, and to make sure something like this never happens again." Lieberman's remarks signaled he was focusing on the question of whether the federal government could have prevented the collapse of Enron. His comments did not suggest he was explicitly looking for information on whether Enron had tried to use its political influence to win favorable policies and decisions from the Bush and Clinton administrations. In any case, a major Senate investigation never materialized. And when the Republicans regained control of the Senate in November, such an endeavor became unthinkable.

But for Bush, the trouble was not over, for the Enron mess begat the Harken mess.

"Everything I do is fully disclosed. It's been fully vetted. Any other questions?"

The Enron fiasco was but the first in a long stretch of corporate scandals. Throughout 2002, the business section of newspapers read like a crime sheet, full of stories about WorldCom (which overstated pretax profits by a whopping $3.8 billion), Tyco International (which was run by executives who allegedly misused company money and covered up improper payments to themselves), Xerox (which overduplicated its earnings), Martha Stewart (the domesticity-doyenne who stood accused of insider trading), and other alleged corporate malfeasants. Of particular embarrassment to the administration would be Halliburton, the oil-services company that Cheney headed before signing up as Bush's running mate. It came under investigation for using allegedly improper accounting practices, when Cheney had been its CEO, to pump up its revenues on paper—a move that had been approved by its auditor, Arthur Andersen of Enron fame.* But what

---

*Cheney had managed to escape a previous controversy about his Halliburton past, which had caused him to shuffle the truth. In July 2000, he said that as Halliburton CEO he "had a firm policy that we wouldn't do anything in Iraq, even—even arrangements that were supposedly legal." But the *Washington Post* found that two Halliburton subsidiaries had signed contracts to sell more than $73 million in oil equipment to Iraq while Cheney was head of Halliburton—a legal deal occurring under the auspices of the U.N.'s oil-for-food program in Iraq. Cheney aide Mary Matalin suggested Cheney was unaware of these deals because they had been part of a joint venture inherited by Halliburton. But the head of one of the subsidiaries said Cheney must have at some point learned of these sales.

would cause the White House even more discomfort was Bush's past as an official in a much smaller corporation called Harken Energy.

It took a while for the ghosts of Harken to catch up to Bush. As one corporate scandal after another was breaking, the present was posing enough challenges for him. Bush, the first MBA president and a businessman himself, was under pressure to respond to the orgy of boardroom misdeeds—especially since they were accompanying, if not causing, a declining stock market. In a speech in March, he announced a "plan to improve corporate responsibility" that included ten planks, each related to the Enron scandal. When he unveiled his proposal he did not use the E-word. But Bush's proposal noted, for instance, that every investor in a publicly owned company "should have quarterly access to the information needed to judge a firm's financial performance, condition and risks" and that "corporate leaders should be required to tell the public promptly whenever they buy or sell company stock for personal gain."

Bush's initiative did not take the heat off him. Congress was toiling away on corporate accountability legislation—with some members proposing actions going much further than Bush had urged. By summer, with corporate crookedness still dominating the headlines, the White House decided it needed to have Bush deliver yet another major address on corporate responsibility. As the speech approached and as corporate controversies continued, Bush's record as a private businessman—a subject few journalists had bothered to explore during the 2000 campaign—became news. Bush could thank *New York Times* columnist Paul Krugman for this. In a series of columns, Krugman had taken several whacks at Bush's stint as a director of Harken. Author/columnist Molly Ivins, a longtime Bush antagonist, and a few other journalists had previously written in depth about Bush's curious Harken dealings. But when a *Times* columnist throws punches, the jabs get noticed. Krugman's columns prompted a new—and more intense—round of media scrutiny of Bush's days as an oilman.

What prompted the most questions was Bush's 1990 sell-off of stocks in Harken Energy, an oil company based in Dallas. Bush was on Harken's board of directors and its audit committee, and the critical issue was whether he had dumped most of his Harken stock because he had picked up inside information about the firm's shaky condition. But there was more to the tale than that.

Harken had bailed out Bush in 1986 by buying his own down-and-almost-out oil venture, Spectrum 7. Bush received about $500,000 in Harken stock for his piece of Spectrum 7, and Harken signed him up as a $120,000-a-year consultant.

Why had Harken, run by a Republican fund-raiser named Alan Quasha, saved Bush's company from ruin? It wasn't Bush's record as a businessman. This deal marked the second time in Bush's career as a failing-upward oilman that a floundering Bush venture had to be rescued by an outside firm. But business failures aside, he still was the son of the vice president. Bush later denied he had benefited from his surname. In 1994 he told the *Dallas Morning News* he had succeeded in the business world due to "hard work, skillful investments, the ability to read an environment that was ever-changing at times and react quickly." He insisted he had never profited because of his lineage. "I was the son of the president of the United States," he added. "But that in itself can be a drag at times." Perhaps.

In July 2002—as Bush's Harken past was being exhumed by reporters—I encountered George Soros, the global billionaire and funder of liberal causes, at a reception in Washington. Soros had been one of the major investors in Harken when it absorbed Bush's Spectrum 7. What was the deal with Harken buying up Spectrum 7 and saving Bush? I asked. He replied that he had not known Bush. But Soros explained, "He was supposed to bring in the Gulf"—meaning Persian Gulf—"connection. But it didn't come to anything. We were buying political influence. That was it. He was not much of a businessman."*

Three years after Bush (and his potential political influence) was acquired by Harken, the firm won a 35-year exploration contract with the emirate of Bahrain in the Persian Gulf—an odd arrangement, since this small company had no previous experience in international or offshore drilling. A Houston oil-business analyst told *Forbes* the ven-

---

*Had it not been for Soros and his Harken partners, what might have become of Bush? Because a liberal billionaire and his corporate allies sought political juice in 1986, Bush's corporate career was preserved and artificially inflated. Consequently, he was able to enter politics, citing his business experience, and land in a position where he could implement policies that would make Soros gag.

ture was "hard to imagine." Some industry observers wondered if Harken's Bush connection had been a factor.

In June 1990, Bush sold over 212,000 Harken shares—about two-thirds of his entire Harken holdings—for $4 apiece and bagged $848,000. At the time, Harken, from the outside, seemed a sound company. It had posted some losses, but it had lined up the Bahrain deal (which looked impressive though never would become a success). Harken, however, was slipping. It had hidden much of its losses by selling a subsidiary, more or less, to itself in a deal the Securities and Exchange Commission later ruled a phony transaction. This is what happened: in 1989, Harken sold 80 percent of a subsidiary, Aloha Petroleum, to a partnership of Harken insiders for $12 million, but $11 million of that was financed by a note held by Harken itself. Harken claimed an $8 million profit on the deal, and that allowed it to state losses of $3.3 million in its 1989 annual report. But in 1990, the SEC gave Harken a hard time about the Aloha sale, and in February 1991, Harken amended its annual report and declared 1989 losses of $12.6 million.

But when Bush sold his shares, the extent of Harken's 1989 losses remained hidden from the public because of this sham sale. And Bush managed to dump his stock—to a buyer who has never been identified—before news of the company's enormous losses for the second quarter of 1990 became public. It was not until August that the firm announced it had dropped $23 million that quarter. After that news hit, the company's stock plummeted by more than 20 percent; months later it had fallen to $1.25. (It later rebounded.)

Bush had sold at a very fortunate time—when 1989 losses had been concealed and recent losses not yet divulged. And he had very much needed the money from this sale. He used these funds to pay off a $500,000 bank loan he had taken the previous year to buy an interest in the Texas Rangers baseball team—an interest that would earn him $16 million when the club was sold for $250 million in 1998. (Bush's original interest in the Rangers would have won him about $2 million from the 1998 deal, but due to financial bonuses written into the contract to benefit Bush and the other co-general partner, he ended up with a much larger slice of the pie.)

The Center for Public Integrity, which in 2000 first revealed news of the shady Aloha Petroleum deal, noted there was no evidence

Bush had been aware of the slippery accounting on this transaction. But had it not been for such financial shenanigans, Bush's Harken stock would likely have been worth less when he sold it to raise funds to cover his Rangers investment. Harken's Enron-like practices may well have helped Bush become a multimillionaire.*

Did Bush have an inkling in June 1990 that it was an opportune time to sell most of his Harken stock? A month before the sale, Harken had appointed Bush, who served on the firm's audit committee, to an internal committee studying the restructuring of the company, which might have placed him in even more of a position to learn about the company's troubles. A *U.S. News & World Report* investigation in 1992 concluded that at the time of the sale there was "substantial evidence to suggest that Bush knew Harken was in dire straits." Whether he knew or not, Bush failed to disclose his stock dump right away, as the SEC required. Instead, he notified the SEC eight months after the federal deadline.

Once Bush finally informed the SEC of his stock sale, the SEC started investigating him for possible insider trading. But in August 1991 its staff concluded there was "insufficient evidence to recommend an enforcement action" against him. The investigators said that before selling his stocks Bush had received information indicating that operating losses were expected to be $4.2 million, but they claimed this was consistent with the firm's recent trend of losses and did not amount to insider information. In a 1992 memo, the SEC investigators noted, somewhat carefully, "Based upon our investigation, it appears that Bush did not engage in illegal insider trading because it does not appear that he possessed material nonpublic information."

---

*The Rangers franchise became so valuable partly because the city of Arlington, Texas, raised local taxes and condemned private property in order to build a new $190 million stadium for the team. That is, Bush—a tax-cut advocate, a fan of property rights, and a champion of welfare reform—became independently wealthy because he was part of an enterprise that pushed for higher taxes, that violated property rights, and that benefited from corporate welfare. In a 1994 interview with the *Dallas Morning News*, Bush claimed that the Rangers had not been plotting with the city to grab people's land: "The Rangers aren't even involved. The condemnations are being handled by the city." But the newspaper reported, "Internal Rangers memos and letters concerning the property transactions . . . indicate that the team has been an active participant in the land acquisitions."

But the SEC investigators never interviewed Bush. And those skeptical about the SEC's ability to investigate the son of a sitting president could point to the fact that the SEC chairman at the time, Richard Breeden, had been nominated by Bush's father and that the agency's general counsel, James Doty, had earlier represented Bush during his purchase of the Texas Rangers baseball team. (Doty recused himself from the SEC inquiry.) During the SEC investigation Bush was represented by Robert Jordan, who had been a partner of Doty at the Baker Botts law firm, where Breeden had also been a senior partner. (Jordan later was appointed U.S. ambassador to Saudi Arabia by Bush II.)

The Harken deal was all very Enron-ish. An insider selling stock before the price tumbled. A politically wired executive escaping financial misfortune. A company covering up losses—which likely inflated its stock price—by using a shell outfit. All this made it somewhat disingenuous for Bush to be parading as a corporate reformer 11 years later—particularly since he was decrying corporate schemes that "used artful and intricate financial arrangements" and calling for more timely notification when corporate executives buy or sell company stock. And now that Harken was once more in the headlines, Bush, as he had done through the years, continued to issue unpersuasive explanations about his Harken actions.

In response to Krugman's wallops, reporters on July 2, 2002, asked Bush about Harken. "Everything I do is fully disclosed," he snapped. "It's been fully vetted. Any other questions?" His reply was an echo of what he said when asked about the deal during his 1994 gubernatorial campaign: "I was exonerated." In 1993, the SEC had sent Bush a letter informing him it had concluded "enforcement action" was unnecessary. But the letter also contained legal boilerplate stating that this "must in no way be construed as indicating that the party [Bush] has been exonerated or that no action may ultimately result."

At a July 3, 2002, press briefing, Fleischer tried to explain why Bush had been eight months late in notifying the SEC of the stock sale. He noted that in 1990 Bush had filed a Form 144 with the SEC; this was a notice that Bush intended to sell some of his Harken shares. Fleischer claimed that the delay in Bush's filing of Form 4 (the notification of the actual transaction) had been due to a "mix-up" by Harken lawyers.

But Fleischer's account differed from the explanation Bush offered during his 1994 governor's race. Back then, his campaign claimed he had filed the required report and that the SEC must have misplaced it. Bush at that point told the *Houston Chronicle* he was "absolutely certain" he had complied with the law. An SEC spokesman at the time told *Time* that no one at the agency ever found the lost document.

So which was it? A lost form or lousy lawyers? When was Bush telling the truth—or not telling the truth? As a *New York Times* news story noted, "Mr. Fleischer could not completely explain the inconsistency." For his part, at a July 8 press conference, Bush said, "As to why the Form 4 was late, I still haven't figured it out completely." Which was not what his campaign had said in 1994.

Misplaced or mixed up—neither excuse addressed the fact that the 1990 late-filing was not the only time Bush had violated SEC rules. A 1991 SEC memo, prepared by the agency's enforcement division and obtained by the Center for Public Integrity, stated that Bush had four times missed deadlines for reporting his stock trades to the SEC. The tally included the infamous 1990 sale of Harken stock, as well as Bush's acquisition of 212,152 shares of Harken stock in 1986 (17 weeks late), a 1986 exercise of Harken stock options worth $96,000 (15 weeks late), and a 1989 exercise of Harken stock options valued at $84,375 (15 weeks late). Bush had been a serial late-filer.

At that July 8 press conference, reporters also pressed Bush about the bogus transaction that kept $8 million in Harken losses under wraps at the time Bush sold his Harken stock. "All I can tell you," he said, "is—is that in the corporate world, sometimes things aren't exactly black and white when it comes to accounting procedures. And the SEC's job is to—is to—is to look and is to determine whether or not—whether or not—whether or not the decision by the auditors was the appropriate decision. And they did look, and they decided that earnings ought to be restated, and the company did so immediately upon the SEC's findings. . . . There was no malfeance [*sic*] involved. This was an honest disagreement about accounting procedures."

That was akin to saying that when one is caught with a hand in a cookie jar and forced to return the cookie, all that had transpired was simply a honest disagreement. Bush was soft-peddling. The case actually was black and white. Harken tried to pull a fast one, was caught, and had to restate its earnings.

And had Bush been involved in the bogus deal? When asked, he did not reply directly. Instead, he said, "You need to look back on the directors' minutes." Two days later, White House Communications Director Dan Bartlett said the administration did not possess the minutes and would not bother asking Harken to release them. In other words, Bush was refusing to say whether he had been a party to this Enron-like business conduct. According to an internal Harken document obtained by the Center for Public Integrity, Bush had chaired a special committee of Harken board members created to review the terms of the $11 million note used to finance the transaction. But this document did not resolve the question of what Bush knew about the suspicious sale. That remained murky—which apparently did not upset the White House. Bush aides also told reporters that they would not ask the SEC to make public all the records of its investigation of Bush.*

Had Bush been in-the-know about Harken's impending losses when he sold his stock? In 1994, Bush told the *Dallas Morning News* he had been unaware: "I absolutely had no idea and would not have sold it had I known." Yet E. Stuart Watson, another director at the time who served on the audit and restructuring committees with Bush, told the newspaper that he and Bush were constantly informed of the company's finances and knew losses were to be announced. (Bush said Watson was "mistaken.") An April 20, 1990, letter from Harken's president to the company's board did warn of a "liquidity crisis." And, according to the Center for Public Integrity (which collected dozens of Harken records from this period), "other internal documents refer to a 'severe cash crisis' and 'critically tight cash flow.'" And in May 1990, Harken's banks were putting pressure on the company. Bush had been surrounded by signs of Harken's troubles, but what precisely he knew remained a question.

In mid-July 2002, the news broke that 16 days before Bush had sold his Harken stock, he had been sent the company's "weekly flash

---

*The White House did not go out of its way to clear up questions about Bush's Harken actions. At a July 16, 2002, press briefing, a reporter asked Fleischer, "The president's accountant said yesterday that a Texas bank freed up ... 130,000 shares of Harken stock that were being pledged for the loan the president took out for the Texas Rangers. Do you happen to know what the president did to get that collateral free?" The press secretary replied, "No, Ron, I'm not the president's accountant." Fleischer did not offer to find out what had happened.

report," which provided information from subsidiaries on projected earnings. The report predicted a second-quarter loss of about $4 million—an amount of losses the SEC concluded did not count as an insider warning. The *Washington Post* noted this "latest information leaves unresolved whether Bush knew his biggest asset was about to shrink and unloaded before other investors found out, or whether he sold only because, as he says, he wanted to pay off his loan."

Speaking for Bush, Bartlett said that Bush and other board members "knew that there were going to be some losses [in the second quarter of 1990]—in the neighborhood of $9 million," not the $23 million loss that would be posted. Bartlett's statement contradicted Bush's 1994 claim that he had been in the dark about these losses. More intriguing, the $9 million figure was more than twice the projected losses that Bush, according to SEC investigators, had known about, more than the amount predicted in the flash report. Where did Bartlett get the $9 million figure? He didn't explain. But if the SEC investigators had realized that Bush traded his shares after learning of a $9 million—rather than a $4 million—loss, would that have caused them to view Bush's stock sell-off differently? Perhaps a $9 million loss—four times the loss of the previous quarter—had been a reason to sell.

In this summer of corporate scandals, Bush also faced questions about Harken's unusual deal in Bahrain. In 1991, when the *Wall Street Journal* examined the Bahrain project, Bush would not speak to the newspaper. But he provided brief responses to a list of written questions, including one that asked whether his involvement with Harken had provided the company credibility in the Arab world. "Ask the Bahrainis," Bush replied. Alan Quasha, the former Harken chairman and its second-largest shareholder, was more forthcoming. "You'd have to be an idiot," he said, "not to say it's impressive" to have the Bush name attached to Harken. In 1994, while running for governor, Bush was willing to say more. He told the *Dallas Morning News,* "I expressed concern at the board meeting that the company not participate in a project overseas. I didn't think the company was prepared to do that. . . . I had absolutely nothing to do with the Bahrain deal."

In July 2002, Bush again declared that he had opposed the Bahrain venture. But minutes from a 1989 Harken board of directors meeting became public a few days later and they showed Bush had voted in favor of the venture. In response, the White House claimed Bush had spoken against it during deliberations but had followed a company tradition of having unanimous votes on major matters. The board minutes did not reflect any Bush doubts.

"We must usher in a new era of integrity in corporate America."

Toting all his Harken and Enron baggage, Bush on July 9, 2002, attended a luncheon at a Wall Street hotel and delivered his second big speech on corporate responsibility. "America's greatest economic need is higher ethical standards," he proclaimed, adding, "We must usher in a new era of integrity in corporate America." He tossed a few choice words at corporate evildoers, blasting business leaders who have been "obstructing justice and misleading clients, falsifying records . . . breaching the trust and abusing power . . . earning tens of millions of dollars in bonuses just before their companies go bankrupt, leaving employees and retirees and investors to suffer." But he mentioned no names. Not Enron, WorldCom, Global Crossing, Adelphia, Arthur Andersen. And not Halliburton.

Bush called for "a new ethic of personal responsibility in the business community." And he unveiled a list of initiatives to add to those he had unveiled in March. He hailed his creation of a federal "corporate fraud task force" that would "function as a financial crimes SWAT team." He proposed doubling the maximum prison terms for mail or wire fraud from five to ten years. He promised new money and enforcement personnel for the SEC. He "challenged every CEO in America" to describe in plain English in the company's annual report his or her compensation package. And he also "challenged" compensation committees to end company loans to corporate officers.

Despite these impressive-sounding proposals, his package was more of a do-something placeholder than a get-tough plan. He failed to include the two most talked about proposals for cleaning up corporate America: compelling firms to count executive stock options against profits and preventing accountants from doing consulting work for firms they audit. Such consulting work had caused accounting firms to become too close to the companies they inspected, and analysts maintained this had led to weaker accounting procedures that enabled corporate misconduct. Nor did Bush explain why he was opposing stricter reforms then pending in a Senate bill. These included preventing accounting firms from offering certain consulting services to their audit clients, establishing an independent board to oversee auditors of public companies, allowing the SEC to ban company executives and CEOs deemed "unfit" to serve, and creating a new category of felony for defrauding shareholders. (Nailing corrupt CEOs was sometimes difficult under existing fraud laws.)

As *U.S. News & World Report* put it, Bush's "address was not a stirring call to arms. Instead, he advocated a stronger enforcement of existing laws, urged businesses to police themselves better, and proposed a variety of modest measures . . . far less than what many on Congress favor." *Newsweek* reported, "The president's widely panned Wall Street speech—tough in tone but containing few legislative specifics—was kept cautious on the advice of business-world alumni, among them Vice President Dick Cheney (late of Halliburton) and domestic-policy chief Joshua Bolten (of Goldman Sachs)." And the *New York Times* noted, "While chief executives praised the President's speech, saying it would help restore confidence in American business, many professional money managers expressed disappointment that there were not more specific proposals for cleaning up corporate America." The bottom line: the corporate class felt relieved; those representing the victims of corporate crime were unimpressed and argued that no new, Bush-created era of corporate integrity was dawning.

Tepid or not in his proposals, Bush had engaged in his own sort of false disclosure. His corporate fraud task force was no SWAT team poised to swoop down on crooks in suits. FBI and Justice Department officials told the *Times* that it was a coordinating body and a clearinghouse for information, with no responsibility for investigations or prosecutions. And Bush's call to double jail terms for convicted corporate crooks seemed more important than it was. The key matter was increasing the chances a felonious businessperson would be caught and punished. Adding a few years to what *might* be the punishment was not likely to discourage a would-be corporate swindler who already knew he or she would lose his or her livelihood and reputation and face jail time if caught. And then came a sadly comic grace note to the speech. Two days afterward, the *Washington Post* reported that Bush in 1986 and 1988 had taken low-interest loans totaling $180,375 from Harken and used the money to buy Harken stock. It was a practice he had condemned in his Wall Street address.

Bush had little credibility as a champion of corporate reform—either in deed or in word. As a businessman, he had been associated with several of the practices he now condemned. So it was no surprise that a week after he lectured Wall Street, the Senate—ignoring his objections—voted 97-0 for a corporate reform package largely crafted by Democrats that exceeded Bush's plan. Even Bush's Republican allies were willing to defy him and dismiss his warnings that the Senate measure went too far. The bill created a new regulatory board to investigate and prosecute the accounting industry, limited consulting work by accounting firms, established a new corporate fraud felony, and prevented Wall Street investment firms from punishing research analysts who produced bad-news reports. The Senate, though, had not been as fierce as some corporate critics desired. For instance, it yielded to an intense industry lobbying campaign and blocked a provision calling for *studying* whether stock options should be included on expense reports.

Bush tried to ride the wave, rather than be bowled over by it. He declared the Senate had "acted on a tough bill that shares my goals and includes all of the accounting and criminal reforms I proposed." He neglected to note he had opposed many of its key provisions. And two weeks later, there was Bush signing the legislation in a televised ceremony in the East Room of the White House, praising the law and maintaining that "the era of low standards and false profits is over." He also took credit for the legislation, remarking, "My administration pressed for greater corporate integrity. A united Congress has written it into law." As if Congress had written *his* less-stringent proposal into law. Now that the spotlight was on him, Bush and his administration had decided to embrace the law they had previously wished to weaken.

But it did not take Bush long to prove his insincerity. During the signing ceremony, Bush noted, "Corporate misdeeds will be found and will be punished. This law authorizes new funding for investigators and technology at the Security [*sic*] and Exchange Commission to uncover wrongdoing." And he promised that his administration would use the "new tools" of the law "to the fullest." But two and a half months later, Bush reneged. The law had called for increasing the SEC's budget from $438 million to $776 million. Congress had approved the extra funding so the SEC could meet the new responsibilities it had been handed by the new law. Of the funding increase, $102 million was earmarked for personnel raises, $98 million for 200 additional prosecutors, investigators, and auditors, and $108 million for better computers and reviving the SEC's New York offices destroyed on September 11. In mid-October, though, the Bush administration announced it was only requesting $568 million for the commission. That is, Bush would only give the SEC 38 percent of the budget boost backed by Congress. This funding level, the SEC's spokesman told the *New York Times*, "doesn't allow for a lot of new initiatives." So much for using the law "to the fullest." Months later, Bush called for a bigger increase in the SEC's budget—but one that would not kick in until the fiscal year 2004. In the meantime, the SEC would have to do more with not enough funding. Bush's avowed commitment to combating corporate crookery was not on the money.

When Bush placed his signature on the corporate reform law, he observed, "Under this law, CEOs and chief financial officers must personally vouch for the truth and fairness of their companies' disclosures." Such a standard, unfortunately, could not be applied to the chief officer of the U.S. government. Bush's statements about his own corporate past, his administration's relationship with white-collar crooks, and his supposed reforms were hardly encouraging for anyone desiring a new era of responsibility. When it came to all of this, Bush cooked the books.

12. Selling a War

> "Intelligence gathered by this and other governments leaves no doubt that the Iraq regime continues to possess and conceal some of the most lethal weapons ever devised."

It was fitting that Bush would reach for a dishonest phrase to kick off a yearlong and disingenuous campaign to lead the nation to war and occupation in the Middle East. "Axis of evil"—these three words, as used by Bush, were technically untrue. Nevertheless, in his first State of the Union address, delivered before Congress on January 29, 2002, Bush employed this term to lump together three oppressive and anti-American regimes that each had a record of developing unconventional weapons. Referring to North Korea, Iran, and Iraq, Bush vowed, "The United States of America will not permit the world's most dangerous regimes to threaten us with the world's most destructive weapons." This was the start of Bush's public crusade against Saddam Hussein, an effort that Bush braced with lies and exaggerations, from day one until the bombs were launched.

The definition of an "axis" is an alliance of nations that coordinate their foreign and military policies. That could not be said of Iraq, Iran, and North Korea—particularly Iraq and Iran, which had fought each other in a bitter war through most of the 1980s. Bush's axis was more poetical than actual. But his use of this emotionally charged designation, concocted by speechwriters, was quite purposeful. It was crafted to both accentuate a threat and imply a response. After all, if a powerful state is faced with an "axis of evil," what option does it have other than to smash the offending axis? And Iraq resided at the top of the to-be-smashed list.*

After unveiling these three misleading words, Bush spent 14 months trying to make the case that Saddam Hussein was an imminent danger to the United States because he possessed weapons of mass destruction *and* was in league with the evildoers of 9/11. He proved neither one of these key assertions. Veracity lost out to rhetoric. But Bush got his war.

Bush always had the option, in arguing for war, of playing it straight, telling the public that the evidence pertaining to weapons of mass destruction and a link between Iraq and al Qaeda was inconclusive, but that the United States could not take a chance. He could have forthrightly explained that he and U.S. allies had different views of how to handle Hussein and that he felt obligated to follow his own principles. If there were other reasons beyond the purported immediate threat from Hussein that justified sacrificing American lives and taking Iraqi lives, Bush could have fully shared those. Instead, in the long prelude, truth became a casualty *before* the war. Bush, his vice president, his secretary of state, his defense secretary, his national security adviser, and other administration officials distorted evidence, misrepresented facts, hurled unsubstantiated charges, and switched stories and rationales in their attempt to win support at home and abroad for a war against Iraq. They fibbed their way to battle.

There was some truth amid all this. Administration officials were certainly accurate when they assailed Hussein as a murderous tyrant who oppressed millions. They were also right that this brute could not be believed when he claimed he did not have awful weapons, and they were right to be concerned about the prospect of a Hussein armed with biological, chemical, or nuclear weapons. But too often the Bush crowd tampered with, or outright avoided, the truth to justify their war. On what was literally the most serious of presidential matters—involving thousands of lives and deaths and the future security of the United States, if not other parts of the world—Bush and his lieu-

---

*A month after the "axis of evil" speech, Bush felt compelled to reassure one member of the unholy trinity. "We're peaceful people," he said. "We have no intention of invading North Korea. South Korea has no intention of attacking North Korea, nor does America." Was this an indication that Bush had gone too far in his rhetoric?

tenants could not be trusted. Of all the lies Bush had told as president, none so brazenly challenged the bond between the government and the governed as did the lies that led to the invasion of Iraq. By relying upon deceit to guide the nation to an elective war, Bush violated the most fundamental principles of democracy. His war was an attack on the notion that an informed populace should be—and must be—the ultimate judge of presidential conduct.

"The president has made no decision about the use of force."

The axis-of-evil speech in January 2002 understandably fueled talk of war. Yet in public Bush and his team consistently claimed he was not committed to war against Iraq. "There are a number of means that we're pursuing," Condoleezza Rice said on March 1. "But the president has made no decision about the use of force." In mid-March, Bush told reporters, "All options are on the table." A week after that, Ari Fleischer was asked, "Will the U.S. now invade Iraq and go after Saddam Hussein?" He maintained that Bush had "not made any decisions about that phase in the war on terror."

But for months, there had been pressure inside the administration for war. Before the fires of 9/11 had been doused, senior Bush administration officials were urging a war against Saddam Hussein. The day after September 11, Donald Rumsfeld and Paul Wolfowitz pressed Bush to make Iraq a target in the first round of the war on terrorism, according to Bob Woodward's *Bush at War*. Days later, Wolfowitz even argued at a National Security Council meeting that Iraq would be an easier target than Afghanistan. Bush initially resisted such importuning. But at a September 17 NSC session, he remarked, "I believe Iraq was involved [in 9/11], but I'm not going to strike them now. I don't have evidence at this point."

The Bush administration's desire for military confrontation with Iraq had a history predating September 11. Bush's father had driven Hussein out of Kuwait during the Persian Gulf War of 1991, but Bush I had not taken the fight to Baghdad. In the minds of many conservative foreign policy partisans, he had left the job undone. His son inherited that unfinished business. He also had a personal beef, since Hussein reportedly had tried to assassinate the elder Bush in 1993. During the presidential campaign, Bush told an interviewer, "If I found in any way, shape or form that [Hussein] was developing weapons of mass destruction, I'd take 'em out." On another occasion, he tough-talked: "Saddam just needs to understand that if I'm the president, he's going to have a problem." Moreover, traditional hawks and neoconservative pundits and defense intellectuals had for years called for war against Hussein; several of these think-tank warriors had obtained senior positions in the Bush II administration. In 1998, for instance, Rumsfeld, Wolfowitz, William Bennett, William Kristol, Richard Perle, R. James Woolsey, and others wrote to President Clinton and pressed him "to take the necessary steps, including military steps [in Iraq], to protect our vital interests in the Gulf." U.S. policy, they declared, "should aim, above all, at the removal of Saddam Hussein's regime from power"—by force if need be. These "vital interests" were not tightly defined. Did these hawks mean the United States' influence in the region, the security of its ally Israel, access to the oil reserves of Iraq, or the general benefits that would come with a Hussein-less Middle East? It was probably a mix. But the 1998 letter contained not a word about liberating Iraq from Hussein's brutality or bringing democracy to the Iraqi people—goals its authors and Bush would later cite as a benefit of invading Iraq.

By March 2002, despite the assertions of Rice and Fleischer, Bush may well have been already set on the war many of his supporters and aides had been urging for years. That month, according to a subsequent *Time* article, Bush poked his head into Rice's office while she was conferring with several U.S. senators about Iraq. He waved his hand dismissively and said, "Fuck Saddam, we're taking him out." *Time* had more than this anecdote to suggest Bush's die was cast—and that he and his aides were misleading the public about his looking-at-all-options posture. The magazine maintained that in late March Cheney told a lunch of Senate Republicans that they could not repeat what he was about to say to them. And this, reported *Time*, was what came next: "The question was no longer if the U.S. would attack Iraq, [Cheney] said. The only question was when." These two episodes were evidence suggesting the Bush campaign against Iraq was dishonest at the creation—that war was the goal, that the administration, for appearances' sake, would only pretend it was considering other responses.

In the meantime, the Bush administration, in the first half of 2002, was dramatically altering U.S. military strategic doctrine, codifying a theoretical framework that would cover its campaign against Hussein. In a June 2002 speech to West Point cadets, Bush outlined a new guiding principle of U.S. policy: preemptive war. "If we wait for threats to fully materialize, we will have waited too long," he said. "We must take the battle to the enemy, disrupt his plans and confront the worst threats before they emerge." A key phrase was "before they emerge." What would be the standard for judging a threat that had not yet "emerged"? Bush did not say. But Iraq was his test case for this new doctrine of preemptive warfare.

"The president of the United States and the secretary of defense would not assert as plainly and bluntly as they have that Iraq has weapons of mass destruction if it was not true, and if they did not have a solid basis for saying it."

In the months after the State of the Union speech, Bush officials started pushing their argument in the media and in congressional testimony that the Iraqi dictator was a direct threat to the United States. But the campaign did not swing into full throttle until September. As White House Chief of Staff Andrew Card told the *New York Times*, "From a marketing point of view, you don't introduce new products in August." (And this rollout just happened to coincide with the emotion-rich anniversary of the September 11 attacks.) From that point on, Bush and the administration repeatedly made their case against Saddam Hussein on high-profile occasions. On September 12, Bush delivered a speech at the United Nations. A week later Bush sent a draft resolution to Congress requesting authorization to launch a war against Iraq when he deemed best. On October 7, from Cincinnati, he presented a prime-time address on Iraq. While campaigning for Republican candidates in the fall of 2002, Bush constantly raised the issue at rallies. He continued to warn of the peril from Iraq after the

United States persuaded the U.N. Security Council on November 8 to pass Resolution 1441, which outlined an enhanced inspection regime for Iraq's disarmament. The case for war was a central part of Bush's 2003 State of the Union address. On February 5, 2003, Secretary of State Colin Powell delivered an extensive briefing at the U.N. Security Council that was designed to justify military action against Iraq. And, last, there was Bush's March 17 speech, in which he gave Saddam Hussein 48 hours to leave Iraq or see his country invaded.

Throughout all of this, Bush's argument had two foundations: Saddam Hussein possessed usable weapons of mass destruction, and he could slip them to a group such as al Qaeda at any time. The possession argument was obviously the more important of the two. Without chemical, biological, or nuclear weapons, Hussein could not be considered much of an imminent risk to the United States. There was no doubt that Hussein had in the past possessed WMDs. He had used chemical weapons against the Kurds and Iran in the 1980s. He had WMD programs that he had tried to hide from U.N. inspectors during the early years of an inspections program that ran between 1991 and 1998. There were also WMD materials (and possibly weapons) not completely accounted for when the U.N. inspections came to an end. But Bush's case for war depended not on the past, but on what Hussein currently held. And in claiming Iraq had weapons of mass destruction that could endanger the United States, Bush and his aides relied more on assertion than evidence. They argued mainly by repeating the charge, rather than revealing proof.

In an August 26 speech, Cheney declared, "Simply stated, there's no doubt that Saddam Hussein now has weapons of mass destruction. There is no doubt he is amassing them to use against our friends, against our allies, and against us." Cheney cited convincing reasons for believing that Hussein desired WMD and that the Iraqi dictator had in the past tried to defy weapons inspections and could be expected to do so again. But he presented no facts to back up the claim that Hussein at this point had a WMD arsenal of significance that could be deployed by him or anyone else against the United States.

In his speech at the United Nations, Bush detailed Hussein's decades of infamy and cited the numerous times the U.N. Security Council had declared Iraq in breach of resolutions ordering Iraq to rid itself of unconventional weapons. But Bush's most important point was that "Saddam Hussein's regime is a grave and gathering danger." And what made him most dangerous was his weapons. Bush declared that "United Nations inspections [in the 1990s] . . . revealed that Iraq likely maintains stockpiles of VX, mustard and other chemical agents and that the regime is rebuilding and expanding facilities capable of producing chemical weapons." But this was sleight of hand. How could inspections that ended four years earlier reveal the present-day "rebuilding and expanding" of WMD facilities?

Ignoring the four-year time lag was not Bush's only trick. In a crafty and disingenuous practice, Bush and his aides were misrepresenting the findings of the past U.N. inspections to depict Saddam Hussein as neck-deep in WMDs. During the Cincinnati speech, Bush noted that in the mid-1990s Iraq had admitted it produced 30,000 liters of anthrax and other deadly biological agents. "The [U.N.] inspectors, however, concluded that Iraq had likely produced two to four times that amount," he said ominously. "This is a massive stockpile of biological weapons that has never been accounted for, and capable of killing millions."

Bush was citing the U.N. inspectors to prove Iraq had stockpiles of dangerous weapons. But the U.N. inspectors had not "concluded" that Iraq had generated these amounts of weapons and that such "massive" stockpiles existed. The U.N. inspection force that searched Iraq in the 1990s—the U.N. Special Commission (UNSCOM)—maintained that it had dismantled the key facilities Iraq had used to develop chemical, biological, and nuclear weapons and that it had destroyed significant amounts of chemical and biological weapons. But the UNSCOM inspectors did encounter discrepancies in the accounting of Iraq's weapons and WMD material. They found that Iraq *could have* produced more weapons than the inspectors had uncovered or Iraq had acknowledged. That did not mean, though, Iraq was maintaining massive WMD reserves. Bush was deceptively turning unaccounted-for material into here-and-now weapons

For example, Iraq claimed it had produced 8,445 liters of anthrax and then had destroyed this supply, as well as all of its unconventional weapons. The U.N. inspectors deduced that Hussein's regime had maintained the production capacity to manufacture 22,000 to 39,000 liters. Had Iraq used its full capacity and produced all that anthrax? The inspectors were not sure. It was a possibility that required further examination. The U.N. inspectors were able to determine that anthrax growth media had been burnt and buried by Iraq, but they could not tell how much. So they suspected 10,000 liters of anthrax had not been destroyed and might still exist. But to the U.N. inspectors, this was an unresolved question—and a serious one—but not an established fact. A similar situation involved Iraq's VX nerve agent. Regarding botulinum toxin, U.N. inspectors estimated that Iraq could have manufactured twice as much of this lethal bacteria as it said it had. But they also noted that it was unlikely the remaining quantity—if it did exist—would be significantly potent, since the material degrades over time. U.N. inspectors also doubted Iraq's claims that it had disposed of all of its sarin-filled warheads, but they also thought that these weapons would likely no longer be viable.

UNSCOM inspectors left Iraq in 1998 with questions and concerns about Iraq's chemical and biological weapons, but Bush was blatantly mischaracterizing the U.N. inspectors' work, as he falsely suggested that the U.N. inspectors believed gargantuan stockpiles of WMDs remained in Iraq. In an interview in 2000, Rolf Ekeus, the former executive chairman of UNSCOM, summed up the 1990s inspections: "UNSCOM was highly successful in identifying and eliminating Iraq's prohibited weapons—but not to the degree that everything was destroyed. . . . In my view, there are no large quantities of weapons. I don't think Iraq is especially eager in the biological and chemical area to produce such weapons for storage. Iraq views those weapons as tactical assets instead of strategic assets, which would require long-term storage of those elements, which is difficult. Rather, Iraq has been aiming to keep the capability to start up production immediately should it need to."

U.N. inspectors had been sure they had destroyed much of Hussein's unconventional arms, but unsure as to what remnants—if any—remained. Perhaps they had been wrong, and Iraq had managed to hide large stockpiles from them. But Bush did not offer evidence of that. Instead, he twisted the findings of the U.N. inspectors. Nuances and uncertainties were willfully ignored by Bush officials. Insistence took the place of proof, as the administration declared over and over

that Saddam Hussein—no question about it—was armed with significant amounts of the world's worst weapons.

On September 13, 2002, Rumsfeld observed, "There's no debate in
the world as to whether they have those weapons. . . . We all know
that. A trained ape knows that."

On September 28, Bush asserted, "The Iraqi regime possesses biological and chemical weapons, is rebuilding the facilities to make more,
and according to the British government, could launch a biological or
chemical attack in as little as 45 minutes after the order is given."

On December 2, Wolfowitz said, "[Bush's] determination to use
force if necessary is because of the threat posed by Iraq's weapons of
mass destruction."

On December 5, Fleischer remarked, "The president of the United
States and the secretary of defense would not assert as plainly and
bluntly as they have that Iraq has weapons of mass destruction if it
was not true, and if they did not have a solid basis for saying it."

On December 12, Rumsfeld maintained, "It is clear that the Iraqis
have weapons of mass destruction. The issue is not whether or not
they have weapons of mass destruction."

On January 7, Rumsfeld commented, "There is no doubt in my
mind but that they currently have chemical and biological weapons."

On January 9, Fleischer insisted, "We know for a fact that there are
weapons there."

But it was not a fact—not when these statements were being made.
After the war, *U.S. News & World Report* revealed the existence of a
September 2002 report by the Defense Intelligence Agency that said,
"There is no reliable information on whether Iraq is producing or
stockpiling chemical weapons, or where Iraq has—or will—establish
its chemical warfare agent production facilities." The assessment noted
that "a substantial amount of Iraq's chemical warfare agents, precursors, munitions, and production equipment were destroyed between
1991 and 1998 as a result of Operation Desert Storm and UNSCOM
actions." The report did state that "Iraq probably possesses [chemical
weapons] in chemical munitions, possibly including artillery rockets,
artillery shells, aerial bombs, and ballistic missile warheads," but that
"we lack any direct information" on this subject. In other words, the
Pentagon's intelligence analysts assumed Iraq had chemical weapons,

but it had not confirmed this presumption. And a DIA report produced in November reached the same conclusions. Yet before and after these reports were written, Bush and his aides—including Rumsfeld, who oversaw the DIA—were stating that Iraq definitely possessed chemical weapons. In communicating absolute certitude about the existence of the threat of Iraq's WMDs, they were defying their own experts.*

After the war, it also turned out that the British claim—embraced by Bush—that Iraq could deploy chemical and biological weapons within 45 minutes had been unsubstantiated. (That would cause a tremendous row for British Prime Minister Tony Blair.) And Bush administration officials would tell the *Washington Post* that the White House had not bothered to consult the CIA about the British allegation before Bush repeated it.

All in all, the WMD situation in Iraq was far more complicated than Bush let on. There might be weapons; there might not be. There had been discrepancies during the inspections, and it was a safe assumption that Iraq had retained some production capabilities and the expertise that could be used to manufacture some unconventional weapons. If Hussein had lied to the U.N. inspectors and had hidden away chemical and biological weapons, that would be a disturbing matter and require forceful action. But there was only suspicion, not confirmation. There was no evidence of "massive" reserves of weapons. But Bush and his administration refused to convey an accurate description of the unaccounted-for weapons. They exploited the discrepancies and Hussein's intransigence, hinted they possessed conclusive intelligence when they did not, and transformed possible weapons into a threatening arsenal. They were conjuring up a stockpile to fit their policy.

---

*The DIA report was somewhat contradicted by an October 2002 National Intelligence Estimate that said, "Baghdad has chemical and biological weapons." After the war—when the administration was caught in a controversy over its prewar statements about Iraqi WMDs, the White House released an eight-page excerpt from this NIE. It contained this assertion about chemical and biological weapons but did not reference much in the way of evidence. For instance, it estimated that Iraq had between 100 and 500 metric tons of chemical weapons agents, but conceded, "We have little specific information on Iraq's [chemical weapons] stockpile." And following the war, a CIA internal review noted that intelligence analysts had relied on circumstantial and inferential evidence in reaching conclusions such as the ones in this NIE.

"I don't know what more evidence we need."

When it came to nuclear weapons, Bush and his aides stretched further in their efforts to portray Iraq as an immediate danger. A Saddam Hussein wielding nuclear weapons was a frightening prospect, perhaps worthy of preemption. But was this a real worry? In early 2002, a CIA review of weapons proliferation did not warn of any nuclear threat from Iraq. But months later, the administration was making it seem as if Hussein were minutes away from a nuclear bomb (which he would then immediately hand off to Osama bin Laden). In August 2002, Cheney declared, "Many of us are convinced that Saddam Hussein will acquire nuclear weapons fairly soon." But on the basis of what information? Cheney did not say. And he was contradicted by Senator Chuck Hagel, a Nebraska Republican on the intelligence committee, who noted that the CIA had "absolutely no evidence" that Iraq had or would soon have nuclear weapons.

To prove Hussein was going nuclear, Cheney's boss tried to cite evidence. Yet he only succeeded in perpetuating the threat-mongering. During a September 7 joint news conference, Bush and Blair claimed an International Atomic Energy Agency (IAEA) report released that day had noted Iraq was engaged in new construction at several nuclear-related sites. "I would remind you," Bush told reporters, "that when the inspectors went into Iraq [in 1991] and were denied, finally denied access [in 1998], a report came out of the Atomic—the IAEA, that they were six months away from developing a weapon. I don't know what more evidence we need."

A snide response could have been, *evidence that actually existed.* The IAEA denied it had produced any report showing significant construction at Iraq's nuclear facilities. And in 1998, the IAEA had not claimed Iraq was six months from producing a nuclear bomb. The agency had reported the opposite. "There are no indications," the IAEA noted then, "that Iraq has achieved its programme's goal of producing nuclear weapons." The IAEA said that its inspectors had "taken actions to destroy, remove and render harmless the known components of that programme" and that "there are no indications of Iraq having retained any physical capability for the indigenous production of weapon-usable nuclear material in amounts of any practical significance . . . nor any indication that Iraq has otherwise acquired such material." Iraq's nuclear weapons program in 1998, according to the IAEA, was fundamentally kaput. In beating the drums of war, Bush was fabricating proof.* At the same time, his team was relying on melodrama. "There will always be some uncertainty about how quickly [Hussein] can acquire nuclear weapons," Rice said. "But we don't want the smoking gun to be a mushroom cloud."

During his U.N. address, Bush offered other evidence of an ongoing Iraqi nuclear weapon program, noting that "Iraq has made several attempts to buy high-strength aluminum tubes used to enrich uranium for a nuclear weapon." But scientific experts challenged the claim that these tubes were only suitable for a nuclear weapons program. The Institute for Science and International Security released a report maintaining, "By themselves, these attempted procurements are not evidence that Iraq is in possession of, or close to possessing, nuclear weapons." The *Washington Post* reported that U.S. intelligence officials differed on whether Iraq intended to use these tubes for a nuclear program, with some maintaining the aluminum was destined for launch tubes for artillery rockets. And a white paper released by the British government that month noted there was "no definitive intelligence" indicating the tubes were part of a nuclear program. The debate over the tubes would continue, but they could hardly be considered end-of-the-story evidence.

During his October prime-time speech from Cincinnati, Bush again maintained Hussein was in hot pursuit of nuclear weapons. He cited satellite photos that he said revealed Iraq was "rebuilding facilities at sites that have been part of its nuclear program in the past." Yet after U.N. inspectors searched these sites weeks later, IAEA chief Mohamed

---

*In defending Bush, the White House, according to the *Washington Times,* later said that he had actually been referring to a 1991 IAEA report that maintained Iraq had been within six months of building a nuclear bomb. But an IAEA spokesperson said there was no such 1991 report, either. The White House also pointed to articles in the London *Times* in 1991 and the *New York Times.* But neither cited an IAEA report, and each noted only that Iraq in 1991 had been six months away from developing uranium-enrichment procedures, not "developing a weapon," as Bush claimed. And these were the very components that U.N. inspectors later destroyed. Then the White House, shifting its story once more, said that it was a recent International Institute for Strategic Studies report that had concluded Iraq could develop a nuclear bomb "in as few as six months." But that report had come out two days *after* Bush had made his statement about a 1998 IAEA report. And that IISS report— which the IAEA took issue with—said that Iraq could assemble nuclear weapons within months only if it could obtain fissile material from foreign sources, no easy task.

ElBaradei reported, "At the majority of these sites, the equipment and laboratories have deteriorated to such a degree that the resumption of nuclear activities would require substantial renovation." In Cincinnati, Bush also declared, "Iraq possesses ballistic missiles with a likely range of hundreds of miles—far enough to strike Saudi Arabia, Israel, Turkey and other nations—in a region where more than 135,000 American civilians and service members live and work." But U.N. weapons inspectors later found that the missiles in question could travel less than 200 miles—not far enough, the *Washington Post* noted, "to hit the targets Bush named."

"Atta, who was the lead hijacker, did apparently travel to Prague on a number of occasions. And on at least one occasion, we have reporting that places him in Prague with a senior Iraqi intelligence official a few months before the attack."

Bush administration officials not only misrepresented what was known (and what they knew) about Hussein's weapons of mass destruction to create the impression the Iraqi dictator was loaded with weapons that could harm the United States. They also maintained he would supply these arms to anti-American terrorists without ever demonstrating this was a plausible possibility. In May 2002, Rumsfeld testified in the Senate that "we have to recognize that terrorist networks have relationships with terrorist states that have weapons of mass destruction, and that they inevitably are going to get their hands on them and they would not hesitate one minute to use them." In July, Richard Perle, then chairman of the Defense Policy Board, a Pentagon advisory group, told PBS, "It is likely that chemical weapons, biological weapons in the possession of the Iraqis derived during the Cold War from the Soviet Union, are now being disseminated to terrorists."

Some Middle East experts, including hawkish ones, such as Richard Butler, the former chief weapons inspector in Iraq, did not regard a WMD transfer as probable. They argued that Hussein (a secularist) and bin Laden (a fundamentalist) were neither strategic nor tactical allies and that Hussein was unlikely to share WMDs—a valuable source of power—with others, especially parties over which he exerted no control. But if the administration could show Hussein had maintained operational links with al Qaeda, then their nightmare scenario (Hussein arms bin Laden with WMDs) would have to be considered a serious peril. And if they could demonstrate any connection between Hussein and 9/11—well, that would be game, set, match, a reason to bomb Baghdad immediately and unilaterally.

To connect Saddam Hussein to 9/11 and al Qaeda, Bush officials and their outside-the-government allies first peddled the dramatic story of a meeting between a 9/11 hijacker and an Iraqi intelligence officer. In October 2001, media reports cited unnamed Czech officials who said that in the spring of 2001 Mohamed Atta, the apparent ringleader of the September 11 hijackers, met with an Iraqi intelligence officer in Prague. Advocates of toppling Hussein waved this flag for months. An unnamed senior Bush official spoke to reporters about "meetings" (note the plural) between Atta and Iraqi intelligence. Columnist William Safire cited this contact as an "undisputed fact" tying Hussein to September 11.

The significance of this event, though, could only be determined if one knew the purpose of the meeting. It was possible—though not probable—that Iraqi intelligence was assisting al Qaeda and knew of its 9/11 master plan. But perhaps this intelligence officer was acting on his own. Or maybe he was trying to penetrate al Qaeda. Unless one had knowledge of what was said during this supposed meeting, its relevance could not be judged.

But it increasingly appeared that this supposedly incriminating meeting in Prague never even happened. That inconvenient fact, though, would not stop the administration from continuing to cite it. In April 2002, *Newsweek*'s Michael Isikoff reported that "the Czechs quietly acknowledged that they may have been mistaken about the whole thing. U.S. intelligence and law enforcement officials now believe that Atta wasn't even in Prague at the time the Czechs claimed." A U.S. official told the newsmagazine, "Neither we nor the Czechs nor anybody else has any information he was coming or going [to Prague] at that time." Nevertheless, Richard Perle asserted, "I am quite confident the meeting took place."

On May 21, 2002, Ambassador Frank Taylor, the State Department's coordinator for counterterrorism, noted the Prague meeting had "not been confirmed." Still, the Bush hawks yearned to use this piece of ammunition. In August, *Newsweek* reported that Wolfowitz had met with two FBI officials in an effort to get the FBI to endorse reports of the Prague meeting. FBI Counterterrorism Chief Pat D'Amuro and a case agent voiced skepticism, and Wolfowitz challenged them. "The sole evidence for the alleged meeting," the newsmagazine noted, "is the uncorroborated claim of a Czech informant. The informant says he saw Atta meeting with an Iraqi spy on April 9, 2001. But the FBI can't find any evidence—such as airline or passport records—that Atta was in Prague that day." In September 2002, both the *Washington Post* and the *New York Times* quoted U.S. intelligence officials dismissing the Atta allegation. The *Post* put it this way: "CIA officials who scrutinized the report's source—an Arab student not considered particularly reliable who relayed the information to the Czech government—concluded there was no evidence to support the claim."

But as the Bush administration revved up its anti-Hussein campaign in early September 2002, Cheney had no compunction about playing this unproven—if not debunked—card. On *Meet the Press*, Cheney said he did not want "today" to allege that Iraq was tied to the 9/11 attacks. But he did not seem to mind raising the subject and referring to the Atta-in-Prague story to connect Iraq to September 11: "Mohamed Atta, who was the lead hijacker, did apparently travel to Prague on a number of occasions. And on at least one occasion, we have reporting that places him in Prague with a senior Iraqi intelligence official a few months before the attack on the World Trade Center." Yes, the administration had "reporting," but apparently it had been false reporting from one unreliable source. Cheney was referring to bad intelligence to link—nod, nod, wink, wink—Iraq to the 9/11 murderers. This was one of the more dishonest stunts pulled by an administration war hawk.

The Atta-Iraqi story would finally be laid to rest on October 21, 2002, when the *New York Times* reported that Czech President Vaclav Havel "has quietly told the White House he has concluded that there is no evidence to confirm earlier reports" of the meeting. It seemed that Atta had gone to Prague in June 2000, not April 2001. "Now," the paper noted, "some Czech and German officials say that their best explanation of why Mr. Atta came to Prague was to get a cheap airfare to the Untied States."

The Iraqi intelligence connection was, at best, ephemeral, if not wholly manufactured. But the administration tried hooking Hussein to al Qaeda another way. At an August news conference, Donald Rumsfeld proclaimed it "is a fact that there are al Qaeda in a number of locations in Iraq." When CNN anchor Wolf Blitzer asked Rice in early September if the Iraqi government was linked to al Qaeda, she responded, "There is certainly evidence that al Qaeda people have been in Iraq. There is certainly evidence that Saddam Hussein cavorts with terrorists." (Asked the same day if Iraq has been "working with and supporting al Qaeda," Powell took a different line: "We cannot yet make a definitive conclusion that such a thing has occurred.") But the presence of al Qaeda in Iraq only had meaning if Hussein was providing these fighters sanctuary or somehow scheming with them. The *Washington Post* quoted a senior U.S. intelligence official who said there was no evidence Hussein had "welcomed in or sheltered" the terrorists. And another U.S. official commented, "They aren't the official guests of the government" and described these al Qaeda fighters as largely "on the run."

But when the White House on September 19 sent to Congress a draft resolution that would authorize Bush to use military force against Iraq, it attempted to turn the presence of these on-the-run al Qaeda fighters into a casus belli. The proposed legislation—essentially a blank check for Bush—noted, "Members of al-Qaida, an organization bearing responsibility for attacks on the United States, its citizens, its interests, including the attacks that occurred on Sept. 11, 2001, are known to be in Iraq." Could the White House have been more vague? Al Qaeda members were also known to be in 60 different countries, including the United States. The presence of an unstated number of al Qaeda members in Iraq meant nothing. Were these fiends hanging out with the Islamic fundamentalists active in the Kurdish areas of the north? Or were they plotting with Hussein in one of his presidential palaces? In a Rose Garden speech and a radio address, Bush remarked, "There are al Qaeda terrorists inside Iraq." But he did not say how many, how he knew this, what these terrorists were up to, or with whom they were collaborating. The aim was not to prove an assertion but to conflate Iraq with al Qaeda any way possible.

Rumsfeld joined in. On September 26, he declared he had "bulletproof" evidence that Hussein was tied to bin Laden. But he did not share whatever it was with the public. The next day, a spokesman for Senator Bob Graham, the Democratic chairman of the intelligence committee, told *USA Today* that Graham had seen nothing in classified intelligence reports that confirmed any connection between Hussein and al Qaeda.

"The current Iraqi regime has demonstrated its continuing hostility toward, and willingness to attack, the United States."

The Bush strategy was clear: hype the threat presented by Iraq, exaggerate and embellish. Overstate Hussein's potential as a menace to America; overstate his ties to al Qaeda. The White House's draft resolution, for instance, maintained, "The current Iraqi regime has demonstrated its continuing hostility toward, and willingness to attack, the United States, including by attempting in 1993 to assassinate former President Bush and by firing on" U.S. forces patrolling the no-fly zones in Iraq. The alleged plot to kill Bush's father and the Iraqi military's attempts (serious but futile) to shoot down U.S. warplanes warranted condemnation. But it was disingenuous to equate those hostile actions with a "willingness to attack" the United States directly.

Bush's draft resolution also claimed there was a "high risk" that Iraq would use weapons of mass destruction "to launch a surprise attack against the United States or its armed forces or provide them to international terrorists who would do so." Hussein was a brutal dictator who had murdered his way to power and who had used chemical weapons against his local enemies. But mount a "surprise attack" against the United States? There were no indications he had ever pondered that. (Such a move would be suicidal.) And while the prospect of a WMD transfer—as a theoretical possibility—was a legitimate concern, the White House was reckless in deeming it a "high risk."

In early October, Bush ratcheted up his rhetoric about the threat from Saddam Hussein, as he both attempted to convince the U.N. Security Council to approve a tough resolution against Iraq and tried to persuade Congress to pass the legislation handing him the power to launch a war. In speech after speech—many of them on the campaign trail—he excoriated Hussein as a direct threat to Americans. At a political fundraiser in New Hampshire, he called Hussein "a man who hates so much he's willing to kill his own people, much less Americans." And Bush noted, "We must do everything we can to disarm this man before he hurts a single American." During the Cincinnati speech, Bush pronounced the Iraqi dictator a "significant" danger to America and said, "Iraq could decide on any given day to provide a biological or chemical weapon to a terrorist group or individual terrorists. Alliance with terrorists could allow the Iraqi regime to attack America without leaving any fingerprints."

Bush was using loose language. He raised the prospect of Iraq supplying WMDs to terrorists, but his administration had yet to prove Iraq currently possessed such weaponry. And was he right to claim Hussein was plotting to kill Americans? No, not at all, said one key source—the Central Intelligence Agency.

At an October 8 hearing of the Senate Intelligence Committee, Senator Bob Graham read from a letter sent to him by CIA director George Tenet. In that note, Tenet reported the CIA had determined that "Baghdad for now appears to be drawing a line short of conducting terrorist attacks with conventional or CBW [chemical and biological weapons] against the United States." The CIA also had found, "Should Saddam conclude that a U.S.-led attack [against Iraq] could no longer be deterred, he probably would become much less constrained in adopting terrorist actions." And the agency noted, "Saddam might decide that the extreme step of assisting Islamist terrorists in conducting a WMD attack against the United States would be his last chance to exact vengeance by taking a large number of victims with him."

Tenet's letter also referred to an exchange at an October 2 secret hearing in which Senator Carl Levin, a Democrat, asked a senior intelligence official, "If [Saddam] didn't feel threatened . . . is it likely that he would initiate an attack using a weapon of mass destruction?" The intelligence official (unnamed in Tenet's letter) replied, "My judgment would be that the probability of him initiating an attack—let me put a time frame on it—in the foreseeable future, given the conditions we understand now, the likelihood I think would be low."

The bottom line, according to the CIA: Saddam was not likely in the near future to hit the United States or share his weapons with al Qaeda unless the United States assaulted Iraq. He was not plotting to attack the United States. This was not the threat assessment Bush was presenting to the American public.

Bush's exaggeration of the threat did not appear to irk Congress. On October 10, the House voted 296 to 133 to grant Bush you-pick-the-date authority to attack Iraq. The next day, the Senate followed suit 77 to 23. And Bush kept his rhetoric red hot. When a terrorist blast killed over 180 people in Bali, Indonesia, he pointed to the tragedy as another reason for vigorous prosecution of the war on terrorism. The bombing was linked to al Qaeda. But Bush focused less on al Qaeda and more on Hussein, claiming the Iraqi dictator hoped to deploy al Qaeda as his own "forward army" against the West, despite the fact that the Bali incident was unconnected to Hussein or Iraq.

Bush didn't need to have his facts correct to push public opinion in the direction he desired. By the end of October, according to a *Time* poll, nearly three-quarters of Americans surveyed believed Hussein was currently assisting al Qaeda; 71 percent thought it was likely Hussein had been involved in the September 11 attacks.

"He's a threat because he is dealing with al Qaeda."

Bush kept the volume high on his Saddam-is-a-threat chorus. And his avoidance of facts hit a high—or a low—during a press conference on November 7, two days after his Republican Party had triumphed in the congressional elections. A reporter tossed him the following question: "Your CIA director told Congress just last month that it appears that Saddam Hussein 'now appears to be drawing a line short of conducting terrorist attacks against the United States,' but if we attacked him he would 'probably become much less constrained.' Is he wrong about that?"

Bush replied: "I'm sure that he said other sentences. . . . I know George Tenet well. I meet with him every single day. He sees Saddam Hussein as a threat. I don't know what the context of that quote is. I'm telling you, the guy knows what I know, that he is a problem and we must deal with him. . . . Well, if we don't do something he might attack us, and he might attack us with a more serious weapon. The man is a threat. . . . He's a threat because he is dealing with al Qaeda."

Was Bush unfamiliar with Tenet's letter and the CIA's conclusion that an attack from Hussein was unlikely? The letter had caused a major dustup, spurring newspaper headlines. Had Bush never discussed—or been briefed on—these CIA findings? He could have replied that he disagreed with the CIA, or that the CIA assessment was based on inference more than evidence, or that he believed that Hussein presented a long-term threat and had to be confronted before it was too late. Instead, Bush practically denied the existence of the CIA's report.

In replying to this question, Bush also contradicted the CIA's assessment by stating unequivocally that Hussein was an immediate danger because he was currently working with al Qaeda. This was an explosive charge that, if true, could indeed justify war. His "dealing with al Qaeda" remark should have been a stop-the-presses news flash. ("President Definitively Says Hussein in League with Al Qaeda.") Yet no major media organ ran that story. And Bush was not pressed to explain the comment. (By now, did members of the media consider reckless embellishment from Bush not newsworthy?)

Shortly after Bush made this over-the-top charge, the *New York Times* reported, "The Bush administration has said it has evidence of contacts over the years between Iraqi intelligence and Qaeda operatives. . . . But American intelligence officials say there is no evidence that Iraq has become involved in Qaeda terrorist operations." Bush's assertion that Hussein was "dealing" with al Qaeda went far beyond what the CIA had concluded. After the war the *Washington Post* reported that the classified October 2002 National Intelligence Estimate on Iraq that had circulated within the Bush administration weeks before Bush made this claim "portrayed a far less clear picture about the link between Iraq and al Qaeda than the one presented by the president, according to U.S. intelligence analysts and congressional sources who have read the report." The newspaper noted the estimate "contained cautionary language about Iraq's connections with al Qaeda and warnings about the reliability of conflicting reports by Iraqi defectors and captured al Qaeda members about the ties." Bush did not bother to absorb such cautions and warnings.

During Bush's autumn 2002 campaign-of-rhetoric against Iraq, news stories often contained information contradicting his assertions. But Bush officials were not merely misstating facts and interpretations, there were indications they were rigging the government's intelligence and analytic procedures to ease the path to war. David Albright, the director of the Institute for Science and International Security (which wrote a report challenging the administration's view that Iraq's acquisition of aluminum tubes was evidence of an active nuclear weapons program), alleged that government experts who disagreed with the administration's conclusion that the tubes were meant for bomb-making were told to keep quiet.

USA Today—under the headline, "U.S. Assertions Go Beyond Its Intelligence"—reported, "The Bush Administration is expanding on and in some cases contradicting U.S. intelligence reports in making the case for an invasion of Iraq, interviews with administration and intelligence officials indicate." That sounded like Bush was committing fraud. "Some [intelligence] agency officials," the paper noted, "say privately that they do not want to be pushed into going beyond the facts to provide justification for a war. . . . CIA analysts have reported that Saddam wants weapons for prestige and security, not for an attack on U.S. interests that would almost certainly bring a devastating U.S. response." Cheney and Rumsfeld, the newspaper noted, had pressured the CIA to confirm reports that al Qaeda members were "hiding in Iraq with Saddam's blessings." The agency could not. "Nevertheless," the paper said, "Rumsfeld, Cheney and Rice have accepted these reports as accurate." Several weeks later, the *Los Angeles Times* reported a similar story. It noted that "senior Bush administration officials are pressuring CIA analysts to tailor their assessments of the Iraqi threat to help build a case against Saddam Hussein." The paper's sources wagged an accusing finger at Rumsfeld and Wolfowitz.

If there was the slightest truth to the *USA Today* and *Los Angeles Times* articles, they ought to have triggered a scandal. Was intelligence being manipulated to shape the outcome of a public debate that would determine whether American lives would be lost? But these reports caused no outcry. I called both the House and Senate intelligence committees and inquired if either intended to investigate whether Bush officials had attempted to doctor intelligence to improve the administration's case for hitting Hussein. Neither responded. And no inquiry materialized—before the war.

"I think it is probably not a good thing for the United Nations to be laughed at and sneered at and disobeyed and . . . to not be significant enough."

Bush and his aides mischaracterized the nature of the threat. They also were shifty in discussing their intentions and dishonest in discussing options other than war. Democrats in Congress, a few Republicans, and critics (at home and abroad) who feared Bush was heading toward a unilateral attack against Iraq had caused enough of a fuss to compel him to seek support from the United Nations. The result was that on November 8, the U.N. Security Council, after eight weeks of negotiations, unanimously adopted Resolution 1441—based on a revised U.S. draft—which outlined an enhanced U.N. inspections regime for Iraq's disarmament. The Bush administration hailed the vote a success. Bush had gone to the United Nations and won a resolution that tightened the noose around Hussein. See, he did believe in diplomacy, administration officials maintained. He was not a cowboy unilateralist eager for war, as critics charged; he was willing to work with the international community to disarm Iraq. At this point, Bush was maintaining that his primary concern was disarmament—not regime change, not liberating Iraq, not transforming the strategic balance in the Middle East, not projecting U.S. influence in the region, not gaining control of the world's second largest oil reserves, not revenge, not taking care of unfinished business.

But were the Bush officials being truthful? Was Bush willing to give inspections a chance as an alternative to war? Or was he in his own mind already committed to war and disingenuously mounting these U.N. maneuvers to appease critics and assist Tony Blair, whose anti-Hussein alliance with Bush was not widely supported at home?

Administration statements over the previous months had suggested that Bush was not really interested in disarmament-via-inspections, as opposed to disarmament-via-war. Part of the case for war that Bush had been pitching all along was that inspections did not work and that there was no other available course. Bush had not yet come out and declared inspections pointless and war inevitable, but there had been few signals from the White House that it believed in—or wanted—inspections. There were far more indications it desired the removal of

Saddam Hussein. Days before Bush's September 12 U.N. speech, Powell had said, "Disarmament is the issue." But when Cheney was asked whether the goal was "disarmament or regime change," he replied, "The president's made it clear that the goal of the United States is regime change."

Cheney had derided weapons inspections as an effective remedy to the dire situation at hand. At the end of August 2002—while the United Nations was trying to reintroduce weapons inspectors into Iraq—Cheney said in a speech, "A return of inspectors would provide no assurance whatsoever of [Hussein's] compliance with U.N. resolutions [compelling him to disarm]. On the contrary, there is great danger that it would provide false comfort that Saddam was somehow back in his box." And to reinforce his argument, Cheney dishonestly dismissed the work U.N. inspectors had done in Iraq between 1991 and 1998. He referred to the case of General Hussein Kamel, Hussein's son-in-law, who was in charge of Iraq's WMD programs and who defected in 1995 and spilled information on Iraq's weapons programs. "We often learned more as a result of defections than we learned from the inspection regime itself," Cheney said. At the United Nations, Bush, too, suggested that Iraq's biological weapons program had only been discovered because of this defector.*

In a sharp response to Bush's implicit criticism of the inspections process, Rolf Ekeus wrote a piece in the *Washington Post* that noted that the U.N. inspectors' important discovery of Iraq's biological weapons program in 1995 had not been due to Kamel's defection. U.N. inspectors had on their own uncovered Iraq's biological weapons four months before Kamel fled Iraq. "The discovery of Iraq's bioweapons program was the work of smart inspectors, not a godsend," Ekeus maintained. He also noted that U.N. inspectors had found and demolished stockpiles of chemical weapons and (as the IAEA had reported repeatedly) critical technology for uranium enrichment. "Our experi-

*Neither Bush nor Cheney mentioned that when Kamel was debriefed by U.N. inspectors in 1995, he told them, according to a transcript, that weapons inspectors were playing an "important role in Iraq. . . . You should not underestimate yourself. You are very effective in Iraq." He also said, "all chemical weapons were destroyed. I ordered [the] destruction of all chemical weapons. All weapons—biological, chemical, missile, nuclear were destroyed." Perhaps Kamel was lying to mislead or flatter the inspectors. Nevertheless, Cheney and Bush did not share this part of the Kamel episode with the public. *Newsweek* broke the story in late February 2003.

ence from those years," he wrote, "proves beyond doubt that Iraq has the ambition and ability to acquire weapons of mass destruction. But it also shows that international weapons inspectors, if properly backed by international force, can unearth Saddam Hussein's weapons programs."

The Bush administration had not only dismissed the value of inspections, it had equated the call for more inspections with foolish, wishful thinking. During his U.N. speech, Bush falsely depicted the argument against war: "To assume this regime's good faith is to bet the lives of millions and the peace of the world in a reckless gamble." This was an insult to U.S. allies. The influential U.N. members who opposed war at this juncture did not do so on the assumption of Hussein's "good faith." They advocated reviving intrusive inspections and pursuing other means before contemplating war. It was not enough for Bush to mischaracterize his own arguments, he had to do the same to the arguments on the other side. Such dishonest debate conveyed the impression that the only alternative he was willing to accept (at the end of the day) was war.

So the administration's embrace of Resolution 1441 was questionable. The measure specified that Iraq would face "serious consequences" if it did not fully cooperate with the inspections process and disarm. But in a classic diplomatic dodge, "serious consequences" was not defined. Bush could argue later that it meant war. But for the time being there would be a new inspections process—and Bush talked as if he supported it. In a November 20, 2002, speech in Prague, he said, "Our goal is to secure the peace through the comprehensive and verified disarmament of Iraq's weapons of mass destruction." Was he being honest in emphasizing disarmament? Having falsely trumped up the WMD threat from Iraq and Hussein's connections to al Qaeda, Bush did not deserve to be taken at his word about his own intentions. Only he knew what he was truly aiming for.*

The Bush administration also had been disingenuous in professing a desire to enhance the authority of the U.N. As Bush was preparing for

---

*Neoconservative columnist and war-against-Iraq advocate William Kristol, writing after Congress authorized Bush to use force, offered something of a defense for such slipperiness: "The president now becomes a war leader.... [H]is task is not to educate or persuade us. It is to defeat Saddam Hussein. And that will require the president, at times, to mislead rather than to clarify, to deceive rather than to explain."

his U.N. address, Rumsfeld argued, as had other Bush officials, that Hussein must be punished (invaded, that is) for defying previous U.N. resolutions. "I think," Rumsfeld said, "it is probably not a good thing for the United Nations to be laughed at and sneered at and disobeyed and . . . to not be significant enough. . . . And for the United Nations to acquiesce in that, it seems to me, is an unfortunate thing." But the Bush administration had frequently turned its back on the United Nations, opposing the Kyoto protocol on global warming, spurning the International Criminal Court, boycotting a U.N. conference on a comprehensive nuclear test ban treaty, refusing to ratify the U.N. Convention on the Rights of the Child, rejecting a draft U.N. agreement to enforce a biological weapons ban, opposing a U.N. initiative against torture that established an inspections process, and more. Was Rumsfeld—in expressing the Bush White House's supposed concern for the standing of the U.N.—being dishonest or merely insincere?*

"Nobody, but nobody, is more reluctant to go to war than President Bush. . . . He does not want to lead the nation to war."

The final phase of Bush's prewar campaign began with his second State of the Union speech. By then, a new inspections process had started: Iraq had provided weapons inspectors with a 12,000-page declaration claiming it possessed no WMDs, but had failed to account fully for proscribed WMD materials it previously possessed; chief U.N. inspector Hans Blix had called Iraq's statement "not enough to create

---

*That month Rumsfeld, who had been a special envoy to the Middle East in 1983 for the Reagan administration, seemingly told another fib. In late December 1983, he had met with Saddam Hussein in Baghdad as part of a new U.S. tilt toward Hussein. At the time, Iraq was using chemical weapons in its war against Iran. Talking to CNN in September 2003, Rumsfeld claimed he had "cautioned" Hussein about using such weapons. Three months later, the *Washington Post* reported that declassified State Department notes of Rumsfeld's 90-minute chat with Hussein indicated he had not raised the subject. The Pentagon then told the *Post* that actually Rumsfeld had discussed the matter not with Hussein, but with Iraqi Foreign Minister Tariq Aziz. Yet the official records showed that Rumsfeld had merely mentioned Iraq's use of chemical weapons in passing. As a result of Rumsfeld's 1983 sit-down with Hussein, Washington and Baghdad developed closer relations. This led to increased U.S. arms sales to Iraq, including precursors for chemical weapons—even as Hussein's Iraq was engaging in chemical warfare against Iran and the Kurdish resistance.

confidence"; the Bush administration had accused Baghdad of being in "material breach" of Resolution 1441; and Bush had declared "time is running out." Iraq was providing U.N. inspectors access to facilities, and the initial inspections were finding scant evidence of unconventional weapons. But the Bush administration continued to insist that Iraq had weapons of mass destruction that threatened the United States—and that U.S. intelligence had proof of this. Speaking at the Council on Foreign Relations, Wolfowitz asserted, "It is a case grounded in current intelligence, current intelligence that comes not only from sophisticated overhead satellites and our ability to intercept communications, but from brave people who told us the truth at the risk of their lives. We have that; it is very convincing." Still, Fleischer said, "nobody, but nobody, is more reluctant to go to war than President Bush. . . . He does not want to lead the nation to war."

On January 28, 2003—a year after the "axis of evil" speech—Bush, one more time, presented a case against Saddam Hussein. During his State of the Union address, he declared, "America will not accept a serious and mounting threat to our country." He noted that Hussein's government had not fully explained what had happened to biological and chemical weapons or WMD materials it once had. And he ran through a litany of weapons Hussein *could* have: over 25,000 liters of anthrax, over 38,000 liters of botulinum toxin, as much as 500 tons of sarin, mustard and VX nerve agent, and 30,000 or so munitions capable of delivering chemical agents. It was a dramatic way of presenting *possible* threat as a *definitive* threat—without assessing the actual probability this stuff existed and was still potent. And there was more reason to fear: Bush informed the American public that the International Atomic Energy Agency "confirmed in the 1990s that Saddam Hussein had an advanced nuclear weapons development program." This was another brazen attempt to mislead, for Bush had left out the fact that the IAEA maintained it had years ago demolished this "advanced" nuclear program. And the day before Bush's speech, U.N. inspectors had said there were no signs of a vigorous nuclear weapons program in Iraq.

Ignoring the IAEA's past and present findings, Bush pointed to what he maintained was evidence that Iraq was indeed close to a nuclear bomb. He again claimed that Iraq had been caught trying to purchase aluminum tubes "suitable for nuclear weapons production" and that the British government had learned that Hussein recently had attempted to buy "significant quantities of uranium" from Africa. Neither piece of evidence was conclusive; one was apparently based on forgery.

The aluminum tubes issue had come up before; Bush had cited them during his speech to the United Nations in September. In the months since, scientists and intelligence analysts had been debating whether the aluminum tubes were destined for a nuclear program. Three weeks before Bush's State of the Union address, the IAEA had reported the tubes were "not directly suitable" for uranium enrichment but were "consistent" with manufacturing ordinary artillery rockets. CIA analysts, according to media reports, tended to believe the tubes were indeed part of a nuclear program, while Department of Energy experts and State Department officials thought otherwise. (Months later, *Newsweek* reported that Hussein had not been secretly buying the tubes; "the purchase order was posted on the Internet.") And days before the State of the Union speech, the *Washington Post* reported, "There is no evidence so far that Iraq sought other materials" necessary for constructing an uranium enrichment facility. Bush did not concede that the truth about the tubes—whatever it was—was hotly contested. Rather, he presented disputable fact as rock-solid confirmation of an ongoing nuclear program.

The other half of Bush's case—the uranium-from-Africa charge—was not merely disputable, it seemed to have been predicated on a hoax. The British government had first publicly charged in September that Hussein had been seeking uranium in Africa. Then in December, the State Department released a "fact sheet" that claimed Iraq had attempted to purchase uranium from Niger. But weeks after Bush highlighted—and legitimized—this important accusation in his State of the Union address, the IAEA reported that the Niger allegation was phony. It had found that documents supposedly showing that Iraq had tried to acquire uranium in Niger were easy-to-spot fakes. U.S. and British intelligence had obtained these papers and then shared them with the IAEA. As various news accounts noted, one of the documents was signed by Niger's president, but the childlike signature was clearly not his. Another bore the name and signature of a Niger official who had been out of the government for years. Bush made a serious and misleading charge in a presidential speech on the basis of bad information—apparently because the White House had been so eager to win support for war.*

During the State of the Union speech, Bush stuck with his principal—though unproven—argument: Hussein had WMD and was in cahoots with al Qaeda, and this created a risk that had to be countered not with additional or more intrusive inspections, but with war. Bush did observe that war against this brutal dictator would lead to "liberation" for the repressed Iraqi people. But his justification for military action was clearly—and solely—the weapons Hussein supposedly possessed: "If Saddam Hussein does not fully disarm, for the safety of our people and for the peace of the world, we will lead a coalition to disarm him." And Bush promised that in a few days Colin Powell would present information and intelligence to the U.N. about Iraq's weapons program and its links to terrorist groups. He was leaving the heavy lifting to him.

"Iraq is harboring a terrorist network, headed by a senior al Qaeda terrorist planner."

Eight days later, the secretary of state appeared at the Security Council and laid out the government's best case against Iraq. It was the culmination of the administration's yearlong effort to persuade the public to support war in Iraq. Finally, the administration was going to supply proof that Saddam Hussein had terrible weapons and was working with al Qaeda. Yet while Powell—the senior Bush official with the most credibility at the United Nations—offered specific pieces of evidence, he also served up embellished evidence. And he commingled truth with half-truth.

Powell's presentation was a sophisticated PR endeavor that came with a slide show. He played audio tapes indicating Iraqi military personnel had hidden one prohibited (but unspecified) vehicle, had ordered an

---

*Bush's use of the uranium-from-Africa allegation—which had been merely one sentence in the State of the Union speech—months later ignited one of the most intense controversies of his presidency. The firestorm produced conflicting accounts from the administration of whether this line had been based on the Niger charge or other unsubstantiated reports of Iraqi uranium shopping in Africa. But it seemed that the Niger caper had been the piece of most interest to the White House, and the primary evidence regarding that allegation turned out to be forged papers. See Chapter 14.

ammunition site cleaned out before inspectors arrived, and had instructed a commander to remove the words "nerve agents" from wireless communications. He claimed intelligence sources indicated the Iraqi government was hiding documents and moving biological and chemical weapons to keep them from being discovered by U.N. inspectors. Indeed, Powell repeatedly asserted that intelligence—including satellite photography and reports from sources—demonstrated that Saddam Hussein was not just developing weapons of mass destruction, he had them.

Powell displayed a satellite photo of a weapons munitions facility and stated it had been used to store chemical weapons; he pointed out a decontamination vehicle as telltale evidence. He showed another shot of a chemical complex and maintained part of it had been bulldozed and graded to conceal the presence of chemical weapons. He claimed that "we know from sources" that Iraq had dispersed rocket launchers and warheads containing biological warfare agents to various locations in western Iraq and hidden them in large groves of palm trees. He showed the Security Council a diagram of a mobile biological weapons lab that he claimed Iraq had developed and that could produce in a month enough biological agents "to kill thousands upon thousands of people." It was not a diagram of a real unit, but a drawing based on four intelligence sources, including two defectors, one of whom claimed the units worked only on Fridays because the government believed U.N. inspectors would not conduct inspections on the Muslim holy day. As for nuclear weapons, he did not mention the uranium-from-Africa charge, but he pointed to those aluminum tubes. Powell did note there were "differences of opinion . . . about what these tubes are for." But he argued the case for believing they were to be part of a nuclear weapons program, even though the intelligence analysts of his own State Department had concluded it was "far more likely" that the tubes were intended for another purpose. (The view of the State Department analysts was included in a dissent to an intelligence estimate that would not become public until after the war.)

Powell effectively demonstrated that Iraq had not met all its obligations under 1441 and was in "material breach." He painted a grim portrait of an ugly and repressive regime that was out to fool the United Nations. But he did not unveil direct evidence that Hussein currently maintained a deployable and significant WMD arsenal and had a reason and the ability to use it. For example, Powell said, "Saddam Hussein has never accounted for vast amounts of chemical weaponry. . . . Saddam Hussein has chemical weapons." But the absence of an accounting—troubling as it was—did not necessarily mean these weapons existed. Chief U.N. inspector Hans Blix would later say, "To take an example, a document which Iraq provided suggested to us that some 1,000 tons of chemical agent were 'unaccounted for.' I must not jump to the conclusion they exist." Powell supplied no hard data confirming Iraq possessed these unconventional weapons in dangerous supplies. There were no photos of actual weapons, no firsthand reports from sources who could be independently evaluated. So why head straight to war and occupation, rather than try more intrusive inspections?

The administration's response to a question like that was Hussein's purported links to al Qaeda. To bring this point—and the threat—home, Powell claimed a "sinister nexus" existed between Iraq and al Qaeda. And to prove this, he offered details. It was the first time that the administration had presented what appeared to be a serious case regarding its allegations of an ongoing al Qaeda–Iraq partnership.

"Iraq today," Powell said, "harbors a deadly terrorist network headed by Abu Musab al-Zarqawi, an associate and collaborator of Osama bin Laden and his al Qaeda lieutenants." Zarqawi, according to Powell, had overseen a terrorist training camp in Afghanistan specializing in poisons and after the Afghanistan war "the Zarqawi network helped establish another poison and explosives training center camp . . . in northeastern Iraq." He maintained the Zarqawi outfit was teaching its operatives how to produce ricin—a pinch of it will kill you—and other poisons. And he reported that Zarqawi—who had been linked to the murder of a U.S. Agency for International Development official in Jordan the past October—had received medical treatment in Baghdad the previous spring and stayed there for two months. His network, Powell added, had "been operating freely in the capital for more than eight months." This did seem like damning material.

In his U.N. presentation, Powell had made good use of the material he had available. He described patterns of Iraqi behavior that would allow a reasonable person to assume that Hussein had been trying to hide weapons-related equipment, or weapons research programs, maybe even weapons themselves. But much of what Powell said, upon examination, turned out to be overstated or open to dispute—particularly his claim of a "sinister nexus" between Hussein and bin Laden.

In presenting one of his key pieces of evidence, Powell apparently misled his audience at the Security Council. The second audio tape he played was a conversation that had transpired on January 30 in which an officer at the headquarters of Iraq's Republican Guard had issued instructions to an officer in the field. The HQ man informed the other officer that "they are inspecting the ammunition you have for the possibility there is by chance forbidden ammo." Powell maintained that the HQ officer then said, "And we sent you a message yesterday to clean out all the areas. Make sure there is nothing there. Remember the first message: evacuate it." Powell claimed this was proof the Iraqis were concealing weapons of mass destruction from U.N. inspectors. "This is all part of a system of hiding things and moving things out of the way and making sure they have nothing left behind," he said.

But the official State Department transcript of this intercepted conversation varied greatly from Powell's rendition. In the department's version, the headquarters officer reminded the field office, "And we sent you a message to inspect the scrap area and the abandoned areas." He said nothing about cleaning out these areas, nothing about making sure the site was clear. He did not say "evacuate it." This was a significant discrepancy. An order to "inspect" an area that will be examined by U.N. weapons inspectors is not as incriminating as one to "clean out" a site. What accounted for this stark difference? When Gilbert Cranberg, a former editorial page editor of the *Des Moines Register,* asked the State Department's press and public affairs office for an explanation, officials referred him to the department's website. "The material there," he wrote in a piece for the *Washington Post,* "simply confirmed that Powell had misrepresented the intercept."

As for Powell's satellite photos, Jonathan Tucker, a former weapons inspector who specialized in biological and chemical weapons, said they probably did indicate Hussein possessed chemical weapons, but "not huge amounts." Kelly Motz, another weapons specialist, told the *Washington Post* that "on the question of whether Iraq still has an active program, the evidence is still circumstantial and open to interpretation." Tucker was also dubious about those bioweapons labs on wheels. "The sources apparently were defectors, who have not always been reliable or credible," he said, adding, "I would be more comfortable if there were photos." Another former weapons inspector, Raymond Zilinskas, who was a microbiologist, said to the *Post* that the 24-hour,

Fridays-only production cycles Powell had mentioned were insufficient for cooking up significant levels of anthrax or other pathogens. "You normally would require 36 to 48 hours just to do the fermentation," he said. "The short processing time seems suspicious to me." He and other experts said that Powell's schematic drawing represented a theoretically possible design but that workable mobile labs presented significant challenges, such as waste disposal. "This strikes me as a bit far-fetched," Zilinskas remarked. (After the war, the bioweapons labs would take on much significance, and the administration would still not have a solid case.)

Powell had stretched the most when he portrayed Zarqawi as the missing link between Hussein and al Qaeda. Newspaper articles that appeared before and after his slide show seriously undermined this assertion. The *Washington Post* interviewed European officials and U.S. terrorism experts and reported that "Powell's description" of this link "appeared to have been carefully drawn to imply more than it actually said." Judith Yaphe, a senior fellow at the National Defense University who worked for 20 years as a CIA analyst, observed, "You're left to just hear the nouns, and put them together."

The Baghdad-Zarqawi connection was unconfirmed. The *Washington Post* noted, "A senior administration official with knowledge of the intelligence information said that evidence had not yet established that Baghdad had any operational control over Zarqawi's network, or over any transfer of funds or materiel to it." The day of Powell's presentation, the newspaper reported that "U.S. intelligence officials have said up to now that they had no direct evidence that Zarqawi met with Iraqi leaders." The *Post* later noted that, according to senior U.S. officials, "although the Iraqi government is aware of the group's activity, it does not operate, control or sponsor it." And three days before Powell's U.N. appearance, the *New York Times* had reported, "Intelligence officials say there is disagreement among analysts about whether there are significant connections between Ansar-al-Islam [the militant Islamic outfit running Zarqawi's supposed poison camp in northeast Iraq] and the Baghdad government."*

*The *New York Times* also reported, "Some analysts at the Central Intelligence Agency have complained that senior administration officials have exaggerated the significance of some intelligence reports about Iraq, particularly about its possible links to terrorism, in order to strengthen their political argument for war."

Zarqawi's link to al Qaeda was also iffy. "Senior administration officials," the *Post* reported, "said that, although Zarqawi has ties to bin Laden's group, he is not under al Qaeda control or direction. 'They have common goals,' one intelligence analyst said, 'but he [Zarqawi] is outside bin Laden's circle. He is not sworn al Qaeda.'" And in testimony to the Senate armed services committee, CIA chief George Tenet said that while Zarqawi had received funds from bin Laden, he and his network were "independent" of al Qaeda.

So the relationship between Hussein and Zarqawi was not so definite, and the connection between Zarqawi and al Qaeda was not so tight. But that had not prevented Powell from exaggerating (or misrepresenting) two sets of ties and using Zarqawi to draw a straight line from Hussein to bin Laden. This disingenuous A-to-B-to-C exercise smacked of desperation. With this performance, Powell stepped over a line. The Bush official who previously had appeared a reluctant warrior, who had fretted over the consequences of a unilateral U.S. move toward war, was now on board Bush's Baghdad express, as he accepted the administration's policy and adopted its truth-bending practices.*

But why should Powell have worried about the hazy and misleading details of his briefing to the Security Council? None of the finer—or truthful—points about the Iraq–bin Laden connection seemed to inconvenience his commander-in-chief. Two days after Powell's showcase at the United Nations, Bush declared that Iraq was "harboring a terrorist network, headed by a senior al Qaeda terrorist planner." Powell had not tagged Zarqawi as an al Qaeda *leader*. But that hadn't stopped Bush from overstating an overstatement. That day, the Pentagon issued formal orders deploying the Army's 101st Airborne Division to the Middle East and sent an additional aircraft carrier to the Persian Gulf.

And when bin Laden in mid-February released a taped message exhorting Muslims in Iraq and elsewhere to resist an American invasion, Powell pronounced the tape evidence that the al Qaeda leader was "in partnership with Iraq." This was more desperate dissembling. In his remarks, bin Laden had blasted Hussein's Ba'ath regime as one of "hypocrites," "apos-

---

* *U.S. News & World Report* later reported that when Powell first read over the intelligence material he was to use in his briefing to the Security Council, he junked much of it, calling the material "bullshit."

tates," and socialist "infidels." Muslims, he explained, should fight the "crusaders" for the "cause of Allah," not the sake of Hussein. These comments could not be honestly cited as proof of a "partnership."

With few Democrats willing to challenge Bush on going to war against Iraq—and many supportive of his drive toward invasion—Bush's fact-stretching (or lies) did not become a political issue. But they did bother some pundits and commentators. *New York Times* columnist Thomas Friedman weighed in on February 19, 2003. "I am also very troubled," he wrote, "by the way Bush officials have tried to justify this war on the grounds that Saddam is allied with Osama bin Laden or will be soon. There is simply no proof of that, and every time I hear them repeat it I think of the Gulf of Tonkin resolution. You don't take the country to war on the wings of a lie. Tell people the truth. Saddam does not threaten us today. He can be deterred. Taking him out is a war of choice—but it's a legitimate choice." Bush, though, did not take this unsolicited advice. In a February 26 speech, he said, "The safety of the American people depends on ending this direct and growing threat [from Iraq]." He noted that "acting against this danger" would contribute to stability in the Middle East and benefit the repressed population of Iraq. But the primary reason to go to war was to protect the nation.

"America tried to work with the United Nations to address this threat because we wanted to resolve this issue peacefully."

By the start of March the endgame was ending. Blix and ElBaradei had released mixed progress reports on the ongoing inspections in Iraq. Hussein had agreed "in principle" to inspectors' demand that Iraq demolish its Al Samoud 2 missiles, which exceeded a 150-kilometer limit. And Bush, who had been sending troops to the region for months, was on a very public and bitter collision course with members of the Security Council. His administration had been pushing for a new Security Council resolution mandating military action; France, Germany, and others had been urging an enhanced inspections process. On March 5, France, Germany, and Russia announced they would "not allow" a new resolution on military action. At a prime-time news conference on March 6—only the eighth news conference of his presidency—Bush repeated many of the unproven assertions and misrepresentations of the previous year. Hussein, he said, possessed weapons of terror (no specifics mentioned); funded, trained, and protected terrorists "who would willingly use weapons of mass destruction against America"; and posed a "direct threat" to the United States.

In the post-9/11 world, any possibility of a brutal dictator with anti-American sentiments acquiring nuclear, biological, and chemical weapons had to be considered worrisome and worthy of a vigorous response. Bush and his crew were right about one crucial matter: one could not assume that the absence of evidence (of weapons of mass destruction) was the same thing as evidence of the absence (of WMDs). The U.S. government has an obligation to identify potential foes and potential attacks and develop the means to neutralize them early. Perhaps it might even be prudent in some circumstances to move against such threats before undeniable proof can be obtained, more so if the targets are known murderers, torturers, and thugs who do not deserve the benefit of the doubt. One could have argued that while the actual danger posed by Hussein (and whatever weapons he *might* possess or *might* develop) was difficult to assess, the United States could not risk guessing wrong.

Bush's problem was that a case for war based on the *potential* threat from Iraq was, obviously, not as compelling as a case predicated on an immediate threat. If a nation faces a possible danger, it has the luxury of weighing—and debating—various aspects of going to war: the moral legitimacy of the action, how other governments and populations will react, the possible consequences and costs, and, most importantly, the alternatives. Bush and his officials consistently refused to engage in any public discussions about the war's costs. Much of this sort of deliberation though, could be shoved aside if the United States were confronting a clear-and-present danger. Consequently, Bush pumped up the threat—depicting it in stark and melodramatic but inaccurate terms—in order to transform a judgment call into an imperative and to make the need for war immediate.*

---

*"There are very good reasons to end Saddam Hussein's brutal reign over Iraq but terrorism is not one of them," Daniel Benjamin and Steven Simon, who were in charge of counterterrorism at the National Security Council in the late 1990s, write in *The Age of Sacred Terror*. "There is little or no history of cooperation between Iraq and al Qaeda." They add, "There is little evidence that state sponsors like Iraq and Iran provided al Qaeda with meaningful assistance."

Highlighting—if not contriving—the threat from Hussein's WMDs, Bush argued there was no time to wait, no time to try alternatives to all-out war. He and his officials refused to entertain the possibility of coercive inspections—that is, inspections backed by military force. (This could have included imposing a no-fly zone across almost all of the country, or mounting military raids against suspected WMD sites.) In this vein, at the March 6 press conference, Bush said—as he had before—"The risk of doing nothing, the risk of hoping that Saddam Hussein changes his mind and becomes a gentle soul, the risk that somehow that inaction will make the world safer is a risk I'm not willing to take for the American people."

With this statement, Bush was presenting a dishonest dichotomy: war or nothing. If that was the choice, war might have been unavoidable. Yet the nations opposing Bush's push for war—France, Germany, Canada—had proposed other responses involving more aggressive and intrusive inspections. Most opponents of a war against Iraq at this time pointed out that inspections had worked to constrain and contain Hussein in the 1990s and could do so again—even if Hussein did not fully cooperate. The real choice—which Bush refused to recognize—was invasion or beefed-up inspections. He was free to explain why he believed tighter and more coercive inspections would not work. Instead, he dismissed his opposition by untruthfully suggesting it was naively counting on Hussein's transformation into a saint. This was one of the critical distortions he wielded to sell his war.

Bush also claimed the war was necessary to preserve the relevance of the United Nations. Was this an honest argument? U.N. Security Council Resolution 1441 promised there would be "serious consequences" if Hussein did not comply with its disarmament orders. It had not defined those consequences. Yet Bush was saying that unless the Security Council embraced *his* definition—war right now—it was a pointless body. "The credibility of the Security Council is at stake," he maintained. But what if the Security Council had decided to toughen up the inspections and conduct them for another five months? Why would that be evidence of meaninglessness? It was Bush who was placing the Security Council in a position of irrelevance by threatening to go to war over its objections.

On March 7, Britain introduced a U.S.-supported measure that would basically authorize war if Iraq failed to demonstrate its unconditional commitment to disarmament by March 17. France signaled it would veto such a measure and then Russia joined in the veto threat. If Bush attacked Iraq, it would be a war unsanctioned by the United Nations.

In the last days of the prewar period, Bush and his team piled it on. Appearing on *Meet the Press* on March 16, Cheney proclaimed Hussein was "trying once again to produce nuclear weapons and we know that he has a long-standing relationship with various terrorist groups, including the al Qaeda organization." He added, "We believe [Hussein] has, in fact, reconstituted nuclear weapons." Cheney may have meant to say "nuclear weapons programs." But in either case, he was making a claim the administration could not back up. On March 7, IAEA director ElBaradei had stated, "After three months of intrusive inspections, we have to date found no evidence or plausible indication of the revival of a nuclear weapons program in Iraq." The White House did not even bother at this point to produce any new information to challenge the IAEA findings or to corroborate these same-old disputable assertions. (A long-standing relationship with al Qaeda?) Cheney also said without hesitation, "We will, in fact, be greeted as liberators."

The next day Bush, in an address to the nation (and the world), gave Hussein 48 hours to get out of town. It was a declaration of war, and it was draped with the usual disinformation. Speaking from the Cross Hall of the White House, Bush said, "Intelligence gathered by this and other governments leaves no doubt that the Iraq regime continues to possess and conceal some of the most lethal weapons ever devised." *No doubt*—those were Bush's words. Unequivocal. Unambiguous. Bush was telling the public he knew for sure. He had undeniable proof. He raised the specter of Hussein passing nuclear weapons to an al Qaeda "aided, trained, and harbored" by Iraq. "The danger," Bush solemnly said, "is clear: using chemical, biological, or, one day, nuclear weapons, obtained with the help of Iraq, the terrorists could . . . kill thousands or hundreds of thousands of innocent people in our country." War was necessary to defeat this threat. And Bush claimed that a liberated Iraq would "set an example to all the Middle East of a vital and peaceful and self-governing nation" and "advance liberty and peace in the region."*

"America, " Bush remarked, "tried to work with the United Nations to address this threat because we wanted to resolve this issue peacefully." But was that the truth? His so-called diplomacy at the United Nations had been focused on winning Security Council support for a U.S.-led invasion. He had not considered other options, and in his public statements—including this one—he refused to acknowledge that actions short of invasion and occupation had ever been proposed.

Bush's final pre-war remarks capped off a deceptive campaign that had been fueled by unsubstantiated, inaccurate, untruthful, or misleading statements about Iraq's WMD arsenal, Saddam Hussein's supposed links to al Qaeda (and 9/11), Hussein's intentions, the Bush administration's intentions, and the alternatives to war. And none of this had been a secret. The day after Bush issued his ultimatum, the *Washington Post* published a piece on page A13 that began, "As the Bush administration prepares to attack Iraq this week it is doing so on the basis of a number of allegations against Iraqi President Saddam Hussein that have been challenged—and in some cases disproved—by the United Nations, European governments and even U.S. intelligence reports." The headline was damning: "Bush Clings to Dubious Allegations About Iraq." Bush's road to Baghdad—whether the war was justified or not—had been paved with lies. The next evening, about 90 minutes after Bush's deadline expired, U.S. forces began bombing Iraq.

---

*A classified State Department report revealed days earlier by the *Los Angeles Times* concluded it was unlikely that installing a new government in Iraq would encourage the spread of democracy in the region. The paper found that if some sort of democracy did take root in Iraq—a prospect it deemed improbable—it could well lead to an Islamic-controlled government antipathetic to Washington. Was it possible for Bush to be dishonest by being overly or unduly optimistic?

13. Return of the Tax Policy Cheat

"That sounds fair to me."

At the start of 2003, as Bush was beginning his third year in office, the man once derided for smirkiness and boobery, who won the White House because a Democratic Party official in Palm Beach botched a ballot design, who seemed a good bet to join his father in the Single-Term Wing of the Hall of Presidents, who was dismissed as a rube by leaders overseas, now stood as the most powerful—and perhaps the most unfettered—president in recent history. In the wake of September 11, Bush expanded the authority of the presidency and the federal government he oversaw (military tribunals, secret detentions and the like). He increased official secrecy. He was prosecuting a mostly clandestine war against terrorism, which even included—on at least one known occasion—the CIA covertly assassinating suspected enemies with remote-controlled drones in Yemen. He had claimed the right—with Congress's assent—to declare war on Iraq on his own and, with little political opposition (within the United States), was leading the country toward an invasion and occupation in the Middle East. The previous fall, by dauntlessly campaigning like a partisan zealot, Bush had thwarted a historical trend favoring the Democrats and had practically single-handedly won control of both the Senate and the House for the Republicans.

He was standing tall. But the economy was not. In the past two years, 2 million Americans had lost their jobs. The unemployment rate was nearing 6 percent. An era of federal budget surpluses had turned into one of deficits. And that dramatic turnaround could not be blamed entirely on 9/11. Bush's first set of tax cuts were partly responsible for the expanding deficits, and these tax cuts had not led to much in the way of economic growth. The economy had expanded by just 0.3 percent in the previous quarter.

Bush remained a popular wartime (of sorts) president, but public opinion polls showed that his handling of the economy did not generate sweeping popular confidence. For the sake of his political future, he had to demonstrate that while he was waging his war on terrorism abroad he could redress the nation's woes at home. The previous December Bush had implicitly acknowledged that his management of the economy could stand improvement when he dumped his economic team—Treasury Secretary Paul O'Neill and Chief Economic Adviser Larry Lindsey. But even though he canned Lindsey and O'Neill, Bush was not about to alter the main course of his economic policy. With the economy still in a slump, he held fast to his favorite answer to any economic question: tax cuts, tax cuts, tax cuts. And he proposed a second round of tilted-to-the-rich tax cuts much larger than expected. To sell them, Bush would again reach for the tools that had served him well during the first tax-cut battle: fibs, fabrications, and fuzzy numbers.

"This growth and jobs package [will] provide an immediate boost to the economy."

Bush's new set of tax cuts—a brazen package—was the lead element of an aggressive policy assault waged on various fronts. Bush's budget bean counters were clamping down on domestic spending, cutting environmental protection, public housing, and family literacy programs. For his 2004 budget proposal, Bush was slashing $300 million—18 percent—from the Low-Income Heating and Energy Assistance Program. (In 2000, he had said he would "make sure we fully fund LIHEAP." The New York *Daily News* now called him "our icicle-in-chief.") He even proposed cutting 5 percent for the No Child Left Behind Act, the education program that supposedly was his signature domestic social initiative. Congress had authorized $32 billion for the program; Bush wanted to devote $22.6 billion to it. Democrats howled he was breaking a promise to supply sufficient funding. Bush was also preparing to return to the Senate several controversial court nominees rejected the previous year by the Democrats. The man who had once vowed (incessantly), "I'm a uniter, not a divider," seemed to have adopted a new motto: "In your face!"

No more so than with his tax cuts, which he unveiled on January 7 at the Economic Club of Chicago. The $726 billion, ten-year proposal was bolder and twice as big as most political and economic observers had anticipated. It included immediately implementing tax cuts passed in his first package but scheduled for 2004 and 2006 and speeding up the planned expansion of the child tax credit, which also had been part of Bush's first round of tax cuts. Its most controversial, surprising, and expensive provision called for eliminating most taxes on stock dividends. This one measure accounted for half of the entire plan. Bush also proposed boosting the amount of expenses a small firm could write off, expanding the bottom tax rate, and reducing the so-called marriage penalty ahead of schedule. (His proposal also provided for some extra unemployment benefits and devoted about one-half of 1 percent of its total to a new program setting up accounts for unemployed workers searching for work.) Considering the package's tremendous cost and its timing—deficits at hand, the military preparing for war, and homeland security costs increasing dramatically—this was a brash move on Bush's part.

At the speech in Chicago, Bush hailed the benefits of his tax proposal. It would allow middle-income Americans to keep an average of nearly $1,100 more in 2003. Eliminating the tax on dividends would assist seniors. This "growth and jobs package" would provide "an immediate boost to the economy," and the "need for this plan" was "urgent." These statements ranged from unduly hopeful to outright dishonest.

Bush's main argument for the plan was that it would invigorate the economy. But most of the package was slated to kick in after 2003 and had little to do with this "urgent" task. By Bush's own calculations, $98 billion of his $726 billion proposal—13.5 percent—would go to reducing taxes in 2003. The Center on Budget and Policy

Priorities estimated that more than 90 percent of the tax cuts' costs would not be incurred until after 2003. Could these near-term tax cuts—which at most equaled less than 1 percent of the size of the economy—be expected, as Bush said, to energize the economy? Material prepared by the White House Council of Economic Advisers, Bush's own experts, indicated, according to the *New York Times*, that the "main purpose" of the tax proposal "was not to fix the economy's current weakness but rather to advance a longer-term agenda of reducing taxes and increasing future growth." The newspaper added, "No matter what the costs, the White House estimates confirm the opinion of most outside economists that Mr. Bush's tax plan would do little to help the economy this year."

Yet that was not how Bush promoted the package. He did not say, I'm against quick fixes and here is a long-term restructuring. Instead, he advertised the plan as economic help for the here and now. The White House claimed that this initial boost would create 190,000 jobs in 2003. That was better than no new jobs, but not a large number relative to the overall workforce. And if the first year of these new tax cuts had actually been designed for job creation, it would mean that Bush was proposing to spend $500,000 in tax cuts for each job created.

"Ninety-two million Americans will keep an average of $1,083 more of their own money."

By now it was old hat. If Bush was pushing a tax plan, he would describe it as deliverance for the middle class. This time out, Bush's most manipulative swipe at the truth came when he said, "These tax reductions will bring real and immediate benefits to middle-income Americans. Ninety-two million Americans will keep an average of $1,083 more of their own money." The Tax Policy Center found that, contrary to Bush's assertion, nearly 80 percent of tax filers would receive less than $1,083, and almost half would pocket less than $100. The truly average taxpayers—those in the middle of the income range—would receive on average $265.

As he had done during the debate over his first tax cuts, Bush was using the word "average" in a flim-flam fashion. To concoct the misleading $1,083 figure, the administration took the large dollar amounts high-income taxpayers would receive and added that to the modest, small, or non-existent reductions middle- and low-income taxpayers would get—and then used this total to calculate an average gain. His claim was akin to saying that if a street had nine households led by unemployed individuals but one with an earner making a million dollars, the *average* income of the families on the block would be $100,000. Mathematically true, but a meaningless calculation.

The $1,083 average—which Bush and his lieutenants would repeat in the months ahead—was a statistic designed to create a false impression, to provide Bush cover from the inevitable criticism that he was again favoring the well-to-do with a package mostly benefiting big-money earners. It was, for all intents and purposes, a lie.*

In another sly maneuver, Bush and the White House stressed that the dividend tax elimination (estimated cost: $364 billion) would be a boon for the elderly. In his speech introducing the proposal, Bush said, "For the good of our senior citizens . . . I'm asking the United States Congress to abolish the double taxation of dividends." But this reduction, too, was weighted toward the wealthy, since almost two-thirds of all stock, according to the *Washington Post*, was owned by households that earn over $100,000 a year. It was true, as Bush suggested, that the elderly *as a group* would make out well with a dividend exemption. The Tax Policy Center estimated that 41 percent of the benefits of this provision would wind up with people over 65. But most of that money would go to *well-off* seniors. Forty percent of it would land in the bank accounts of the wealthiest 2.5 percent of the elderly (those with incomes above $200,000); almost three-quarters would go to the top one-fifth ($75,000 and above). This was not a plan to help struggling seniors. As the Center on Budget and Policy Priorities observed, "Most elderly have fairly low incomes and would receive little or nothing from this tax cut."

---

*Bush would also use this averaging device to make his plan seem swell for small businesses. In a radio address, he claimed that his proposal would "give 23 million small business owners an average of $2,042 this year." Yet in the real world (as opposed to the world of averages), 79 percent of tax filers with small business income would receive less than this "average" amount, according to the Tax Policy Center. About half of these filers would receive $500 or less. A fifth would get nothing.

All in all, Bush's proposed "relief" was another bonanza for the rich. The Tax Policy Center estimated that nearly 60 percent of the tax cuts would end up in the hands of the top 10 percent of taxpayers (people with incomes above $100,000). It noted that two-thirds of the benefits from the jumbo-sized dividend tax cut would flow to the top 5 percent. Citizens for Tax Justice figured that the top fifth ($77,000 and more) would pocket 77 percent in 2003 and the top 1 percent ($374,000 plus) would bag about a third. The bottom 60 percent ($46,000 and below) would receive 8.5 percent. Put another way, individuals earning between $16,000 and $29,000 a year would net about $99, according to Citizens for Tax Justice. Those making above $374,000 would pick up $30,127. And taxpayers with incomes over a million dollars would receive about $90,000, the Tax Policy Center calculated. The radical *Wall Street Journal* reported, "Overall, the gains from the taxes are weighted toward upper-income taxpayers."*

"Oh sure, you hear the typical class warfare rhetoric, trying to pit one group of people against another."

Bush knew he would be assaulted for advocating yet more tax cuts for the rich while including in the 2004 budget reductions in social programs that generally assist low- and middle-income Americans. Days before he announced his tax plan, he launched a preemptive strike, telling reporters he expected his foes would try "to turn this into class warfare." Bush's stance provoked a natural question: why was handing out more tax cuts to the rich than to middle- and low-income people *not* an act of class warfare, but merely noting who would gain the most *was* class warfare. The task of explaining that fell to Ari Fleischer.

Two days after the tax package was released, a reporter at the daily White House briefing asked why Bush was accusing critics of the tax

---

*The White House chief economist, Glenn Hubbard, argued that cutting income tax rates for the wealthiest was a smart move because half of the top 1 percent are small-business owners who would spend and invest more if their taxes were reduced. Yet Alan Binder, a Clinton administration economist, told the *Wall Street Journal* that the 1990s demonstrated this was not necessarily so. Clinton raised the top rate in 1993, and business investment boomed throughout the rest of the decade.

cuts of practicing class warfare. Fleischer answered, "Well, I'll tell you, it's class warfare to say that there are wrong people in America and these wrong people are not deserving of tax relief. The president doesn't look at the American people and say, I'm from the government, I know who the right people are—I'm from the government, I know who the wrong people are. The president believes that's a divisive approach."

But the president was indeed declaring, "I'm from the government, and I know who the right people are." He was saying that the "right people"—those deserving of the biggest chunk of "relief"—were taxpayers who held stocks that pay out dividends, as opposed to those who held other investments or no investments. Pressed further on the class-warfare business, Fleischer maintained, "It's inaccurate to say that the benefits will go to the wealthy" and that "because it's inaccurate, [this criticism] is used in . . . a way to divide and to play class warfare, in an effort to portray some Americans as unworthy of tax relief and other Americans as worthy of tax relief based on their class."

How could Fleischer claim that a plan that ended most dividend taxes and lowered the top income tax rates did not reward the well-to-do? Well, he did. He did not offer any statistical evidence to counter the distribution analyses of the Tax Policy Center or Citizens for Tax Justice. And by Fleischer's own standard, since Bush had focused on income taxes as opposed to payroll taxes, it could be said that Bush was deeming low-income workers (who do not earn enough to pay income taxes but who are socked by payroll taxes) as Americans "unworthy of tax relief."

Fleischer even managed, by accident, to make a strong argument against Bush's plan. "Let me address," he said, "one thing about why this issue about who benefits from tax cuts, I think, is such a different issue in Washington than it is in the real world. If you make $30,000 a year, and you pay, for example, $2,000 in taxes, and you receive a $1,000 tax cut, you just received a 50 percent cut in your taxes. A thousand dollars to somebody who makes $30,000 a year means all the world to them. . . . Take somebody toward the top end of the scale, somebody who makes $200,000, and they pay $50,000 in taxes. . . . They receive a tax cut that in dollar amounts may be larger than somebody who receives less. To them, that tax cut won't change their life as much as it does somebody who doesn't earn as much. Their life will change more so, more beneficially, than somebody toward the top."

But instead of the $1,000 tax to which Fleischer referred, the average $30,000-a-year earner would receive about $200 from these tax cuts in 2003. Moreover, Fleischer was conceding that the big earners would not see their lives drastically changed by what he and Bush insisted on calling tax relief. So why bother sending them hundreds of billions of dollars at a cost of adding to the deficits for years to come, forcing spending cuts, and possibly being short of money for homeland security and war?

Appearing at a trucking and warehouse firm in St. Louis to promote his proposed tax cuts, Bush dismissed his critics. "Oh sure, you hear the typical class warfare rhetoric, trying to pit one group of people against another." As he spoke, Bush stood in front of a wall of cardboard boxes stamped "Made in USA." It was a picture-perfect scene, imbued with economic patriotism. One problem: most of the boxes in the warehouse said, "Made in China." Workers preparing for the Bush event had placed tape or white stickers over the "Made in China" stamps and had arranged for the "Made in USA" boxes to be placed behind him.

"We will not deny, we will not ignore, we will not pass along our problems to other Congresses, to other presidents, and other generations."

On January 28, 2003, Bush delivered his second State of the Union speech. He claimed credit for his 2001 tax "relief" package (without explaining why he considered it relief to give most of those tax cuts to the top 5 percent); for the education reform legislation (without mentioning the extensive criticism the law had recently received from state officials and education experts worried about its real-world consequences); for the creation of a new Department of Homeland Security (without recalling his initial stubborn opposition to the birth of this superbureaucracy); and for a white-collar-crime crackdown (without referring to the White House's efforts to water down the corporate-crime bill). He ran through a list of policy initiatives—criminalizing late-term abortions, a global anti-AIDS effort,* a research program for a hydrogen-powered car—but he zeroed in on the war against Iraq and the new tax proposal, recycling critical but dubious claims about his tax cuts.

And he was dishonest on other domestic policy fronts. Seniors, Bush asserted, should be able to keep their Medicare coverage "just the way it is"—that is, be permitted to stay with the doctor of their liking—and have the "choice" of a health-care plan that provides a prescription drugs benefit. But according to a variety of media reports, at that time the Bush White House was planning to offer a prescription drug plan only to seniors who enrolled in a private HMO or something equivalent. Seniors would then face this "choice": your doctor or your drugs.† Bush also offered a superficial plug for Social Security reform, reprising his misleading campaign assertion that the financial standing of Social Security could be strengthened by taking money out of the system for personal retirement accounts.††

Reaching for eloquence, Bush proclaimed, "We will not deny, we will not ignore, we will not pass along our problems to other Congresses, to other presidents, and other generations. We will confront them with focus and clarity and courage." Except for at least one issue: the federal deficit.

---

*Bush pledged to spend $15 billion over five years on the AIDS initiative, with much of the money going to Africa. Activists in the anti-AIDS field assumed this meant $3 billion a year. But six months later, the White House opposed legislation funding the program at that level. Instead, it called for spending $2 billion, claiming that was all the money that could be used efficiently.

†Weeks after the speech, administration officials, stunned by the criticism their Medicare prescription drug proposal had drawn, released a revised plan. Under this scheme, seniors could stay in the traditional Medicare program and receive prescription benefits. But these benefits would be limited. Seniors who joined a managed-care plan would be given more comprehensive drug coverage.

††One of the Bush administration's more blatant lies had involved Social Security. In July 2002, Fleischer said, "The president does, of course, believe that younger workers who right now are going to receive no money for their Social Security taxes that are taken out of their paycheck deserve to have more options." No money? That was not so. According to then-current estimates, the Social Security trust fund would not be exhausted until 2041 (provided that no steps were taken to bolster the program). Anyone retiring before then could expect to receive full benefits. And after that crunch point, the program would still be able to pay 73 percent of benefits, and 66 percent by 2076. There would be a shortfall, but a gap is quite different than zilch. Fleischer was continuing a Bush tradition: create a false panic about Social Security in order to build support for privatization.

■ ■ ■

Unlike the tax-cuts debate of 2001, the 2003 sequel was occurring within a budgetary environment shaped by deficits and a whole new set of costly federal obligations. In 2001, Bush had argued his tax cuts would be covered by the surplus. Now Bush officials readily conceded that he was proposing big tax cuts at a time of deficits. But their attitude was, No big deal, and, besides, it's not our fault. The first half of this defense was arguably a matter of opinion (though the Bush administration offered its opinion in a deceptive fashion); the second half was a falsehood.

On January 7, 2003, White House Budget Director Mitch Daniels summed up the administration's position: "The president places a very high priority on limiting and eliminating deficits, but there are some circumstances forced on him that created these deficits in the first place: a war that came to us a year-plus ago, the need to defend the homeland in ways we never have had to before, and now, as the president sees it, the need to turn a moderate recovery into a strong recovery. And those priorities simply come first in his eyes." A week later, Daniels observed that budget deficits would exist for the "foreseeable future," but he assured they would be "modest." Early the following month, Bush declared, "My administration firmly believes in controlling the deficit and reducing it as the economy strengthens and our national security interests are met." He noted, "A recession and a war we did not choose have led to the return of deficits." The deficits, he was saying, were due to events beyond his control.

This excuse was in keeping with something of a joke Bush had repeated several times the previous year. "You know," he would say, "when I was campaigning in Chicago in the general election, somebody said, 'Would you ever deficit spend?' I said, only if we were at war, or if there was a national emergency, or we were in a recession. Little did I realize we'd get the trifecta." The line often earned a laugh for Bush. But reporters could not find a trace of Bush having uttered this "trifecta" remark during the 2000 campaign. On *Meet the Press* in June 2002, Tim Russert said, "We have checked everywhere and we've even called the White House as to when the president said that when he was campaigning in Chicago, and it didn't happen." Bush, it appeared, had made up a story to defend himself. The *Post* managed to discover a similar comment from a 1998 speech: "Barring an economic reversal, a national emergency, or a foreign crisis, we should balance the budget this year, next year, and every year." But those words had been spoken by Vice President Al Gore.

The "trifecta" line was part of a dishonest Bush attempt to backtrack. During the presidential campaign and in the months of his presidency before September 11, Bush had proclaimed that he would steer clear of deficits and not touch the Social Security surplus. But his first tax cuts, according to the Congressional Budget Office, had contributed to the return of the federal deficit *before* September 11, 2001. After 9/11, though, Bush opportunistically blamed the deficit on that tragedy.

He even claimed that without his tax cuts, the deficit would be worse. On November 13, 2002, he remarked, "We have a deficit because tax revenues are down. Make no mistake about it, the tax relief package that we passed . . . has helped the economy, and . . . the deficit would have been bigger without the tax relief package."

That was not what the Congressional Budget Office had said. And when Bush in early January 2003 introduced his new tax-cuts proposal, he made a similar point, asserting the cuts will lead to "higher revenues for the government." Fleischer said the next day that due to these "additional revenues" the tax-cuts package will "pay for itself."

Welcome to the return of supply-side economics. Bush, the son of the man who once ridiculed Reagan's policies as "voodoo economics," was now championing a central tenet of Reaganomics—lower tax rates will yield more revenues. Contending that Bush was behaving in a fiscally responsible manner, his aides claimed that less (in terms of tax rates) would produce more (in terms of tax revenues). So there was no need to fret about Bush's tax cuts adding to the deficit.

In the midst of Bush's Reaganomics revival, the Spinsanity.org website keenly noticed that the 2003 *Economic Report of the President,* released by Bush's Council of Economic Advisors, contradicted this high-flying, don't-worry rhetoric. In the dry language of economists, the study stated, "The modest effect of government debt on interest rates does not mean that tax cuts pay for themselves with higher output. Although the economy grows in response to tax reductions (because of higher consumption in the short run and improved incentives in the long run), it is unlikely to grow so much that lost tax revenue is completely recovered by the higher level of economic activity." Translation: supply-side fantasies were just that. Bush's own economists were saying that cutting taxes would not lead to the greater revenues Bush Inc. was promising. Who was not telling the truth?

"Give [Bush] a choice between Wall Street and Main Street and he'll choose Main Street every time."

As Bush campaigned for his new round of tax cuts, the lies kept piling up. Two weeks after Bush premiered his plan, Karl Rove, in a meeting with reporters, said Bush's proposed repeal of the dividend tax was aimed at "the little guy." But a revised Tax Policy Center analysis maintained that 70 percent of the benefits would go to the top 5 percent ($133,000 and above). Rove, though, did not address that analysis. Instead, he hailed his boss as a populist: "Give him a choice between Wall Street and Main Street and he'll chose Main Street every time."

As proof, Rove maintained that 45 percent of all dividend income goes to people making $50,000 or less. If that were true, then eliminating the dividend tax could be regarded as a lift for the little guy. But on the facts, Rove was not even close. Forty-six percent of all taxpayers who *claimed* dividend income had an income of $50,000 or less. But they only *accounted* for 14.7 percent of all dividend income, according to the Tax Policy Center. The little guys would get a little portion—6.8 percent—of the biggest provision of Bush's budget-busting tax plan.

Bush resorted to his own fibs. Defending his call to speed up the reductions in income tax rates scheduled for later years, he denounced Congress for stringing out his 2001 tax cuts over several years. "Congress," he huffed, "decided these were good measures, just that they [had to] phase them in over three or five or seven years. . . . If the tax relief is good five years from now, it makes a lot of sense to put the tax relief in today." But the 2001 tax cuts had been phased in to keep Bush's trillion-dollars-plus package from being even more expensive than it was so it could fit within *his* overall budget framework. And the phase-in had been *his* idea, not Congress's. Here was what Bush had said in early January 2001: "The tax relief package that I talked about in the campaign was phased in based upon projections so that we wouldn't run a deficit." Now he was dishonestly blaming Congress for his own decision.

In late February 2003, Bush and Fleischer cited a survey by "*Blue Chip* economists" that they said concluded the economy would grow 3.3 percent if Bush's tax package was passed. But Randell Moore, editor of the *Blue Chip Economic Forecast,* a monthly newsletter that surveys the nation's top economists, told *Newsday,* "I don't know what [Bush] was citing." He added, "I was a little upset. It sounded like the *Blue Chip Economic Forecast* had endorsed the president's plan. That's simply not the case." The White House insisted Bush's claim had been justified because the *Blue Chip* survey had forecast 3.3 percent growth for 2003 while assuming that "some version" of the Bush package would be enacted that year. But Moore noted that a *Blue Chip* survey taken in January *before* Bush announced his plan had forecast 3.3 percent growth.

There seemed no end to dissembling in defense of tax cuts. Bush argued his tax cuts would produce 1.4 million new jobs by the end of 2004. This was not a lot for an economy that included about 130 million jobs, and that was, historically speaking, a modest figure. The White House's estimate was based on a preliminary analysis contained in a report by the consulting firm Macroeconomics Advisers. "But," the *New York Times* reported, "the White House has never mentioned the caution in the second paragraph of the firm's report. The forecasters predicted that if the tax cuts were not offset within a few years by reductions in government spending, interest rates would rise, private investment would be crowded out, and the economy would actually be worse than if there had been no tax changes." Bush was not proposing long-term spending cuts to offset all his tax cuts. Consequently, the economic experts upon which the White House was relying were predicting Bush's package spelled bad news for the country.

To counter the tilted-to-the-rich criticism, Bush's Treasury Department released figures claiming that under his tax cuts, taxpayers earning $30,000 to $40,000 would receive a whopping 20.1 percent decrease in their income taxes and those in the $40,000 to $50,000 bracket would see a 14.1 percent reduction. The Bush economic team had used this particular form of misleading accounting two years earlier. They knew that percentages can sometimes seem more persuasive than the actual amounts. The *New York Times* explained it well: "The problem with figures like those is that a large percentage of a small amount of money may be less important to a low- or middle-income family's lifestyle than a small percentage of a large amount of money would be to a rich family. For example, a $50 tax cut would be a 50 percent reduction for a household that owed only $100 in taxes to start with, but that small amount of money would not significantly improve the family's well-being." According to the congressional Joint Committee on Taxation, a family with an income of $45,000 would receive a tax reduction of $380 (less than 1 percent of its post-tax income), while a household making $525,000 would receive $12,496 (3 percent of its after-tax income). These numbers were a more accurate reflection than the percentages hawked by the administration. Why didn't Bush stick to the real numbers and tell the public that working-class taxpayers would likely receive a couple hundred dollars and millionaires would pick up tens of thousands of dollars? That probably would have been bad for business.

To beat back another criticism of his so-called jobs-and-growth program—that it did not include assistance for states clobbered by fiscal crises—Bush maintained that the 2004 budget he submitted contained $400 billion worth of grants to states. "That's a 9 percent increase," he said at a National Governors Association meeting. Yet the number-crunchers at the Center on Budget and Policy Priorities found that in the Bush budget grants to state and local government increased only 2.9 percent, without taking into account inflation. And if mandated federal Medicaid funding was removed from the picture—in order to determine if Bush was really responding to the needs caused by the economic downturn—grants to state and local governments *dropped* by 2.8 percent, when adjusted for inflation. Once more Bush stood accused of fudging numbers.

"We didn't squander a surplus. We never had it. It was a forecast. It wasn't real dollars in hand."

What Bush and the White House could not spin away was the incoming tide of red ink. It looked like a tsunami. And despite their assertions that the "trifecta" of 9/11, a war, and a recession was responsible for the deficits, the evidence kept coming in that Bush's obsession with tax cuts was also a significant cause.

In early March 2003, the Congressional Budget Office issued a devastating report. It noted that without Bush's tax and spending plan, the federal government would run almost a $900 billion surplus over ten years. In other words, deficits were not inevitable. Bush was choosing—or creating—them. The numbers the CBO predicted were staggering. *Without* Bush's tax-cuts plan and his spending proposals, the federal deficit for 2003 would be $246 billion—nearly a quarter more than the CBO had predicted just two months earlier. If Bush got lucky and passed his tax cuts and spending proposals, the deficit would hit $287 billion in 2003 and $338 billion in 2004. (The largest U.S. budget deficit until then had been $290 billion in 1992.) As for the big picture, the CBO said that under the Bush-gets-want-he-wants scenario, deficits would continue through 2013, with the U.S. government racking up $1.8 trillion in debt. (None of these projections included the costs that would come from war and occupation in Iraq or a new—and expensive—prescription drug benefit under Medicare, which Bush said he supported.)

A potential disaster lay ahead (and these estimates would soon be eclipsed by much worse numbers). The year 2013 is when the baby boom generation will start to hit retirement, placing a greater burden on the federal budget. If these deficit projections were to come true, the federal government at that point would be burdened by a tremendous amount of debt just as baby boomers begin collecting Social Security and drawing on Medicare. In response to these CBO numbers, economists expressed their fear a fiscal calamity was being set in motion. Yet the White House held tight to its position: the projected deficits were not as important as the task of cutting taxes and creating jobs.

A *Washington Post* editorial slammed Bush for fiscal recklessness. "First, what happened to the surplus?" it asked. Two years earlier, the CBO had predicted a $5.6 trillion, ten-year surplus, which allowed Bush to claim his initial $1.3 trillion tax-cuts package was affordable. At that time, Bush and his tax-cutting allies pooh-poohed the criticism that the surplus projections might not pan out. Now the White House was defending itself with an argument it had once dismissed. "We didn't squander a surplus," John Snow, Bush's second treasury secretary, told Congress. "We never had it. It was a forecast. It wasn't real dollars in hand." Exactly. That had been the critics' point: don't lock in to mega–tax cuts on the basis of budget predictions that might not come to pass. Yet the Bush administration—two years later—was expropriating their opponents' position in order to absolve itself.

And Bush officials continued to refuse to admit that their first tax cuts had anything to do with the current fiscal situation. It was, they claimed, the fault of that darn sluggish economy and, of course, the terrorists. But a report released in early March 2003, by the Committee for Economic Development, a group of mainstream business leaders, stated, "While a substantial portion of the current fiscal deterioration can be blamed on the economy, responsibility for the fiscal set-back in later years lies squarely on the shoulders of policymakers"—and that included the tax-cutters of the Bush administration.

The *Post* observed that the U.S. government's books looked even worse than the CBO's numbers indicated. The $1.8 trillion deficit projected by the CBO, it noted, included a $2.6 trillion Social Security surplus—money that was supposed to be reserved (through accounting devices) for the expanding population of retirees. The non–Social Security deficit would actually be $4.4 trillion. And other factors not considered by the CBO—fixing the Alternative Minimum Tax, the costs of the war in Iraq, realistic estimates of future government spending—only made the projections uglier. How did all this square with Bush's state-of-the-union promise to resort only to "a deficit that will be small and short-term"? It didn't.

A month later—in early April—the CBO revised its 2003 deficit estimate, noting the projection was approaching a record $400 billion. It also said Bush's budget and tax-cuts plans were "unlikely" to improve the economy. The White House simply dismissed the report.*

"Why are they for a little bitty tax relief package? If they believe tax relief is important for job creation, they ought to join us."

Bush's lies did not win over Congress. The Senate voted to preserve a budget opening for tax cuts totaling $350 billion, half the price tag for Bush's proposals. The House settled on a $550 billion figure. Still,

---

*"Congressional Budget Office data," the Center on Budget and Policy Priorities observed, "indicate that in 2003 and 2004, the cost of enacted and proposed [Bush] tax cuts is *more than three times as great* as the cost of war, even when the cost of increases in homeland security expenditures, the rebuilding after September 11, and other costs of the war on terrorism—including action in Afghanistan—are counted as 'war costs,' along with the costs of the military operations and subsequent reconstruction in Iraq."

Bush refused to throttle back on the misrepresentation. In mid-April, he flew out to Ohio to flag his plan. Speaking at a ball-bearing company—which happened to have donated $260,000 to Republican candidates and the GOP during the 2000 elections—he scoffed at the skeptics in Congress: "It seems like to me they might have some explaining to do. If they agree that tax relief creates jobs, then why are they for a little bitty tax relief package? If they believe tax relief is important for job creation, they ought to join us."

That was simplification at its most, well, simple. His foes, including Republicans, had varying reasons for opposing Bush's plan or for preferring a less expensive package of $350 billion—the "little bitty" initiative to which Bush dishonestly referred. For Bush to suggest that tax and fiscal policy were as straightforward as more tax cuts (whatever the cuts) automatically equals more jobs was disingenuous. As Joel Slemrod, a tax economist at the University of Michigan, told the *Washington Post*, under this line of reasoning, Bush could support eliminating all taxes in order to create jobs: "Logically, the statement that more tax cuts are better is certainly wrong." The art of tax policy has always been to ascertain the right mix and levels of taxes. For instance, Joel Prakken of Macroeconomic Advisers (the firm that developed the computer model used by the White House for its job-creation estimates) was now saying that beyond 2007, Bush's tax plan would do more harm than good.

At the Ohio event, Bush repeated his false claim that Congress (not he) had been responsible for phasing in his first tax cuts. He repeated the misleading statistic that seniors receive half of all taxable dividend income. And he said—perhaps the biggest lie of the day—"This nation has got a deficit because we have been through a war." The nation had entered deficit-land before September 11, partly due to Bush's first set of tax cuts. In-the-red spending can have benefits and, at times, be an appropriate course of action, but Bush declined to accept credit for his contribution to the new deficits and to concede that a cost of his tax cuts would be a grim fiscal challenge down the road.

In fending off the charge that his tax cuts would wildly favor the rich, Bush dismissed such criticism as "Washington, D.C., political rhetoric." And to prove his point he painted a false picture of his tax cuts. In one routine speech, he said, "You'll hear all kinds of rhetoric about how this plan is not fair. Well, let me describe to you what it means to the family of four making $40,000 a year. It means their taxes would go from $1,178 a year to $45 a year. . . . That sounds fair to me."

Bush made it seem as if his plan was nothing but gravy for the middle class. Some families could end up pocketing the tax savings he claimed, though most earners in this income range and below would receive less. But the tax cuts that Bush was talking about in his example—increasing the child credit, expanding the 10 percent bracket and reducing the so-called marriage penalty—added up to $157 billion, according to the Center on Budget and Policy Priorities, or less than one quarter of Bush's package. He could have provided this same "relief" to middle- and low-income taxpayers without running up a gargantuan tab. Addressing the fairness issue with the example was dishonest, for Bush's critics were complaining not about these tax cuts but mostly about his call to abolish dividend taxes and to accelerate the upper-bracket rate cuts. Those were the provisions that inflated the costs of the proposal and caused it to benefit the well-off disproportionately.

Bush failed to persuade Congress to stick with his original plan. In the House, GOP leaders crafted a $550 billion bill structured much differently than Bush's proposal. For instance, rather than elimi- nate taxes on dividends, it would lower taxes on dividends and capital gains and would impose short time limits on Bush's more middle-class-oriented tax cuts. But the Republican sponsors of this plan expected that these particular tax cuts would not actually expire. After all, would lawmakers and the president in the future allow middle-class taxes to increase? Establishing the expiration dates was a way of artificially lowering the ten-year cost of the bill. If one assumed these tax cuts would live past their phony sunsets—and most experts assumed this— the actual cost of the bill would be about $1 trillion more than Bush had asked for. And the House plan was even more generous to the wealthy than Bush's package, according to the Tax Policy Center. In response to the House initiative, the Bush administration said half of a dividend income tax cut was not good enough. It wanted it all. And when Senate Republicans settled on a $350 billion tax-cuts bill that included a downsized version of the dividend tax exemption, Fleischer commented, "Insufficient, but it's progress."

On May 9, 2003, the House Republicans passed the $550 billion tax-cuts legislation 222 to 203. Six days later, the Senate Republicans, 51 to 49, passed their $350 billion plan, which included more generous tax breaks for corporations and investors. But the Republican senators, like their House colleagues, had resorted to arithmetic artifice. Their bill called for its dividend tax cut and other provisions to expire in 2007. But no one believed these deadlines would stick, either. That meant the real cost of the measure would be closer to $700 billion. "It is a measure of how far fiscal discipline has slipped," complained Robert Bixby, executive director of the Concord Coalition, a budget watchdog group, "that the Senate would even consider such hocus-pocus in the wake of the Enron accounting scandal."

But with Bush's blessing, the House and Senate Republicans started to hammer out a compromise, and on May 23 each body passed a $320 billion tax-cuts package, with Cheney casting the deciding vote in the Senate. Most dividends and capital gains would be taxed at 15 percent, with this provision comprising almost half of the package. Income tax rate reductions would be accelerated. Middle-income families would get a $400 check for each child, due to expanding the child credit. Businesses would be able to write off more expenses. The so-called marriage penalty would be reduced. But using a host of sunset gimmicks, the GOPers managed to disguise what would likely be the real cost of the plan: at least $800 billion, and possibly $1 trillion. And most of the tax cuts would wind up with the wealthy. According to the Center on Budget and Policy Priorities, taxpayers with incomes over a million dollars would receive $93,500 in 2003; half of U.S. households would get $100 or less. And in an appropriate coincidence, the day the bill was passed, the Senate approved raising the nation's $6.4 trillion debt ceiling by almost $1 trillion—the biggest boost in history. With these tax cuts, the U.S. government was probably going to need that line of credit.

"This is a Congress which is able to identify problems facing the American people and get things done."

Bush had previously derided a $350 billion package as "little bitty." But he called the final $320 billion bill "good for American workers, it is good for American families." Perhaps he was comforted by the fact that the bill would really end up costing over $800 billion. "This is a Congress," he said, "which is able to identify problems facing the American people and get things done." Whatever the merits of enacting these tax cuts in the face of widening deficits—would reducing taxes on capital gains and dividend income for the wealthy lead to more jobs?—congressional Republicans had engaged in deception. They had failed to acknowledge and confront the real costs of their legislation, and Bush embraced this shiftiness, which reflected his own rig-the-books approach to tax policy.

He also kept ducking the fiscal consequences of the tax cuts. After the bill passed, he remarked, "I will also work with Congress to bring down the budget deficit that has resulted from war, recession, and terrorist attacks. Faster growth in the economy will bring more revenues into the federal treasury." Once more, he was blaming only the "trifecta" for the deficits and claiming—against the views of his own economic experts and many others—that his tax cuts would lead to more tax revenues. The *Financial Times* was aghast: "The long-run costs of financing huge U.S. fiscal deficits, which stretch far into the future, will weigh heavily on future generations. With little of the tax cut having an immediate effect, the necessary short-run economic stimulus will be negligible. . . . The lunatics are now in charge of the asylum. Including 'sunsetting' provisions to cut the ten-year cost of the tax measures is an insult to the intelligence of U.S. people. . . . In response to this onslaught, there is not much the rational majority can do: reason cuts no ice; economic theory is dismissed; and contrary evidence is ignored."

When Bush signed the tax cuts, he lauded the package as one that "will deliver substantial tax relief to 136 million American taxpayers. We are helping workers who need more take-home pay. We're helping seniors who rely on dividends. . . . We're helping families with children who will receive immediate relief." No mention, though, of millionaires. Bush made it appear as if the worst-off taxpayers were getting the most. But half of all taxpayers would receive $100 or less. (Is that a "substantial" amount?) Much of the dividend "relief" would wind up with higher-income seniors. As for relieving families with children, after Bush signed the bill, news reports revealed that the final version had dropped a child tax credit measure that would have assisted nearly

12 million children in families earning slightly more than the minimum wage. This provision would have cost $3.5 billion—or 1 percent of the total price tag.* Also after the tax cuts became law, the Tax Policy Center released an analysis showing that 8.1 million lower- and middle-income earners who pay income taxes would receive no tax reductions under this legislation. Fleischer, though, had asserted that people in the lowest tax bracket would "benefit the most" from the tax cuts.)

"We have taken aggressive action," Bush said, "to strengthen the foundation of our economy so that every American who wants to work will be able to find a job." Was Bush really claiming that because of this bill there would be no more unemployment? Maybe not, but he talked up the jobs-creation angle more than was warranted. His aides claimed this assortment of tax cuts would add one million jobs to the economy by the end of 2004. The conservative Heritage Foundation estimated that total employment in the United States would increase by 3.2 million jobs in this time period, but that only 500,000 would be attributable to the tax cuts. And Mark Zandi, the chief economist of Economy.com, a forecasting firm, told the *New York Times* that although the tax cuts would create 480,000 jobs through 2004, over the next decade they would *cost* jobs. Weeks later, at the end of June, the unemployment rate rose to 6.4 percent, the highest level in nine years. In the first half of the year, the economy had lost 236,000 jobs.

Bush's lies did not help him obtain exactly the tax package he desired. His vision of ending dividend taxes for wealthy investors went unfulfilled. But with the Democrats and many economists

---

*The Senate quickly moved to pass a $10 billion bill to grant an expanded child tax credit to 6.5 million low-wage families, though Republicans who voted for the measure were not happy about it. They just didn't want to be portrayed as having explicitly screwed the poor while handing tax breaks to millionaires. The House GOP leaders were not equally discomfited. "There are a lot of things that are more important than that," House majority Leader Tom DeLay remarked. The House Republicans then passed an $82 billion tax cuts bill that covered this provision but that also—opportunistically—extended tax cuts just passed. This measure, supposedly a fix to help the working poor, would provide 96 percent of its benefits to middle- and upper-income taxpayers. The Bush White House said it supported the bill.

opposed to any tax cuts resembling those Bush had originally urged, he could claim a major victory in having pressed Congress to adopt tax cuts totaling $320 billion—especially when the true cost of these tax cuts could be three times that amount. Even at its official price tag, this tax-cut package was the third largest in history, and Bush had won its passage after pushing through the biggest tax cuts in history two years earlier.

His success was more than a matter of size. He had revived the less-is-more supply-side ideology that had been relegated to the fringes of polite economic conversation in the years after the Reagan era. He had exacerbated deficits that would generate extreme pressure to shrink government and cut social programs. In an angry editorial, the *Washington Post* observed, "Whatever relief any such measure will provide, it cannot offset the enormous damage that will be done to low-income families and low-income children over the next few years by the tax cuts. . . . Let's be honest: Underfunded state and federal budgets mean fewer after-school programs for poor children, fewer health benefits through state Medicaid programs and fewer housing benefits, just to begin with." Bush, though, was not being honest. He had not bothered to detail what deep cuts in government services he would support in the coming ten years.

Bush had also managed to restructure the tax burden of the nation to the distinct advantage of wealthier Americans. As the *Post* noted, "The effective federal tax rate on households earning more than $416,000 will have fallen from 32.7 percent when Bush took office to 26.9 percent by 2010, while their share of federal taxation will have dropped from 24.3 percent to 22.8 percent." The rich would get richer, and other income earners would pay a larger share of the nation's tax bill. Bush had brought about this change without being forthright about it. He had often touted his tax cuts as relief for the middle class. Yet in his speeches he did not add, *And, by the way, our goal is to have middle-class Americans assume a higher percentage of our tax burden.* There are various ways to measure tax benefits and burdens, and economists constantly debate them. But the *Post* noted there was no debate on this trend: "Conservatives and liberals alike agree that Bush's tax policies have shifted more of the tax burden to the middle class." Would Bush say, "That sounds fair to me"?

In mid-July 2003, the White House released its latest forecast for the

2004 deficit: $450 billion. This was 50 percent higher than its estimate of five months earlier and almost $200 billion more than the CBO estimate of March. It marked a $577 billion reversal from the $127.3 *surplus* of 2001. The White House claimed that this deficit was "manageable," that huge federal deficits were merely a temporary phenomenon, that the deficit would fall to $226 billion by 2008, and that the current budget deterioration was mostly the fault of the slow economy. "The tax cuts proposed by the president and enacted by Congress are not the problem," said Josh Bolten, the recently installed White House budget director.

The irate anti-deficit hawks at the Concord Coalition disagreed. They observed, "Much of the deficit growth can be attributed to either legitimate short-term needs . . . or to . . . lower-than-expected revenues. Yet, the largest single change in the near term came from the 'Jobs and Growth' package [the tax cuts Bush won]." The coalition called the Bush package "deceptive," noting that it "may indeed provide some short-term fiscal stimulus but any such benefit will likely be outweighed over the long term by a reduction in national savings and investment due to the resulting future deficits. It is crucial in this regard to recognize that the actual revenue loss will be much higher than the official $350 billion estimate." And the Center on Budget and Policy Priorities (CBPP) noted that the long-term deficit numbers released by the Bush White House were based on unrealistic assumptions (including declining military expenditures in 2004 and no funding for the occupation and reconstruction of Iraq after September 2003). "The administration's new budget forecast," the CBPP maintained, "significantly understates the expected deficits in the future."

With his push for tax cuts in 2003, Bush successfully repeated his deception-ridden performance of 2001. But there was a dramatic difference. In 2001, he played fast and loose with what appeared to be a healthy-sized surplus. (Bush claimed the surplus would still be standing after his tax cuts; his opponents argued otherwise. Time—several months—proved he was wrong and they were right.) Two years later, during a time of deficits, Bush lied to justify a package that would place the nation deeper into the hole.

The leader who often said he was ushering in a new era of responsibility would not take responsibility for the outcomes of his own economic policies. He would neither concede the deficit-deepening impact of his first set of tax cuts nor would he address the projected deficit-expanding results of the second. And he consistently hid behind mathematical and accounting trickery, using phony averages and religiously adhering to the claim his tax cuts would boost tax revenues and redress deficits even after his own economists declared otherwise. Bush was stuck in a world of fiscal fictions, and he had imposed those fictions upon current—and future—generations of Americans.

14. In Iraq

"We'll reveal the truth."

George W. Bush had a good war in Iraq. The major fighting lasted only three weeks. U.S. forces suffered relatively light casualties, with 138 American troops killed. Saddam Hussein was vanquished; his repressive rule was toppled. If regime change had been the stated goal of the war, then Bush would have had a clearly defined success. But in the long run, up to the invasion, Bush had repeatedly said that the primary reason for resorting to military action was to protect Americans from the threat posed by Saddam Hussein's weapons of mass of destruction. Bush and his national security team—including ex officio members deployed in think-tank bunkers and op-ed command centers—had emphatically asserted that Iraq possessed dangerous levels of WMDs (no doubt about it) and that it was "urgent," as Bush said, to find, secure, and destroy these weapons before they were used against Americans. They also had talked about birthing a democratic government in Iraq—where U.S. troops would be warmly embraced as liberators—without acknowledging obvious obstacles and potential traps.

On these crucial matters, the war offered proof that Bush had not leveled with the American public (and the world) during the on-to-war months. Once U.S. troops were in Iraq, the administration and the Pentagon showed less-than-intense concern over WMDs. If Bush had been truly serious about preventing terrorists from obtaining terrible weapons, his administration's actions in Iraq did not reflect that. More noticeably, the U.S. military failed during the war and in the months afterward to locate the weapons that Bush had claimed as *the* cause for the invasion. And the post-war period demonstrated that Bush and his pro-war colleagues had not been straightforward about the challenges of occupation and, perhaps worse, had not been prepared to deal with the consequences of military victory. The fog of *prewar* was easier to see through once the war had been fought.

"Every victory in this campaign and every sacrifice serves the purpose of defending innocent lives in America and across the world from the weapons of terror."

During the war, the Pentagon engaged in assorted spinning. After early developments suggested the invasion was not going to be as smooth as some Bush officials had indicated, Donald Rumsfeld tried to disavow his role in creating the war plan then under fire. At a Pentagon briefing, he noted, "The war plan is Tom Franks' war plan," referring to General Tommy Franks, head of the U.S. Central Command. Journalists and commentators widely interpreted the remark as an attempt to distance himself from a plan that he actually had shaped thoroughly. Rumsfeld also claimed the anti-Iraq military coalition was "larger than the coalition that existed during the Gulf War in 1991." But this was inartful embellishment. The current military operation was almost entirely a U.S.-British affair; many of the 46 nations cited as coalition members were only participating by endorsing the invasion. The 1991 coalition had included 34 nations that provided troops, aircraft, ships, or medics; dozens more endorsed the action. When U.S. soldiers in a highly publicized episode killed ten or so civilians—including five children—who had approached a checkpoint in a vehicle, the Pentagon claimed the troops had followed procedure and fired warning shots. But the *Washington Post*'s William Branigin, who witnessed the episode, reported the troops had failed to fire a warning shot in time. After the vehicle was destroyed, the unit's captain yelled over the radio at the platoon leader, "You just [expletive] killed a family because you didn't fire a warning shot soon enough." Following the U.S. military rescue of Private Jessica Lynch from a hospital in Nasiriya, Brig. General Vincent Brooks, deputy director of operations for Central Command, told reporters, "There was not a firefight inside of the building . . . but there were firefights outside of the building, getting in and getting out." Two months later, Marine Lt. Colonel David Lapan, a Pentagon spokesman, told Associated Press that the rescue team had not been fired upon (though supporting troops had been shot at).

Pumping up a coalition that existed mostly in name, putting out CYA statements, refusing to concede a war plan had obvious problems, hyping one of the more dramatic (and cinematic) moments of the war—none of this was surprising behavior for the Pentagon. But the war and its aftermath revealed a more profound dishonesty, for the Bush administration's conduct in Iraq was far out of sync with its breathless pre-war rhetoric about Saddam Hussein's WMDs. In stark contrast to his claim that the war was absolutely necessary to counter the direct danger these weapons presented, Bush failed to mount anything resembling a serious and top-priority hunt for the WMDs that supposedly imperiled America.

Once U.S. troops hit Iraq, the administration kept reminding the public of the immediate menace posed by Hussein's unconventional weapons. On March 20, 2003—the first full day of the war—Rumsfeld said, "We have a serious task before us, and it is to remove that regime and find the weapons of mass destruction, and replace it with a government that does not want those weapons." The following day, he remarked, "Our goal is to defend the American people, and to eliminate Iraq's weapons of mass destruction, and to liberate the Iraqi people." He assured the public that U.S. forces would "identify, isolate, and eventually eliminate Iraq's weapons of mass destruction, their delivery systems, production capabilities, and distribution networks." Rumsfeld noted that "we will . . . ensure their weapons of mass destruction will not fall into the hands of terrorists." Days later, he remarked, "We're there to eliminate the weapons of mass destruction in that country." On March 30, he even said he was sure of where such weapons could be found: "We know where they are. They're in the area around Tikrit and Baghdad and east, west, south, and north somewhat."

Bush, too, kept referring to the vital necessity of tracking down the WMDs. On March 25, he headed to the Pentagon to unveil his war budget request of $74.7 billion (after having refused for months to provide any estimate of how much the war might cost). In his remarks, he noted, "Our coalition is . . . bound together by the principle of protecting not only this nation, but all nations from a brutal regime that is armed with weapons that could kill thousands of innocent people." The next day, he traveled to MacDill Air Force Base in Florida, home of Central Command and Special Operations. He spoke of liberating the Iraqi people, but the main task was taking care of WMDs. "Every nation in our coalition," he said, "understands the terrible threat we face from weapons of mass destruction. . . . Every victory in this campaign and every sacrifice serves the purpose of defending innocent lives in America and across the world from the weapons of terror."*

On April 9—the day U.S. troops took Baghdad—Rumsfeld once again emphasized the WMD mission: "We still need to find and secure Iraq's weapons of mass destruction facilities and secure Iraq's borders so we can prevent the flow of weapons of mass destruction materials and senior regime officials out of the country."

"We have high confidence that they have weapons of mass destruction. This is what this war was about and is about."

Throughout the fighting, U.S. and British troops found no weapons of mass destruction. There had been reports of WMD discoveries. One U.S. unit thought it had uncovered a chemical weapons facility. (It had not.) Other troops found three 55-gallon barrels with chemicals they

---

*At MacDill, Bush also said, "We've destroyed the base of a terrorist group in northern Iraq that sought to attack America and Europe with deadly poisons." He was referring to the redoubt of Ansar-al-Islam, a militant group that did appear to have been interested in developing poisons. Powell had cited Ansar-al-Islam during his U.N. show-and-tell as proof of the "sinister nexus" between al Qaeda and Saddam Hussein. But Bush was exaggerating the threat from this band of extremists. After the war, Los Angeles Times reporter Jeffrey Fleishman visited its decimated camp in Kurdish-controlled Iraq, and he noted, "Documents, statements by imprisoned Ansar guerillas and visits to the group's strongholds before and after the war produced no strong evidence of connections to Baghdad and indicated that Ansar was not a sophisticated terrorist organization. The group was a dedicated, but fledgling, al Qaeda surrogate lacking the capability to muster a serious threat beyond its mountain borders. The main intent of the group's 700 to 800 guerillas was to battle the secular U.S.-backed Kurdish government in Northern Iraq."

deemed suspicious. (The drums turned out to be holding pesticides.) A National Public Radio reporter quoted a "top military official" who said U.S. forces had come across 20 or so medium-range rockets containing sarin and mustard gas. (The Pentagon denied knowledge of such a discovery.) At one point, U.S. military officials said they had intercepted a coded message indicating Iraqi forces were preparing to use chemical or biological weapons. (Such an attack never came; military officials later admitted this intelligence was bad.) Had Bush and his administration been wrong about the presence of large amounts of WMDs in Iraq? On April 10, Fleischer remarked, "As I said earlier, we have high confidence that they have weapons of mass destruction. This is what this war was about and is about."

Despite such talk, as the war drew to a close, it became evident that Bush and the Pentagon had no comprehensive plan for quickly locating and securing the weapons of mass destruction they had passionately warned about. Nor had they implemented any extensive scheme to prevent a much-discussed nightmare scenario: in the chaos caused by war, terrorists, crooks, or government officials grab chemical and biological weapons and WMD-related materials (if any did exist) and spirit them out of Iraq. Bush and his warriors were taking what could be considered a lackadaisical approach to locating and safeguarding such weapons and materials. "I don't sense that this was much of a priority," Fred Ikle, an undersecretary of defense in the Regan administration, later told the *New York Times*.

On April 11, Rumsfeld even made it seem as if dealing with WMDs was now a secondary task: "When there happens to be a weapon of mass destruction suspect site in an area that we occupy and if people have time, they'll look at it." *If people have time?* What had happened to his high-priority WMD mission? Certainly, the first responsibility of U.S. military units was to win the battle of the moment. But front-line troops could have been accompanied by WMD-seekers assigned to examine and secure the hundreds of suspected sites. After all, the objective of this war supposedly was to make sure Saddam Hussein could not hand off chemical or biological weapons or nuclear material to terrorists who would use them against the United States.

As Rumsfeld said on April 9, "The thought that . . . those materials could leave the country and in the hands of terrorist networks would be a very unhappy prospect. So it is important to us to see that that doesn't happen." Yet the window of opportunity for WMD-craving terrorists had been wide open for weeks. Rumsfeld's "unhappy prospect" might well have already occurred, or could be happening in the confusion following the war's conclusion. But Rumsfeld and the administration had apparently not planned seriously for this contingency.

That became clear on April 17—a month after the war had started—when Rumsfeld noted that only "for the first time in the last few days" were the Pentagon's WMD teams able to conduct serious searches in the most promising areas. That made it seem as if the hunt for unconventional weapons and WMD materials had just started. Rumsfeld offered one surprising reason not to worry about the delay: "I don't think we'll discover anything, myself. I think what will happen is we'll discover people who will tell us where to go find it. It is not like a treasure hunt where you just run around looking everywhere hoping you find something. I just don't think that's going to happen. The inspectors didn't find anything, and I doubt that we will. What we will do is find the people who will tell us." Days later, Rumsfeld claimed that he had "believed all along" that U.S. forces would find no WMD without the assistance of Iraqi tipsters, completely defying his earlier claim that "we know where they are."

At the White House, Fleischer adopted the same position, saying, "The chance of success depends not on finding something by bumping into it during the course of travel through Iraq, but it really depends on information that is provided to the United States or to the coalition." And Bush, during an April 25 interview with Tom Brokaw, said, "It's going to take time to find them. And the best way to find them is to continue to collect information from the humans, Iraqis who were involved in hiding them." But imagine if Bush, Rumsfeld, and the others had said this prior to the war: *We're invading another country to eliminate its weapons of mass destruction—which we know are there—but I doubt we'll find them unless locals tell us where they are.* Would that have persuaded the public this war was absolutely necessary?

Locating weapons of mass destruction might have been a tough assignment, especially because any Iraqi WMD programs would have been well hidden to foil U.N. inspections. But what called into question the prewar sincerity of Bush was the undeniable fact that he had not ordered an extensive and massive WMD search-and-secure operation that could have kicked off as soon as the war ended or even before.

There were, of course, military units assigned the task of looking for the weapons. But news from Iraq regarding the WMD hunt then under way was not heartening. In mid-April, Judith Miller, a *New York Times* reporter embedded with one of four specialized military teams searching for WMDs, noted that "two of the four mobile teams originally assigned to search for unconventional weapons have since been reassigned to investigate war crimes or sites unrelated to weapons." War crimes were important. But more so than finding weapons that can kill thousands and that happened to be the basis for the war? Only about 150 actual WMD-seekers were then at work within Iraq—that hardly made for a wide-ranging operation—and some were complaining they were short on vehicles, radios, and encryption systems. And nothing incriminating had even been located at the sites Secretary of State Powell had so confidently cited in his briefing to the U.N. Security Council in February.

What was most shocking was the Bush administration's actions—or lack thereof—regarding Iraq's nuclear facilities. Bush had maintained that Saddam Hussein was a danger partly because he was close to developing nuclear weapons. That may have been an overblown claim based on little—or phony—evidence. But the United States and the rest of the world did know that Iraq possessed radioactive materials that could be useful to anyone looking to develop a nuclear weapon or construct a dirty bomb. The IAEA had catalogued much of Iraq's nuclear holdings. But during the war, the U.S. military did not bother to secure quickly Iraq's major nuclear sites. A *Washington Post* story by Barton Gellman noted that before the war the vast Tuwaitha nuclear repository held about 4,000 pounds of partially enriched uranium and more than 94 tons of natural uranium, as well as radioactive cesium, cobalt, and strontium. Yet, Gellman reported on April 25, "Defense officials acknowledge that the U.S. government has no idea whether any of Tuwaitha's potentially deadly contents have been stolen, because it has not dispatched investigators to appraise the site. What it does know, according to officials at the

Pentagon and U.S. Central Command, is that the sprawling campus, 11 miles south of Baghdad, lay unguarded for days and that looters made their way inside."

A week later, Gellman revealed that a similar screwup had happened with another Iraqi nuclear site. He reported that a specially trained Defense Department team had not been dispatched to guard the Baghdad Nuclear Research facility until May 3, after a month of "official indecision." Radioactive waste stored there would be quite attractive to a dirty-bomb maker. The unit found the place ransacked. The survey conducted by the team, Gellman noted, "appeared to offer fresh evidence that the war has dispersed the country's most dangerous technologies beyond anyone's knowledge or control."

And five other nuclear facilities had been looted as well. Hundreds of unknown individuals—maybe more—had had access to scientific documents that would help anyone desiring to manufacture a nuclear or dirty bomb. Files and containers that held radioactive materials were missing.

When one American team uncovered a strong source of radiation—perhaps cobalt-60—at a long-abandoned test range, a member of the unit told the *New York Times* that the U.S. military in Iraq had no specific policy for handling found radioactive material. Other news reports said signs of radiation sickness had appeared in villages near Tuwaitha. When the electricity went out during the war and a water-pumping station didn't work, some of the locals broke into the nuclear complex, emptied hundreds of barrels containing uranium ore and other radioactive material, stole the drums, and used them to store water for drinking, cooking, and bathing. For almost three weeks, the *Times* reported, these people drank and bathed in water containing radioactive material.

Not until the end of May did the Bush administration start to make arrangements to permit the International Atomic Energy Agency to enter Iraq and visit the nuclear sites—six weeks after IAEA Chief Mohamed ElBaradei had first warned the United States of the potential problem these facilities posed. In June, IAEA officials secured the uranium at the Tuwaitha site and purchased back most of the stolen barrels for three dollars each. They concluded that most of the prewar uranium was accounted for. But, according to the Associated Press, they were "unable to determine whether hundreds of radioactive materials used in research and medicine across the country were secure. Officials fear such material could be used to make crude radioactive bombs."

"We know he had them. And whether he destroyed them, moved them, or hid them, we're going to find out the truth."

Toward the end of April, Bush administration officials, speaking off the record, were telling journalists it was possible no WMDs would be unearthed. A front-page story in the *Washington Post* noted, "With little to show after 30 days, the Bush administration is losing confidence in its prewar belief that it had strong clues pointing to the whereabouts of weapons of mass destruction concealed in Iraq, according to planners and participants in the hunt. After testing some—though by no means all—of their best leads, analysts here [in Kuwait] and in Washington are increasingly doubtful that they will find what they are looking for in the places described on a five-tiered target list drawn up before fighting began." The newspaper hammered an obvious point not then being raised in much of the media: "If such weapons or the means of making them have been removed from the centralized control of former Iraqi officials, high-ranking U.S. officials acknowledged, then the war may prove to aggravate the proliferation threat that President Bush said he fought to forestall." In other words, whoops. At the same time, for what it was worth, captured senior Iraqi officials, according to Associated Press, were telling U.S. interrogators that Iraq had no WMDs before the war. (And, according to the *New York Times*, two of the most senior al Qaeda leaders in U.S. custody—Abu Zubaydah and Khalid Sheikh Mohammed—had told the CIA during separate interrogations that their terrorist organization had not worked with Hussein's regime.)

At a Pentagon press conference on May 7—nearly a month after U.S. forces took Baghdad—Stephen Cambone, the undersecretary of defense for intelligence, noted that the Defense Department was *still* at work assembling what it was calling the Iraq Survey Group, which would be sent to Iraq to search for individuals, records, and materials related to weapons of mass destruction. This unit would assume the work of the 75th Exploitation Task Force, a smaller military group that had been in charge of the WMD hunt, and it would be composed of 1,300 experts and 800 support staff. But the hunt for unconventional weapons would be merely one of its tasks. The team was also being established to uncover information related to Saddam Hussein's regime, his intelligence services, terrorist outfits that might have had a presence in Iraq, war crimes, and POWs. Cambone emphasized that the Iraq Survey Group's WMD responsibilities would be "only a part" of this "very large undertaking." And this unit was not scheduled to arrive in Iraq until the end of May.

Before the war, Cambone reported, the Pentagon had compiled a list of about 600 suspected WMD sites. "As it stands now, we have been to about 70 sites that we were looking to cover," he said, adding that U.S. military teams had also visited another 40 that were not on the original list. This hardly appeared to be the anti-WMD blitzkrieg that could have reasonably been expected by anyone who had listened to Bush's prewar rhetoric. If Saddam Hussein's weapons were such an imminent danger that the United States had had no choice but to spurn further inspections and invade and occupy, why had Bush not put together the Iraq Survey Group earlier? Why hadn't it been ready to roll as soon as U.S. boots were on the ground? The war had come as no surprise to the Bush administration.

For his part, Bush insisted his prewar statements had been on target. Speaking on April 24 at an Ohio factory that manufactured Abrams tanks, Bush said of Saddam Hussein and unconventional weapons, "We know he had them. And whether he destroyed them, moved them, or hid them, we're going to find out the truth." But he noted, "It's going to take time."

White House officials, though, were starting to cover their tracks. On May 4, the *New York Times* reported that Bush's "senior aides, in interviews in recent days, had begun to back away from their prewar claims that Mr. Hussein had an arsenal that was loaded and ready to fire. They now contend that he developed what they call a 'just in time' production strategy for his weapons, hiding chemical precursors that could be quickly loaded into empty artillery shells or short-range missiles. But no evidence has been found that he did so, and Mr. Bush's comments reflected a growing concern in the administration that opponents of the war would claim that the United States exaggerated the evidence against Iraq in order to justify an attack that was intended to depose Mr. Hussein." Some Bush officials were saying— privately, not publicly—there might not be *any* WMDs discovered.

At a May 7 White House briefing, Fleischer was pressed on whether the United States had failed to act to prevent Iraqi weapons of mass destruction from being dispersed. The exchange was illuminating.

QUESTION: Ari, everybody's getting into this trap a little bit about whether WMD will be found, which may not be the issue, because, A, you may not find them, they may have been destroyed, whereas the president said they may have been dispersed, which raises the question that they could have somehow been spirited out of the country by terrorist groups and the like. What information do you have about that eventuality happening? I mean, isn't it presumptuous to presume that the American people are safer when you can't account for whether weapons have been taken out of the country or weapons materials have been taken out of the country?

FLEISCHER: Well, I think the real threat here came from a nation-state headed by Saddam Hussein and his henchmen, who showed they were willing to use weapons of mass destruction before. . . . That's the basis for saying that people are safer. If you're asking the question, on what basis does the president conclude people are safer, that's the answer.

QUESTION: I thought the concern was [weapons of mass destruction] falling into the hands of al Qaeda. Wasn't that the rationale?

FLEISCHER: Well, I'm continuing. The president said that the removal of the regime has diminished the threat and increased our security, and I think that's unquestionable. It was, after all, the regime that used weapons of mass destruction in attacks previously. Of course we always have concerns about any place that has weapons of mass destruction passing them along. But given the routing of the Iraqi regime, it certainly makes that much harder to do. . . .

QUESTION: I know that, but you're making these pronouncements without answering the direct question, which is, what does this administration know about not only what has been found —you're still checking —but what weapons materials or actual weapons may have been taken out of the country?

FLEISCHER: Well, we don't have anything concrete to report on that.

Precisely. The risk identified by the White House prior to the war was not, as Fleischer suggested, that Saddam Hussein would use WMDs against the United States, but that he would slip them to terrorists who would do so. Now Fleischer was claiming that the danger to the United States had decreased because a dictator who had used chemical weapons against regional foes in the 1980s was gone. He also said America was better off because the Iraqis who would arrange a WMD handoff were out of commission. But were the WMDs also out of commission? Could he assure Americans that such transfers had not occurred during or following the war? He had nothing to say about that.

I n mid-May, members of the 75th Exploitation Task Force said they were ending their search for unconventional weapons and would leave the country in June. Army Colonel Robert Smith, one of the task force's officers, told the *Washington Post* that the unit's leaders no longer thought "we're going to find chemical rounds sitting next to a gun. . . . That's what we came here for, but we're past that." Task force members complained they had lacked vital tools and, according to the newspaper, "consistently found targets identified by Washington to be inaccurate, looted and burned, or both." Army Colonel Richard McPhee, who commanded the 75th, noted that there had been no solid plan for protecting possible WMD sites: "You've got two corps commanders being told, 'Get to Baghdad,' and, oh, by the way, 'When you run across sensitive sites, you have to secure them.' Do you secure all those sites, or do you get to Baghdad? You've got limited force structure and you've got 20 missions."

The 75th had focused on a small list of 19 high-priority sites and 68 non-WMD sites that might hold useful clues, and it had managed by mid-May to have inspected 17 of the former and 45 of the latter. The task force had uncovered nothing. Its officers were disappointed and frustrated. "Why are we doing *any* planned targets?" Army Chief

Warrant Officer Richard Gonzales, who led the MET Alpha team, said. "Answer me that. We know they're empty." In one less-than-encouraging episode, U.S. military WMD hunters smashed through padlocks to reach a suspected weapons storage facility and found, instead, a cache of vacuum cleaners.*

The WMD hunt would be carried on by the Pentagon's new Iraq Survey Group. Yet, the *Post* reported, the survey team was already cutting back on its WMD staff for lack of work—even before it had been deployed. Colonel McPhee told the *Post* he believed the war had stopped Saddam Hussein's unconventional weapons programs: "Do I know where they are? I wish I did . . . but we will find them. Or not. I don't know. I'm being honest here." More honest than his commander-in-chief.

"We found the weapons of mass destruction."

Less than two months after the war Bush had not a scandal on his hands but one big inconvenient question: Where were the WMDs? News broke that the CIA was reviewing whether its prewar assessments of Saddam Hussein's WMD program had been wrong. (Oddly, the review had been triggered months before the war by Rumsfeld, who was then worried that CIA analysts had not found indisputable connections between Iraq and al Qaeda.) The House intelligence committee in May asked CIA Director George Tenet "to reevaluate U.S. intelligence" on WMDs and the supposed al Qaeda–Iraq link. "This could conceivably be the greatest intelligence hoax of all time," said Representative Jane Harman, the senior Democrat on the committee. "I doubt it, but we have to ask." Senator Jay Rockefeller IV, the top Democrat on the Senate intelligence committee, blasted the CIA's estimates on WMDs as "wholly unimpressive" and also called for an inquiry.

But the issue was not only whether the CIA had screwed up, but

---

*At the same time the 75th Exploitation Task Force was looking for weapons, a covert Army Special Forces unit named Task Force 20 was also on the case. But it, too, had little luck. Before the war began, a team from this group, according to the *Washington Post,* struck a military base in western Iraq looking for chemical-armed Scud missiles that U.S. intelligence suspected were there. The team found no weapons.

whether the administration had overstated the information contained in the intelligence assessments it had received from the spies. In mid-May, Hans Blix, the former chief U.N. inspector, said he was "beginning to suspect" that Iraq had no weapons of mass destruction. He also criticized the evidence Bush had presented as "shaky."* In an editorial, the *New York Times* welcomed the CIA's internal review but urged outside investigations.

All these stirrings placed the administration on the defensive—and caused Bush officials to both repeat their past claims and to reconfigure their current lines (or lies). During a public speech, Rumsfeld was asked why U.S. troops had not encountered any chemical or biological weapons. "We knew they had chemical programs from the past," he replied. "And we knew they were talking about these programs in one way or another." Rumsfeld pointedly did not repeat his previous assertion that Iraq—no question about it—had an arsenal of actual chemical and biological weapons. And he added, "It is also possible that they decided that they would destroy them prior to a conflict." If Iraq had done so, why had it escaped the attention of U.S. intelligence and why had the U.S. military found no traces of this destruction? Rumsfeld did not elaborate.

Bush seemed irritated—if not rattled—by the postwar questions about the MIA WMDs. While he was visiting Poland in late May, a Polish television reporter asked him, "Weapons of mass destruction haven't been found. So what argument will you use now to justify this war?"

"We found the weapons of mass destruction," Bush exclaimed. "We found biological laboratories. . . . And we'll find more weapons as time goes on. But for those who say we haven't found the banned

---

*As time went on—and unconventional weapons were still not found—Blix's pronouncements became sharper. In an interview with the *New York Times,* he questioned why the Bush administration had expected to find large stockpiles of chemical and biological weapons in Iraq. "What surprises me, what amazes me," he said, "is that it seems the military people were expecting to stumble on large quantities of gas, chemical weapons and biological weapons. I don't see how they could have come to such an attitude if they had, at any time, studied the reports" of the U.N. inspectors. He added, "Are reports from here totally unread south of the Hudson?" No, those reports had indeed been read in Washington, but they had been cited dishonestly by the White House to make the argument that Iraq maintained massive WMD stockpiles. And during an appearance at the Council on Foreign Relations, Blix took a clever swing at the Bush administration's prewar position on WMDs: "It is sort of fascinating that you can have 100 percent certainty about weapons of mass destruction and zero certainty about where they are."

manufacturing devices or banned weapons, they're wrong. We found them."

Bush was referring to two tractor-trailers obtained in Iraq by U.S. forces earlier that month. The CIA and the DIA had produced (and posted on the CIA website) a six-page report that concluded these trailers were mobile biological weapons plants, and the agencies noted their resemblance to the bioweapons labs Powell had cited during his prewar presentation to the United Nations. But there was one thing missing from the CIA's and the DIA's case: evidence of biological agents. Not a trace of pathogens had been detected on these supposed labs. In interviews with me, two scientists who were former weapons inspectors—including David Albright, head of the Institute for Science and International Security—said that it would have been virtually impossible for the Iraqis to have scoured clean a bioweapons lab that had ever been used.

Albright's ISIS released a statement noting, "No biological weapons agents were found on the trailers. Instead, the government's finding is based on eliminating any possible alternative explanations for the trucks, which is a controversial methodology under any circumstances. Given the high stakes for the United States to prove the existence of weapons of mass destruction (WMD) in Iraq, this methodology is particularly suspect." Other technical experts expressed doubt about the CIA analysts' conclusion. Former Iraqi officials claimed the vehicles were designed for producing hydrogen for weather balloons—an explanation rejected by the CIA and the DIA. But the *Los Angeles Times* reported that the U.S. military had its own fleet of vehicles designed to do the same, and it quoted one (unnamed) veteran U.S. intelligence official in Iraq involved in investigating these vehicles who said he was convinced the tractor-trailers were made to produce hydrogen. "We didn't find what we expected to find," he said. And in late June, the *New York Times* revealed the existence of a classified June 2 memorandum produced by the State Department's intelligence division that disputed the CIA's and DIA's findings about these trailers.

Had the CIA and DIA rushed to a convenient conclusion? Whichever side was ultimately right about the trucks, this all-important piece of evidence was hotly contested. It was not solid enough to support Bush's we-found-them declaration or to justify a war. Had Bush really invaded Iraq because Hussein's government had built two mobile labs that might be used for bioweapons but that had not yet produced anything?

"The issue of WMD has never been in controversy."

In England, Prime Minister Tony Blair was having a tougher time than Bush on the missing-weapons front. His former foreign secretary accused him of misleading Parliament and the British people and pointed to a September 2002 dossier produced by 10 Downing Street that said Saddam Hussein was in the position to deploy chemical or biological weapons within 45 minutes. Well, what happened to those weapons? The British press reported this sensational claim—which had been borrowed by Bush—had been based on information from a single Iraqi defector of uncertain reliability. Other members of Blair's own party issued similar charges; headlines accused him of lying. The BBC reported that Blair's office had requested that the dossier be "sexed up." A Parliamentary inquiry began, and Blair proclaimed, "I have absolutely no doubt about the existence of weapons of mass destruction."*

In the United States, Bush officials kept urging patience and kept downplaying the significance of the MIA weapons. "The issue of WMD has never been in controversy," Wolfowitz said, "where's there been a lot of arguing back and forth about whether the Iraqis have been involved in terrorism." But that was not true. Much of the pre-war debate had been about the seriousness of the WMD threat from Iraq. Wolfowitz further maintained "there was no oversell" of the WMD threat, but he acknowledged there "had been a tendency to emphasize the WMD issue." Somehow Bush, Cheney, Rumsfeld, Wolfowitz, Powell, Rice, and Fleischer had each forgotten to share that important piece of information—*we're just emphasizing here*—with the public. In an interview with *Vanity Fair,* Wolfowitz did concede that the WMD argument had been quite convenient: "For bureaucratic rea-

---

*On June 9, Blair's government acknowledged it had been wrong to publish in February a second white paper on the military threat posed by Saddam Hussein. The document— dubbed the "dodgy dossier"—had included plagiarized portions of a 12-year-old doctoral thesis by a California student.

sons, we settled on one issue, weapons of mass destruction, because it was the one reason everyone could agree on." It just happened to be the only one deployed by Bush that made the immediate safety of the country the paramount issue.*

While the administration insisted time would answer all questions— and while news talk shows debated the missing weapons of mass destruction and members of Congress spoke of investigations—more indications of prewar deception emerged. *New York Times* columnist Nicholas Kristof quoted a Defense Intelligence Agency official who charged, "The American people were manipulated." Greg Thiel- mann, a former official in the State Department's intelligence office, said, "The al Qaeda connection and nuclear weapons issue were the only two ways that you could link Iraq to an imminent security threat to the U.S., and the administration was grossly distorting the intelli- gence on both things." The newspaper also reported that the internal CIA review was looking closely at whether the October 2002 Intel- ligence Estimate exaggerated the development of Iraq's WMD pro- gram. One issue was if the CIA, which had not been able to obtain high-quality intelligence about Iraq's unconventional weapons pro- grams after 1998 (when U.N. inspectors left Iraq), had reached con- clusions about Iraq's present efforts on the basis of intelligence obtained before 1998.

In the months before the war, major newspapers had reported that intelligence analysts were complaining they were being pushed to tai- lor their conclusions to support the Bush administration's dramatic pronouncements on Iraq's weapons and the supposed ties between Hussein and al Qaeda. Now the *Washington Post* revealed that Cheney and his chief of staff had repeatedly visited CIA headquarters to dis- cuss the intelligence on Iraq with analysts and that some of these ana- lysts "felt they were being pressured to make their assessments fit with the Bush administration's policy objectives." Intelligence officials said that Wolfowitz had also leaned on analysts to produce assessments that supported the case for war. At least three complaints were filed with

---

*In late April, ABC News' John Cochran reported on the network's website that "officials inside government and advisers outside told ABC News the administration emphasized the danger of Saddam's weapons to gain the legal justification for war from the United Nations and to stress the danger at home to Americans." Cochran's report continued: " 'We were not lying,' said one official. 'But it was just a matter of emphasis.' "

the CIA ombudsman about the possible politicization of intelligence on Iraq.

Then in early June, *U.S. News & World Report* revealed the existence of the September 2002 Defense Intelligence Agency report that said there was "no reliable information" on whether Iraq had produced or stockpiled chemical weapons or had even reestablished the means to produce such weapons. Responding to news of the DIA report, Fleischer said, "We continue to have confidence about Iraq's possession of chemical and biological weapons." He added, "The precise location of where Iraq had chemical and biological weapons was never clear, but the fact they had it was never in doubt, based on a reading of the intelligence." Not this intelligence.

When Powell was asked about this DIA report on *Fox News Sunday,* he fired off a completely disingenuous defense. He claimed, "The sentence that has gotten all of the attention"—the one stating there was no "reliable" information of Iraqi chemical weapons stockpiles—was followed immediately by a "sentence that says that [the DIA] had information that [chemical] weapons had been dispersed to [Iraqi military] units." Powell's characterization of the DIA report gave the impression that there was no doubt Iraq had manufactured deployment-ready chemical weapons, but his description of the report was inaccurate. The next sentence actually read: "Unusual munitions transfer activity in mid-2002 suggest that Iraq is distributing CW munitions in preparation for an anticipated U.S. attack." "Suggest" was the key word there. And, as Powell and others sure knew by this point, during the war the United States had uncovered no evidence indicating Iraq had dispersed chemical weapons to its troops. So the DIA *suspicion* Powell cited to defend the administration had only been an unconfirmed *assumption*—not a definitive finding—and it had been proven wrong by subsequent events.

"If there's a problem with intelligence . . . it doesn't mean that anybody misled anybody."

Powell, Rice, and other Bush officials were trying hard to defend the administration's prewar remarks. Tenet denied his analysts had cooked any books. On Capitol Hill, some Republicans resisted the call from

Democrats for full-blown probes, but they promised to review—at first behind closed doors—what the intelligence community knew about Iraq's weapons before the war and whether Bush had hyped that information. (In two private hearings, Christian Westermann, a senior intelligence analyst at the State Department and an expert on biological and chemical weapons, maintained he had been pressed to shape his analysis on Iraq and other subjects to match administration policy, according to the *New York Times*.) The Bush administration leaked information claiming that Iraq had hidden chemical and biological weapons equipment within commercial facilities. That may well have been the case. But it was still not the same as maintaining threatening stockpiles.

During a visit to U.S. troops in Doha, Qatar, on June 5, Bush proclaimed, "We'll reveal the truth" on Iraq's weapons. But he added, "One thing is certain: no terrorist network will gain weapons of mass destruction from the Iraqi regime, because the Iraqi regime is no more." That was true by definition. But if Saddam Hussein had not had ready-to-go weapons, then no war had been needed to achieve this end. Days later, Bush subtly shifted his rhetoric, maintaining, "Intelligence throughout the decade showed they had a weapons program. I am absolutely convinced, with time, we'll find out that they did have a weapons program." A *program*, though, is different than a *stockpile*. A program could be merely a research effort; a stockpile would involve actual weapons. Before the war, there was plenty of reason to suspect Iraq had programs of some sort. But Bush had promised his war would net weapons, not programs.* Fleischer claimed that Bush was not retreating from his previous position: "The president has repeatedly said that Iraq had weapons of mass destruction. . . . We still have confidence in that information. . . . They're still there."

During this visit to this U.S. military base in Doha, Bush, according

---

*In a June 8, 2003, article, the *Sunday Times* of London quoted an Iraqi general who maintained Saddam Hussein had set up secret cells to research, but not produce, chemical and biological weapons. "It was all just theory," the unnamed officer said. "The aim was to keep us up to date and ready so that if [United Nations] sanctions were lifted or we needed to produce chemical or biological weapons again, we could start up immediately." He insisted no WMDs could be found in Iraq. If this Iraqi was telling the truth, his comments were an indication that, despite Hussein's desire for WMDs, sanctions and inspections had constrained Iraq's weapons programs.

to an account in *Time*, held a meeting with his top Iraq commanders and asked them, Where are the weapons of mass destruction? Turning to L. Paul Bremer, the former ambassador, now heading the U.S. occupation in Iraq, he said, "Are you in charge of finding WMD?" Bremer said he was not. Bush asked General Tommy Franks. He, too, said no. Then the aides raised the name of Stephen Cambone, the undersecretary of defense for intelligence. "Who?" Bush asked. Was Bush really unaware of who was managing what was supposedly his top priority in Iraq?

As the tussle over what the administration had known and had said about the WMD threat ensued, Wolfowitz also tried to create some wiggle room. When he appeared at a House armed services committee hearing, Representative Gene Taylor, a conservative Democrat, said he had voted for the war only after being persuaded personally by Wolfowitz. Now Taylor wanted to know if the intelligence about the threat from Iraq had been wrong or misrepresented. "A person," the congressman said, "is only as good as his word. This nation is only as good as its word."

Wolfowitz answered, "If there's a problem with intelligence . . . it doesn't mean that anybody misled anybody. It means that intelligence is an art and not a science." How true. But the administration's onto-war remarks had reflected none of the subjectivity of art. The Bush team had treated intelligence as neither art nor science, but marketing.

The WMD controversy lingered. "Until WMD are found, or their absence accounted for, there is urgent explaining to be done," conservative columnist George Will observed. Referring to the Bush team, Republican Senator Chuck Hagel remarked, "This is a cloud hanging over their credibility." Like Wolfowitz, General Richard Myers, chairman of the Joint Chiefs of Staff, also trotted out a defense that emphasized the inherent uncertainty of intelligence. "Intelligence doesn't necessarily mean something is true, it's just, it's intelligence, you know, it's your best estimate of the situation," he said not so eloquently during a Pentagon press briefing. "It doesn't mean it's a fact. I mean, that's not what intelligence is, and so you make judgments."

Myers was in a sense correct, though he was being disingenuously modest about U.S. intelligence capabilities. Intelligence can at times produce hard data—say, a photograph of a secret weapon. Yet often intelligence estimates are best-guesses based on the limited amount of information an intelligence service has managed to collect. In the prewar period, however, Bush and his aides had not said that their "best estimate" was that Hussein possessed unconventional weapons and maintained operational ties to al Qaeda. They proclaimed it was a fact that he had both these weapons and these contacts. Wolfowitz himself had said the previous January that the case for war was "grounded in current intelligence" and "very convincing."

But now Wolfowitz and Myers, seeking cover, were explaining that intelligence is frequently ambiguous. (In testimony before the Senate, General John Abizaid, Bush's nominee to head the U.S. Central Command, said that prewar intelligence on Iraq's WMDs had been "perplexingly incomplete.") In adopting this defense, Wolfowitz and Myers (unintentionally) indicted the Bush administration. They were conceding—implicitly—that Bush and other officials had pushed the country to war with black-and-white assertions when the information they possessed was far less definitive. These remarks suggested that Bush had purposefully deployed rhetoric unsupported by the intelligence.

Toward the end of June and the start of July, information began seeping out of the ongoing investigations that buttressed the charge that Bush had been dishonest with the public before the war. First, Representative Harman, the ranking Democrat on the House intelligence committee, delivered a statement on the House floor and shared some early findings of her committee's review of the WMD controversy. "When discussing Iraq's WMD," Harman said, "administration officials rarely included the caveats and qualifiers attached to the intelligence committee's judgments. . . . For many Americans, the administration's certainty gave the impression that there was even stronger intelligence about Iraq's possession of and intention to use WMD." She reported that the committee was still investigating "whether the intelligence case on Iraq's WMD was based on circumstantial evidence rather than hard facts." On the subject of the Iraqi–al Qaeda connection, Harman noted her committee's investigation "suggests that the intelligence linking al Qaeda to Iraq, a prominent theme in the administration's statements prior to the war, [was] contrary to what was claimed by the administration."* Harman's statement was only a preliminary report from a moderate Democrat—who had voted for the war and was no partisan hothead—but it was the strongest official indication to date that Bush had indeed misled the United States into war.

Then similar findings emerged from the internal CIA review. In interviews with reporters, Richard Kerr, a former CIA deputy director who was leading the examination of the CIA's prewar intelligence on Iraq, said that his unfinished inquiry had so far found that the intelligence had been somewhat ambiguous, that analysts at the CIA and other intelligence services had received pressure from the Bush administration, and that the CIA had not found any proof of operational ties between al Qaeda and Saddam Hussein's government. Kerr was not trying to be difficult. (He made sure to talk to reporters the day before July 4, which guaranteed minimum media coverage.) His remarks were primarily pro-CIA. He said that intelligence analysts had resisted pressure and done a fine job, considering the limited amount of material they had to work with. Kerr noted that U.S. intelligence analysts had been forced to rely upon information from the early and mid 1990s and possessed little hard evidence to evaluate after 1998 (when U.N. inspectors left Iraq). The material that did come in following that, he said, was mostly "circumstantial" or "inferential." It was "less specific and detailed" than in earlier years, "scattered." CIA intelligence reports, according to Kerr, included the "appropriate caveats" regarding their less-than-definitive conclusions.

Though Kerr did not say so outright, these comments were further confirmation there had been no incontrovertible intelligence that Iraq had chemical or biological weapons or that Hussein had

---

*About this time, the U.N. committee on terrorism released a draft report on al Qaeda and noted it had found no evidence of links between these terrorists and Saddam Hussein's government. And *Newsweek* published an article reporting it had obtained German law enforcement records that indicated that Abu Musab al-Zarqawi, the terrorist that the Bush administration had claimed as the missing link between al Qaeda and Baghdad, was not a middleman. "The secret German records—compiled during interrogations with a captured Zarqawi associate—suggest that the shadowy Zarqawi headed his own terrorist group, called Al Tawhid, with its own goals and may even have been a jealous rival of al Qaeda," the newsmagazine said.

been, as Bush had declared, "dealing" with al Qaeda. A former CIA deputy director was implying that Bush had misrepresented the intelligence.*

"When it's all said and done, the facts will show the world the truth."

Though Harman's and Kerr's remarks—which received little media notice—were signs that the ongoing inquiries could produce problems for Bush, they posed no immediate trouble. Instead, the White House became ensnared in Nigergate—a controversy over one line in the State of the Union address Bush delivered the previous January. Trying to show that Hussein was in hot pursuit of nuclear weapons, Bush had said, "The British government has learned that Saddam Hussein recently sought significant quantities of uranium from Africa." This allegation had been based—primarily or partly (this became a matter of dispute)—on the charge that Iraq had tried to buy uranium from Niger. But the Niger claim had been supported by documents subsequently determined by the IAEA to be amateurish forgeries.

In June and July 2003, a brouhaha erupted over how this particular sentence had found its way into Bush's mouth. News stories noted that former Ambassador Joseph Wilson IV had been dispatched to Niger by the CIA in February 2002 to check out the story and had concluded there was nothing to it. A senior CIA official told Knight Ridder newspaper that the intelligence agency had informed the White House in March 2002 that it could not confirm the Niger allegations. "Three senior administration officials said Vice President Dick Cheney and some officials on the National Security Council staff and at the Pentagon ignored the CIA's reservations and argued that the president and others should include the allegation in their case against Saddam," according to the Knight Ridder report. The news service added, "The revelation of the CIA warning is the strongest evidence to date that

---

*The October 2002 National Intelligence Estimate had said that "Baghdad has chemical and biological weapons." But Kerr claimed CIA analysts in general had underscored the limits of the intelligence.

prowar administration officials manipulated, exaggerated or ignored intelligence information in their eagerness to make the case for invading Iraq."

The White House denied it had ignored warnings about using this allegation in its brief against Hussein, and maintained that at the time of the State of the Union speech it believed that the Niger charge was true. "Maybe someone knew in the bowels of the agency," Condoleezza Rice said, "but no one in our circles knew that there were doubts and suspicions that this might be a forgery." And on June 13, Sean McCormack, a spokesman for the National Security Council, said that Bush stood by the main thrust of the sentence in dispute. "Those [forged] documents were only one piece of evidence in a larger body of evidence suggesting that Iraq attempted to purchase uranium from Africa," he remarked. "The issue of Iraq's pursuit of uranium in Africa is supported by multiple sources of intelligence. The other sources of evidence did and do support the president's statement."

The controversy centered on who knew what when about the phoniness of the Niger charge. Media reports noted that in September 2002, Tenet had privately told members of Congress that the CIA had information suggesting Iraq had attempted to buy uranium in Africa but that the agency had doubts about the credibility of the report. And the October 2002 National Intelligence Estimate on Iraq had contained a footnote reporting that State Department intelligence analysts viewed the uranium-from-Africa tale as "highly dubious." Why had this allegation continued to survive?

In early July 2003, Joseph Wilson went public with his own account of his trip to Niger. Writing an op-ed for the *New York Times*, he explained how he had concluded in February 2002 that the Niger charge was "highly doubtful." He wrote, "The question now is how [my conclusion] was or was not used by our political leadership. If my information was deemed inaccurate, I understand (though I would be very interested to know why). If, however, the information was ignored because it did not fit certain preconceptions about Iraq, then a legitimate argument can be made that we went to war under false pretenses." And he told the *Washington Post*, "It really comes down to the administration misrepresenting the facts on an issue that was a fundamental justification for going to war. It begs the question, what else are they lying about?"* The next day, July 7, a British parliamentary committee report questioned the Blair government's use of the Niger charge, noting that the CIA had debunked this intelligence. This undercut Bush further, for in the State of the Union speech he had attributed the buying-uranium-in-Africa charge to the British government. (The British report also found that Blair had not misled Parliament regarding the threat from Iraq's WMDs but that he had mishandled intelligence on Iraq's weapons.)

Bush then caved. The day the British report came out, the White House released a statement that said, "Knowing all that we know now, the reference to Iraq's attempt to acquire uranium from Africa should not have been included in the State of the Union speech."

But that was not the end of it. Weeks earlier, the White House had claimed the Niger charge had not been the only reason for Bush's assertion. Now Fleischer conceded that the sentence in question had been wrong "because it was based on the yellow cake [uranium] from Niger." But then Michael Anton, another spokesperson for the National Security Council, said that the Niger documents "were not the sole basis for the line" in the State of the Union speech. Yet he added, the "other reporting that suggested that Iraq had tried to obtain uranium from Africa is not detailed or specific enough for us to be certain that such attempts were in fact made." Good spin. The White House was trying to have its (yellow) cake and eat it, too, saying the Niger material was not the only evidence in pocket, but that the other evidence was not really evidence.

And the issue still remained: how had this misleading information gotten into Bush's speech? Who was responsible for that lapse? Bush and Rice claimed that the CIA had vetted the speech. "If the CIA—the director of central intelligence—had said, 'Take this out of the speech,' it would have been gone," Rice said. "We have a high stan-

---

*For challenging the White House, Wilson got slammed. A week later, conservative columnist Robert Novak identified Wilson's wife as an undercover CIA operative who worked in the tough field of weapons counter-proliferation, and he cited "two senior administration officials" as his sources. Assuming Novak was reporting accurately what his sources had told him, that meant Bush officials either had blown the cover of a covert operative who was trying to protect the nation from the threat of WMDs or had wrongly branded Wilson's wife—who was known to friends as an energy analyst at a private firm—as a CIA officer. In either case, this was an ugly act of revenge—a political hit job—that might even have impaired the intelligence community's anti-WMD efforts.

dard for the president's speech." But on the same day Bush and Rice blamed the CIA, the *Washington Post* reported that back in September 2002, the CIA had tried to persuade the British government to remove from an official intelligence report a reference to an Iraqi attempt to purchase uranium in Africa. Why had the CIA told the Brits to drop the charge but okayed its use in a presidential speech?

On July 11, Tenet released a statement that did not quite answer the question, but it offered a few hard-to-miss clues. Like a good bureaucratic soldier, he assumed full responsibility for the "mistake" and noted that the CIA had managed to keep this allegation out of other public speeches by Bush officials. But his statement hinted that White House officials—eager to throw whatever charges they could at Hussein—had been behind the decision to keep the line in the State of the Union address. Tenet maintained,

> Portions of the State of the Union speech draft came to the CIA for comment shortly before the speech was given. . . . Although the documents related to the alleged Niger-Iraqi uranium deal had not yet been determined to be forgeries, [CIA] officials who were reviewing the draft remarks on uranium raised several concerns about the fragmentary nature of the intelligence with National Security Council colleagues. Some of the language was changed. From what we know now, [CIA] officials in the end concurred that the text in the speech was factually correct, i.e. that the British government report said that Iraq sought uranium from Africa. . . . This did not rise to the level of certainty which should be required for presidential speeches, and CIA should have ensured that it was removed.

One did not have to be an intelligence officer to read the (barely) coded message. Tenet was signaling that NSC officials at the White House had taken the lead in keeping the doubtful and misleading sentence in the speech and that the CIA vetters had okayed the line only after it had been fiddled with to make the British government—not U.S. intelligence—the source of the charge. The White House had tossed out the allegation and pinned it on the British, even though its own intelligence services had decided the charge was too thin to cite. Bush aides had resorted to a dishonest maneuver.

The whole Niger dustup, though, was a bit overblown. Bush had uttered plenty of other untrue or disingenuous statements before the war, even in the State of the Union speech in question. But in the Senate, Republicans voted down a Democratic measure calling for an independent commission to examine how the Bush administration used—or misused—intelligence in pressing its case for war. Republican Senator Chuck Hagel, though, did remark that the case for war was looking "weaker and weaker." He told CNN, "There's credibility involved here, there's our word, there's the trust of this country involved. . . . There's a cloud hanging over this administration." And in the middle of the Niger controversy, Greg Thielmann, the former State Department intelligence analyst, wryly observed, "This administration has had a faith-based intelligence attitude: 'We know the answers, give us the intelligence to support those answers.' When you sense this kind of attitude, you quash the spirit of intellectual inquiry and integrity."

The White House was unable to quickly smother Nigergate—which should have been a small matter. Perhaps that was because Bush officials could not bring themselves to say, *We messed up, we were too keen to use every available piece of information to make our case.* Instead, administration figures—including Rumsfeld and Rice—tried to defend Bush's use of the line even after the White House acknowledged it should not have been included in the speech.

Regarding this point, Fleischer, on his last day in the job, once again performed amazing acrobatics. A reporter asked, "But you're trying to have it both ways. You're saying it shouldn't have been in the speech, but it still may be true. But you really don't know. Why don't you simply retract and withdraw the statement?" Fleischer replied, "Well, we said it should not have been in the State of the Union." The journalist followed up: "But you're still trying to suggest that it may be true in the end [that Iraq was seeking uranium from Africa]."

"That's because," Fleischer said, "in the face of allegations that [the line] was false, I think it's important for people to have a realistic understanding of Iraq's attempt to pursue nuclear weapons. . . . They needed to get uranium from somewhere. They previously had a history of getting it from Africa. And the reporting at the time indicated that there were suspicions they were getting it from Africa."

"The bottom line," the reporter asked, "is, though, that you don't know for certain one way or not?"

"I've said that many times," Fleischer answered.

It was bizarre. The White House was saying it had no strong evidence to back up the line. But it refused to admit the sense of the sentence was incorrect—though the administration did concede it should not have appeared in the speech. (A few days earlier, Fleischer had come up with another head-scratcher: "I think the burden is on those people who think [Hussein] didn't have weapons of mass destruction to tell the world where they are.")

When Bush was forced to address the Niger business, he could not help but provide his critics more ammunition. During a photo opportunity at the White House—in which he declared, "I think the intelligence I get is darn good intelligence"—he told White House reporters, "When I gave the speech, the line was relevant." No, it was not—according to Tenet. By the time of the speech, Tenet had said in his mea culpa, the CIA had concluded that the uranium-from-Africa charge should not have been part of a presidential speech.

Bush then changed the subject and tossed out a whopping lie: "We gave [Hussein] a chance to allow the inspectors in, and he wouldn't let them in. And, therefore, after a reasonable request, we decided to remove him from power." Not at all. Hussein had permitted the U.N. inspectors to enter Iraq and examine suspect sites there. His overall record of cooperation with the inspectors had been mixed. But the United States had not bombed and invaded because Hussein had banned the inspectors. In an effort to dodge the accusation that he had misled the nation into war with his uranium-from-Africa comment, Bush was misleading the public about the reason for the invasion.

"There are some who would like to rewrite history."

Nigergate opened the door for a bigger question: Had Bush oversold the case for war? *Time* magazine ran a cover piece under a large headline: "Untruth and Consequences." Its article focused on the Niger business, but the magazine also noted that prewar assertions by Bush on other WMD matters—biological weapons in Iraq, Hussein's use of aluminum tubes for a nuclear weapons program, and Iraq's links to al Qaeda—had not yet proven true.

Before the Niger affair exploded, on June 16, 2003, Bush spoke to small-business owners in New Jersey, and he responded—in a way—to the charge he had misled the public on WMDs. "The nation," he said, "acted to a threat from the dictator of Iraq. Now, there are some who would like to rewrite history—revisionist historians is what I like to call them. Saddam Hussein was a threat to America and the free world in '91, in '98, in 2003. . . . And one thing is for certain: Saddam Hussein is no longer a threat to the United States." This was not argument; it was reiteration. Bush, conspicuously, did not mention WMDs as he now reminded people that Hussein had been a threat to the United States. Nor did he explain why it was revisionism to wonder, on the basis of evidence, if his prewar statements had been disconnected from reality. That wasn't rewriting history; it was judging truthfulness.

Bush yielded no ground. During a White House event on July 2, a reporter asked him the key question: "On weapons of mass destruction, is it fair to say now, after two months of looking for them, that there is a discrepancy between what . . . you and your top officials described as the threat from Saddam Hussein and what was actually there on the ground?" Bush replied, "No, Saddam Hussein had a weapons program. Remember, he used them. He used chemical weapons on his own people." Hussein had certainly attacked the Kurds and Iranian troops with chemical weapons—but years earlier, before the first Gulf War, before the U.N. inspectors had found and destroyed much of his arsenal. Prior to his invasion of Iraq, Bush had not argued that Hussein posed a direct threat to the United States because he had fired off chemical weapons at regional foes two decades earlier. But with the absence of the WMDs in Iraq, this was the best he could come up with.*

A week later, in the midst of the Niger scuffle, Bush held a press conference in Pretoria, South Africa, while he was on a five-nation tour of Africa. He sidestepped questions about whether he had used false information to argue the case for war. And when a reporter

---

*Days earlier, Rolf Ekeus, the executive chairman of UNSCOM in the 1990s, had written in the *Washington Post* that Hussein had sought unconventional weapons mainly to gain a military advantage over neighboring Iran. "The Iraq policy after the Gulf War," Ekeus observed, "was to halt all production of warfare agents and to focus on design and engineering, with the purpose of activating production and shipping of warfare agents and munitions directly to the battlefield in the event of war."

asked, "Do you still believe they [Iraq] were trying to buy nuclear materials in Africa," he refused to answer the query. Instead, he quipped, "One thing is for certain, he's not trying to buy anything right now." No surprise, Bush would not take serious the accusation that he had fiddled with the truth to get his war. He again dismissed questions about his prewar statements as part of "a lot of attempts to try to rewrite history"—a sounds-good/means-nothing non-answer. He added, "There's no doubt in my mind when it's all said and done, the facts will show the world the truth."

The Niger episode continued on, and media reports kept churning out new information. That General Carlton Fulford Jr., the deputy commander of the U.S. European Command, had also been sent to Niger in February 2002 and had found that the uranium supply there was secure. That the CIA had managed to delete a reference to Iraq's alleged uranium shopping in Niger from a Bush speech the previous October. That the CIA that month had sent two memos to the White House expressing strong doubts about the uranium-from-Africa claim. That a CIA officer claimed he had told a National Security Council official that the agency doubted the British intelligence the White House wanted to cite in the State of the Union speech (an account the White House denied). That the State Department and the CIA had obtained the forged documents about the supposed Niger deal three months before Bush's State of the Union speech.

And the Bush team kept trying to extricate itself from the Niger mess by dissembling. Rice declared, "The notion that the president of the United States took the country to war because he was concerned with one sentence about whether Saddam Hussein sought uranium in Africa is purely ludicrous." But Rice then engaged in her own historical revisionism: "The president took the nation to war to depose a bloody tyrant who was building a weapons of mass destruction program and had weapons of mass destruction . . . who was a threat to American interest in the Middle East." But that was not how Bush had sold the war. He had not maintained that Hussein was a threat to "American interest in the Middle East." He had depicted the Iraq dictator as a threat—right now—to Americans in their own towns and cities.

As questions about the yellow cake affair mounted, the White House cranked up the usual damage control. At press conferences, Scott McClellan, the new press secretary, said that it was time to move on, that the issue had been addressed, that this was nothing more than a campaign "to rewrite history." In a stab at closure, the White House declassified and released eight pages from the 90-page October 2002 National Intelligence Estimate on Iraq. That paper had concluded that "Baghdad has chemical and biological weapons. . . . [I]f left unchecked, it probably will have a nuclear weapon during this decade." The administration's point was that before the war Bush had reason to believe there were WMDs in Iraq. But the intelligence report did add, "We lack specific information on many key aspects of Iraq's WMD programs." And its warning about Iraqi nuclear weapons came with an important qualifier: *if left unchecked*. The NIE excerpt also included the assessment that Baghdad was unlikely to attack the United States or to assist terrorists in an assault against the United States, unless Hussein feared he was about to be struck by Washington. And it contained the (previously reported) strong dissent from State Department intelligence analysts who believed that the known evidence did not "add up to a compelling case" that Iraq was pursuing an active nuclear weapons program.

The NIE excerpt was meant to bolster the White House's defense. But the day the administration released it, Bush officials, in a background briefing for reporters, noted that Bush and Rice had not read the NIE—the most authoritative prewar assessment from the intelligence community—in its entirety. Not once before sending U.S. troops to war? How, then, could Bush on March 17, 2003, have said with confidence that U.S. intelligence "leaves no doubt that Iraq continues to possess" WMDs? Didn't such a statement imply he had reached an informed judgment on the state of the intelligence? But he hadn't even read the stuff.

After over a month of Nigergate bumbling—during which the White House tried to blame the CIA—on July 30 Bush and Rice finally assumed responsibility for the mess, obviously attempting an admit-wrong-and-get-this-behind-us move. Interviewed on PBS, Rice said, "I certainly feel personal responsibility for this entire episode"— particularly the lapses in the vetting process for the State of the Union speech. At a press conference, Bush said, "I take personal responsibility for everything I say." Asked if he had exaggerated the links between al Qaeda and Hussein and could offer "definitive evidence" proving this connection, Bush said it would "take time for us to gather the evidence" in Iraq. (But hadn't he already made the charge many times?) Asked if he had taken the country to war on "flimsy or . . . nonexistent evidence," he replied, "I strongly believe that Saddam had a weapons program." He did not say *weapons*.

As for the still-missing WMDs, Bush and his aides continued to say, *We're going to find them*. After Tony Blair—in a rousing speech to Congress—said that "history will forgive" if his and Bush's prewar WMD claims ended up wrong, Bush declared, "We won't be proven wrong." Standing next to Blair during a brief White House press conference, Bush was asked, "Does it matter whether or not you find these weapons?" He replied, "I believe we will find the truth."

Whether or not biological or chemical weapons or an active nuclear weapons program would eventually be uncovered, Bush and his national security aides had violated a prewar commitment to the United States and the world by not mounting a more assiduous WMD search. Looters beat the United States to Iraq's nuclear facilities. If Iraq had WMDs, if al Qaeda types were in Baghdad, and if these terrorists were seeking unconventional weapons in Iraq—the fundamental prewar claims made by the administration—then there was a good chance the potential horror Bush & Co. had exploited to whip up support for their war had come true. Even if the downsized WMD component of the late-to-the-game Iraq Survey Group were to unearth dangerous goods, its members would likely never know what they missed—and where and with whom that material might be today.

When the war was drawing down, Bush said, "People have got to know that we are serious about stopping the spread of weapons of mass destruction." That might not have been a lie—because he was talking about North Korea. But Bush had been serious about blocking the spread of Iraqi WMDs only to the extent that doing so justified the obliteration of the regime of Saddam Hussein. Destroying the Iraqi government was a task Bush accomplished rather well, and, presumably, it would benefit the people of Iraq. But Bush either had misled the American public with his prewar WMDs-are-falling incantation or he had neglected to do all that was possible to counter the peril he himself had identified. Whichever was closer to the truth, his victory in Iraq was tainted.

"The images you are seeing on television you are seeing over and over and over, and it's the same picture of some person walking out of some building with a vase."

Bush's triumph was also tainted in the first weeks of the postwar era by his administration's inability to handle effectively many of the challenges of the occupation. Bush had not outright lied; he had not said that providing security and revitalizing a nation of 24 million would be easy. But Bush and his advisers had been somewhat disingenuous before the war by ducking questions and declining to address concerns about the difficulties of bringing democracy and security to postwar Iraq. A case in point: in February, General Eric Shinseki, the Army chief of staff, testified that it could take several hundred thousand troops to secure Iraq after the war. Wolfowitz quickly dismissed him as being "wildly off the mark." Rumsfeld, too, dressed him down. Obviously, the administration, in the march to war, had an interest in lowballing post-war needs and dilemmas. But, as events quickly demonstrated, Shinseki had been closer to the mark than Wolfowitz.

The days and weeks following the fall of Baghdad showed the Bush administration and the Pentagon had not been committed to postwar security. The national library and museum trashed, hospitals ransacked, widespread looting—Rumsfeld wouldn't even voice regrets about the unrest. In fact, as the chaos became an issue in the media, Rumsfeld dissembled to ward off criticism. At an April 11 Pentagon briefing, he tried to dismiss the extent of the plundering: "The images you are seeing on television you are seeing over and over and over, and it's the same picture of some person walking out of some building with a vase, and you see it 20 times and you think, 'My goodness, were there that many vases?' Is it possible that there were that many vases in the whole country?" Members of the Pentagon press corps laughed at the quip.

He kept up the performance, claiming that when U.S. troops "see looting, they're stopping it, and they will be doing so." That was not entirely true. Sometimes troops intervened; other times they maintained their positions. Junior military officials told reporters they often had neither the orders nor the resources to act as a police force.

Sticking to his defense, Rumsfeld reeled off what became one of his more famous comments: "Stuff happens! But in terms of what's going on in that country, it is a fundamental misunderstanding to see those images over and over and over again of some boy walking out with a vase and say, 'Oh my goodness, you didn't have a plan.' That's non-sense. . . . Freedom's untidy. And free people are free to make mistakes and commit crimes and do bad things." Rumsfeld was being absurd—claiming that all the looting involved one vase. But he had a reason to hide behind this line.

These messy developments had indeed been predicted by the Defense Department. Yet Rumsfeld's Pentagon had decided to over-look such warnings—partly because they had been following Rums-feld's edict to invade Iraq with lower troop levels than military traditionalists favored. "Months before the invasion of Iraq," the *Washington Post* reported in mid-April, "Pentagon war planners antici-pated the fall of Saddam Hussein would usher in a period of chaos and lawlessness, but for military reasons, they chose to field a light, fleet invasion force that could not hope to quell such unrest when it emerged, Pentagon officials said."

Was the public ever informed that the U.S. military would rush troops to guard the oil ministry in Baghdad but would not be able to protect the three dozen hospitals in the city—even though Bush had promised in a prewar speech that "we will deliver medicine to the sick"? (He just didn't say when.) Bush also had promised food aid. But in the days after U.S. troops took Baghdad, frustrated international aid workers, who were unable to initiate major humanitarian efforts in Iraq due to the lack of security, were calling upon the Bush adminis-tration to make relief a greater priority.

Bush responded to criticism about the United States' handling of the opening days of the occupation with a blast at naysaying. "You know, it's amazing," he said on April 13. "The statue [of Saddam Hussein] comes down on Wednesday and the headlines start to read, 'Oh, there's disorder.' Well, no kidding. It is a situation that is chaotic because Saddam Hussein created the conditions for chaos. He created conditions of fear and hatred. And it's going to take a while to stabilize the country."

That was true. But Bush was dodging the question of whether his administration had sufficiently planned for what was almost certain to be a confusing and difficult time. During the presidential campaign, Bush had famously derided nation-building. But with the war he had assumed the most ambitious nation-building task the United States had attempted in decades. And he botched the takeoff. Most nation-building experts say that the quick imposition of security is essential for a democratic transition. A prewar Council on Foreign Relations report—crafted by a panel of Democratic and Republican establishment experts—had warned the Bush administration that U.S. forces should enter Iraq with the "mission to establish public security and provide humanitarian aid. This is distinct from the tasks generally assigned to combat troops." Bush did not take the advice.

"My impression of what's taking place is that the folks in General Franks's organization and in General Garner's [reconstruction] organization have done an outstanding job and are continuing to make things better in almost every corner of that country."

In mid-April, Senator Richard Lugar, the Republican chairman of the foreign relations committee, charged that Bush and his team had been "ill-prepared" for the postwar period. And on May 9, the *Washington Post* reported that military commanders were complaining that Rumsfeld's plan to prosecute the war with a smaller number of fast-moving troops—while a battlefield success—had left them with too few people to provide security.

The *Post* story portrayed an American occupation hindered by poor planning. "A month after U.S. forces seized Baghdad," it noted, "the Pentagon's occupation authority remains plagued by insufficient resources and inadequate preparations, fueling complaints from Iraqis and doubts about the Bush administration's promise to reconstruct the country swiftly and set its politics on a new, democratic course. . . . U.S. officers, acknowledging Iraqis' complaints about lax security, have pleaded that their troops are stretched too thin." Essential services—water and electricity—were intermittent, and Iraqis were waiting in mile-long lines for gasoline. The health system was near collapse. Looting was ongoing. Crime was on the rise. Relief workers were attacked. Iraqis were settling old scores with revenge killings. There was no functioning police force in the capital. The U.S. occupation operation lacked language interpreters. "The planning was ragged," a senior U.S. official in Baghdad told the *Post*, "and the execution was worse."

British Foreign Secretary Jack Straw expressed disappointment with the occupation. "Results in the early weeks," he told Parliament, "have not been as good as we would have hoped." But the Bush crew was not so candid. As the media reported crime and violence was spreading in Baghdad, Rumsfeld declared on May 9, "My impression of what's taking place is that the folks in General Franks's organization and in [retired] General [Jay] Garner's [reconstruction] organization have done an outstanding job and are continuing to make things better in almost every corner of that country." Yet days later, the news broke that Bush was dramatically overhauling the U.S. occupation, withdrawing Garner, the first civilian viceroy, and other U.S. officials, and replacing them with a new team. Was this shake-up a sign of White House concern over "unforeseen difficult circumstances"? a reporter politely asked Fleischer. The press secretary would not acknowledge any such unease.

In subsequent weeks, the occupation continued to be problem-ridden. In mid-May, U.S. occupation officials were predicting that the money and time needed to reconstruct Iraq would be much greater than anticipated. The number of U.S. and British troops in the country numbered near 200,000. At a May 22 hearing of the Senate foreign relations committee, Senator Joe Biden, a Democrat, asked Wolfowitz, "When is the president going to tell the American people that we're likely to be in the country of Iraq for three, four, five, six, eight, ten years, with thousands of forces and spending billions of dollars? Because it's not been told to them yet." He was charging the administration with dissembling by avoidance. Wolfowitz replied, "It's possible that things will go faster."

A week later, in response to the increased activity of an armed Iraqi resistance, Lieutenant General David McKiernan, commander of U.S. ground forces in Iraq, announced a new military push against the opposition, which had been ambushing and killing U.S. soldiers. "These are not criminal activities, they are combat activities," McKiernan said. He added, "The war has not ended." Instead, it had become a counterinsurgency operation incorporating house-to-house sweeps and military raids that occasionally killed civilians—actions that fueled Iraqi resentment toward the occupation. A new sort of military action was at hand. Yet Bush spoke little about the mission creep—from (relatively) peaceful occupation to troublesome pacification—and the new sets of challenges the United States and its troops were facing in occupied Iraq.

In Washington, former Army secretary Thomas White—who had been fired by Rumsfeld shortly after the major combat in Iraq ended—told *USA Today* that Pentagon officials "are unwilling to come to grips" with the scale of the United States' post-war obligation. He complained that senior Defense Department officials had belittled the need for a huge occupation force prior to the invasion. "This is not what they were selling before the war," he said, in a clear jab at Rumsfeld and Wolfowitz. Had the Bush administration before the fighting purposefully misrepresented what the U.S. commitment would have to be during the occupation? White had an obvious gripe with Rumsfeld, but this was a serious charge.

Toward the end of June, Senators Lugar and Biden visited Iraq and concluded that the United States would have to maintain its military presence there for a minimum of three to five years. Lugar told reporters, "There now needs to be real truth-telling by the president." That was a harsh statement from a fellow (and usually mild-mannered) Republican—a not-so-veiled accusation that Bush was not being honest with the public.

"The reason I don't use the phrase 'guerilla war' is because there isn't one."

In one absurd moment, Rumsfeld, appearing before Pentagon reporters, refused to characterize the ongoing and deadly resistance in Iraq as guerilla warfare. "The reason I don't use the phrase 'guerilla war' is because there isn't one," he said. Then CNN correspondent Jamie McIntyre read him the Defense Department's definition of the term: "military and paramilitary operations conducted in enemy-held or hostile territory by irregular ground indigenous forces." McIntyre added, "Seems to fit a lot of what's going on in Iraq." Rumsfeld shot back: "It really doesn't."

But it did. So said retired colonel W. Patrick Lang, the former chief of Middle Eastern affairs at the Defense Intelligence Agency, noting what was transpiring in Iraq was "exactly" a guerilla war in the nascent phase. Retired Army general Barry McCaffery said the same. Days later, Senator Pat Roberts, the Republican chairman of the intelligence committee, remarked, "We're now fighting an anti-guerilla effort." And two weeks after Rumsfeld denied U.S. troops were facing a "guerilla" insurgency, General John Abizaid said American forces were facing "a classical guerilla-type campaign" in Iraq. "It's low-intensity conflict, in our doctrinal terms," he explained "but it's war, however you describe it." Yet Rumsfeld declined to be straight with the public. And during an appearance before the Senate armed services committee, Rumsfeld told the senators—only after being pressed—that U.S. military operations in Iraq were costing about $3.9 billion a month, almost double the $2.1 billion estimate the Pentagon had derived in April. (And the tab for reconstruction and the civilian side of the occupation was running higher than the administration had calculated.) After Rumsfeld's testimony, Senator John McCain expressed irritation that the Bush administration had not been up front about the full costs of occupation: "I think the American people need to be told, 'Look, we're going to be there for quite a while, and it's going to cost us quite a bit of money. People should be given some estimate of what we can expect." Days later, the *Washington Post* reported that defense and congressional aides were expecting that the bill for the war and the occupation could reach $100 billion through 2004.

Bush had not fully or directly spelled out the costs and span of the U.S. commitment. He had avoided the topic both before the war and in the months after Baghdad fell. But on July 1, he finally acknowledged that the occupation in Iraq could be "a massive and long-term undertaking." Still, he gave no sense of how "massive" or how "long-term"—or what he expected the costs to be, in dollars and in lives. The next day, during an appearance at the White House, Bush challenged the anti-American Iraqi resistance. "Bring 'em on," he declared.

"We will, in fact, be greeted as liberators."

Had Bush and his national security officials conveyed unrealistic expectations to the public before invading Iraq? While selling the war, some Bush officials had implied that the occupiers would have an easy time in Iraq. On March 11, Wolfowitz proclaimed, "The Iraqi people understand what this crisis is about. Like the people of France in the 1940s, they view us as their hoped-for liberators." Three days before the war began, Cheney said, "We will, in fact, be greeted as liberators." These were simplistic assessments. Were they a reflection of sincere but unfounded optimism? Or were they naive by design, because such assertions strengthened the administration's case for war?

There were celebrations and warm welcomes for U.S. and British forces in some spots. In the north, the Kurdish opposition embraced U.S. troops and conducted missions with U.S. Special Forces. Many liberated Iraqis exuberantly expressed their disdain for the immoral and murderous regime of Saddam Hussein at the first possible moment. A band of Baghdad residents cheered the televised toppling of a Saddam Hussein statue. But even before the war was won, it was evident that the postwar political situation would be much more complicated and difficult than the Bush administration had suggested with its we-will-be-welcomed statements.

In many cities, dancing in the street quickly turned to stomping in the street. When John Donvan, an unembedded ABC News reporter visited "liberated" Safwan, a southern border town, early in the war, he found the residents there more resentful than appreciative. "We learned," Donvan reported, "that just because the townsfolk don't like Saddam, it doesn't mean they like the Americans trying to take him out. . . . They were angry at America, and said U.S. forces had shot at people in the town. They were also angry because they needed food, water, and medicine, and the aid promised by President Bush had not appeared. . . . They asked us why the United States was taking over Iraq and whether the Americans would stay in Iraq forever. They saw the U.S.-led invasion as a takeover, not liberation." On March 31, the London *Times* reported that refugees outside Basra were throwing stones at British forces. One refugee, who shook his fist at the British, told a reporter, "I have no love for Saddam, but tell me how are we better off today when there is no power, nor water. There are dead bodies lying on our streets, and my children are scared to go to bed because of the shelling."

Shi'ite Muslim clerics, in particular, were not cheering their liberators. As hundreds of thousands of Shi'ites turned out for religious events spiced with America-go-home sentiment, their fundamentalist leaders moved to fill the power vacuum and to demand a rapid exit of the Americans. In some parts of the country, Sunni Muslims joined the Shi'ites in calling for a fast end to the occupation. In Mosul— where residents had defiantly displayed Iraqi flags a day after U.S. troops entered the city—American soldiers violently clashed with an angry crowd of thousands and killed several civilians. In Fajullah, U.S. troops shot protesting Iraqis and killed 15. (The Americans claimed they had been fired upon; Iraqis challenged this account.) Remnants of Hussein's Ba'athist regime were regrouping to form an underground and violent opposition. Postwar Iraq was wild and woolly—far more so than Bush administration officials before the war had indicated it would be.

The rise of Shi'ite Power had not been part of Bush's Iraq plan. "As Iraqi Shi'ite demands for a dominant role in Iraq's future mount," the *Washington Post* reported, "Bush administration officials say they underestimated the Shi'ites' organizational strength and are unprepared to prevent the rise of an anti-American, Islamic fundamentalist government in the country."

The administration had a challenge for which it had not "wargamed." But the Shi'ite resurgence was not an unforeseeable event. "Nobody who knows anything about Shi'ites and Iraq is surprised by this," said Judith Kipper, director of the Council on Foreign Relations' Middle East Forum. "There were people in the government who knew this. But they were on the desks, not in the room where decisions were made." Joseph Wilson, who had been the last acting ambassador in Iraq, noted, "The Shi'ites always had aspirations. And the clerics have a constituency, an organization, a pulpit, an agenda, ambition and a trained militia. What else do you need?"

On April 24, 2002, *The New York Times* reported, "Administration officials have been surprised by the ferocity of the anti-American sentiments being voiced in some quarters of Iraq." But no administration official would state this in public. Questioned about what seemed to be widespread anti-America sentiment displayed during an important religious observance in Karbala, Fleischer spinned away, characterizing the passions displayed as "the message of a few" and noting Iraqis were "experiencing the joy of being liberated."

"There were some in our country who doubted the Iraqi people wanted freedom."

In a speech to Arab-Americans in Dearborn, Michigan, on April 28, Bush proclaimed, "Every day Iraqis are moving toward democracy." That was true of *some* Iraqis; others were trying to move toward theocracy and others were trying to return to the days of Ba'athist glory. But those Iraqis who were interested in moving toward democracy were being frustrated by the American occupation. In the weeks after the war, U.S. officials vowed the transition to self-rule would be quick. But on May 6, the United States and Britain abruptly reversed course and put off indefinitely a plan to allow Iraqis to form a national assembly and interim government by the end of the month. In the ensuing weeks, the Bush administration concentrated power within the U.S. military occupation authority, which sparked disappointment and resentment among Iraqis eager to see the start of democracy and self-determination. Then on June 1, the United States announced it would handpick up to 30 Iraqis to serve on an interim council that would advise the U.S. officials running the occupation. Iraqis would not be selecting their own leaders. Shortly after that, former ambassador L. Paul Bremer, the head of the American occupation, canceled a municipal election in Najaf that had been organized by the local American military commander. It would have been the first election in the new Iraq. Next, U.S. military commanders in cities and towns across the country called off local elections, with Bremer expressing his fear that if were there to be elections, the veterans of the Ba'athist regime and Islamic fundamentalists would fare the best.

In early July—in what he called a "tactical adjustment"—Bremer announced the governing council of Iraqis he was establishing would have executive power and be able to appoint and oversee ministers running the country, craft a budget, and send diplomats abroad. He was doing his best to deal with the resentment caused by the administration's backtracking on self-rule. Western and Iraqi officials were saying that he also needed an Iraqi body to share responsibility and blame.

Two days after the formation of the governing council, Bremer enthusiastically remarked, "The timing of how long the coalition stays here is now in the hands of the Iraqi people." But that was not quite the truth. The United States was an occupying power and would stay in Iraq until the man in the White House—not the Iraqi people—decided it was time for America to leave.

In his Dearborn speech in April, Bush had declined to discuss the troubles of postwar Iraq. Instead he focused on those instances when Iraqis had cheered or assisted U.S. troops. "Yes," he said, "there were some in our country who doubted the Iraqi people wanted freedom, or they just couldn't imagine they would be welcome—welcoming to a liberating force." But what person of any significance in the prewar debate had argued Iraqis did not desire freedom? Bush was peddling a self-serving fiction. As for how Iraq had greeted the "liberating force," the record spoke for itself. He was denying—or twisting—reality once more to suit his own ends.

Shi'ite defiance, unleashed fundamentalism, Ba'athist resurgence, lawlessness, loose chemical and biological weapons or components, looted nuclear facilities, when-we-have-time WMD inspections, popular resentment, armed resistance—none of this had made it into Bush's prewar disclosure statements. Instead, Bush and his aides had raised the rosy prospect of a domino effect spreading democracy from postwar Iraq to other states in the region—even though a classified State Department analysis had fiercely challenged that view. Bush and the war supporters could argue that the outcome was worth the costs and the chaos. Indeed, the murderous Saddam Hussein was out; the Iraqi people were no longer at his mercy. Yet this had been liberation accompanied by deception and misrepresentation.

On May 1, Bush flew out to the USS *Abraham Lincoln* aircraft carrier to deliver a premature victory speech. It was the mother of all photo-ops. He came in on an S-3B Viking jet and emerged from the aircraft—on live television—in a full flight suit. Bush, who had never explained what appeared to be a missing year in his Texas Air National Guard service, looked as if he were striding out of the film *Top Gun*. The images were a political consultant's dream.* The trip, in a sense, marked the end of the war—that is, the war as spectacle. His televised (in primetime) flight-deck address to the carrier's crew—beneath a huge red, white, and blue "Mission Accomplished" banner—came across as a grand (but false) finale for his Iraq endeavor.

Bush declared that "major combat operations in Iraq have ended. In the battle of Iraq, the United States and our allies have prevailed." But combat operation would continue for months in an unpacified and dangerous Iraq, with U.S. military deaths averaging several a week.

Bush told his audience, "We've begun the search for hidden chemical and biological weapons and already know of hundreds of sites that will be investigated." But a slow and undersupported WMD hunt had been under way for weeks, had uncovered no traces of WMD, and had caused some military and administration officials to doubt there were any weapons to be found.

Bush said, "No terrorist network will gain weapons of mass destruction from the Iraqi regime, because the regime is no more." But that disingenuous comment sidestepped two issues: whether Iraq had been in any position to hand such weapons to terrorists and, if it had, whether terrorist networks might have actually obtained WMDs because of the conditions created by Bush's invasion.

Bush also proclaimed, "We have removed an ally of al Qaeda." But there had never been any proof that Saddam Hussein's regime had recently collaborated with Osama bin Laden. In triumph, Bush would not stop misinforming the public.

But the most important line in the speech came when Bush stated, "The battle of Iraq is one victory in a war on terror that began on September 11th, 2001, and still goes on." The accuracy of this asser-

---

*Before the event, Fleischer said Bush had no choice but to travel by fighter jet because the aircraft carrier would be beyond the reach of the Marine One helicopter. Yet the day of the speech, the *Lincoln* was 30 miles out of San Diego, well within helicopter range. When reporters and Democrats raised questions, Fleischer rejiggered the explanation, noting Bush had wanted to go through the experience of a tailhook landing on a carrier. And after the event, Fleischer claimed that the cost of a jet flying to the carrier was essentially the same as the cost of a helicopter. He did not mention that Marine One and two other helicopters had to fly to the carrier anyway in order to take Bush and his entourage home.

tion was worth a debate. Had the action in Iraq truly been part of an effort against terrorism? Or had Bush exploited 9/11 to justify war against Iraq? Had the war marked real progress in the anti-terrorism campaign? Were al Qaeda or other anti-American terrorist outfits weaker because Bush had smashed Saddam Hussein's evil regime? (Weeks after the fighting concluded in Iraq, car bombs in Riyadh, Saudi Arabia, ripped apart three compounds housing Americans and other Westerners, killing eight Americans and seventeen others; Saudi officials fingered al Qaeda as responsible.) Would Bush's defeat of Saddam Hussein and the subsequent occupation discourage or encourage future acts of terrorism? These were open questions. But Bush's choice of words was significant, perhaps ominous. Iraq had been not a *war* but a *battle*. He was suggesting that there were other battles ahead and that this honesty-challenged commander-in-chief might again feel compelled to lead the country into combat. If his past was any guide, Bush could be expected once more to sacrifice truth for war.

Conclusion: How He Gets Away with It (So Far)

"I believe everybody should be held responsible for their own personal behavior."

On November 8, 1993, George W. Bush was skipping across Texas in a King Air plane dubbed *Accountability One*. It was the kickoff of his first campaign for governor—a campaign that would exploit themes of responsibility and integrity and that would launch him on a swift and successful-beyond-his-expectations career in the family business. At a speech that day at a Houston hotel, Bush spelled out his personal and political philosophy: "I believe everybody should be held responsible for their own personal behavior. All public policy should resolve around the principle that individuals are responsible for what they say and do."

Bush has not been held responsible for his lies. Seven years after he first packaged himself as the candidate of trustworthiness, he was elected—so to speak—president of the United States, following a campaign in which he ran as the friend of honesty and integrity. That was one of the biggest lies of his public life. He was no more honest (no more a uniter, no more a straight-talker, no more a foe of do-anything/say-anything partisan politics) than the average politician and elected official—and arguably a lot less.

How has he managed to get away with this, through a presidential campaign, through tax-cut battles, through two wars?

A facile answer is, because much of the media lets him. It is not quite as simple as that. But Bush has greatly benefited from news media practices and norms. This was especially so during the 2000 campaign, the period in which Bush was first introduced to a national audience. At the time, Cokie Roberts of ABC News and National Public Radio observed, "The story line [of the election] is, Bush isn't smart enough and Gore isn't straight enough. In Bush's case, you know he's just misstating as opposed to it playing into a story line about him being a serial exaggerator." So, Bush wasn't really lying, he was only making lots of mistakes, and Gore was the real fibber.

Such a view extended beyond Roberts' desk. Gore was whipped within the media any time he made a false remark—or any comment that could be depicted (rightly or wrongly) as not entirely true. Bush did not receive this sort of treatment. Was it because reporters harbored resentment toward the less affable Gore, who projected a know-it-all aura that could irritate? Nearly two years after the election, *Washington Post* White House reporter Dana Milbank, who covered the 2000 campaign, said, "I think that Gore is sanctimonious and that's sort of the worst thing you can be in the eyes of the press. And he has been disliked all along, and it was because he gives a sense that he's better than us." Or did journalists handle Bush differently because they shared Roberts' low opinion of him and believed that the lies and misstatements of a guy perceived to be not so bright were less intentional or less noteworthy than those of a smarter-than-thou vice president? After all, you don't expect dim bulbs to always have their facts in order. It was probably a combination of dislike of Gore's personality and disregard for Bush's intellect that prompted journalists to whack Gore and to cut Bush slack. (Bush's awkward relationship with the English language did receive much critical media attention, becoming something of a surrogate issue for the sensitive subject of his intelligence. But verbal tangles are easier for reporters and voters to dismiss than lies.)

Bush was helped because many political reporters cover campaigns as if they are sporting events, and these journalists are not always enthusiastic about sorting out the finer policy details to assess the veracity of candidates. After the first presidential debate, CNN's Larry

King asked *Nightline* anchor Ted Koppel what he had made of all the point-counterpoint concerning the "top 1 percent, 1.3 trillion, 1.9 trillion bit," referring to exchanges on Bush's proposed tax cuts. Koppel replied, "Honestly, it turns my brains to mush. I can't pretend for a minute that I'm really able to follow the argument of the debates. Parts of it, yes. Parts of it, I haven't a clue what they're talking about."

In that debate, Bush had misled the public about his tax cuts and budget numbers, his campaign finances, his Social Security plan, his prescription drug benefits plan, and Gore's budget proposals. But none of this affected the reviews in the media. CBS News' Bob Schieffer said, "Clearly tonight, if anyone gained from this debate, it was George Bush. . . . He seemed to have as much of a grasp of the issues [as Gore]." R. W. "Johnny" Apple of the *New York Times* opined, "Neither man committed an obvious gaffe; Mr. Bush avoided stumbling over his own syntax or comically mispronouncing words as he had in the past." Larry Sabato, a political scientist at University of Virginia and popular sound-bite source, observed, "The surprise for many people was that Bush was perfectly competent." Pollster John Zogby noted, "Mr. Bush showed he was fully in command of the facts." Presentation counted far more than accuracy.

Bush has also been fortunate—as a candidate and as a president—in that many reporters from the major news outlets are often uncomfortable interjecting judgments that are too sharp into their coverage. Unless others are doing it. Once Gore-is-an-embellisher became a campaign motif, many reporters were happy to publish or broadcast any new piece of data supporting that theme. But before such a tipping point is reached, journalists usually are cautious about wagging fingers and accusing someone who might become president of lying. During the campaign, Howell Raines, then the editorial page editor of the *New York Times,* ordered Paul Krugman, a feisty, liberal columnist for the paper and a harsh Bush critic, not to use the word "lie" when assailing Bush's proposals.

Bush played the system well. The *New York Times'* Frank Bruni observed, "For all his advisers' complaints about the sins of the news media, most mainstream journalists felt an obligation, first and foremost, to report what a candidate was saying before they went on to parse, analyze, and belittle it. So Bush tried to make sure that he said only so much; he made journalists feast on a main course of his most carefully considered sentences and most carefully constructed themes by not putting anything else on their plates. His aides were similarly loath to provide side dishes or garnishes. If you asked them what Bush had for breakfast, the reply might be, 'The governor believes that no child should be left behind,' or, 'The governor wants the American dream to'—you guessed it—'touch every willing heart.' . . . I exaggerate, but less than you might think." At one point in the campaign, Bush spokesperson Mindy Tucker told reporters that the campaign had decided a daily news conference was no longer "in our best interests." She explained: "We have a message of the day, and we're going to stick to it. We are not going to have one big, fat news conference on our schedule where you can come and ask what you think is the news of the day."

Bush, Bruni noted, was assisted—perhaps saved—by the reluctance of media outfits, which generally relish scoops, to intervene with too heavy a hand in the events they cover. When Bush's old DWI arrest was disclosed just days before the 2000 election—and when one issue was whether he had lied about his past arrest record—he "caught a big, big break," Bruni explained. "News organizations don't like to publish or air incendiary, potentially prejudicial stories about candidates in the final days [of a campaign]; they don't want to be seen as, or accused of, trying to tip the election one way or another. So they hurry to run all of their most critical dissections of candidates' records or personal histories well before the last minute, and if something like Bush's drunken-driving arrest pops up in the home stretch, well, they cringe. They pause. And, sometimes, they end up giving the candidate more of a pass than he or she might otherwise receive." Bruni, in consultation with his editors, covered this piece of news in what he later called "a tempered way"—meaning it was buried within a story that led with the "news" that Bush had attacked Gore for trusting too much in the federal bureaucracy. How the *Times* handled this story was especially significant, for many in the media world—especially producers and bookers for television and radio shows—take their cues from that paper. "Bush and his advisers," Bruni concluded (a bit too late), "didn't end up taking as much heat for it as they perhaps deserved."

"I'm the master of low expectations."

Once he moved into the White House, Bush avoided the heat as well. And he seemed to understand the dynamics at work. Shortly after he took office, about two dozen members of the White House press corps were invited to an off-the-record chat with him. During the session, according to a participant, a CNN reporter asked Bush if he was constantly underestimated. "I hope so," he replied, and everyone laughed. "Keep on lowering that bar for me, boys," he added. The diminished expectations of the campaign press corps had resulted in Bush's statements receiving less intense scrutiny. Perhaps he was hoping for more of the same. Indeed, in June 2002, while traveling home from the Middle East after participating in U.S.-brokered peace talks, Bush told reporters, "I'm the master of low expectations."

In the White House, he has mostly enjoyed good press—particularly after September 11.* He has not often been called on his fibs and fabrications in the mainstream media. At the White House Correspondents' Association gala dinner in May 2002, Bush told the crowd of several thousand journalists and guests, "You asked some pretty tough questions, but to tell you the truth, I don't think you have laid a glove on me." (He also joked that he had chewed out Ari Fleischer, telling him, "Ari, I'm sick and tired of you not fully answering all of the wonderful questions." The audience laughed.)

It was not until ten months after the attacks on the World Trade Center and the Pentagon that the White House press corps "showed its teeth," according to Milbank. What peeved the reporters was that Bush, responding to a question about his actions at Harken Energy, told them to "look back on the directors' minutes," but then the White House refused to ask Harken to release these private records. This

---

*The Bush White House's media operation was top flight. His handlers often arranged for him to strike heroic-looking poses. The trip to the USS *Lincoln* was one of their well-plotted attempts at image enhancement. When Bush delivered a speech at Ellis Island on the first anniversary of the September 11 attacks, the White House rented three barges of giant lights and floated them in the New York Harbor, so the Statue of Liberty, appearing behind Bush, would be illuminated just right. When tornadoes struck the Midwest in May 2003, Bush stood stoically in the Missouri rain—without an umbrella—and expressed his concern. With water running down his face, he also defiantly vowed to bring to justice the terrorists that had recently blown up several compounds for Westerners in Saudi Arabia and killed eight Americans. "They understand the visual as well as anybody ever has," Michael Deaver, Ronald Reagan's chief image man, told the *New York Times*.

episode, which followed recent skirmishes concerning terrorism intelligence failures and Enron, prompted White House reporters, according to Milbank, to strike "a more skeptical tone than the one that greeted Bush's first-year policy initiatives and his handling of the terrorism war." But the administration did not look worried. "We've seen this cycle before—it comes and it goes," Fleischer said. "The president is trusted by the American people and is liked by the American people, and the press is bored by that [Harken] story." Fleischer was mostly right. The Harken story faded, and much of the White House press corps retracted their fangs. Only after the question of Iraq's missing weapons of mass destruction emerged during uranium-from-Niger did Bush find himself in an awkward situation concerning his honesty. But even then the initial media and political response in the United States was nothing like the frenzy with which Tony Blair had to contend in Britain.

It is not easy for reporters who cover the president to call him a liar. There is a natural deference to the office and its holder. And it becomes more difficult to challenge a president when his approval ratings soar as the public sees him prosecuting wars to protect Americans. Confrontation can also carry a price. The Bush White House has a vindictive streak, and journalists who poke too hard at the administration can find themselves frozen out.

When Milbank wrote a page-one piece for the *Post* in October 2002 entitled, "For Bush Facts Are Malleable; Presidential Tradition of Embroidering Key Assertions Continues," the White House struck back. The morning the story appeared, a senior administration official called the authors of *The Note*, a daily political newsletter produced by ABC News and posted on its website, and trash-talked Milbank. This official—unnamed by *The Note*—challenged Milbank's assorted examples of Bush's distortion, which included the time Bush cited a nonexistent IAEA report to claim Saddam Hussein was "six months away from developing a [nuclear] weapon." According to *The Note*, the White House official "took the unusual step of saying: 'This was a story that was cooked and ready to go before any due diligence of the facts,' by a reporter who 'is more interested in style than substance.'" The official conceded that Bush had offered a wrong citation for his claim about Iraq's nuclear weapons program, but he insisted the underlying fact was true. But it wasn't. (See pages 213–214 of this book.) So here was a lie upon a lie from the White House—prompted by the desire to tarnish one reporter and probably also meant as a warning to other journalists who might impugn Bush's honesty.

Milbank had not used the word "lie." But he came close. He noted Bush had made "dubious, if not wrong" assertions, that "his rhetoric has taken some flights of fancy," that his "statements on subjects ranging from the economy to Iraq suggest that a president who won election underscoring Al Gore's knack for distortions and exaggerations has been guilty of a few himself." This was not the kind of language usually found in White House coverage. But it did not appear until almost halfway through a presidency that had been lubricated with lies from the get-go. Liberal pundits, such as Michael Kinsley and Paul Krugman (who after the election was permitted to use the L-word), had dared to tag Bush a liar. (I had done so, too, in columns for *The Nation* and elsewhere.) But Bush's serial lying—about war and peace, tax cuts, health care, social policy, environmental security—had not become a main feature for most of the media. As Ben Bradlee, the former executive editor of the *Washington Post,* remarked in 1997, "Even the very best newspapers have never learned how to handle public figures who lie with a straight face. No editor would dare print this version of Nixon's first comments on Watergate for instance: 'The Watergate break-in involved matters of national security, President Nixon told a national TV audience last night, and for that reason he would be unable to comment on the bizarre burglary. That is a lie.'"

That is a lie. The mainstream news organizations could have used that phrase in many a story about Bush. When he said the estate tax forced families to sell their farms. When he said he only got to know Lay after becoming governor. When he said that budget deficits were the result of 9/11. When he said he would produce a plan to "reduce" global warming emissions. These were all lies. Yet most media outfits did not see it as their mission to stamp "lie" on a demonstrably untrue Bush remark or to question Bush's truthfulness. In October 2002, when the CIA, under pressure, released the findings of its analysts, who had concluded Saddam Hussein was not likely to strike at the United States unless he felt threatened, the *Washington Post* front-page headline read, "Analysts Discount Attack by Iraq." The *New York Times* said, "CIA Warns That a U.S. Attack May Ignite Terror." These newspapers could have reasonably announced, "CIA Suggests Bush Misleads Public on Threat from Iraq." But that's not how they do business.

It's not that the traditional media has failed to create a record of Bush's lies or covered up for him. Bush lies could readily be found in the *New York Times*, the *Washington Post*, the *Wall Street Journal*, the *Los Angeles Times*, and other influential media enterprises. News stories frequently have noted when a Bush assertion was contradicted by an expert, a report, or the existing record. Many of the examples in this book are drawn from such articles. But, more often than not, the contradiction is not the story, not the subject of the headline; it is merely found in a reference several paragraphs into a piece. Rarely was the gap between Bush and reality emphasized. Consequently, Bush's untruthful ways have not—as of this writing—become a defining theme of his presidency, but his lies have been hidden in plain sight.

"Someone running for the highest office of the land should stick to the facts. Pretty soon it's going to have a corrosive effect on his campaign if he's not telling the truth."

Why has Bush lied so often? To get what he wants. There usually is a tactical or strategic purpose to his deceptions. During a bitter fight with Senate Democrats in May 2003, Bush claimed there was a "crisis in our judiciary" because Democrats were blocking a few of his judicial nominees. He blamed Democrats for an "unacceptably high" number of empty seats. Yet when Bush was declaiming this state of affairs, the federal judiciary had the lowest vacancy rate in 13 years. In fact, 2002—when Democrats controlled the Senate—was the best year since 1994 in terms of the numbers of judges confirmed. The judicial nomination process had not functioned smoothly for years, but Bush was decrying a phony "crisis" in order to win approval of several nominees that Democrats had opposed out of concern they were too conservative. It was reminiscent of Bush's use of overheated rhetoric about the coming "collapse" of Social Security to gain support for a partial-privatization plan. Then there were his untrue assertions that farm families were being wiped out by the estate tax—another crisis that did not exist—and, of course, his statements about weapons of mass destruction in Iraq.

He also broke promises and shaded the truth for crass political gain. During the campaign, Bush declared, "I'll work to end tariffs and break down [trade] barriers everywhere, entirely, so the whole world trades in freedom." As president, he proclaimed, "Open trade is not just an economic opportunity, it is a moral imperative." And he preached a tough-love approach: "We must understand that the transition costs of open trade are dwarfed by open trade's benefits." But then in March 2002 this moralistic free-trader imposed tariffs on imported steel to assist the struggling U.S. steel industry and said the move was necessary for the United States "to remain a free-trading nation." Had he had a change of heart? He didn't acknowledge any. Conservative activists opposed to the tariff who had met with White House aides told reporters that Bush's decision was all politics, that Bush—who as a candidate had assailed the overlap of policy and politics in the Clinton White House—was looking to win over steelworkers in key states (such as Pennsylvania, Ohio, and West Virginia) for the 2004 election. A reporter asked Fleischer, "Were political considerations involved in the president's decision on steel?" The press secretary said, "No," but before he could finish his reply, the White House press corps burst out laughing.

Bush made use of misstatements and false claims to prop up his policy positions. In 2003, while promoting a proposal to add a prescription drug benefit to Medicare, he repeatedly said that senior citizens on Medicare need to have a choice of affordable plans that provide drug coverage: "If it's good enough for the employees and members of Congress to have choice, it's good enough for our seniors to have choice." The plain implication was that Bush favored giving seniors as good a choice as legislators received. Yet the Medicare drug bill approved by Republicans in the House and Senate—which the White House cheerleaded—did not offer seniors the same extensive options offered by the federal employees' system. That system—enjoyed by members of Congress and Bush, as well—included a plan covering 80 percent of prescription drug costs. The proposed drug benefit in the

House bill covered about 55 percent. Despite Bush's remarks, what was good enough for Congress was too good for seniors.

In a similar fashion, Bush triumphantly hailed a new nuclear arms agreement he reached with Moscow. "Today, I'm pleased to announce," he said in May 2002, "that the United States and Russia have agreed to a treaty which will substantially reduce our nuclear arsenals to the agreed-upon range of 1,700 to 2,200 warheads." Not exactly. The U.S. nuclear arsenal—which numbered about 7,000 warheads—will likely not be reduced as dramatically as Bush suggested. Many or most of the 5,000 warheads scheduled for retirement will not be destroyed but kept in storage or maintained as "spares." They can be reactivated, perhaps quite quickly. And this agreement had no timetable. There was a deadline; each side has to reduce its ready-to-fire warheads to the 1,700-to-2,200 range by the end of 2012. But that means these two nuclear powers can maintain operational arsenals much larger than the agreed-upon levels until the final hours of December 31, 2012. And the following day, if the agreement has not been extended, each side will be free to return thousands of warheads to its launch-ready force.

On occasion, it seems Bush has lied because he just gets carried away. During one of those moments when Bush was trying to demonstrate he was indeed interested in resolving the Israeli-Palestinian conflict, he called Israeli prime minister Ariel Sharon "a man of peace." Probably not even Israelis who voted for the hawkish Sharon—who titled his memoirs *Warrior*—would honor him with that phrase. Sharon's appeal to many Israelis was based on the fact that he was *not* a fan of the peace process. And an Israeli commission had found Sharon partially responsible for the 1982 massacre of 1,000 or so Palestinian civilians by Lebanese militia in the Sabra and Shatila refugee camps in Lebanon. Enabling the slaughter of civilians is not usually the mark of a "man of peace."

Bush has lied to obtain power and has lied while using it. And so far—*so far*—he has not suffered for repeatedly violating the truth. Unfortunately, lying often works for presidents. American history does not teach presidents that they must expect to pay a direct and immediate price for deception. Reagan, who constantly spilled misstatements and false information, was elected twice. Clinton saved his candidacy in 1992 by falsely denying he had ever had a sexual relationship with Gennifer Flowers (a fact he was forced to acknowledge six years later in a sworn deposition in a sexual harassment case). And he survived an impeachment trial that focused on his lies about sex. Many of Clinton's Republican tormentors could not believe the American public did not rise up en masse against a president who had defiled the Oval Office and lied about his acts of sacrilege. They kept waiting for popular outrage to catch up to their own. It never did.

In 2003—before the WMDs controversy—Democrats initiated an effort to challenge Bush's credibility. Trying to turn the public against a popular wartime leader, they repeated the mantra *He says one thing but does another.* They were right. But at that time, the Democrats did not have an easily recognizable overarching message of opposition to Bush, and attacking Bush's integrity appeared to be a desperate Plan B. This strategy did not produce any perceptible results.

In her book *Lying: Moral Choice in Public and Private Life,* author Sissela Bok adopts a somewhat optimistic view of what happens to liars in public office. She writes,

> A public lie on an important matter, once revealed, hurts the speaker. . . . But the problem for liars is that they tend to see *most* of their lies in [a] benevolent light and thus vastly underestimate the risks they run. . . . These risks are increased by the fact that so few lies are solitary ones. It is easy, a wit observed, to tell a lie, but hard to tell only one. The first lie "must be thatched with another or it will rain through." More and more lies may come to be needed. The liar always has more mending to do. . . . And it is inevitable that more frequent lies *do* increase the chance that some will be discovered. At that time, even if the liar has no personal sense of loss of integrity from his deceitful practices, he will surely regret the damage to his credibility, which their discovery brings about. Paradoxically, once his word is no longer trusted, he will be left with greatly *decreased* power—even though a lie often does bring at least a short-term gain in power over those deceived.

If only. In the real world of American politics, lies, when discovered, do not always disgrace or disqualify leaders. The public has a high tolerance for them. Many Americans expect them and are not surprised by lies from on high. Such cynicism—an understandable response to the extensive spin of modern-day politics—serves to grant public officials who lie even greater latitude. During the 2000 campaign, Bush asserted, "Someone running for the highest office of the land should stick to the facts. Pretty soon it's going to have a corrosive effect on his campaign if he's not telling the truth." He was not speaking about himself. But he proved this statement false.

Does Bush believe his own lies? Did he truly consider a WMD-loaded Saddam Hussein an imminent threat to the United States? Or was he knowingly employing dramatic license because he wanted war for other reasons? Did he really think the average middle-class taxpayer would receive $1,083 from his second tax-cuts plan? Or did he realize this was a fuzzy number cooked up to make the package seem a better deal than it was for middle- and low-income workers? Did he believe there were enough stem cell lines to support robust research? Or did he know he had exaggerated the number of lines in order to avoid a politically tough decision? Did he really consider Ariel Sharon a "man of peace"?

It's hard to tell. Bush's public statements do suggest he is a binary thinker who views the world in black-and-white terms. You're either for freedom or against it. With the United States or not. Tax cuts are good—always. The more tax cuts, the better—always. He appears impatient with nuance. What does he say about those nations that are *with* the United States but not *for* freedom at home, such as Saudi Arabia, Pakistan, and Uzbekistan? Not much. Asked in 1999 to name something he wasn't good at, Bush replied, "Sitting down and reading a 500-page book on public policy or philosophy or something." Bill Clinton, by comparison, relished diving into the intricacies of an issue. Bush likes life clear-cut. And perhaps that causes him to either bend the truth or to see (and promote) a bent version of reality.

He has a tendency to cast people, organizations, and situations in the starkest terms. In November 2002, as he was attempting to develop a case for war, he insisted that Saddam Hussein was currently "dealing" with al Qaeda, an assertion not supported by any public evidence. The CIA had only claimed that there had been *some* links between al

Qaeda members and Iraqi officials at *some* time. Had Bush's desire to justify an attack upon Saddam Hussein caused him to resort to passionate but inaccurate hyperbole? Or might it have been that in the world according to Bush one anti-American brute *must* be in league with another anti-American brute because there are only two sides, us and them? Earlier, Bush had portrayed al Qaeda leaders, as evil as they were, as being intent on killing *all* Americans—when their actual (and perverse) motivations involved other aims. He has often over-demonized actual demons in order to sell his preferred course of action.

His simplistic framing of issues frequently works in his political favor. Missile defense? If the issue is defend the United States from madmen with nuclear weapons or not defend the United States from madmen with nuclear weapons, isn't the choice clear? Perhaps Bush purposefully embraces and promotes two-dimensional analyses of complicated subjects in order to buttress his positions. Maybe it's all a clever ruse. Maybe he knows al Qaeda is driven by theology-based geostrategic goals, but he sticks to the elemental freedom-versus-evil account because that is more likely to rally the American public. So is he binary by design, or by birth? It's probably some of each, which explains why he seems so comfortable when he is misleading the public. His nature reinforces his means—or vice versa.

Does Bush buy his claim that he is a uniter not a divider, that he has changed the tone in American politics, even after the numerous times he has engaged in slash-and-burn politics, partisan finger-pointing, and my-way-or-the-highway maneuvers? He might. Self-perception can be a tricky business. He can point to the bipartisan No Child Left Behind education legislation he worked on with Senator Edward Kennedy (who later accused Bush of violating the spirit of this political venture by not fully funding his own initiative). And Bush did bring together Republicans and Democrats to support his actions against al Qaeda, the Taliban, and Saddam Hussein. One anecdote about Bush offers reason to think that even if he believed his own PR he didn't believe that all that uniter stuff should get in the way of victory. In their biography of Karl Rove, *Bush's Brain,* journalists Wayne Slater and James Moore recount a moment when Bush stood "awkwardly" next to John McCain in a television studio before the start of the South Carolina Republican primary debate during the 2000 campaign. McCain, who had been hit by savage and slanderous attacks, turned toward Bush. Shaking his head, McCain simply said, "George." Bush replied, "John, it's politics." McCain shot back, "George, everything isn't politics." Did Bush mean that whatever-it-takes tactics shove aside principles? The exchange is not conclusive, but it hinted that Bush was conscious, to an extent, of the deception he and his campaign had been mounting.

Given all the times he has fiddled with the truth, does Bush think of himself as an honest fellow, the politician of integrity he campaigned as in 2000? Well, don't most people regard themselves as honest, even if they acknowledge that now and then they slip? After his first meeting with Russian president Valdimir Putin, a former KGB officer, Bush said he had "looked the man in the eye . . . [and] was able to get a sense of his soul." And, Bush declared, Putin was "trustworthy." But peering into a person's soul is tough work. It is hard to know whether Bush considers his fibs, embellishments, and misrepresentations the honest-to-God truth or whether he cynically hurls falsehoods to fool the public. But a believer or a deceiver, the result is the same.

"First and foremost is to tell the truth."

With his misrepresentations and false assertions, Bush has dramatically changed the nation and the world. He has turned the United States into an occupying power. Via his tilted-to-the-wealthy tax cuts, he has profoundly reshaped the U.S. budget for years to come, most likely ensuring a long stretch of deficits that will make it quite difficult for the federal government to fund existing programs or contemplate new ones. He did all this with lies. They were essential to Bush's successes. Imagine if before the invasion of Iraq, he had appeared on national television and said,

> My fellow Americans, there may be threatening amounts of weapons of mass destruction in Iraq. There may not be. We're not sure. The intelligence is not conclusive. And if unconventional weapons are there, it may take weeks after military victory before we can launch a major effort to find and secure them. By then, they could be gone—that is, if they were there in the first place—

and perhaps end up in the hands of people who mean us harm. And after we defeat Iraq's brutal regime, the people of Iraq may welcome U.S. troops as liberators. Then again, within days, many of them could be shouting, "Yankee, go home," and calling for a new government dominated by fundamentalist religious leaders, as disorder and lawlessness spreads and an armed guerilla resistance kills several U.S. soldiers a week. We don't know. Nor do we really know the extent of any operational links between Saddam Hussein and al Qaeda—if such links do exist. Or whether Saddam Hussein does intend to share what weapons he might have with others who wish to attack us. Still, I believe the *potential* risk posed by Saddam Hussein is so great that we cannot let what we do not know to stand in the way of decisive action. We cannot afford to guess wrong. We cannot afford to spend another month, week, or day on enhanced weapons inspections. With that in mind, I have ordered . . .

With such a truthful pitch, would he have been persuasive in arguing that war was unavoidable? The answer is obvious. He had to lie to get the war he desired. If he had played it straight, there would have been far more opposition. And if he had used undistorted facts and figures during the tax-cuts battles, he would have been in a deep hole. Lies were his lifelines.

Does Bush lie more than his predecessors, more than his political opponents? That is irrelevant. Bush is guiding the nation during difficult and dangerous times, in which a credible president is much in need. Prosperity or economic decline? War or peace? Security or fear? This country has a lot to deal with. Lies from the White House poison the debates and discussions that must transpire if Americans are going to confront and overcome the challenges of this century at home and abroad.

Presidential lying threatens the country. To render informed and wise choices about the crucial and complicated controversies of the day, people need truthful information. What if the fellow with the most powerful megaphone is supplying the public wrong information? The president often is in a position to define and dominate a debate, more so than other political players. He can influence the national discourse unlike anyone else. What a president tells the public matters greatly—especially when the policy issues of the day are complex and tough to navigate. A lie from the White House—or a fib or a misrepresentation or a fudged number—can go a long way toward distorting the national discussion.

In February 2003, a Pew Foundation poll found that 57 percent of Americans believed Saddam Hussein "helped" in the 9/11 attacks. Why did a majority assume this, when there was no evidence that remotely suggested Saddam Hussein had anything to do with September 11? Might these people have been influenced by Bush's continuous and exaggerated references to a connection between Saddam Hussein and al Qaeda?* It is tough to suss out popular opinion and figure what molds it. But there is no doubt that disinformation or misinformation from the president cannot lead to a better-informed public.

One day when Bush was campaigning for president, he accused a Republican foe of dishonesty and declared, "First and foremost is to tell the truth. There's a lot of young people who get disillusioned when they see political figures say one thing and do another; political figures who say, I'm going to campaign one way, and campaign another way; political figures who, when they take the oath of office, don't uphold the dignity and honor of the office. So step one is to . . . tell the truth." And on his first full day on the job, while swearing in his White House staff, Bush reminded his cadre, "On a mantelpiece in this great house is inscribed the prayer of John Adams, that only the wise and honest may rule under this roof." But Adams's prayer has once more gone unanswered. A liar is in the house again. There has been no restoration of integrity. Bush's promise was a lie. The future of the United States remains in the hands of a dishonest man.

---

*A poll conducted by the University of Maryland's Program on International Policy Attitudes and released on July 1, 2003, found that 71 percent of Americans said they believed the Bush administration had implied Hussein was involved in the 9/11 strikes.

Acknowledgments

Writing is a solitary endeavor; producing a book is not. This volume is the work of many. At the top of the list is Jonathan Miller, whose contribution far surpassed the routine responsibilities of a research assistant. He gathered and pored over reams of material, as he relentlessly chased after and checked facts. He also supplied valuable editorial input and much-appreciated companionship. He was a partner in this project.

Gail Ross was not only my agent but a one-person support structure. She was this book's first champion and always there whenever a need arose.

I thank all my colleagues at Crown Publishers. Steve Ross, the publisher, was an enthusiastic supporter from the start. All writers should feel so encouraged by their publishers. My editors at Crown—Chris Jackson and Emily Loose—shared their keen insights and kept the editorial process moving at a fast clip, without losing sight of quality and substance. Their support for the book was essential. The other members of the Crown team—Amy Boorstein, Tina Constable, Leta Evanthes, Doug Jones, Kristin Kiser, Alex Lencicki, Genoveva Llosa, Elina Nudelman, Philip Patrick, Tim Roethgen, Caroline Sincerbeaux, and Jim Walsh—were committed to this project and helped bring this book to its audience (quickly).

I am grateful to *The Nation* and its editor, Katrina vanden Heuvel, for providing institutional support and for allowing me to explore the themes of this book in various articles for the magazine and its website. Likewise, Alternet.org (captained by Don Hazen) and TomPaine.com (guided by John Moyers and Ellen Miller) posted—and paid for—a weekly column in which I was able to develop material used in this book. Jacqueline Kucinich did a wonderful job of fact-checking. Historian Rick Shenkman helped with the lies of past presidents.

I owe special thanks to journalists who have covered George W. Bush on the campaign trail and in the White House. Many have done excellent reporting, as they vetted his remarks and actions. In part, this book rests on their notepads. Several White House correspondents were kind enough to share with me their observations of Bush and their favorite examples of his untruthfulness. They, of course, must go unnamed. A special nod of thanks goes to a particular television correspondent. I am also thankful for the fine work of reporters in Iraq and Afghanistan; they bravely covered the reality on the ground, which often was at odds with the rhetoric from the White House and the Pentagon. And several congressional aides—again, no names—assisted me, as I navigated the details of various policy debates.

My appreciation extends to the various conservatives with whom I have regularly sparred on radio and television, particularly those at the Fox News Channel: Tony Blankley, David Brooks, Linda Chavez, Monica Crowley, Sean Hannity, William Kristol, Rich Lowry, Michelle Malkin, Clifford May, Bill O'Reilly, Bill Sammon. These sound-bite exchanges proved quite valuable in sharpening the arguments in this book. Thanks, too, to those moderators who facilitated these face-offs: Jim Angle, David Asman, Alan Colmes, John Gibson, Shepard Smith, Tony Snow, Greta Van Susteren, Linda Vester, and Brian Wilson at Fox, and Warren Olney and Diane Rehm at NPR. I am indebted to the producers and bookers who arranged these debates.

While writing this book, I was encouraged and helped by friends and family: Tony Alfieri, Julie Burton, Sonya Cohen, Marc Cooper, Reid Cramer, Kate Doyle, Anne Glusker, Janlori Goldman, Bonnie Goldstein, James Grady, Ellen Grant, Christopher and Claudia Harvie, Nicholas Kahn, Gudrun Kendon, Peter Kornbluh, Dan Moldea, Bill Press, Steven Prince, Rick Schaeffer, Ricki Seidman, Micah Sifry, Cathy Silverstein, Stephanie Slewka, Raymond van Straelen, Henry von Eichel, Tim Weiner, David Williams, Ruth Corn, Gordon Roth, Kenneth Corn, Diane Corn, Barry Corn, Steven Corn, Amy Corn, Coby Laanstra-Ypma, Fokke Laanstra, and Nynka Laanstra. Jack Shafer was kind enough to read and critique portions of the manuscript. And many thanks to Arianna Huffington, Molly Ivins, and Clarence Page—supporters and partners-in-journalism.

To my immediate family, I owe not only gratitude but lost time. My wife, Welmoed Laanstra, was understanding and (mostly) patient as the book drew me away from family responsibilities. She picked up the slack and enabled me to complete this work. She was an ardent believer in the project. I thank her for the sustenance. To any extent she wishes, this book is joint property. And my two wonderful daughters, Maaike and Amarins, were understanding whenever I explained to them that reading a book or a trip to the park had to be deferred so I could keep on writing—as understanding as a three-year-old and a two-year-old can be. They will not know for years how much their love and joy buoyed a distracted father.

It is customary in writing acknowledgments for an author to share credit with all those who assisted but to accept full blame—to take the fall—for any errors that might have crept into the book. I follow suit.

At one point, while I was furiously typing away, my older daughter asked if I was writing a "real" story. In our household, the children divide the books we read into two categories: "real" or "pretend." I told her that indeed I was working on a "real" book. "Good," she said, without further explanation. In writing a "real" book with an incendiary title and theme, I have tried to be accurate, precise, and careful. If errors slipped into the manuscript, I will take responsibility for my mistakes and issue corrections in future editions (if I am so lucky) or on the website bushlies.com. If only a certain chief executive would be so responsible.

Index

Roberts, Pat, 302
Rocca, Christina, 187
Rockefeller, Jay, IV, 277
Roe v. Wade, 69
Roosevelt, Franklin D., 2–3
Rothstein, Richard, 71–72
Rove, Karl, 35, 76, 180, 252, 321–22
Rudman, Warren, 149
Rumsfeld, Donald, 142n
    Afghanistan war and, 160–65, 168–69,
      172n
    Hussein 1983 meeting, 227n
    Iraq occupation and, 297–98, 299, 301,
      302
    Iraq policy and, 205, 206, 211, 215,
      218–19, 223, 226–27
    Iraq war and, 266, 267, 269–70, 277,
      278
    missile defense system and, 125, 126,
      127, 129
    Niger uranium report and, 291
    on post–Iraq war looting, 297–98
    on U.N.'s standing, 227
Russert, Tim, 250
Rwanda, 4–5

Sabato, Larry, 311
Sadler, Paul, 16
Safire, William, 216
sales tax, Texas, 15
Sammon, Bill, 54n
SAT scores, 19–20
Saudi Arabia, 137n, 138, 307, 313n
Schieffer, Bob, 311
Schlesinger, Jacob, 47–48
Schlesinger, William, 115
schools. *See* education policy
Securities and Exchange Commission,
    192–97, 200–201
Security Council. *See* United Nations
September 11, 7, 131, 133–57, 201, 256n,
    313, 315
    Afghanistan campaign and, 159
    attempt to link Hussein with, 204, 207,
      215–19, 221, 226, 240, 307–8, 324
    budget deficit blamed on, 251, 256,
      257, 315
    Bush approval ratings and, 9, 176
    Bush press treatment after, 313–14
    Bush's expanded power from, 7–8, 241
    Bush simplistic rhetoric on, 134–38
    economic stimulus package, 150–52
    intelligence failure and, 139–45
    investigation of, 139, 144–45
    See also war on terrorism
75th Exploitation Task Force, 274,
    276–77

Shapiro, Matthew, 92
Sharon, Ariel, 318, 320
Shaw, Clay, 61
Shi'ite resurgence, 303–5, 306
Shinseki, Eric, 297
Shipman, Claire, 121
Sibley, David, 17
Sierra Club, 35, 104, 105–6, 184
Simon, Roger, 13
Simon, Steven, 137, 237n
Slater, Wayne, 29, 35, 36, 38, 321–22
Slemrod, Joel, 92, 257
Smith, Robert, 276
Snow, John, 255
Snow, Tony, 106
Snyder, Evan, 121
Social Security
    Bush campaign pledge, 50–51, 52, 63,
      91, 311
    inaugural speech pledge, 65
    partial-privatization plan, 9, 39n,
      42–48, 50–52, 63, 88, 92, 117, 249,
      316–17
    payroll taxes and, 40
    trust fund surplus, 39, 42, 87, 91, 251
    See also Medicare
Soros, George, 191
South Carolina primary, 34–37, 321–22
Southern Partisan, 66
Spectrum 7, 179–80, 191
Staiger, Douglas, 71–72
Star Wars. *See* missile defense system
State Department, 233, 240n, 279, 283,
    306
State of the Union speech (2002), 203–5
State of the Union speech (2003), 208,
    227, 228–30, 248–49, 256
    Niger uranium deal charge and, 230n,
      287–95
steel tariffs, 317
Steeper, Fred, 38
stem cell research, 118–25, 131, 320
Stevens, Robert, 147
Stewart, Martha, 189
stock market
    Enron misdeeds, 175–76
    Harken Energy sell-off, 190–98
    insider trading, 189, 193–94
    personal retirement accounts and,
      43–44, 50
    See also dividend tax
stock options, 198–99
Straw, Jack, 300
Stufflebeem, John, 163, 164
supply-side economics, 251–52, 262
Supreme Court, Florida, 60, 62–63
Supreme Court, U.S., 63

Weiner, Tim, 162–63, 164
Weinstein, Lauren, 58
Westermann, Christian, 283
White, Ronnie, 66
White, Thomas, 181, 301
White House Correspondents' Association
    dinner, 313
Whitman, Christine Todd, 73–77, 112,
    149
Will, George, 284
Wilson, Joseph, IV, 287, 288–89, 289n,
    304
Wilson, Thomas, 168
wiretap laws, 153n
Witt, James Lee, 47
WMD. *See* weapons of mass destruction
Wolfowitz, Paul, 129, 205, 206, 211, 217,
    223, 228, 285, 297, 300, 301, 303
    on selling of WMD threat, 280–81, 284
    September 11 analysis, 137n

Wood, Pat, III, 183
Woodward, Bob, 160, 205
Woolsey, R. James, 206
workplace ergonomic standards, 77n
World Bank, 186, 187
World Trade Center. *See* September 11

Yaphe, Judith, 234
Yemen, 241
Yousef, Ramzi, 141

Zandi, Mark, 261
Zarqawi, Abu Musab al–, 232, 234–35,
    286n
Zilinskas, Raymond, 233–34
Zoellick, Robert, 180
Zogby, John, 311
Zubaydah, Abu, 273

About the Author

David Corn is the Washington editor of *The Nation* and a Fox News Channel contributor. He has written for the *Washington Post*, the *New York Times*, the *Los Angeles Times*, the *Philadelphia Inquirer*, *Harper's*, *The New Republic*, *Mother Jones*, *The Washington Monthly*, *The LA Weekly*, Slate, Salon, TomPaine.com, Alternet.org, and many other publications. He is the author of the novel *Deep Background*, which the *Washington Post* called "an exceptional thriller," and the biography *Blond Ghost: Ted Shackley and the CIA's Crusades*, which *The Washington Monthly* praised as "an amazing compendium of CIA fact and lore." He was nominated for a 1997 Edgar Allan Poe Award.

He has long been a commentator on television and radio and has appeared on *The O'Reilly Factor*, *Hannity & Colmes*, *On the Record with Greta Van Susteren*, *Crossfire*, *The Capital Gang*, *Fox News Sunday*, *Washington Week in Review*, *The McLaughlin Group*, *Hardball*, C-SPAN's *Washington Journal*, and many other shows. He is a regular on NPR's *Diane Rehm Show* and has contributed commentary to NPR, BBC Radio, and CBC Radio. He has been a guest on scores of call-in radio programs.

Corn is a Phi Beta Kappa graduate of Brown University.